ARTISTS WHO THRIVE

ERIN MINCKLEY

Illustrations by the author

ARTISTS WHO TRHIVE
© Copyright 2020, Erin Minckley
All rights reserved.

All rights reserved. No portion of this book may be reproduced by mechanical, photographic or electronic process, nor may it be stored in a retrieval system, transmitted in any form or otherwise be copied for public use or private use without written permission of the copyright owner.

It is sold with the understanding that the publisher and the individual authors are not engaged in the rendering of psychological, legal, accounting or other professional advice. The content and views in each chapter are the sole expression and opinion of its author and not necessarily the views of Fig Factor Media, LLC.

Printed in the United States of America

ISBN: 978-1-952779-11-4
Library of Congress Number: 2020923654

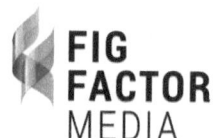

To Anwar and Yassine.
May you see that with enough creativity and hard work,
anything is possible.

To Allison, you have taught me ease and grace. Though
none of it was easy, nevertheless, I am willing. Thank you for
guiding me.

Table of Contents:

LETTER TO THE READER 7

PART 1: LEARNING RESILIENCE 11

CHAPTER 1: REIMAGINING THE ARTIST IDENTITY 14
The Big Peel 16
The Emperor's New Clothes 36
Know Your Worth 41
Flip the Script 51

CHAPTER 2: DOING SHIT YOU DON'T WANT TO DO 57
I am Coachable 58
Being Broke is the Best Motivator 63
Carrying the Rock 75

CHAPTER 3: SAYING NO TO NEGATIVITY 85
Toxic Pessimism 86
This is How I Meant it to Look 100
Limiting Beliefs 106
The Artist's Tongue 117

CHAPTER 4: A HABITAT TO THRIVE IN 129
Self-preservation: The Chameleon 130
Shake it 'til You Make it - A Bun Dance 139

SECTION 2: CREATING NEW RELATIONSHIPS 146

CHAPTER 5: YOUR DYSFUNCTIONAL RELATIONSHIP WITH TIME 149
Lie #1: I'm Flaky 151
Lie #2: I'm Lazy 156
Lie #3: I'm Forgetful 159
Lie #4: There's Not Enough Time 167
The Administration of Life 173

CHAPTER 6: YOU AND MONEY NEED TO MAKE AMENDS 179
Your Money Attitude 180
Types of Income 193
The Struggle is Real... Or Is it? 204

CHAPTER 7: THE HUMANS IN YOUR LIFE 211
Go on a Diet 214
Get a New Network 225

CHAPTER 8: THE NEW LOVE AFFAIR 237
Your Relationship with Your Body 238
The Whitest I've Ever Felt 255

SECTION 3: ACHIEVING RESULTS 264

CHAPTER 9: THE STUDIO MESS CONUNDRUM 271
Hoarders Need Love Too 274
1 TAT (One Thing at a Time) 290
The Studio as a Temple 294

CHAPTER 10: BECOME THE CEO OF YOUR LIFE 303
Start with Your Why 305
Channeling Your Magic 311
Expression of your Worldview 324
Critical Structure 342
Dumping Out the Incompletions 346

CHAPTER 11: ELIMINATING OBSTACLES & HAVING COURAGE 351
Excuses: The Leading Cause of Death to Creativity 352
The Monkeys in my Mind 362
Fear is the Moose on the Trail 370
If Optimism Seems Fishy, Will You Believe Science? 379

CHAPTER 12: MASTERY 385
Manifestation vs. Demonstration 386
Believe It, or Better Yet, Yell it from the Mountain Top 393
Self-Promotion 405
The 90% Rule: Just Press "Go" 424

CHAPTER 13: WRITING YOUR LEGACY 429
Throwing Yourself a Party 435
Surrender 437
Butterfly Conversations 449
Forgiveness: The Ho'oponopono Prayer 453
The Fat Lady Sings 455

ABOUT THE AUTHOR 459
ABOUT THE COVER 459
NOTES 460

Letter to the Reader

Dear Reader,

This is your wake up call.

This book is a manifesto not a self-help or "How To" book. You are beginning the next chapter of your life and I am here to push you to become the author of your own story. I wrote this book to wrap my mind around "what's wrong" with the way artists are portrayed. I am writing to you because you 'get it' and furthermore, because you're a creative person. We speak the same language. This is not a tribute to all the suffering, starving artists of our time. No, I call it a "manifesto" because it is the simplest rules to follow if you want to thrive in our modern world. These strategies for money and time and mindset are rarely talked about and surely never spoken of in art school.

You don't know me, but if you did you'd know I'm a true artist. I paint and draw. I used to make large scale sculptures out of fabric and crazy 3D installations. If you know me from Instagram you know I founded a wallpaper company that has grown to be moderately successful. I want to confess that I started a business to give myself a day job, because frankly I was no good at working for someone else. I have a problem with authority. I have the mouth of a truck driver. I speak my mind a lot and it usually gets me in trouble. I have some things I want to teach you, if you're open to listening.

Whether you want to take the leap into entrepreneurship, or you are already on your way, this boook is for you. If you are where I was a few years ago: tired of the grind, tired of never getting ahead and feeling like society doesn't value your contribution and your art degree has failed you. If you're feeling like "if only there were a way to do more of _____ (insert your creative pursuit of choice)."

In 2012 I received my Master of Fine Arts from the second best art school in the country. I went on to teach screen printing at the School of the Art Institute of Chicago. As a college professor I was making $16k per year and I had two little boys' mouths to feed. I took on two more part-time jobs to make ends meet and in 2015 I broke. One day, at age 33, I came home and decided to quit all my jobs and start a business. It was the ballsiest thing I'd ever done.

As my newfound career took off and I successfully funded my startup with the help of a $20,000 Kickstarter campaign, my marriage tanked. An unstable relationship buckled under the pressure of me possibly becoming the person I was meant to be instead of the keeper of the castle. My husband moved out in May of 2016 and I have been a single mother ever since. Though the chaos of the past few years is not something I would wish to live through again— nor would I wish it on my worst enemy— I am a stronger person for it. The lessons I learned in the oast 6 years are bottled up here for you to uncork. Like a ship in a bottle, I hope this message reaches you when it matters most.

I have climbed a ladder that I created for myself. I'm still climbing. At the end of my ladder is 'Thriving.' Success means something totally different to each of us, and our ladders are all different lengths. You might be closer than you think to the top. Reaching for that place of personal growth and artistic development is a lifelong pursuit, one that is easier if you don't feel so god damn alone. Let's form a cohort or commune of thriving artists who say "See! We're not all losers. We're highly valuable and we can do great things." By lifting up one artist (you) I hope it inspires all of us. Watching you thrive (and knowing I helped in some way) will be one of the greatest achievements of my life. If you, artist/creator of things/entrepreneur can go out into the world and conquer personal milestones while your friends and family watch, you just might prove to folks that artists CAN and will thrive.

This book is meant to be uplifting, powerful, hilarious, and practical. It might be sad at times. I may put you to task so apologies now if I pick apart every excuse you've ever given for why you CAN'T. I've been called "bossy" more times in my life than I'd like to recount, so it's okay if you take my tone to be demanding or a wee bit judgy. It's with the best of intentions that I kick you smack in the ass. It's time to start living your best life as an artist, the one that was meant for special, creative, brilliant people like you.

Happy Reading,

–Erin

Part One

Learning Resilience

Resilience is the capacity to recover quickly from difficulty, failure or disappointment. Resilience knows that failure is not the end of the line, it's part of the process. Learning how to overcome adversity is not something they teach in school, though in art school we have made it part of the culture to critique and poke holes in an artist's argument. So, if you went to art school you will be familiar with resilience techniques to some degree. But at the end of the semester, it is that critique that you work so hard towards. You slave away in your studio, losing sleep and letting your mascara drip under your eyelids a little by morning time. Having pulled so many all nighters working on your art piece, you have learned Process, Technique, and ended on a Form that hopefully you were proud of. When you stand next to your work you try with all your might to explain the piece. Sometimes we speak in metaphors. Sometimes we tell the whole, precarious story of how you made the art. The many staples it took. How hard it was to manipulate the clay in high humidity weather. How it cracked and you had to rebuild it again.

Sometimes, the making holds meaning, just by way of the feelings you had at the time. When I stand next to a mural I painted a year ago, I remember the exact music I was listening to. The boy I was pining over. I see certain areas or brush strokes and I remember how tired I was at the end of a long day. How I pushed to finish.

Resilience is no stranger to us. Artists have adapted to a way of life that is full of struggle for some reason or another. The romantic Jack Kerouac tale of stuffing all your belongings into a suitcase and heading out West. The James Franco melodrama of defining one's self by starting a new medium midway through your career, in essence starting over and being at the bottom of the food chain. We, like Sylvia Plath, the poet, hope of winning our Pulitzer Prize posthumously. We keep our work stocked away in archival envelopes and bubble wrap in hopes that our life's work may make it into the collection of the Guggenheim, the Met, or the Art Institute. Whether you are an author, a painter, a dancer, a designer, an actress, an architect, or just a lousy stick figure drawer this book was written with you in mind. The first section denotes a shift in our collected cultural comradery of the suffering, the starving, the slaving away, the sunken ship of being a true artist. I'd like to propose a different outcome for the story of the creative person who lives their life in the pursuit of success, fame or fortune. I would like for you to thrive in your lifetime. And I would like to announce that the only thing keeping you from doing that is ... you.

Chapter 1

Reimagining The Artist Identity

Let me start by defining the "Artist." I am not talking about people who can draw and paint. I am not talking about musicians with record labels or stage actors like Lin-Manuel Miranda. An artist is defined (by me) as someone who creates or has an imagination. If you are breathing air you likely have ideas and sometimes need to problem solve how to make those ideas come to life. You may be creative in your gardening techniques. You may be creative in karate class. You may be creative in your kitchen, tweaking a recipe from a cookbook, or making up your own recipes. You may like to dance but don't consider yourself an artist. You might knit scarves or tinker in your garage. "You and I and everyone you know are descended from tens of thousands of years of makers… The guardians of high culture will try to convince you that the arts belong only to a chosen few, but they are wrong and they are also annoying. We are all the chosen few. We are all makers by design. Your creativity is way older than you are, way older than any of us. Your very body and your very being are perfectly designed to live in collaboration with inspiration, and inspiration is still trying to find you—the same way it hunted down your ancestors."[1]

This book is for anyone who makes things or "stuff" or "shit" or "work." This book is also for those who want to make things. Who have ideas (or want to have ideas). Anyone who's imagination runs wild, telling stories or making up images or inventing things. This book is for every person, but especially, for those who identify as an artist or creative person or designer. Those of you who have a craft, who've been making since you were young and who deeply want to create a life where these things are acceptable. Maybe even profitable. This is going to be your how-to guide to getting started. To create as if your life depends on it. Because it does.

---

[1] Elizabeth Gilbert, Big Magic: Creative Living Beyond Fear

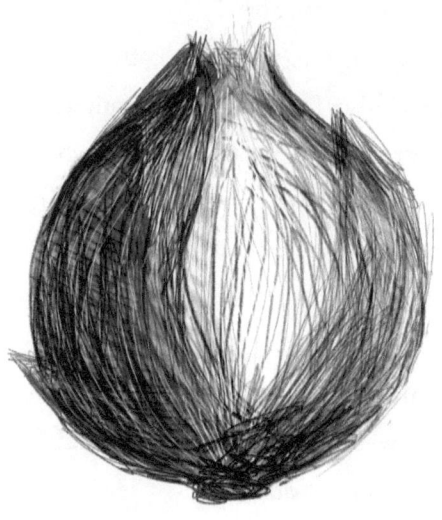

The Big Peel

Depending on where you are at right now, a book on art and business or wealth may seem like the least likely thing you need. You're working a job and trying to raise a family (or yourself). You have a creative pursuit (or you did once) and your hobby is like your habit; a drug you can't seem to quit. Doing it all is an admirable goal. But, I am starting this book with a distinction from every other self-help book out there. I'm starting by stating the obvious: *You're not rich.*

If you consider yourself an artist, you might say: *"Erin, I'm an artist. Artists aren't rich."* I hear you. Like you, once upon a time I believed the same thing. I was drinking from the fountain of Kool-Aid where artists believe they are destined to struggle and starve. Because the starving artist, as a persona, is honorable and/or fashionable. Because there aren't any jobs. Because society devalues us. Because our degree is worthless. Because we have no marketable skills. I want to wrap you in a cozy

CHAPTER 1: REIMAGINING THE ARTIST IDENTITY

blanket by the fireplace and have you elaborate to me all the reasons why this is vividly true for you. Like an impressionist painting of elite white people by the lake, this story is elaborately built with tiny brush strokes and extraordinary attention to detail. It has caused you joy and pain to spend your life singing a sad song to this melody. Each note: angsty and anti-establishment. Hitting the personal all the way to the societal octaves. There is irony and sincerity.

I am here to scratch the record and stop you dead in your tracks. This starving artist fantasy is about to end.

Recently, after revising the manuscript for this book, I decided to pose a question to my Facebook audience about the stumbling blocks that artists face. They stated things I mentioned above: problems with motivation and self-worth. They corroborated with one another using memes of crying chicks, the text below reads "It's just hard." I know that the struggle is ever present and feels more real each and every day. We lost jobs due to the pandemic, juggled our personal lives, and lost our social connections. We feel anxiety about the future and fear for our health and the wellbeing of those we love.

Still, I believe we hold tight to the notion that an artist has no place in this world, nowhere that values him/her/them. The alternative is to address a more dismal truth. **You are struggling or starving because of YOU.** What if the only thing that is holding you back from being a wealthy, healthy, and vibrant version of yourself are your excuses, your shitty mindset, and the seventeen people you know who are also in the same boat? The solution then isn't governmental support of The Arts or more accountable educational systems or the destruction of capitalism! Those things will not happen. Not in my lifetime and not in yours. What are you doing today to better yourself, support yourself, and create a micro-economy for one? What are you doing to make art that matters or expresses your worldview? What are you doing to make sure your legacy is golden?

If you are holding your breath for society to change, it gives you no agency and you're going to run out of air. Fantasy over. You ain't Jack Kerouac. You're not Frida either. Your bohemian lifestyle may qualify you for food stamps. Your Manic Panic hairstyle might turn eyeballs but it's not bringing in dollars, so in this case the advertising campaign is unsuccessful. You are putting yourself half-assed on display and waiting for the art world to discover you instead of going out and tracking down the life you want. The tooth fairy and the art world have nothing in common; they're not going to come into your bedroom in the night and place a dollar under your pillow. The gallerists aren't going to discover you and give you an exhibition just because you've been earnestly dicking around in the studio for ten years. You need to return to primitive survival mode where Maslow's hierarchy of needs is a motivational poster on the wall. If you're starving, you sharpen your spear and leave the cave. You hunt until you find sustenance. (Sorry vegans, I know you hate this metaphor). Find the life you want. At any cost. **This is the new paradigm.**

Let's start with another metaphor. I love metaphors and I will be using them throughout this book. I know you will appreciate them because you too are a visual creature. This chapter is called "The Big Peel" because it is time to peel back the layers of your onion. Yep, you're a stinky vegetable after all of these years of suffering and it makes other people want to cry to be in a room with you. But, somewhere, deep down inside there is a tender and sweet magic that the world needs to know about.

Years of scripts about "creatives" have worn you down and made you put your paintbrush and easel in a closet, laying them to rest for

CHAPTER 1: REIMAGINING THE ARTIST IDENTITY

a "real job" or a more practical life than the colorful one lived by Van Gogh. He is known for being nuts. He chopped his ear off for love. Is that the way you want to be remembered? Do you want people to pity you or admire you? Your parents told you to pick any career but "artist" because they wanted what was best for you. You may have been ridiculed by peers and colleagues for having a creative hobby like making coffee mugs or having a dark room in your basement. These indulgences, aka hobbies, have become your therapy and secret habit you can't kick. It's your addiction that you hide from everyone else. You've tried to quit but you can't.

What would happen if I told you that you could become a millionaire using your passion and talent? And if you did that, you could help people or make the world a better place? Would you believe me? I know you're skeptical but if even 50% of you are curious then keep reading. I will show you simple and practical things you can do to get out of your own head, clean up your room and get on to the best life you've ever had. One thing though: you have to make a vow to yourself to be open: to new ideas, new things, new habits. Try some things you haven't done before- even if you don't think it's going to work. You ready?

Please say thank you to your brain for sharing its doubts. "Thank you for sharing." Your brain took less than 5 seconds to convince you that there is *no way* that you could become a millionaire. Just so you know, I had my doubts too. Art school cost me a fortune ($224,000 by the time I was through with my Master's Degree) and when I leapt out into the real world I thought there was no place for me anymore. My mind deduced that since I went to school to become a teacher and now, I wasn't one, I lived a life of mediocrity and financial instability. I knew that it was possible for artists to become rich and famous, but that fortune wasn't the *purpose* of art. Furthermore, only a select few artists would be able to take that much space in the "Art World."

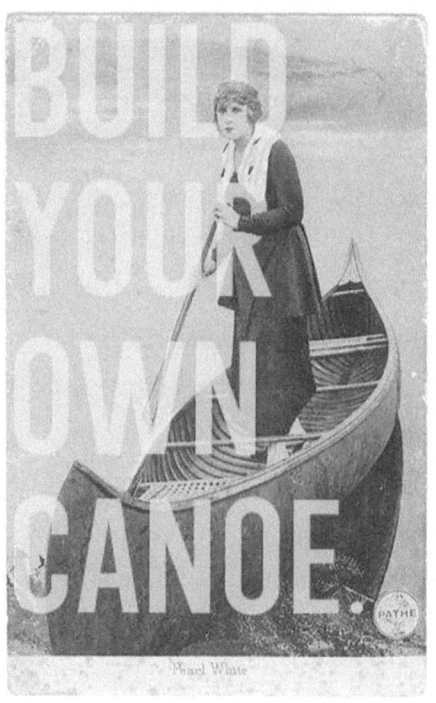

The Art World is a Life Raft

Auspiciously, Jerry Saltz became my advisor in graduate school. For those who aren't familiar with his name he is the author of the book, "How to Be an Artist," the star of a Bravo TV show called, "A Work of Art" that aired in 2011 and oh-by-the-way senior art critic and columnist at NY Magazine and received the Pulitzer Prize for Criticism in 2018.

When Jerry Saltz flew from NYC to meet me in my studio for the first time, I was nervous and excited. I introduced myself and launched into the content of my work. Racial identity, cultural assimilation, narratives of belonging, and what I called "unbelonging." My work was made from found fabric, cut, sewn and woven and hanging like weird 3-Dimensional nests of chaos. Jerry spoke intelligently and was complimentary of my work and ideas. He said that Contemporary Art is straddling the line between authenticity and irony. He said my work belonged in a gallery in NYC and he could see it there right now. I was flattered, in awe, shocked, and invigorated. I whined to him that I was just a broke art student with a kid and didn't know how I'd ever make it to the gallery scene in Chelsea?! He paused as if to change the course of our conversation.

"The Art World… is like a life raft. When a ship wrecks and begins to sink, everyone is vying for a seat in the raft. The ones who make it have life preservers and the ones who don't are all treading water or drowning in the ocean all around. There are only 10-12 seats in the raft, maximum. Three seats are for artists, three are for gallerists, three are for collectors and one more for a curator. If I'm lucky one seat is for a writer."

I interpreted this as a gruesome metaphor, not a message of hope. Realizing that my peers, working furiously in their studios until all hours of the night, were fighting to be a drowning victim in the ocean gave me chills. Like Syrian refugees, we had unrealistic ideas about the freedom that lies on the other side of the Mediterranean Sea. We were ill prepared. We didn't know that peril was ahead if we didn't make a plan. We didn't pack a our pool floaties and now our family and friends might watch as we gasp for our last breaths of air, hoping to survive in the Capital "A" Art World.

I wasn't going to become a statistic like that. I'd love to say that I deserved a seat in that raft. But, I am neither the most talented artist known to man nor the most aggressive to take a life preserver from someone else. I thought about that conversation many times since then. I admire Jerry Saltz very much for telling me straight about his vantage point in the raft that he currently sits in. That said, I had no interest in spending my life devoted to being one of the few in the competitive Art World, not knowing when my time would expire, and I would be replaced by another sexier, more controversial artist.

I have forged a different fate for myself. I figure I've built myself a canoe. It's a humble but well-made boat and there is one seat. I have an oar that is old, but it works and I am paddling in the ocean. I see the drowning painters and potters and picture makers all around me in the dark sea. I watch sometimes when one of their heads sinks underwater like Jack from the movie "Titanic." They really just went on to become an arts administrator and got a desk job. They barely draw anymore. We each see the raft in the distance and it looks glorious.

I read about contemporary artists in the Sunday paper and online. I watch their stories on Art:21. Rather than admire them for their enormous exhibitions or press, I wonder how many sleepless nights lead to that breakeven point; how much time it took to receive that recognition. See, most of the famous artists we know spent decades treading water and waited for their time in the raft and they earned it with their authentic struggle. But what was their quality of life for ten to twenty years? Likewise, I knew right away once I became a professor that I'd potentially teach part-time for 15 years before being tenured. That ocean had a few different life rafts, but occupancy was also limited.

My vision is to teach people how to build their own canoes. So that they can exist in the same ocean called the World. Not the Art

World. Just how to make a nice life for themselves by making art. Experiencing joy and giving magic to others. Whether it's high or low doesn't really matter at all! It's that you aren't drowning. You can be carefree. That's what I hope to package and sell to you by the end of this book. And if you can latch onto my gimmicks and tricks, I think you'll be able to do it. Possibly even better than I have.

Art and Money

What I didn't know [or want to admit] when I left the MFA program at SAIC were these two things: Art and Money are not mutually exclusive. I'll give you the abridged version of this entire book right now. Art loves money and money loves art. I have spent the past five years growing my wealth and changing my habits while being determined to stick to my vision of being rich and doing what I love to do. Money comes towards me. Money has helped me, and I've sought many opportunities to make money. People love original art and they're not even museum goers. They want to spend money to "support" an artist, as much as they want to adopt a cat but don't have space in their home. That's why they send a monthly check to PAWS animal shelter.

There are three things you need to do in order to make money making art: 1) Make Art. 2) Sell the Art. 3) Take that money you made and make more art. Why can't it be that simple? Want to know the moral of this entire book? The one thing that holds you back from doing the same? *It's your mind.*

I could teach you how to start and run a business. I can teach you how to tell your authentic story and market yourself. I can teach you how to price your work, run a successful crowdfunding campaign, design a website and what to do with your money to grow a small fortune. But that's not the point of this book. I want you to cleverly devise your own blueprint for your own canoe. You're a web designer and yoga enthusiast by day, but you love rock music and wish to be designing band posters for First Aid Kit (the band). Or you're a stay at home mom and with nap time approaching you get itchy to list all your old drawings on Etsy and just see what happens. You already have a plan and a dream.

First, before I can teach you how to sell your ideas and skills to the world, I have to return to the "Big Peel." Over years of struggle and hardening, your onion is as hard as a witch's tit in a brass bra on the south side of the equator. Once you peel away the dry, moldy, ugly brown layers of skin on the outside of your onion, you begin to take the rotten stink of "settling" off the table. Take it off the counter, out of the kitchen and put it where it belongs, in the compost pile far, *far* away. Stop settling for mediocre.

Here's how we get down to the sweetest interior part of the onion, where it's tender and compact and precious. Here, your creative magic hasn't been formed or damaged too much by the outside world and hasn't taken any tumbles. There are no scars there and it's 100% authentically YOU. Think about you in first grade, doing your thing. Creating all types of stuff. Honoring all your ideas as 'genius.' You wore a cowboy hat around and didn't care if your pants were backwards. You had courage and your stuffed animals or siblings were your entourage. Let's unearth that guy or gal or person. Let's peel it way back to the place where everything you dream can come true.

That interior magic you possess is what is most valuable. In order to figure out how to present your gifts to others, sell a shit ton of your art and thrive--like, really thrive--you have to make some money. Not a job. Hear me this time. Earn a paycheck that you made for yourself. Be the boss of your own life.

You ready for the "the Big Peel?" I'll go first.

CHAPTER 1: REIMAGINING THE ARTIST IDENTITY

Motherhood and Life After Art School

It was almost the holidays in 2015. I had an infant son and a three-year-old boy and my husband was working as a flight attendant for Delta Airlines. I'd been working three jobs to make ends meet and put my kids into daycare and preschool part-time so that I could work. I was living in a spacious three bedroom apartment in Ukrainian Village, a neighborhood inhabited by many Ukrainians, historically Polish, but now mixed in with Puerto Ricans and a whole mix of other ethnicities. My place was run down, not anything special though the living room was vast and had great sunlight. I used to fight with my downstairs neighbor, Renee, because she liked to play music late at night and the baby would wake up. She had a ceiling fan that made my floor vibrate and I was already lacking sleep, but every attempt to ask her to stop these things so that I could have some quiet were in vain. She'd say *"Why don't you move to the suburbs?"*

I'd lay awake at night and blame a lot of things while listening to that fan go "Wah, wah, wah…" I'd blame my husband and his job for taking him out of the family equation 5 days a week. I'd blame myself for not having chosen a better degree or gotten a better job. After all, I think it was <u>US News</u> that came out with an article about the "Top 5 Most Useless Master's Degrees" and under the MBA, which too many people have and don't utilize, was the MFA. My Master in Fine Arts from the number three school in the country had landed me a part-time teaching gig. I'd taught for two years there when I realized my salary was going to cap out at around $16,000/year. I'd blame Chicago's weather for making the winter so unbearable; the way the wind threatens to rip the top layer of your face off the closer you get to the lake. I'd blame my parents for not helping me enough. I'd blame myself

25

for choosing to have kids because I didn't feel prepared to do this alone. I would blame Delta Airlines for hiring my husband as soon as he came to America. The amount of white shirts I needed to help him iron. The shoe polish, and then he was gone again. I'd become a professional blamer.

For the last year or so the baby would wake up in the middle of the night, around 2:00 AM. He was such a good baby and he'd generally go right back to sleep. But I would put him down in his crib and then sit awake in my bed. Laying in the dark. Trying to figure out how to forge a future for myself and my kids without their father in the picture? I was considering the worst. He was always gone and I was so lonely. Parenting was so fucking hard I wanted to cry most of the time. Being without their dad made me feel pitiful at BBQ's where two parent households traded off who left early to tuck in the babies. I was a single mom while married. Sometimes I had no idea what country or time zone my husband was even in. I was wishing for a partner. I began to obsess about a fictitious other man who could swoop into my life and fill the void.

I am a relatively positive person and I tried to push past the resentment and fear. I'd open my laptop during those late nights awake and try to focus on some digital files I was doing for a wallpaper company I was working for as a freelancer. I was teaching myself how to use Adobe Illustrator while doing their files. Illustrator is not intuitive and many times I lost all of my work when my laptop ran out of juice and I hadn't been religiously saving the edits. As a freelancer, I was charging by the hour but you can't charge for doing the work twice when you screw it up. The hours were flexible, but I didn't have energy to work after a long day of teaching and the kids demanded all of my mental capacity. So, I'd cat nap til 2 AM and then get back to work on a "chintz" floral design with tiny details. Little deer with polka dots less than a centimeter in size, flowers with eastern flair each had teeny tiny marks that needed to be separated into different layers on the artboard. It was tedious. I began to hate that Chintz pattern because it had sucked so many hours of my life away.

I was designing their fabric collection. This particular designer knew nothing about Adobe Illustrator or Photoshop. I was able to charge them about $100/hour for my time and that was the most I'd ever been able to ask for. They were happy to have me work my magic. I felt like an expert. Needless to say my own personal art practice had come to a screeching halt the year I had my second kid. I had no art practice. I did nothing but care for babies and work for money. Work for pleasure or practice or process or progress was not happening. It felt good to be paid because that meant my skills were appreciated. I would have gladly left the teaching gig to be a textile designer full time since I had my doubts about all my 20-something children. Did my students really give a shit about what I had to say? Teaching was part of the common narrative of those who leave art school though.

Teaching the Future Generation

Teaching for peanuts at a prestigious art school was the pinnacle of one's career and an honorable way to be paid. It was either that or becoming a barista at Intelligentsia where fashionable and smart looking artists poured steamed milk into butterfly patterns and counted to thirty while pouring hot water over a coffee filter. My form of suffering involved my inflated ego; those who went to school with me were envious that I'd gotten to teach two classes a semester. They'd congratulate me for my peanut salary. I would oblige by thanking them.

Suffering is what we do as artists. We work in thankless jobs. We earn shamefully low wages. We are "slaves" to our craft. I was an expert at suffering.

So while my nights were a mix of the babies I had created and creations I had yet to give birth to, my days were spent on an imaginary bicycle teaching entitled 20-something babies how to pedal backwards just like me. I was going nowhere fast and getting exhausted doing it. My ego was a kind of schizophrenic dictator telling me to keep up the facade of being a college professor, whilst standing in line for food stamps. I was trying to be the upper echelon and wound up being the bottom tier of the food chain. Each hardship I endured earned me one more crusty onion layer.

My evaluations said I was too hard on my students. Au contraire. I had a hard knocks approach to teaching college. I reminded the undergrad students that their degree was "worthless." That society wouldn't compensate them for their ability to make art or talk about ideas. That if they really wanted to make it, they'd have to work extra hard and that this classroom was just practice for the real world. That some of the most important skills they could learn to practice in the classroom were to:

1) Show up on time They say that half the battle is showing up. The other 50% is doing the work. I can't tell you how many times I had students who were drifting into my college class blaming the elevator for why they were 30 minutes late. The train. The part they don't want to admit is that they hit the snooze button twice and there was a snowball effect which caused them to get on the train three trains after the last one that would have gotten them downtown on time. They didn't plan for any single minute of complication. They also don't care that much because they were paying a fortune to be in my class and they might not even like the class. Those legitimate reasons aside, the skill set that some artists do not have is preparing to be there 15 minutes early. In fact, I'm going to venture to say that almost ALL artists have this problem. Now, I'm not perfect, and I've been known to be 15 minutes late wherever I go, but I will tell you this. If you own a business and you're bringing lunch to an interior design firm of 12 people who are all ravenous by noon and can't wait to take a break and listen to you talk about wallpaper? You sure as heck better be there 15 minutes early. To set up your PowerPoint presentation and set out plastic cutlery. Because if you roll in 30 minutes late? You just lost thousands of dollars of potential business. So, you have to start being the CEO of your own goddam life. Period.

2) Be prepared I can't count how many times I've shown up to a job site to paint a mural or install a wallpaper and realized I forgot the most important piece or part or tool at home. Having to leave to go buy a screwdriver at the nearest hardware store in Chicago can sometimes cost you an hour. Walking to your car, Googling "ACE near me" and parking takes up a good 20 minutes most times. So, when my adult babies showed up to a screen printing for fabric class without any fabric, I rolled my eyes so hard I became a zombie creeper and almost ate their Minecraft-shaped dumb head off. I allowed them to lose an hour to go to the nearest JoAnn's by train and just essentially counted them absent for the day because they'd miss instruction time, studio time and classroom culture time by not being present. So, for fuck's sake let's get serious about preparing the night before. Making a permanent copy of a "List of *What to Bring*" before you go to a job site can help you slow down and double check things before you leave the house and avoid the pitfalls of creative brain deadness.

3) Read the goddam directions Studio messes happen when people don't use the materials correctly and they don't follow the instructions on the packaging. When you share space with 14 other people, who is going to be the one to clean up the mess? You, 20 something entitled private art school princess? Or me, 30 something mother of two kids who is going to have to stay at daycare until 5:30 now because Ashley accidentally used oil based ink instead of water based ink and now the sink is clogged? Yah, the latter. I get really frustrated when your dilemma stems from one simple mistake: "Did you read the directions?" No. This goes for all of life. If you don't know how high to hang a pendant light over an island, you can Google it! Read the directions! And if no directions exist then find a qualified person to ask BEFORE you go and make a mess. Call uncle John who is a contractor. Call a friend who is an interior designer. Look up a lighting showroom in the g- d- phone book. Find the answer somewhere.

I usually had two students per semester who achieved all three, and for the other 14 kids, I pulled in a white board and wrote out their tuition ROI.

Four years. In college. At a prestigious school in one of the largest metropolitan cities in America. Two semesters. Five classes per semester at 3 credit hours each. $49,301 per year meant $197,204 in student loan debt for a degree. Amortized to be about $275K once you factor in how long it would take to pay it off... And that each half hour they missed class cost them $19.50. Now, $19.50 is not a lot of money. But it is the same as the cost of a pack of cigarettes, a latte and a muffin. It was the cost of a burrito and a beer. It was almost four train rides on the "L" at

Art School R.O.I.

$49,301/year ÷ 2 semesters = $24,650

15 credit hours/semester

$4,930 (3 credits)/class

÷ 18 weeks = $273.89/week

÷ 7 hours = $39/hour

different times of the day. It wasn't *a lot*. But it wasn't zero either. And if they consistently showed up 15 minutes late, not only were they in danger of failing the class, but they were losing money left and right.

So I wanted to give them the best bang for their buck. I wanted to teach the class that no one was teaching when I was in grad school. The class where they'd learn how to exist in the real world after school. The one where they'd learn how to present themselves on paper and get a job or apply to an artist residency. Or apply for an exhibition.

I made my students turn in their resume and a cover letter and they complained about "too much writing." And there I was making $32/hour to show up early, stay late, clean up their messes and answer calls from their moms when their grades finally came in and they failed due to seven tardies. I stuck to the academic protocol of the school--since I didn't make up that rule--and I ended up getting fired for it.

The Fall of the Empire

I'll never forget the day I got called into a meeting with the Chair of the Fiber and Materials Studies Department. A stern and well-built woman, with red glasses and short brown hair with one swatch painted bright pink for the Women's March (or some three quarter's life attempt to stay relevant). Dressed as an artist, not an academic, which is to say all black, androgynous and layered, hiding her female form. Her work is well renowned. Her catalog of the last exhibition was written by a well-known Chicago writer. Her exhibitions draw large crowds of people who admire her work.

The list of candidates who wanted my job was long. But she hadn't been the one to hire me. Her tenure had just begun. And I knew she didn't like me. I wasn't fond of her either, but I didn't lead on. I was respectful to her as my elder and because I had just attended school in that very same department. The transition from student to colleague must have been hard for some of the faculty members so I acted accordingly, always a little overly friendly and still accommodating or helpful. I sat at the circle shaped table in her office that was built for maybe three to sit at. She rolled her chair over and began with a compliment. That was never a good sign.

"Erin, you know I like you very much and you are a very talented artist."

This wasn't going to be good.

"Thank you, Joan."

"But it has come to my attention that your style of teaching has lifted some eyebrows..." she went on to describe how she talked with many students about their experience in my class. That I'd been posting about them on my personal social media, which I had. I stated how much they pushed me to be a good teacher, how they made me proud, etc. She mentioned that my presence in the classroom was a bit out of the ordinary. She went on to describe that my role in the department was that of the lowest rung on the ladder. She didn't say that outright and our conversation is hard for me to recollect with exactitude but a quote I will never forget was this:

"Your enthusiasm is a hindrance."

What did this even mean?

Joan politely asked me not to come back the next semester. She explained that there were just too many student evaluations that reported that I was "too hard" on the students and required "too much writing." It was then and there that I was sure I was bamboozled. I'd been in the wrong place this whole time! I'd taught for three years and strived to earn my rank. For what? To be told that I needed to not voice (with enthusiastic tones) my opinions in staff meetings? I was the lowest on the totem pole as an adjunct faculty. It would be years until anyone asked me to submit my own syllabus to teach. Until then, just stick to the program, like everyone else did in their first few years. Don't require too much. Don't fail anyone. Don't ask too much of the students.

Higher education is an ocean of its own. I had once really wanted to teach college but that's not why you get an MFA. You get your degree to refine your philosophy, your mission statement as an artist and in an almost debate tournament-style of argument, you refine how to talk about your work. Artists spent their lifetimes making work that would hopefully someday make it to a retrospective exhibition in a museum like the one across the street. But all I wanted to do was teach. I had taught high school art, but it wasn't for me. My dad was a teacher, so I had always thought maybe I'd be good at it. Turns out, I wasn't as good as I thought I was. Or maybe the life raft was too cramped.

I firmly believe that the students who wrote reviews that I made them write too much are ridiculous. I made them turn in their resume and cover letter so that they'd be more prepared for the "real world!" That was their writing assignment. I was trying to teach the class I never had in art school. The one where an ounce of professional practice was mixed into studio time. If that was too much to ask of a human in their 20's there was something fundamentally wrong with the institution of art schools. Those kids should have their resumes on their desktop ready to send out at the drop of a hat. Phew. I get heated when thinking about all the ways art school fails each of us by the time we leave...

I identified as an academic, a teaching artist. That vision had shattered. I was depressed when I realized I wasn't a teacher anymore. I'd been stripped of my rank and my Master's degree now had no value. I'd gone through all that school to get a teaching job and after two years got fired. What was next for me then? If I wasn't a teacher...why was I here? Why had I spent four years getting my MFA? That was literally the only job my degree was needed for-- teaching at the college level-- otherwise the MFA is not necessary to be a professional artist! It's not necessary to start a business! It's only needed when getting a teaching job. Had I wasted all my time going to graduate school? Oh, and suddenly, when you don't have a job...a panic sets in. *What am I going to do for a living?* What will my peers think when they realize I had two classes a semester, which was really such a triumph for someone straight out of school. Had I squandered that opportunity?

A few years back I'd planned to get pregnant at the end of the summer so that I'd have my second son in June. His summer birthday meant that I would be able to go back to teaching in September. Summer would be my maternity leave. Getting pregnant isn't easy but want to know what else isn't easy? Teaching screen printing classes while you're big and pregnant. Hauling ten-pound frames around and using pressure washers and doing demo's and being on your feet all day is hard.

In the blink of an eye, my life shifted. What I had built crashed down. My identity had to morph like flubber into some other shape. I'd have to use all the inherent skills and worth to make some value somewhere else. Luckily, I'd been working at a second job at a wallpaper factory. There I was learning a lot of new skills. I had something else to fall back on. I was even experimenting with creating some wallpaper designs of my own. But that was just a shot in the dark.

The layers of my onion kind of cascaded to the floor beyond my control. Like the big fat tears bolting out of Alice in Wonderland's eyes when she realizes the tiny door is locked and she made herself enormous by eating the little piece of cake. Her tears flood the room. Thin layers of my crusty onion skin were madly ripping from my core, heavily pounding against the floor, eventually exposing the parts of me I didn't want to admit to. The weak and tender core may not withstand the real world without it's shield. What was I to do now?

In retrospect it was a blessing in disguise.

In the months that followed I started to look at Relativity Textiles as a real business venture. I stayed up many long nights figuring things out. I asked a million questions to a million people. I designed a website, established my LLC, produced packaging that was hand letterpress, assembled a team of interns (who happened to be from SAIC). I was no longer teaching but I filled my mentorship void by telling young women how to be a badass and go out after school and rock their life like I was doing. The career development office loved my story and featured me as a visiting speaker to talk to students about how to run a business. The irony there was immense.

The Emperor's New Clothes

My very first client was Allison Reimus. A Chicago based artist, she was in an art show with me at an "apartment gallery." This is what differentiates Chicago's Art scene from NY or LA. We are so midwestern that we roll up our sleeves and curate exhibitions with lofty titles and real printed catalogs, though the venue is our living room. We invite tons of art friends and offer cheap beer to all. Allison's colorful paintings sat atop my wallpaper. Since I had no recent art to display I hung my experimental black and gold zig zag print up as "Art." Allison liked it so much she asked if I could do it in white and gold to which I just said "yes" without knowing how to make it happen. She asked if I could install it, and I said "yes," though I'd only installed wallpaper once. And that was for this exhibition.

The white and gold "Kilim" wallpaper was inspired by Moroccan rug designs. My husband was from Morocco and I'd been back and forth many times, always inspired by the patterns. Allison wanted it in her nursery, and being that she was an artist, she staged and decorated the room so adorably that it needed to be photographed. Her pictures were submitted (by her) to a monthly competition on a nursery website. All the DIY mamas sent in their rooms hoping to win a product giveaway for baby. And out of the blue, her nursery won "Nursery of the Month." This was in 2015. An outpouring of comments on the blog asked Allison where she'd gotten her lovely wallpaper! I didn't have a website, an email, an online shop, or even a business card.

I had to reinvent myself (or invent myself) very quickly. I had to don a new hat: "Entrepreneur". It came with a new culture. There were always seminars and webinars and speaker panels and mentorship opportunities. There are so many organizations for small business owners who knew nothing about art but were happy to know what I was doing and find resources for me. It was a supportive community. I could get used to this. I was still a creator of something, though not original art. I was a "founder" and created a brand. I manufactured wallpaper and the logo stood for cultural inclusion in the home decor arena. I was subtly tying my art practice into Relativity Textiles, a sneaky artist's approach to selling art by way of a desirable commodity.

One of the members of my group was in PR. I was asking her about magazines and how to get published when she stopped me and said, "I've got to tell you something. Is your website designed on Weebly?" Ooh, lemon juice on the wound! "Yes?" I had designed it myself during one of the 2:00 AM sessions. She politely told me that she wouldn't be sharing her press resources with me until I got a professional website because it looked really amateur. She gave me the number of a web designer and I audibly gulped. I knew this was what needed to happen, but I also did not think I could afford a real website. Didn't they cost a million dollars?

I got way outside my comfort zone when the web guy gave me homework: I was to make four short videos to introduce my brand to my friends on social media. I needed to actively try to find subscribers for an email newsletter also. Eventually, I'd need to sell my brand to the outside world. Things that were made with my hand drawn image on them. My art was going to be a product, and it started with my Sharpie drawings on tracing paper. I drafted this narrative of me as the creator of beautiful objects. Objects that existed in a luxury market. I felt fraudulent at first as a starving artist, speaking about a luxury brand but I didn't have a choice.

Looking at my art as a livelihood was my only way out of the pit of debt I'd dug myself into. It was the only daytime job I could do while being a mother of two little boys with no capital and no formal office space. On my dining room table, my interns and I started sticking labels on the back of hand cut wallpaper samples. Licking all the stamps ourselves. Learning Jedi mind tricks to write email newsletters with a catchy "Call to Action" and scouring the internet for the mailing address of any interior design firm in Chicago who'd publish their whereabouts.

I made my career path to become an entrepreneur instead of a teacher-- instead of an "Artist" with a capital "A." I left teaching to find my true calling. To be the boss. Where no one can politely ask me not to come back. Where I make the rules and where the only people who attend my presentations REALLY want to be there. They'll even come ten minutes early. Where I generally foot the bill, but every success and every failure is my own. Where I was trying to follow my own guidelines that no one had wanted to listen to: 1) Show up on time, 2) Do the work 3) And since there's no goddam directions for how to be an entrepreneur, well, I guess I'll have to write a handbook while I'm at it too.

Too Legit to Quit

What's your melting point story? Where is the place where you pivot and stop doing what's gotten you nowhere up until now? You might have a cushy day job with benefits. You make a spreadsheet and decide that you can never afford to leave said day job and so…? You stay there forever while it sucks out your soul? Or you craft a new narrative and identity too? See, I had a lot of rugs pulled out from under me. Job? Fired. Husband? Moved out. Teaching gig? Nope. Do you think my student loans cared that I was a startup single mom? Nope. What about the daycare lady down the street? I don't suggest you cold turkey everyone and everything in your life with zero budget and no plan. What I did was haphazard and dumb. But it was an extraordinary advantage I had to start from scratch. *I had no other choice but to make it work.* What would it take for you to take that approach? To imagine that if you didn't make a wholehearted leap of faith into something new that you'd have extreme poverty awaiting you. You'd devise a plan. You'd build a canoe.

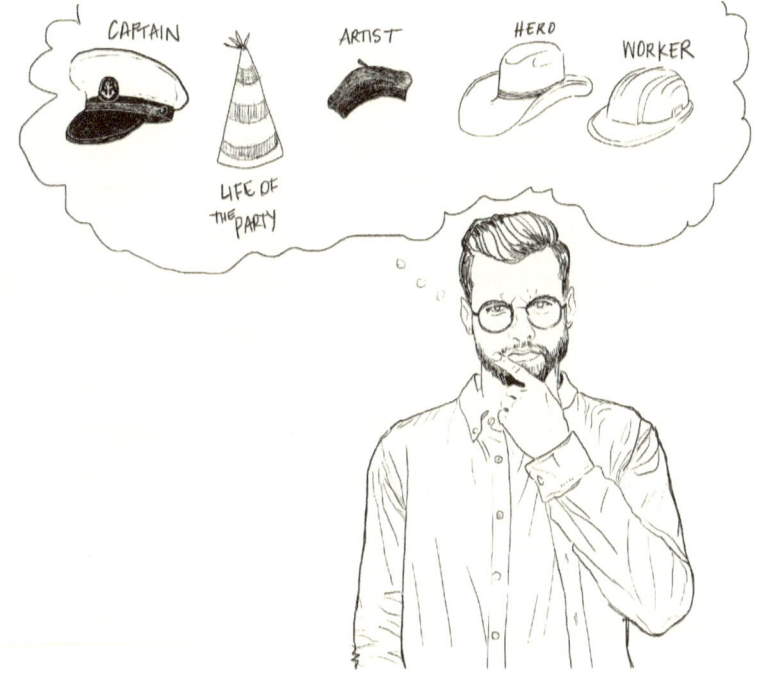

Reinventing One's Self

Once you've hit your melting point or rock bottom as I did, you're down to the soft and sensitive onion center. You're whittled down to a nub which feels very vulnerable. Here's where my identity as teacher and wife was stripped from me. I needed to redefine who I was. At 33 years old, it wasn't so much a mid-life crisis as an awakening to the prescribed path for artists and how it wasn't serving me. In my opinion, going to school for art prepared me very little for how to succeed. Where was I to learn that then? Was the "real world" really the only place left to turn to? I knew for a fact I couldn't go get a day job unless I wanted to be burnt out and snarky forever, so I created a business. But I knew nothing about running a business! As a matter of fact, I didn't consider myself a business person so I was going to have to catch up and learn some new tricks pretty quickly.

Here's where the chance to *edit your story* is super important. You get to define your life as anything you want it to be. You get to wear any hat you want, or many hats. I wanted to be a soccer mom, but also an edgy artist lady with Tibetan prayer flags in my front window. I wanted to not wear deodorant. I wanted to be an expert at something, at the same time, and get paid lots of money to talk about or teach or write about the things I knew a lot about (which were really fuckin' niche and there were limited venues to talk about them!). I wanted to find a way to live the life of a wealthy person so that I could make my own decisions about what I did with my time.

I didn't know how to get there. I didn't know all the steps involved. I didn't know what I didn't know. There were gaps in my understanding of "wealth" and business, and I didn't even know how vast the crevasse was between Here and There. The secret to getting there is to ask a lot of questions. Find someone who knows the answers. Ask for some guidance and don't be afraid to be humbled by how hard it is to start something new and know nothing. It might make you feel foolish, even, but didn't you also feel foolish riding your bike to the grocery store because you couldn't afford a car? And trekking it all back in a messenger bag, not because it was cool to be on a bike but because you literally were that broke?

Some of the keys to breaking free of the old "starving artist" life to become an artist who thrives are below. One is, self worth- value the lovely human you are and if you're in a spot where someone doesn't value you, find a new spot. Two is, flip the scripts- the old timey paradigm of artist suffragette isn't serving you anymore so you're going to need a new definition of a creative person.

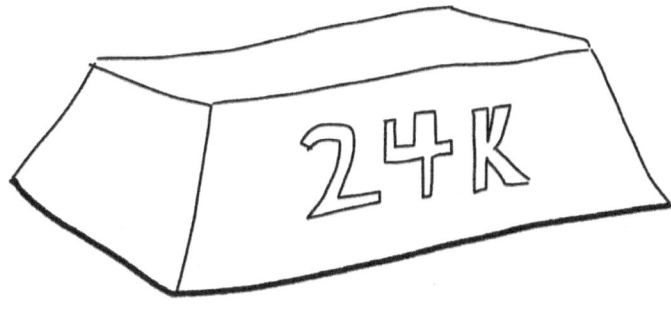

Know Your Worth

I want to share a story with you about knowing your place. I am not sure of the origin of this story, but it might be a parable or a passage from the Book of Mormon. As one of the only non-Mormon children raised in the 1980's in the state of Utah, there are many a story I grew up with that are just embedded in my subconscious like golden tablets hiding in the mountains. Maybe this is one of them.

Before dying, an elderly person told their child, "This is your grandfather's watch and it's a couple of hundred years old. But before I give it to you, please go to the watch shop and see how much they will offer you." The watch would be the son's only inheritance.

The son went to the watch shop and came back to report that the watchmaker offered $6.00 because it was old and would likely need repairs. The old person said that his son must try again. "Go to the coffee shop and see what they offer you," said the father.

The son left and soon returned with his research. "They offered me $3.00."

The old man said, "Go to the museum and show them the watch."

When the son returned, he said to his father "They offered me a million dollars."

"I wanted to let you know that the right place values you in the right way," said his father. "Don't find yourself in the wrong place and get angry if you are not valued. Those that know your value are those who appreciate you, don't stay in a place where nobody sees your value."

The story is a lesson to never doubt your own personal worth. There are places who will undervalue you because they know you are worth a lot, but they want to pay less than your worth. There are employers who will not see your value, and thus offer you a low price or keep you as a peripheral employee that never reaches full time benefits. They maybe need to fill a seat for the lowest amount in order to keep their own boat a float; It's not even about your skills or value sometimes, it's more about their own agenda. Each place of work (and every marketplace) has their own understanding of the cost of the watch (AKA you). However, you are the one who sets the price of your skills, your talent, your contribution and your potential. I'm not talking about the price of your artwork. I'm talking about you.

Sometimes we don't know our own worth until we shop around at a few places getting bids. There I was, with a terminal degree in my field. I was working with world class artists. I was teaching students who could afford a top-notch education. I was spending valuable hours each day preparing very well thought out lessons, helping students form their ideas and hone their screen-printing skills, trying to push them to think about their future career goals. I was cleaning up after them like a maid. I was counsel to countless undergrad and graduate students about whether their letter of intent to an artist residency application was good enough, what to do in a personal situation, how to afford things… and I really was attached to them in my heart. Some are still friends to this day, and a few became my employees once my business was up and running.

However, I was trying to pawn my watch at a coffee shop where they only wanted to give me $3.00.

I didn't know it at the time. I didn't see that all my effort was in the wrong arena and that I wouldn't win Joan or anyone else over no matter what I did. I donned the overalls of Rosie the Riveter and rolled up my sleeves to do the hard work of every female artist who ever lived. I sewed a makeshift white flag and climbed to the roof to mount it, surrendering to my fate. It felt honorable to fit into the army of other faculty members who had devoted their lives to students. These worker bees were all grateful for their jobs and so I must also serve the hive. That was the art world that I had wanted so desperately to be a part of, right?

Not true. It is through the hard knocks lessons that life throws at you where sometimes you learn. I will always be a teacher, even if I don't have a teaching job. I know that each of you have a pocket watch value and perhaps you too have been trying to pawn a million-dollar watch in the wrong place. So this story hopefully resonates with you. Let's turn it into a lesson like "When one door closes, another opens" though that one is overused.

No single opportunity is a make or break moment. Not for your career. Not for personal growth. Not for your fame or fortune. Because, see, each opportunity is testing you. It's calling you to audition, live on stage. You might not get the role or make the team. But you have to audition. And if you make it, that may lead to the next chapter of your creative life or career. But, when you don't get the part, the lesson is to become resilient. Get back up. Dust yourself off. And try again.

What if finding the museum where your worth is clearly priceless is a lifelong pursuit? Let's prepare a strategy for you to create an audience who will pay top dollar to hear you speak. Or buy your paintings. Or hire you to travel the world taking pictures. Let's narrow it down. I have so many activities planned for you. Don't worry about the "how" just yet. We have a few more onion peels to strip away.

Treat Yourself Like a Dear Friend (or Client)

How does an artist get to a place of 'self-worth' when they don't necessarily feel like there's a lot of people around them that value their contribution? How do you put the oxygen mask on yourself before you put it on anyone else? My aim of writing the first chapter is to give you a pep talk. A gentle nudge. A swift kick in the tush. Really, I want you to go about putting time and effort and energy into *loving yourself*. We spent so much time loving everyone else with as much energy as we can. We learned somewhere that if we value ourselves, if we take care of ourselves, if we say, "I'm great!" then we are arrogant or self-centered.

I think a lot of us fear the thought that we may become this self-righteous person if we tell ourselves that we are great. We fight against the notion that we are great because we don't want to come across as being conceited. Therefore, we put all of this energy into loving everyone else and pumping all of our friends up instead, giving everyone else a pep talk when they need it most. We tell them, "you can do it!" while encouraging our friends and neighbors that their decisions are valid and justified and moral. We tell them to follow their hearts. But we don't actually follow ours.

I can see from my own experience that I was afraid to pump myself up or congratulate myself. I was afraid to promote my artwork or my business or myself because I didn't want people to think negatively about me. I actually had this fear that all of the authentic artist friends I had who had been painting away in their studios way harder than me would consider me a "sell out" if I started a business and supported myself. I picture the scene in Princess Bride where Princess Buttercup is presented to the kingdom and an old hag yells out, *"Filth! Rubbish! Garbage!"* I thought that my family would think I was a showoff, obnoxiously marketing my skills as if I was better than them. I thought I was shallow for devoting time to social media and celebrating every 1,000 followers as if it was an actual legit milestone in life. Recognition was a dirty thing to have.

This is an upside-down way of thinking! When you are confident about yourself, the message you tell people is "I am valuable" without saying any words. You command a room; you speak with authority and expertise about your given topic. You assert your opinion. You dress to impress people, and you know what they think? "Who is that?!" They'll want to meet you. They'll gravitate towards you. When you begin to tell your story, they will ask for your card and stay to hear you speak. They'll look up your work. They might even hire you. To the girl with purple hair and a hole in the fanny of your jeans, "They're looking but they're not going to buy." Value your representation of yourself as if you're selling a decorative ostrich egg at Sotheby's. Hold yourself in high esteem! You'd be surprised how many people will approach you at an art fair where you're dressed professionally and ask about your work. When you say "my stuff" instead of "my newest collection of jewelry" how does it feel?

The language we use is important. The way we use our bodies is important. Art school may have led you astray in many ways but here's one fallacy that's bigger than Jeff Koonz's persona: your art isn't going to speak for itself. You have to be the spokesperson for yourself and your art, as if someone hired you to do it. As if someone is paying you to talk about your work. Because guess what? By the time you start selling your art, *that is exactly what the customers are doing.* They're paying for the privilege to know you and shop your collection. They think you're magical so it's time you think so as well. If you have to, PRETEND. Pretend to hold yourself in high esteem because after a while of doing it you just might start to see the shift from others that you were waiting for.

I resist the stereotypes about self-help books being fluffy and new agey... but including this word will turn a lot of people off. "SELF-ESTEEM." There. I said it. I've done a lot of growth work since my marriage fell apart and I started a business with a very public-facing persona. I've had to narrow down who I want to be and pump myself up to become that person. I still work on it every single day. How do you think famous, rich, successful people get to their dreams? Luck? Many of them practice self-esteem. Or hire a team of coaches to push them to practice it. Practicing something that "useless" isn't as immediately rewarding or outwardly noticeable as say going to the gym. Fitness you can see on the outside. Lack of fitness is due to lack of working out. Self-esteem is the invisible emotional fitness that we often neglect. Self-esteem has an impact on everything you do. Being kind to yourself, being coachable, being open to good things will surprisingly have a ripple effect on your business or art practice or job.

When you value yourself, you speak as if you're saying "I am worthy" and "You should pay me money to do something I am good at." You could be talking about the fine materials you use, the countless hours you put into writing your music, the software program you needed to create a 3D model. Talk up the good parts as if you're an expert. If you don't tell people, these things they might not know your value! They might not know that you want to be paid for your work, or your monetary value, or even worse they may assume that you have nothing to offer. Self-promotion or self-affirmation is considered [by artists] to be self-ish. It is considered to be kindness that is one-sided directed only at yourself. Driven by the ego and only in an effort to feed your arrogant, empty heart. Self-aggrandizing is a cardinal sin in the art world because we require (or wish for) the validation of someone with importance and clout. We need a writer to publish a review of our work, a collector to purchase something, a gallery to put our exhibition on the calendar for 2028. If they do validate us, we are ecstatic like we won the lottery. That type of hype is short lived! Day to day there has to be more in it for us to want to keep on truckin'. Also, guess what? We aren't promoting ourselves so that we can be rich. We are trying to share our magic with those who are open to receiving it (or buying it).

We are quick to encourage others and give them praise. We are quick to pay money for things we like, or think are great. We are even willing to spend extra money to support a friend, or a business who is eco-friendly/organic/gluten free, or a business that's locally owned. We are so excited to do something good by supporting the causes we care about, but we don't support our own cause. We don't support the idea that we are valuable or worth tons of money. In fact, we feel bad when someone goes out of their way to buy something from us. We need to flip the script, friend. Because we never got the training to think of ourselves any other way!

Ready, Set, Action!

Let's try a kinesthetic practice or ritual. A body that moves is a brain that grooves, or so says the author of *Limitless*, Jim Kwik. When you act something out it stays with you longer, so when your body is moving and your brain is in thought, it imprints on your memory better than when you're standing still or lying in bed reading. Try this when you can get up and move. Don't skip this part. This is the first part of moving on, moving forward, and redefining yourself.

The most holistic thing you can do is take a Forgiveness Walk. You might want to bring some Kleenex for this. Also feel free to listen to sad, sappy music. Or some new age-y meditation sounds. Begin to walk with an end point in mind. You're going to spend the way there thinking about something specific and the way home something totally different. On the walk to the park or wherever your location is, think through everything you've done that failed. Every relationship that ended and all the crap you could have done differently to make them stay. Tally all the times you've overdrawn your bank account or gotten a parking ticket. Think about applications that were rejected. Times you broke a pot, right as it came out of the kiln. The times you didn't get your security deposit back because you trashed your apartment or something. Really, it's time to lay into yourself and list your mistakes. Go back as far as you want to. Go back to Kindergarten, when you were still innocent and couldn't do anything wrong. I know this sounds like an act of pity or self-hatred but as you speak to yourself, you don't need to yell or berate yourself. Maybe just quietly whisper these grievances with each step, quickly spitting them out under your breath. I like to listen to some music like "spa sounds" as I walk because it drains my energy or makes me weep. But, trust me, there is a point to this.

Moving your body towards a destination, you access another part of your brain called the prefrontal cortex. Once you arrive at a spot where you can sit, put your butt down on a bench, a step, or the ground. I'm asking you now to take up space. We sometimes regret taking up space with our thoughts and feelings, but this is a time when you can be as huge as you want. Really expand your energy out and be large. I like to walk in nature and find a rock to sit on. Now you need to quiet your mind completely. You just spewed out all the poisonous chatter that happens unconsciously throughout the day. *Let your mind get silent.* Since I am a highly visual person, the way for me to eliminate thought is to focus very intently on something. There were ducks in the pond where I walked to and as I sat, they swam near me. I looked at the colors and feathers on their faces. I listened to their sounds. I watched the water part around their bodies making a "v" shape. Almost as if I was going to draw them from memory I took in their details. When a thought creeps in you say to yourself, "this is not time for your input," to your brain. Thank your brain for being humble. Quiet your heart and mind.

When you are ready and you've taken a few deep breaths, head back to your point of origin. You are done with blaming yourself and done with listing things. Done with tallying the shit that's wrong with you. On your walk back, you must resist the urge to be mean to yourself. This is where we are going to act out the friendship role, as if you are talking to a dear friend. You symbolically need to squeeze your own hand or offer a hug. As you walk back, act out Self Compassion; how this may feel to you is up to your sensibility. I tend to be caring and nonjudgmental with myself like a friend would be not a mother figure. I don't dote on myself and say "aww honey, poor you." I just say, it's okay you did that. You're not a bad person. We live and learn. You aren't perfect, nope, but you are human. We all make mistakes. I give myself words of kindness, like "you are a very special and important person." "They don't know you as I know you. You are wonderful, despite your mistakes." "Let's move on and do better next time." "So what if you royally fucked up?! I understand. I hear ya." Yep, you sucked at life in that part. But, it's okay, because you're growing and maturing and living to tell the tale. Now it's time to actively forgive yourself. You give yourself permission to let go of everything you told yourself on the way to the pond. You breathe. Like, guys, this requires a lot of deep breaths. You will see other people maybe. Just smile and say "yes, I'm having a conversation with myself."

Self-Love and Self Compassion and Self Forgiveness is a routine that few artists practice. We are in the habit of being so hard on ourselves, so critical. We collectively, constantly bash our career choice, our habits, our financial status, our lack. We learn then that it is standard and okay to not love ourselves. How do you think we will ever make it to "thriving" if we can't forgive ourselves of our past failures and mistakes? How can we possibly succeed if we let subconscious messaging stream nonstop like the NASDAQ numbers at Times Square? "YOU ARE NOT ENOUGH" is not a way to thrive. Numbing all the past hurts is also a slippery slope. Avoiding the pain or problems by getting "too busy" is another tactic to never deal with the core issues.

Flip the Script

We aren't used to thinking of ourselves in kind ways. We don't see our creative pursuits sometimes as valiant. We don't see our [art] work as work. Defined loosely as "a job that pays us," work is something that all grown-ups must do. We aren't naming ourselves the Founder, Owner and CEO of the brand "my stuff." A required mentality shift is right here in this tidbit of information. By all means, the mentality shift isn't small. It is crucial if you are going to learn to make a living creating things, requires you to **think of the thing that you make as a commodity.** Whether you love baking and dream of owning a custom cake shop or you're forging rings in your homemade metal shop. You will eventually go broke giving them away for free or you will make a killing by refining the recipe and doing it a bunch of times for the highest amount possible. It's not a crime. It's not an aberration. You are literally just monetizing what you love!

Every brand in the world started with one guy or gal who had an idea. They rallied other passionate and skilled people around that idea. And they found lots of "customers" or people who wanted what they were selling. That is the simplest terms of what it is to run a business. What if your art became a commodity instead of just a fart in the wind? A temporary, ethereal remnant of the emotions you had while making it with no meaning after the fact of its birth. **Put a price tag on your time.** Put a budget together with the materials that you used to make your art. That's your basic "COGS" or Cost of Goods Sold. You can't sell an artwork or service for the COGS. Then you'd just break even. You have to also make money on it. So, doubling or tripling or quadrupling the COGS would give you a template for how to scale. Sell enough girl scout cookies and you win a trip around the world.

What if you were forced to redefine not only what you do and how you make money but what an "artist" is? Can an artist be a product designer? Can an artist be a service provider? Can an artist be an idea generator or found a tech start up? Can an artist create floral arrangements? Can an artist be a community activist? Can an artist be a life coach helping other artists bring their vision to life? Can an artist run for political office? And if so, then is their creative pursuit no longer *just* a hobby that they do in their spare time? Reimagining what an artist is and what they can do requires imagination. So, we have that going for us. Imagining things was never hard for us creative people. We can walk into an empty house and see a vision of walls knocked down, floors refinished, new lighting and suddenly this tear down is a luxury home.

If you, were to redefine what an "artist" is, they don't have to be good at drawing. They don't have to like certain things or live a certain way. How should artists deserve to live? What if you… you, yes you… were in charge of rewriting the definition? Whatever you gave as the Wikipedia definition of "artist" would be accepted globally as truth. Pick wisely then because every creative person you know will suddenly clue into the fact that they are capable of being: _____ (fill in the answer here).

You are possibly still looking at me with one eyebrow lifted, skeptical. I don't care if you believe me or not. I'm the case study for this being true, 100%. I define myself as the wearer of many hats and it allowed me the freedom to design wallpaper and start a furniture collection. It allowed me to run a travel business and do super high-end interior design projects. It allowed me to collaborate with some amazing people, sell a quarter of a million dollars in wallpaper and stay home on a Tuesday to chaperone the field trip to the Children's

Museum with my son's kindergarten class. So, you don't have to take my story as evidence that it can be done, but will you hold out an ounce of hope for yourself having the life you've always dreamed of? Hope is important to this process of rebuilding the onion.

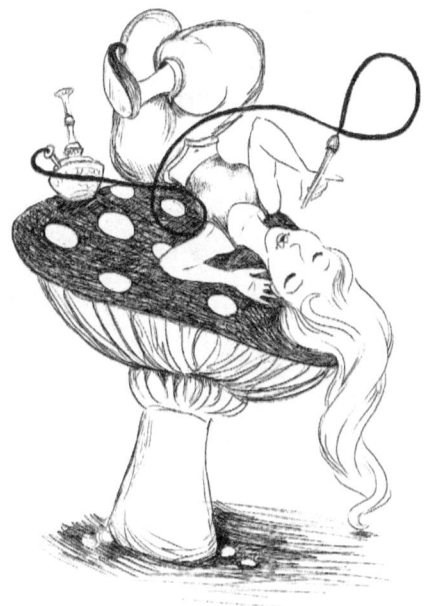

Smoking the Hopium Pipe

My vision for you is not small. It is HUGE. They call those monumental goals BHAGS: Big Hairy Audacious Goals. My mother, the cynic, would call them "delusions of grandeur." Whatever you call them, you should start following them with a sense of curiosity rather than shooting them down right away.

Imagine saying "I am the founder of a luxury wallpaper brand," before you'd ever even sold a roll of wallpaper and you don't have a website yet. Imagine saying "This year I will sell half a million dollar's worth of my wallpaper." I said that in January of 2020. We all know what transpired after that.

Do you ever feel like the people who surround you don't believe you? Like you're a fraud or a nut job? They don't know what you're capable of because *you haven't done it yet*. (Shoot, *you* don't even know if you can do it yet!) They don't believe you because they take three seconds to ask *themselves* "Could I do that?!" and their own answer is "No." So they think you couldn't possibly achieve something big through your own ingenuity and self-expression. They know a Warhol when they see it and you ain't it. They cast their doubts onto you like a rain cloud. They also love to project their fears and failures onto you, especially as the price tag for your dream gets bigger. "You'll *ruin your life* if you _____," "That sounds like such a huge risk and responsibility…"

The thing about goals is that you set them in order to measure what you can achieve; not knowing *if you can or not*. And honestly, most of the time you do not know HOW you are going to get there. Sometimes you don't make it all the way to the finish line. But *that's life*. It's normal because along the way your priorities may shift and change, and you might realize that you don't even want to be running a podcast or a t-shirt business or be an interior designer. So, you pivot! Being able to pivot is called resilience and it's a great quality. It's not called failure, but I digress.

What is the one and only ingredient that is required to achieving your Big, Hairy (or even the Super Tiny) Audacious Goal? What's the one thing that is the secret sauce for making it? Get out a pen because I'm about to reveal the best kept secret.

It's Hope.

Now you can call it faith. If you're not into church or holy books, call it destiny. If you're not into universal timelines, then call it dreaming. Whatever you call it, it's the drug you need to start smoking as soon as

CHAPTER 1: REIMAGINING THE ARTIST IDENTITY

you can get your hands on it and you need to tell other people about your dreams because the more you verbalize it, the more it snowballs into an even better idea. When you say it out loud you begin to believe it yourself. The opinions of others will follow. I've always hated the phrase "fake it til you make it." For me, it was act as the person who you are destined to be even if you're not him/her yet. Others will start to believe it as you prove yourself to the world.

Marc Johnson was working as the Marketing Director for a letterpress company called Rohner back in 2015 when I was still working on this little pipe dream called Relativity Textiles. I went on a tour of their facility and saw young, hipsters operating ancient print machinery. I thought it was the sexiest, most incredible print operation ever built. When copy machines can nearly replicate anything, these guys were foiling and stamping and even creating their own envelopes on machines that were the size of a car. The printing presses were so sturdy they seemed to be made from melted down anvils and grease from a caveman's armpit. I loved this print shop because they printed for Intelligentsia coffee and a custom candle company in Chicago. They made bar mitzvah invitations on leather just because they could. They introduced me to different papers, foils, methods, and it was the most seductive printer's pornography; I wanted to letterpress everything.

Marc had a handsome humility to him. He was funny and blurted out the truth that no one else wanted to say. I leveled with him and he told me that he liked my ideas so much for my wallpaper company that he'd ask the owner to pull a favor for me. They printed my packaging before I'd even completed my Kickstarter campaign and I promised to pay them as soon as the money dropped into my account. Branding was all I needed to sell a luxury item. Marc was also a big fan of craft and he later asked me if we could meet to talk about him potentially becoming an investor in Relativity.

What I learned from Marc was the phrase "Smoking the Hopium Pipe." He was working for a family company, with a marketing degree and perhaps one or two creative bones in his body-- but he wasn't an artist. Marc loved being around things as they were being made. He loved the ancient print process as much as I did. He later went on to work for Chicago's largest wallpaper manufacturer, Maya Romanoff. What Marc taught me as he'd stare at me with a wonder in his eyes was this: I am Superwoman. Here's why. I would speak of my brand as if it was already famous and popular and thriving. Relativity Textiles was still just a pipe dream. I would "sell" him on the idea of it's global inspiration, it's commitment to craft and he would say "You are smoking the hopium pipe, my friend."

It was his silly way to say "How *the hell* are you planning to pull that off!?" I realized he didn't believe me. He deeply wanted to. He thought I was high on hope, dreamy and unrealistic. In contrast, Marc was rooted in reality and numbers and committed to the safety of a day job but all he wanted was to pack a small handkerchief with his moleskine notebook and handmade business cards, tie it to a long stick and jump on my train to Somewhere Else.

Somewhere Else is not a faraway land, no, it's likely not too far away from where you are right now. There are BHAGS and there are SMART goals. I learned about them in different places, but I want to break it down for you now. BHAG = BIG Hairy Audacious Goal. It's the faraway land, the five years in the future, or the "what I would do if I had a million dollars" goal. It may not be realistic for you to achieve that goal right now, which is why it's Big. It would take a lot of work to reach it.

Chapter 2

Doing shit you don't want to do

Resilience is in the mind. And thus we have to train our thoughts. But let's be very clear that not all of this is going to be fun nor is it creative like finger painting all day long. It's WORK. Running a business or getting your creative juices out of the jar they've been in will require elbow grease, determination, lots of hope-y go lucky thinking, but also something that I liken to sports. Doing the reps. If you want to get buff, you'll have to lift the dumbbells more than once. And if you can do ten curls, you may as well wait a minute and do ten more. Then repeat a third time. That's what doing the reps is. Repetition. Repeating. Representin'. Time and time again, doing the shit that's hard. The shit that no one wants to do, most especially you. Before you can afford an army of service providers to do everything for you or create a system where your art practice is automated by robots, you're going to have to do the reps.

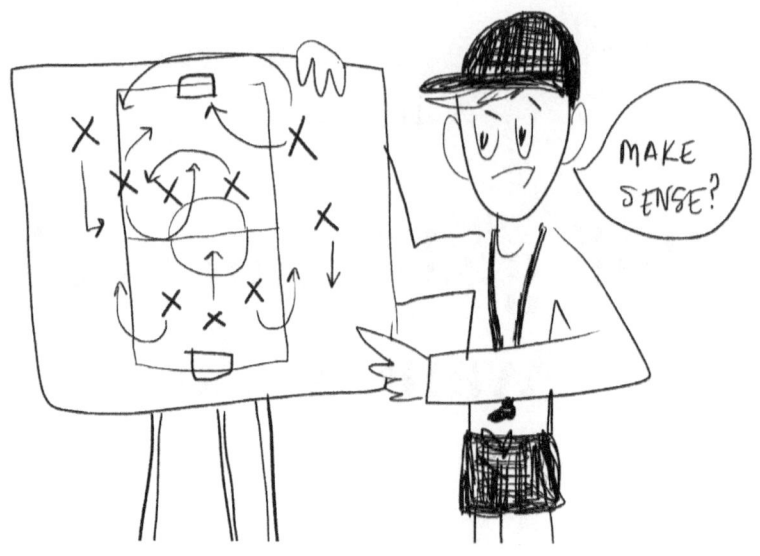

I Am Coachable

Throughout this book I'm asking you to shed some old scripts. I'm asking you to do a little introspection and imagine a new life for yourself. I am also going to ask you to make massive changes to your life. If any of those three steps sound scary, well, you're right. They are. One thing I learned early on is that sometimes when you don't have all the answers, but you know you want things to change, you just start asking lots of questions to everyone you can. "Do you know a web designer?" I would ask people since I wanted to find someone to make my company website, even though I had no budget. Those questions usually lead to discoveries. One of the greatest discoveries landed in my lap thanks to an old college friend who'd become a life coach. She was the typical Type A personality, super beautiful and successful and I wanted to be just like her. So when I heard she was coaching, I signed up right away even though I had no clue what coaching was all about. I knew I wanted to find answers though; through the process she made me find my own answers and ask more questions. It was because I remained open to change and open to feedback and honest about my shortcomings that I was able to grow. This is what I mean by "Being Coachable." I have another story that may illustrate this point a little better.

Freshman year of high school I received the award for Most Improved Player at our annual soccer banquet. I played J.V. and I rode the bench as hard as I could. All the awards for most goals scored, fastest runner, best team captain, best defense were all taken. What was The MIP award and why me? The Most Improved Player award was created for the girl who wasn't the most exemplary at any skill. However, she had a reputation for being coachable. She listened. She tried. She supported her teammates. They saw incremental progress and improved ball skills and they'd cheer her on as she tried to shoot and failed. People generally liked her. But she was not the best and she never made it to Best anything. She never even got to start in a game. But she was trying, and her efforts were recognized with this award.

I didn't consider myself an athlete. At least, I knew that in comparison to other players I was not good at soccer. I was dramatically slower than my peers and my ball skills were crap because I never really took it seriously enough to practice. I still wanted to be good at it though and most of all I wanted to be on the team. Something about belonging to the squad would have elevated my status or made me feel a part of something. That tribal desire to have a kinship over a common goal didn't motivate me to want to be good. In fact, I can remember thinking during the summer conditioning that I hated working out. I hated running in the heat. I hated the coach. What pushed me to go on was actually the surprise of having done the reps. Having pushed through my preconceived notions of how slow I was to eventually beat my record and exceed my own expectations.

By the end of the summer I began to run faster. I distinctly remember the coach leaving a small group of players he was coaching on ball skills to high five me as I took my third lap around the field and surpassed some of my more athletic teammates. I was on top of the world to have earned his congratulations. A simple high five from a man I didn't even like was enough to get me to push harder.

What I'm talking about here is about a willingness or an openness to change. Guys, are you ready to do the reps or run some laps? Are you ready to bust your ass and exceed other peoples' expectations? Are you ready to challenge your own time and get a little faster? How hard will you push before you give up? How much running can you handle before you vomit on the sidelines? How willing and open are you to hear the coach yell at you and persevere, even though I know you want to raise your middle finger and walk off the turf. How game are you, whether you believe it to be true, whether it's your dogma or not, to try something new?

I'll pose this statement and you can try to disagree. Mia Hamm, the Olympic soccer star for the USA was likely *really coachable*. She didn't get good by doing the things that she thought would make her a better player. She got good by being a member of a team, by listening to the educated guidance of an outside force (a coach), by losing/missing the shot a whole bunch and by practicing. Repetition of something simple, over and over and over again actually does make that skill easier. It engrains it into your mind and trains your body to follow. So, if you want to illustrate children's books but you only draw once a year, do you think a publishing house is going to call you out of the blue? Maybe drawing a lot more, filling your sketchbook with good ones and your trash bin with bad ones will get you closer to becoming the Mia Hamm of illustrators.

Just Try It

Being a mother sometimes offers such amazing lessons for life. Having trained little people to do things well reminds me that us big people need some prompts from time to time too. I tell my sons when they're eating a meal that they've never experienced before to "try it" before they tell me "I'm not eating this." Sometimes this results in a child gagging and spitting out their food and honestly …it's a disgusting lesson for both me and the child. But I would rather get my kids in the habit of trying new things and hating it then to just decide it's not for them. For them to stubbornly say from the outset "I don't want to do this," is because it's foreign and slimy and looks bad. Their mind relays little neurons firing upstairs that say "Unsafe! Do not do it!" I'm asking them to challenge those brain messages because 1 time out of 10 they actually admit that the food is good, and they like it. If I allowed them to not eat all the food that they initially reject, they may miss opportunities. They might never know that they love kale chips or red peppers dipped in hummus and thus avoid the foods they could have loved the most! They'd end up like that kid we all know who only eats orange foods like Cheetos and Kraft mac 'n' cheese. Who wants to be that kid?!

So for those of you that feel like self-care and self-affirmation and business strategies are easy? You don't really need this chapter as much as the rest of us… psyche! I'm going to call your bluff. Trust me, if you were at my house for breakfast and refused a spinach smoothie, I would do everything in my power to convince you that it was:

1) healthy,
2) full of vitamins
3) easier than eating a whole salad and
4) it would make me sad if you don't drink it so don't be a piece-of-shit-friend and refuse the food I just worked hard to make you! Ha!

It is important to take advice from people who came up before you did. Even if their advice is a little outdated. I was scouring Chicago for answers about how to run a business and stumbled upon SCORE, at the recommendation of many people in my network. I began working with a free mentor and took a couple of cheap classes on Quickbooks and bookkeeping. The help I received from my mentor was great. She taught me how to price my wallpaper, how to figure out who my target customers were and how to market it.

I finally got wise and hired some consultants. A consultant is basically someone with a niche knowledge and expertise at something. Becky and Al were experts at growing businesses. They met with me once a month for two hours and taught me how to fill up my sales pipeline, how to read my PNL (Profit & Loss statement), how to price my work and where to begin marketing my skill set. We were all over the place trying out new ideas for how I was going to make a buck. They coached me in several ways and some things I was receptive to and others I remained stubborn about.

I had Allison, my life coach, who really helped me to set goals and write them into my calendar. She trained me to have integrity with myself for the things I'd promised to do. She held me accountable in the way that a physical trainer pushes their clients to keep going. She wasn't lifting any weights for me, though I really wished she would.

Being the boss of a company might seem like a dream job to those of you sitting in an office or a cubicle right now but who's going to keep you motivated? Who is the boss's boss? When things got hard for me, I'd come to Allison with questions or areas I wanted to improve, and she helped me realize that the answers were already nearby or in my phone contacts. She made me repeat a phrase that ties in nicely to this thread of thinking about "just try it," which is this: "Nevertheless, I am willing." I was forced to repeat this as I would force you to drink a green smoothie at my house, friend. I urge you to become aware of the potential to grow if only you have someone with more knowledge or a talent for guidance at the helm with you. I urge you to be *willing* and open to simply trying it.

Being Broke is the Best Motivator

I wasn't the most coachable. I remember a conversation I had with Joe Piercy, husband to the Chicago empire of Meg Piercy's genius furniture refinishing business called MegMade. Joe has a degree in business and worked for his parents' shoe company before he jumped into running a business with his wife. He was showing me a spreadsheet of Chicago bloggers and influencers and trying to coerce me into giving away free products so that they'd help me get some eyeballs. {To this day I despise working with social media influencers but MegMade really hit the jackpot with that crowd.} After explaining why my particular product wasn't a good fit for a giveaway because it cost me so much to make, Joe stopped me mid-sentence and said, "Erin, I'm trying to give you tons of ideas about how to grow your business. You have a reason why *everything won't work*." I needed his gentle slap in the face. He really was being so generous to educate me about a world I knew nothing about. He is an expert at marketing, and they've grown so much in recent years that they nearly landed an HGTV show. I was so afraid to spend any money to make money. I was doubtful that anything was going to work.

My excuses were caked in insecurity; I was just a naked onion with nothing to protect me. Thoughts of scarcity made me hold onto every dollar I had with such a firm grip that I didn't think investing any money into anything was going to help me. Later in my business, I realized that putting money into some form of marketing and crossing your fingers was the only way to grow. However, when you're broke it's hard to imagine spending $500-1,000 on something that may or may not pay itself back. That's a mindset issue discussed by Daymon John in "The Power of Broke." I enjoyed reading this Shark Tank superstar's account of how he used to print t-shirts and drive to Black Beauty Shows and open up his trunk. He'd sell his shirts until they were gone and go home with a full pocket and a proud heart. His brand is FUBU. Iconic to pop culture, FUBU was a brand made "for us by us" and signified determination, excellence and going against the grain. It was a hip hop, sportswear brand that elevated black streetwear and gave an identity to a generation.

When I read that book, I recognized that all things have to start small. Not everyone starts with a Kickstarter campaign or some working capital to launch their idea. Not everyone has rich parents. Not every aspiring entrepreneur has a supportive husband like Joe Piercy with a business degree and unlimited love and energy (That guy is seriously the Energizer bunny). The government isn't going to fund your research or your project materials. Then, where's the money going to come from to get started?... Each of us has to start by selling one thing. Literally one. Joe and Meg painted a dresser in their garage and sold it on Craigslist.

CHAPTER 2: DOING SHIT YOU DON'T WANT TO DO

That was how they started. The broker you are, the more desperate, the more starving? It's literally fuel for your fire. It's the special sauce that motivates you to get out of bed and find a customer- any way you can.

I often joke that in the beginning I would've done anything to sell some wallpaper. I liken myself to the caricature of a watch thief who is wearing a trench coat lined with Rolexes on the inside of his jacket. That's what I felt like going to networking events. I'd get super dolled up and grab a glass of wine and head to the center of the party. I started asking people "What do you do for a living?" and when they asked me in return I couldn't wait to respond. "I am a wallpaper designer." It's a great line because no one has ever met a wallpaper designer before. It's like saying you're a circus acrobat. "WOW!" they'd respond and ask to see my work, I'd hand them a sample straight from my purse with my contact information printed on the back. Those-- vinyl stinking, hand cut on my dining room table, labeled by a zero-wage intern-- samples became my business cards and they made a huge impact. It was like I'd opened my coat to show them bright and beautiful patterns that could adorn their walls. And they were impressed.

Little did they know I was a starving artist selling a luxury brand. Many outfits I'd worn to galas and cocktail parties were returned the next day to Anthropologie or Nordstrom's. I didn't know how to dress myself. I wasn't a professional. Most of my clothes have paint spilled on them. The highest price item in my closet came from Target. Nevertheless, I was hustling wallpaper like it was stolen Rolexes. As if I were selling t-shirts from out of my trunk in the parking lot of a convention. I figured the costume I was wearing, the transportation cost to get there, the babysitter I had at home putting my children to bed, all of that was the cost of getting ONE order. Meeting the right people means being in the right place and trying to look like someone they'd buy from. "Networking is being yourself in public," a quote from Bobby Chang founder of Seasons Sodas.

While I spoke of how I grew my little home baked wallpaper enterprise I failed to mention that my marriage of ten years tanked. My husband at the time was skeptical of my ability to "pull this off." Besides that, he'd grown tired of my frenetic artist energy and thought that kids would calm me down. It just made me more antsy and ambitious. We grew apart slowly but the relationship eroded quickly when I realized I couldn't stand to be married for one more minute. I made a call to a divorce attorney from my networking group, of all places. I planned my exit with my therapist. It was my oldest son's fifth birthday when I knew it was over. We'd gone away for two nights at the Wisconsin Dells waterpark. I'd asked my husband to order Thai food from the place in town since there was a takeout menu in our hotel room. I took the baby into the bedroom to put him to sleep. When I returned about 40 minutes later, I was hungry and asked if the food came yet. "I didn't order dinner," he said with a guilty look. "Why?!" I was pissed and feeling like 'Do I have to do everything around here?' He answered as honestly as he could and didn't see his mistake. "I didn't know what you wanted."

After ten years of being married, two children together, bridging the cultural divide between his homeland of Morocco and our life here, him traveling the world and me going to art school, this man didn't know that I like Pad Siew with chicken?! Sounds comical now but that was the deciding moment for me. The straw that broke the camel's back. I told myself, "This is not my husband." What would come after was a really, unexplainably hard road. I lost sight of so many dreams because I was heartbroken, desperate and downright unsure of how to make things work without him. I packed his belongings into two Tupperware

CHAPTER 2: DOING SHIT YOU DON'T WANT TO DO

tubs and set them outside the front door of our second story apartment. He found his own place and it would be months until he started paying me any child support. This is where I had to put my big girl boots on and pull myself up from the bootstraps.

Being hungry is the key to quickly upgrading your life. Getting ideas out of your brain and into the real world. Nothing lights a fire under your ass like being served an eviction notice from your landlord. Getting collection calls about medical bills that were 90 days past due. Or having the principal from your kid's school call to ask when you were making the tuition payment. All of those things and more were *my real life*. I was forced to move out of my apartment when I couldn't afford to make my rent payments anymore. I was truly at zero. But I never stopped hustling. I never stopped smoking the hopium. I never stopped asking questions, trying to meet new people, and trying to find coaches and mentors who could give me advice.

Hitting Rock Bottom

I lived without a car. In Chicago. With two kids. We rode the bus. When my preschooler graduated from the Catholic school system at age 4, I was bragging that finally his schooling would be free. He got into a great school in another neighborhood. His dad and I were fighting so much that he decided to take the car away from me to show me who was boss. He is a flight attendant, so when he went to work, he would take our family Toyota Highlander and park it at the airport in a remote parking lot meant for employees. It would sit for three days there collecting snow and I'd ride the bus with my kindergartener.

This was before I was in court every other month. So, I decided to suffer, as if I had no choice; I really felt at that time in my life that

67

I had no alternative. Fighting for what was fair had left me exhausted and defeated. I usually lost arguments because he had the upper hand and my lawyer's famous line was "You won't be able to teach him how to be a better parent, or a better person." So I would wait at the bus stop in the morning with my kindergarten aged son, wrapped in a scarf and hat and mittens. It was sometimes ten degrees outside or less. His down coat wasn't keeping him warm enough, so I'd hug him tight while sitting on the wooden bench. My down coat wasn't keeping me warm enough either and I loved his squishy tiny body heat next to me. I hugged him for moral support and warmth.

As the bus driver approached, people would stir and line up. I'd get nervous of where I'd left my bus pass, and I'd tell him to find a seat while I fumbled inside the pockets of my purse to find the bus fare card. I tapped the Ventra card on the card reader.

"I'm sorry, ma'am, there's an error," the bus driver said.

Oh no... *Oh shit. This is really happening.* The bus started moving and my kid was in his seat and I realized that my card was on autocharge. It took money from my bank account $25 at a time and then we'd use it as need be. But, today, it seemed I didn't have $25 in my bank account... "Um, I'm sorry. I don't know what's wrong with the card. Maybe it's not working?"

"The error code means there are no funds." the driver replied with a cold stare facing forward to observe the road. At this point, I was holding on for dear life as the bus chugged north on Western Avenue. Potholes or other eminent death urges me to take a seat but I haven't paid. Holding the pole for dear life, I hear him ask me "Do you have any cash?"

Because I had to take two buses to get to my kid's school and two busses to get back, I knew that I had to improvise or else the driver might ask me to get off the bus. Then we'd be walking. It could take me 30-40 minutes to get there. My son would be tired and soaked from the snow since he didn't really have good boots. I'd be sweating and he'd be late to Kindergarten. I'd have to walk back home too…

Inside my mind I was cursing my ex-husband. I was cursing the court system for taking too long to set our hearing date. I was cursing the lawyers, the world. The bus fares. The empty bank account. I cursed all the people in cars who didn't know what a luxury it was. I was so stressed because my son was alone in his seat on public transport and people were staring at me. I was a failure of a mother.

"I can get off." I said to the driver.

"Just take a seat," he said.

I walked over to my son and gave him a side hug. We rode quietly to the next stop. As we were getting off the Western Avenue bus, we ran across the street to barely catch the North Avenue bus. We got on just in time. I held his mittened hand and told the bus driver that my wallet was stolen. That I just needed to get my kid to school. "Can you let us ride for free just this one time?" I recognized this driver. I'd seen them before, and they said "yeah" so we took a seat. Then I started asking my kid which direction we were going. He said East and I was so proud of him. I was at once depressed about the state of things but also proud. And that was such a coping mechanism to see the bright side of all this struggle. To find a positive so that I didn't have to think about how negative things had gotten. I never told my son why I lied to the bus driver and he never asked me, thank God, because kids yell their questions publicly and I didn't want this new bus full of people with their eyes on me. Judging me.

When I tell you these things it's not so that you'll feel bad for me. I'm trying to give context to where I've been and how I've come up with these strategies. I want to assure you because I know where you're at isn't all rainbows and hearts, that there is an end in sight or a *better* place to get to. That striving for "better than this" is something that all humans do, no matter their age, creed, race or geographic location. We aren't all trying to get rich quick, but we are trying to move up a notch on the proverbial ladder. If you're not, I don't know what world you exist in. That you are totally content with where you are. I don't think you would've picked up this book if you weren't looking for some answers.

So when you say *"the struggle is real"* I want you to emotionally reframe it. The current situation that you're in right now is not the worst struggle. The passionate obligation you have to reach your dream life is the challenge. And you have to keep your focus on it. And you have to denounce all those monkeys who will try to convince you that the goal isn't valiant. That, my friends, is the struggle: sticking to the path. Wanting it so bad you can taste it and not relenting until you have it. Because if there is one thing to fear in life, it's this:

If you're in the exact same place a year from now it means you haven't made any progress. Fear no progress. Don't fear the future which you cannot know. Don't fear the lack of knowing how to get there. Those pieces will fall into place.

Denial is Not a River in Egypt

When I launched a Kickstarter campaign in November of 2015, I gave myself an overly ambitious goal: To raise $20,000 in 60 days; right after Christmas. That was what I needed to make my pipedream a reality. I had a lot of support from people who wanted to see my business succeed but on the flip side, I had naysayers in my world who did not believe I could make this elaborate plot work. I was ignoring

CHAPTER 2: DOING SHIT YOU DON'T WANT TO DO

their criticism and skepticism as best as I could, which turned out to be a form of denial. I wasn't willing to fail at marriage while pumping myself up to the world and raise a bunch of money at the same time. So I logged into my husband's Facebook account and wrote this, "Hey friends, I want to promote my beautiful wife and her aspiration to start a business. She's an amazing artist and I hope you can put even $25 into her fundraising efforts by clicking here." I linked the Kickstarter campaign. Several of his friends made generous contributions.

I felt I needed the positive opinion of the people closest to me. So much that I fabricated that support. My mom, my sister, and my soon-to-be ex-husband all had their doubts about whether I could pull off this new life change. I was told to "stop all this foolish stuff," or "Just get a real job and you can save some money for a business later." I was guilted about neglecting my kids by putting so much effort into the wallpaper gig.

I was desperate to please everyone, and it was one of the reasons why it took me so long to leave an emotionally abusive relationship. I wanted the outside world to think that I was successful at being an artist turned business owner. But I also had wanted to succeed at being a wife. I was grasping for success at being a mother, a woman, a partner and friend to the man I chose and feeling like I was failing at all of those things. I wanted to follow through with my obligations, namely the vows I took on my wedding day. I didn't want the pity that came when I was on my own. "Poor single mama," they'd soon call me.

I was trying so hard to convince the world that I was good at what I was doing. But *I was in denial.* I think something powerful happens when we're very honest with ourselves and we say, "I'm failing at _____. I want to quit so badly. I don't even like this." I had failed at marriage. I had failed to hold us together, even with years of therapy and trying all the things. I even believed that our second child would bring us closer together. I failed to meet his needs. I failed to communicate my own. I fell out of love with him and wanted only to be free from our dysfunction. He wanted to be free too, from all my chaos and whimsy and the struggle of reinvention which was a constant pursuit in my life. He told me I was never going to make it. It made me strive harder to prove him wrong, but back then he didn't know what it would become. He had no faith.

I truly think I started a business as a way to channel my energy into something that I knew I could control. I had a lot of hope that I could make this wallpaper business work, and I scarcely talked about my vision and dreams with my husband because it was my secret escape plan. He would never have believed that I could pull it off. I knew that I could push my vision forward and channel all my efforts into it in ways that I couldn't with my marriage. If only you could run a 60-day Kickstarter campaign to reboot your relationships and they'd be fully funded/regenerated with the help of 225 friends pitching in small amounts. Life isn't a campaign. You can't goal set other peoples' change or reinvention. Sometimes you have to let them change on their own terms or accept that they never will change. I had to give up smokium the hopium and praying that my marriage would work; and it was one of the hardest things I ever had to do.

While writing about "giving up" I am reminded of one of my dearest college friends, Heather. One day during varsity soccer practice, Heather decided in the middle of a drill that she really just didn't want to be there anymore. She'd been fielding headers for a corner kick drill, playing defense and her head was throbbing. Concussion imminent, Heather wondered why the hell she was putting herself up to this pain when she really didn't enjoy playing anymore. With the drill in progress,

CHAPTER 2: DOING SHIT YOU DON'T WANT TO DO

Heather walked off the pitch. In a sideline heart to heart with coach (who was notorious for her fiery red hair, short stature, and enormous personality) Heather told her she wanted to quit the team. Heather decided then and there "I'm done."

What balls! Heather had been playing soccer her whole life and her room at home was probably littered with trophies. She was so good at soccer, I considered her the next Mia Hamm. It was something that just came naturally to her. She could walk on the pitch super hungover, barely any special gear or extra practice and just nail the ball into the goal every time. She was possibly the only team captain who ever quit the team mid-season in the history of college sports. I felt like it was so unfair that I was striving to make the team at tryouts and there were girls like her effortlessly ranking top player. I was trying to be coachable, pushing myself every day and she defied the need for the sport at all. There is something to knowing your limitations; something to letting the ship sink while floating away from the wreckage. There's something honorable about it. Maybe neither she nor I "gave up" soccer or marriage. Maybe we just knew when to walk away.

That decision usually happens over time. Many days spent toiling over the outcome that is unknown. Many hours spent wondering what people will think of you when you break the news, "I am getting a divorce." Weeks of going back and forth, bargaining, trying to make it work. So many desperate phone calls made from laundromats asking your best friend who's been divorced twice, "How do you know?... when it's time." Tens of thousands of Kleenexes soiled and tossed into trash bins in all types of places. Crying in therapy. Crying in your car with your sunglasses on. Crying while talking to your husband's mother. So many glasses of wine donated by neighbors who want to console you, not knowing how bad it is at home but seeing your exhaustion with the two boys and the husband who still isn't around. A relationship failing doesn't happen in one day. Yet leaving happens suddenly.

You call the attorney. You ask the hardest questions of your life. You initiate the "ending it" conversation with a very stubborn man. You just take one step in front of the other until you're free.

Walking away is never painless or clean and crisp. Whether you're being fired or breaking up with someone or quitting the team. When you're ending a business partnership and going out on your own. You're moving out because the thought of staying is worse than the aftermath of leaving. Although you're scared of what will come next, you do it knowing something better is out there. Eventually it gets easier. But the judgements that other people have about your choices will never be as critical as the question in your mind later in life when you say, "What if I would've just walked off the field one day?" What types of situations or relationships do you have in your life that are holding you back from progress? Where can you feel the heavy weight each day, the one thing you cannot control or fix? Is it a person you've been dragging through life or a job that is going nowhere? Is there something that you haven't wanted to part with because it's defined you? Stevie Nicks said it best, "I've been afraid of changin' cause I built my life around you."

CHAPTER 2: DOING SHIT YOU DON'T WANT TO DO

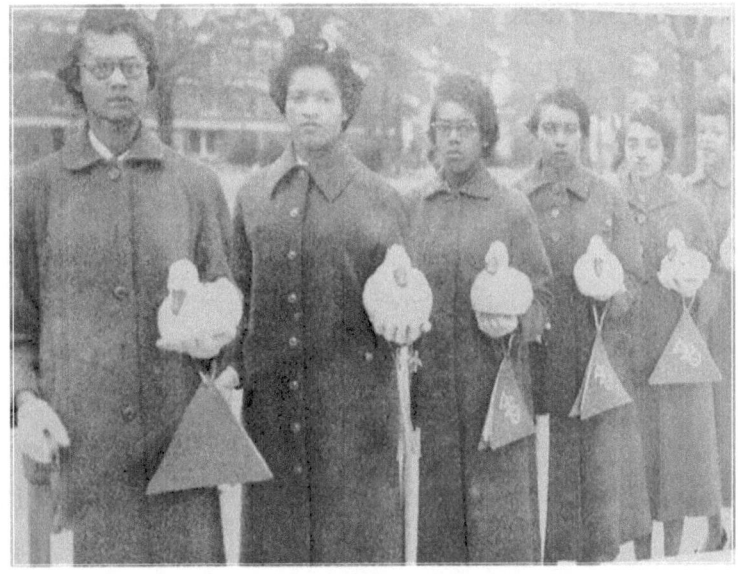

Carrying the Rock

In 2001 I pledged a sorority, which was one of the most unlikely things that you would have heard me do if you were a high school friend of mine. I shocked my family because they thought that I was insane to do something so mainstream. In truth, I had nearly shaved my head and died my boy haircut black right before leaving for college. I was vegan and an artist-- not Alicia Silverstone from *Clueless*. The Alpha Theta Phi sorority wasn't for ditsy babes. It was more like a fraternity since most of the girls who were Theta's were athletes or activists. Many Theta's were leaders at the school. They threw the best parties and considered drinking a sport. As a small liberal arts university, we had only local chapters, not national Greek organizations. For that reason, the hazing protocols and pledging traditions were not very well policed and many of the things that I encountered as a pledge cannot be repeated. In fact, the Greek organizations may not even be practicing these barbaric rituals I am about to recount in 2020's because the hazing is now very well regulated. I am sad that the new members aren't going to undergo these "traditions" and also relieved that they won't be blindfolded and left in the woods anymore. Because *that shit was scary*.

One tradition that had likely not been around since our founding mothers established the sisterhood in 1919 was to carry a rock. Wherever we went, we had to carry a rock that our "big sis" had painted turquoise blue. It was our burden to bear for the 6 weeks that we fought to earn our rank. It was about as big as a loaf of bread, sometimes smaller. The rock could not be put in our backpacks. We could put it down for class, mealtime, sports, and sleep. Otherwise, should a Theta sister see us on campus, we ought to be carrying our rocks at all times.

This reminder that we were not yet ranked was heavy and annoying. I was young and was free for the first time ever. College was so much fun, but I had decided to become a Greek member and I didn't even know why. Was it because I had been so desperate to be popular in high school but never did? Was it because the hot guys I met at the first few all school dances were Greek, so I thought I'd meet more dudes if I was too? Here I was carrying around a rock painted blue, an envelope called a "pledge book" and wearing some turquoise ribbon safety pinned onto my shirt ALL DAY every day for six weeks! And I didn't have a single reason for doing it other than to see what it was like. As if the experience chose me, I didn't choose it-- I was enduring humiliation and awkwardness for the sake of living on the edge and trying new things. I wanted to belong to something so badly that all the trauma I was inflicting upon myself was worth it, if by the end I was a part of the club.

As a rebel at heart, I wanted to throw my rock in the nearest dumpster and move on with my life but something in me had to persevere. To show them that I could do it, even though I didn't want

CHAPTER 2: DOING SHIT YOU DON'T WANT TO DO

to. To follow through on my commitment to these bitches, even though I didn't know what lay ahead. Much of that experience was unpleasant, and I often questioned *"Who are these girls* that are asking me to do this?! I don't even know them. I don't even care about them. Why the hell should I play these stupid pledging games?"

The rock is with you now. You are carrying the torch whether you know it or not. It's your **creative destiny.** The rock is your doubt about whether you are good at drawing or not. The rock is the fact that your grandfather was a concert pianist and you are an okay guitar player. The rock symbolizes the gifts that you carry that you aren't using. It symbolizes the hard work ahead of you that you need to do in order to get your magic out into the world. The rock is heavy because it's always nagging you to stop what you're doing and pay attention! It's the thoughts that keep you awake at night or make your fingers twitch when you enter an art supply store. Making art isn't always fun and cool; it's a cross to bear. You could try to quit being creative, but the fact of the matter is you would be a horrible person to be around if you tried.

You can ignore the rock, disregard it, roll your eyes, toss it in the trash, or hold onto it until the purpose becomes clear. You're carrying it *not* because you have a choice. It is your gift and your burden. It might be something that you would like to get rid of, but you have a talent in you that you can choose to use or not. It seems to me a waste of time to carry it your whole life without regarding it as important. Without being proud of it and showing it to others. Without being grateful that you get to carry this rock, rather than some other God given talent or skill. Like those who are destined to be soldiers or judges or police officers. Like those who are destined to be doctors or surgeons or engineers. Sounds like a lot of pressure. I'd gladly take the rock labeled "Artist" than the one called "Politician."

So from one simple experience a lesson can be applied to all of life. Here it is: *You don't have to like it.* You just have to do it.

It's not easy or pleasant, but the rock is yours to carry. Until you've succeeded to a point that you can put it down. That means that doing the work of answering to your true calling isn't always going to be rewarding or fun. It's not all hearts and rainbows to be an artist, either. There's a lot of mental load to carry and a lot of societal baggage to dismiss on a constant basis. Realize that you have it whether you like it or not and use it to your advantage. Because otherwise, it's just a heavy stupid thing you're carrying around for no goddam reason.

The Most Difficult Burdens

I want to write a small section about grief, trauma and shame. These are real burdens that make motivation and positivity damn near impossible sometimes. Mental health and physical health also impact the accuracy of your internal barometer of self-worth and what you're capable of because sometimes your body doesn't cooperate with your mind. Finding your own magic isn't easy when you feel entirely vulnerable to the point that you can't move. It's as if all the layers of the onion are peeled back and you're just a sliver of a shard of what was once onion shaped. Suddenly, you are exposed.

This is when you have to take a step back and say to yourself, "Maybe now isn't the right time to be peeling the onion." These are the times of our lives when peeling the onion could be dangerous and cause more harm than good. That's when you need to spend more time covering that onion with some healthy and strong layers of self-love and forgiveness. Practice gratitude and celebrate tiny victories, like getting out of bed. Eventually you'll move on to bigger things.

CHAPTER 2: DOING SHIT YOU DON'T WANT TO DO

I first discovered I had a brother at age 31. He is an English teacher and author and father of the two most beautiful humans ever made. His stunning wife is a therapist and teacher too and they live on a quaint hillside outside of Portland, Oregon. I was told of his birth story while pregnant with my second child and I met him at his home one Thanksgiving in 2013. My mother had given my brother up for adoption through the Catholic church and never thought she'd get to meet him face to face. But, as fate had it, the vault of records was opened in 2011 and my mom and her son exchanged information and letters. Their reunion seemed like both closure and that raw onion exposure all at once for both of them.

My mother carried around "shame" like a Theta rock her whole life. As a sixteen-year-old Catholic school girl who ended up pregnant with the baby of her half-Chinese, half-Japanese boyfriend my mom was pretty fucked. She was sent to live with an elderly Catholic family who cared for her until the day she went into labor. Her son was born in 1969. She said she'd refused to look at his face when he was born for fear she'd fall in love with him. My mom spent her lifetime keeping this story a secret, and apart from her brother and sisters, no one knew that she was a mother. Not even me. Not even her gynecologist.

One summer, before I found out about my brother, I was traveling in Morocco when my mom called a little panicked. The call was breaking up, but she said she was having surgery the next day. They'd found a huge cyst in her uterus. I told her that I'd get on the first flight back from Morocco to be with her. I didn't think, just jumped on a plane with my son and returned to Salt Lake City to sit by her side. She was drugged up on painkillers and needed help getting up to pee. I made her chicken soup and sat around with her talking until she fell asleep. It wasn't until years later that I put two and two together about the cyst in her uterus.

Her body had held the trauma and grief for so long that those emotions calcified into a cyst *the size of a human baby*. Right in her uterus she literally grew a rock. Those emotions of grief coupled with her own disintegrating marriage to my dad and her failing health solidified inside her body and could have killed her. The body is not immune to your mental burdens. They crystalize or turn into lava and escape somehow. They can cause you physical discomfort and pain.

The human body can be pushed to many extremes. To climb Mt. Everest. To jump into ice cold lakes in winter. To endure marathons, childbirth and to endure cancer and chemotherapy. The human mind endures all types of Olympic sports every single day which can lead to action or inaction. Suffering or strength. Those types of ailments of the heart and mind, when not dealt with and overcome create a lifetime of unresolved hurt and eventually become dangerous to the human body. So, a note on serious conditions is this. No amount of "Girl Power!" calendars or green spinach smoothies are going to solve your massive trauma. When some people are "struggling" with which car to buy or where to send their resume, you might be overcoming sexual assault, drug addiction or the death of a loved one. Though all things are relative, your worries are larger than life. *You are not on the same playing field*. And that's perfectly okay because first you need to heal.

Your first goal is to get to a place of emotional safety. Once you've begun the process of closure on the pain of the past, then, *and only then* should you begin the powerful journey of self-actualization. Meet those most basic needs on Maslow's pyramid first. Put the oxygen mask on and wait until you start to feel safe. Seek therapy, find support groups, choose a faith-based practice, meditate. Whether it's meditation or church, you have to do the hard work-- the lifelong pursuit-- of overcoming trauma *first*. Simultaneously you can be using art and creativity exercises to reestablish a sense of hope and curiosity and self-exploration. But this is that moment where I hug you and say, it's going to be okay not to peel back the onion or pursue being a thriving artist just this second. You will get through your Most Difficult Burden. Most of all, be kind to yourself and take it slowly when you need to.

Seeing People from the Hero's Heart

We all look at others from a lens of either judgement or envy. Seriously, I think we have two ways of seeing people. Either they're not doing it right (the way we would or the way we think they should) OR they're doing better than we are. Pity is a dirty feeling because at once we feel guilty to be above someone else or further along than them. But it assumes that it's our job to help them, guide them, advise them. We get frustrated when they don't do things a certain way. We lose our temper with them or we look down on them as less than. We can even view them with disgust.

When we are looking up to someone, we can be jealous. *Jealousy*, in my opinion can be a good motivator. I want what they have. I want the lifestyle, the material things, the friendships they seem to have. As long as the things you are jealous about are in line with your values, ex. I want to own a single-family home because I would view myself as a good mother and provider, then I can aim to embody that goal. But when looking with jealousy, be careful not to cross into the territory of envy. **Envy** is when you want something that someone else has for yourself, negating them deserving it. You want them to not have that thing, because if you can't have it, no one deserves it. Example, an artist with a gallery show is receiving a lot of press for selling all of their paintings. You want yourself to be in their shoes and you are jealous, but you fixate on the reasons why that person isn't a good artist, or a good enough person to be deserving of the fame or attention they are receiving. You want them to not be selling their work.

An important frame of mind is to see one another through a "Green Lens[21]." It states that you ought to see everyone from the green lens or generous/empowering point of view. When we look at someone with pity or with envy, we are discounting their legitimacy to take up space in that moment being exactly who they are. We don't allow a belief that they are just doing their best with what they have. We sometimes even think that they are purposely acting a certain way to annoy us or cause problems for us. To see someone from the positive lens is to state that they are a hero, whole and complete. They don't need anything in that moment because they are enough. They contribute to each interaction (even if that means you are having to do some personal growth work when they're frustrating you! Their place is to help push you to become more patient.) They have talents and skills and goals and dreams just like you and their strategy might not be perfect. They might not be your definition of a butterfly just yet, but they are working on getting there at their own pace. You can't force them to see what you have already seen. You can't teach them what you know and expect them to see the light. You have to let go and let them come to their own conclusions at the time that is meant for them to grow. And *the hardest part* is that sometimes people never grow in the way you want them to.

What would people you admire do? Are they coachable? Do they know their worth? Don't they also have burdens and guilt? What would it be like to live a life that others admired? To have others see you as a

---

[8] Maria Nemeth, founder of the Academy of Coaching Excellence sited here for her PDF the Green Lens.

hero. Are you willing to live an authentic life, surrounded by those you admire? Are you willing to do some hard work to get there? Would it be okay for you to stop surviving and begin thriving? Let's face it, there are some ugly qualities that I no longer want to carry around with me. I had to become a fish out of water to realize that I'd been living in water a very long time. All my life, in fact. I lost a lot of people dear to me in order to learn this lesson. But, read on, my friend and we will explore your greatest obstacles. They're not angry demons or scary monsters hiding in your closet. They're familiar old scripts and scrolls of old, hidden amongst your treasures and magic. Let's parse through the hard stuff to get to the best part.

Chapter 3

Saying No to Negativity

Your brain will challenge you. People in your life will challenge you. I'm writing the first section of this book so that if you follow the plan step by step you will undoubtedly come to a point where there is friction, disappointment, rejection and inevitably a feeling of failure. Someone once told me, before I'd hit the break-even year, that only I know when it's time to quit. I never quite knew... For the first three years it always felt like it was time to quit! I never felt prepared! I never felt confident. I always was the ballsiest one in the room, with the loudest voice and the strongest message. Even still, I have questioned myself at every stage along the way, "Am I doing this right?" or "Should I throw in the towel?" I had to include this chapter for those moments when you want to scream at the book and say, "See!? I didn't get the _____, you lied to me!" Smoking hopium isn't enough. Doing the reps isn't enough. Having a network isn't enough. On their own, each chapter isn't enough to get you to be profitable. It's the finesse of all the things simultaneously, the juggling, the prioritizing, the hierarchy of needs. That said, I want to end this section with some real talk. There will be doubts: yours, other peoples'. Here's how we aim to combat the negative talk and reason with our own minds.

Toxic Pessimism

Artists are somehow the keepers of the world's beauty and some of the most negative people you'll ever meet. They have strong opinions, which to me isn't offensive. They have scripts and lots of evidence to show how artists aren't appreciated. They have destructive attitudes about themselves and the power of their work, limiting them from seeing their own magic for what it is. These pessimistic traits are the poison of our everyday. If we aren't careful about how pessimistic attitudes contribute to our own demise, we will slip into depression even with therapy and coaching, hope or goal setting. The language we use to speak to ourselves is therefore super important in how we live out our destinies.

My position of conquering negative with positivity is not new. It involves a little bit of faith; not knowing how the story will unfold. Learning resilience is a weird concept that I want to concisely summarize. It's an equation of one part:

- Tenacity. Having the balls to get out into the world and prove yourself. Perform. Or just be on the team. Try, fail, try harder, learn, try again, and master it.
- Courage. Because once you've done something embarrassing or frightening you can do it again the next time with a little less hesitation. Confidence is gained gradually as you try new things.
- Optimism. We'll talk a lot about this later but it's the product of tricking the mind into caring more about the potential for outcomes to be "good" than to consider all the ways your idea

will light on fire and burn to the ground.

When we fail, we can automatically blame ourselves or get negative about the circumstances around us that didn't set us up to win, or we can tally up our failures and fixate on them. But the key to my success is trying to stay malleable, flexible, and able to change. Resilience for me has always meant:

- getting back up after a swing and a miss (or a full on strike out), dusting myself off, and trying again.
- or going back to the dugout and waiting for my next turn at bat.
- or just realizing you have another chance.
- finding a new audience. I've failed in certain circles and thrived in others. Try a lot of scenarios and test which ones work best for you.

Don't discount the power of pessimism to fully unravel your game plan. It's the words that never come out from our mouth, the ones that our mind says to our heart, that are sometimes the most detrimental. If you want to master resilience you truly have to work on conquering negativity.

Marsha Linehan, PhD. developed a technique for suicidal psychiatric patients called DBT or Dialectical Behavior Therapy. It focuses on emotional triggers and thoughts that being dead would actually feel better than being alive . She describes that she needs to, as a doctor, climb down into the pit of despair that the patients are in. Once she's in hell with them, she teaches them tricks for climbing up the ladder and she says she literally pushes them out of the pit. This is the extreme case where things will feel hopeless to the point that ending one's life is the best option (in their mind) but even then, there are tricks for busting ass up the ladder of life and out into the fresh air of freedom.

I like psychology because it gives us reasons for our behavior. It helps explain why we think the way we do. It is very analytical and intellectual, using the mind and forms of assessment. It also has a way with labeling things, and sometimes with such harmful terms that it can create stigmas and limitations on us and on people in society. If you tell someone you are bipolar, what do they assume about you? If you admit you're taking medication for ADHD, there are some pretty uneducated responses you'll get from the general public. There are a range of clinical terminologies that can confine people to labels, and I don't like that part. I do think everyone should tell a complete stranger all of their deepest most intimate secrets of the heart and mind. Because it's often better than telling your parents, your spouse or your co-workers this information!

So, while a person's condition may require treatment, it is for each of us to decide if that's worthwhile. Yes, this work requires the help of a professional. Cognitive Behavioral Psychology is extremely common, but it's on the far end of a spectrum of "thought work" where you get a diagnosis and have a plan to get well. I think sometimes people believe that they can just "stay positive" and make a path to thriving. But I firmly disagree. I think people get themselves into their funk on their own, using their intellectual mind to start a swirling tornado of thoughts around a given issue. Getting out of the eye of the storm is something that needs professional help nine times out of ten. If you desire a life creating with purpose, climbing the ladder from the hell that you're in to where the light shines may require the help of a professional. *Even borderline personality disorder is treatable.* So, stay focused and optimistic as we scaffold our way up to resiliency.

CHAPTER 3: SAYING NO TO NEGATIVITY

Pessimism is always having something to complain about. You know the friend (or relative) who is always like the moping Eeyore in *Winnie the Pooh*? Or the "Anger" from the movie *Inside Out* (These characters could have used a session with Dr. Linehan big time). Or how about the friend who is always frustrated and down on their luck? I have to joke about days that were full of unexpected complications. Full. Here's how my made-up scenario would go: I'd overdraft my checking account while running out of gas. When I got to the station, I locked my keys in the car. Getting out my cell phone to dial for help, the phone died. Hives erupted all over my body. And my tampon leaked out just enough that I'd be tying my sweatshirt around my waist for the rest of the walk home.

My life was a shit storm.

The problem wasn't me. It was a confluence of rare and unfortunate circumstances, events; all of which were avoidable. My lack of proper prevention and precision made the odds stack up against me. My general mood was a magnet for foul encounters too. The grumpiness was at an all-time high. I'd stub my toe, someone would laugh, and I'd flip them off, and run into a pole while looking their way. You know those days? Am I the only one? If I had the opportunity to sit down with myself as my future CEO, I would have said, "Listen. You're a hot mess. What's going on?" There would be ten minutes of blabber about why all these things were someone else's fault. How I was worthless, and I'd never get ahead. But truth be told, I just needed a little precision in my life. I needed a plan. Each week I needed to fill the gas tank, get an app to monitor my bank statements, have three phone chargers (one home, one in the car, and one that is portable--and make sure it was

89

charged!) and carry some cash for "just in case" moments. But I had no back up plan. No maxi pad for life.

I was eating shit sandwiches. I was living with such a pessimistic attitude that nearly everything bad was magnetically pulled towards me in a universal effort to prove me right. No matter what could go wrong, it was going wrong. Murphy's Law seemed to have been written for my Irish life!

What I didn't realize was that no one wanted to spend time with me. No one wanted to do anything but give me $5 like the homeless man selling *StreetWise* magazines on the corner, so that they'd feel better and I'd go away. No one wants to date Eeyore or kick it with him after work.

I had a neighbor named Liz. She was generous and bossy and the team captain of the neighborhood. Her house became home base for all the kids and moms with empty wine glasses. We all gravitated there around "Happy Hour" which ranged from 4:45 PM to 10:45 pm on any given night, especially weekends.

Liz was my refuge. She cooked for the kids and we talked. I knew she wasn't going to divulge details of her marriage or personal life because she was just a really private person (she has healthy boundaries). But she always asked me about my life because it was always evolving and there was usually some drama. She cared about my wellbeing. And I obliged by over sharing as if I was on the therapist's chaise (because I have poor boundaries.) She likened me to one of her friends who'd recently gotten a divorce. Only difference is that the other lady was dating the CEO of McDonald's and had such horrible circumstances because she had to pack her suitcase routinely and fly to the Bahamas with her boyfriend. Hard eye roll. Liz said casually one night, "I can't be around her too much though. She's always such a drain. The

CHAPTER 3: SAYING NO TO NEGATIVITY

drama that follows her and her ex, the court case, the money… it's too much. I always feel drained when I spend a long day with her. She's so pessimistic and I'm like 'look at all the good in your life!' It gets frustrating to always hear her woes." The friend actually seemed so privileged even though she was fighting a similar custody battle as me.

She didn't know it, but I knew in that exact moment that many people were saying the same thing about me! Maybe even Liz had said this about me too! She was too kind to lead on that I was a drag, but what if I was?! What if other people I had once been close to had fallen away from me because I am the PigPen from the "Peanuts" caricature? With chaos all around me like a tiny tornado?! Maybe I stink like an onion???? Is that how people see me? Is that how people sense my arrival? …

Toxic pessimism is like friend repellant for normal, good, stable people who work hard and have healthy boundaries. Liz listened to my garbage life story with all of her judgement reserved away. She didn't ever criticize me. She also didn't share so in some way I thought I was the only one who had any problems. But Liz had boundaries. She was probably talking about her issues with a shrink. Or a coach. Or a preacher. Who knows? This advice comes in handy once in a while: There are three kinds of relationships. One is your therapist, one is the person you're dating (or a close friend), and one is your client/customer. You shouldn't be sharing the same information with these three categories of people!

What you admit in therapy shouldn't be repeated on a date. What you talk about in a date should never be the same as what you talk about during a client presentation. The way you speak to a client shouldn't be brought into therapy. Each serves a purpose. One person is paid to listen, one person is there to share joyful experiences with you, the last is paying for your service. When your friends turn into the role of the shrink, what do you think they feel like? They feel like either they should be paid to listen and share all their wine with your whining ass or, they feel it's a one sided equation. Unless you're both equally bitching about stuff, which can sometimes also be an exhausting exchange, you can't expect your friends to take that on. It's too much and it's not their job to counsel and console you. This work is for you to do!

Are you above all of this? Are you guilty of abusing your friends' kindness? Maybe you have your shit together a little more than my past self-did, in which case you are above it all. Maybe your problems are locked in a vault and you don't think you need to talk about them. Maybe you've got the friends who constantly complain and it sucks your energy to hang out with them. If you're wondering why you can't seem to shed the losers in your life, it could be because you are making company with those whose dumpster fire of a life is more chaotic than yours. In any case, begin to assess the company you keep and monitor if there is balance and harmony. If you're taking up too much airtime with your drama. Ask yourself if that's the type of friend you want to be.

Mantras for Forward Momentum

I can't remember just when I started talking smack to myself. It must have been in the months after my husband moved out because those were some of the most challenging times of my life. I regretted having started a business at the exact same time, though I didn't know any different. I had all these things to do and no time to do them. I had no support, or so it felt. I had one son who hadn't even made it to his 2nd birthday and those times are a blur for everyone I know. Through it all, I clued into negative voices inside my head.

I was trying to get everywhere so fast. Between the backpacks, sippy cups, strollers, purse, and my art, I would typically get tangled up and tripped up and always felt like a klutz. And when it wasn't me falling over, my kids were falling down and I never had any g- d- band aids in my purse. I gave myself a really hard time about being miles away from perfect.

Once I began listening to the voice I used to speak to myself, I took the driver's seat and started to navigate my own mind. I realized certain scripts were on repeat like "Dummy!" or "God, I can't even do this right?!" when I'd lock myself out of the house and have to knock on my neighbor's window to let me in. I had many not very nice things to say to myself. I had a pretty negative opinion of me and some of that was informed by phrases others would offer but mostly I'd make up the mantras myself. "You're never going to make it," or "It will never be easy."

What I wanted was someone to tell me that I was doing a *great job* but no one was there to say that. So I realized I had to step up or nothing would change. I became the beacon in my own life. When things felt like an avalanche chasing me, I had to provide guidance and hopeful affirmations to myself instead of waiting for approval from the outside world. I started to replace the absurd comments spit out by my mind with nice things. Gentle sayings. Even if they were a little fluffy and cute, I wanted to hear them sometimes when the day had been hard. I began to recite a mantra. "Go Slow and Be Nice to Yourself." As I was closing the door to my apartment, I would say that and it probably prevented many a stubbed toe. When I would rush, I noticed I'd make more mistakes. I noticed I was trying to hurry but also do things well. That wasn't the best strategy for nailing my daily routine. So

I made these loving suggestions to myself and it worked. Kinda.

Self-directed kindness is such a chore. Like, giving yourself a break is the last thing you think of. We are all aiming for varying degrees of perfection but then there's always going to be a natural margin of error. Running out of gas on the highway should only happen once in a lifetime. But I swear to God it happened ten times in the last six years to me. Am I a fucking dunce? Should I be thrown in jail? No. Give me a break, Me! I now keep gas cans in the trunk.

Record some of your intrinsic self-talk. Take note. Bookmark the times throughout the day when you're really laying into yourself. And take a moment to back off. Notice those thoughts. Find a one liner that's an "emotional bubble bath" phrase. Calming, soothing, gentle, and kind--even relaxing. Start by telling yourself something new, no matter how hokie you think this crap is. Relieve yourself of the need to always go fast, always be perfect, always do ten things at once.

Because nobody is good at all that stuff all the time. And if they are, I want to read THEIR book to gain some insight into how to perform at lightning speed and achieve greatness effortlessly.

When You are Raised to Think the Worst

Pessimism is a trait I inherited. Likely from a long line of Irish immigrants whose cynical limericks still plaster the walls of my uncle Randy's hallways. Growing up in Ireland and sailing across the ocean to the new land was a dance with death. Being a Mick in Chicago could land you in the Patty wagon. Irish were treated as the scum of the earth (although one rung higher than Italians, if you can imagine that), possibly because many of them were drunk all the time and liked to cause trouble. My great-great-grandfather was a gas lamp lighter living in a two-bedroom flat in Chicago with his wife and kids and brother. His son would go on to play professional baseball for the Cubs! I'm sure they'd have a good laugh at my book about resilience! I do know there's a dark limerick waiting for me in hell. My uncle literally used to carry a sign during the St. Patrick's Day parade that read "May you be in heaven a half hour before the devil knows you're dead." Thank you, Grandpa Edward Stack for passing on this "wisdom."

My mom taught me every swear word I know. My dad taught me my sense of humor. The subconscious residue of my parents is everlasting. Mom was like Joan of Arc, busting into ye' old brain and say things like "You're a fuckin' idiot!" when my train pass had expired and slayed my hope of ever making it to the appointment on time. Dad would belch loudly and say "Well.... they never bought you any beer," if I lost the potential for a big sale. When I recklessly spend my last dollar, my mom's voice can be heard inside my brain saying, "It's just money." They trained me to see the worst in myself; to make light of a situation that really mattered but didn't go as planned. These are traits of negative self-image and they're toxic for my emotional and mental health. I didn't realize it until I started purposefully redirecting my self talk to be more like the mum and pop that Harry Potter always wished he'd had growing up.

Pessimists have a way of ruining the party; they damper one's ability to thrive. Pessimism is the opposite of seeing the silver lining. They can usually always find something to complain about. Watch out for your deep desire to find bad news. As you embark on a journey to reach your own greatest potential, you may shock people. Your new life choices and self-worth may beget some pretty catty comments from those around you. Friends may think you're selling out--because you are selling art. Acquaintances may dish out backhanded compliments like my ex-boyfriend from college did:

JL: "Wow, Minckley! I never expected you to do anything like this! It's so cool." What is demoralizing about this statement is that he never thought I'd make anything of myself. That I hadn't ever shown a propensity to succeed or that I wasn't the first one he (or anyone I went to college with) expected to become wealthy or famous.

Me: "Huh? You never thought I'd make something of my life?" It was up to me to prove myself to the world. I didn't need to take this comment and marinate on it. I didn't need to let it be true for me. It was probably meant to be uplifting and show me how much he thought of me. I could choose to interpret it as 'I'm not good enough' or 'He thinks highly of me now.'

Just because people don't see your potential or incremental progress as a monumental leap towards the unknown goal, don't let that rain on your parade. One day, you'll turn around to face the past and see what you've made. Others will act as if it happened 'all of a sudden' but really, it's usually painfully slow. Progress is progress. Even 1% improvement is improvement. "Slow and steady wins the race" said the tortoise.

Much like the "Go Slow, and Be Kind" mantra, you may have to throw yourself a party from time to time. Sometimes celebrating the small stuff is against your inner Irish pessimist's nature. He's yelling "Ooh, aren't we fancy!" in an Austin Powers accent. But you can treat yourself to a night out, a glass of wine, a cake with a candle and it's not even your birthday. Celebrate little milestones you hit along the way with small rewards. What celebration tells your inner pessimist to "fuck off?" The ritual of celebration proves to yourself that you are WORTH celebrating. That you've come this far. And it tricks the mind into wanting to reach the next small milestone because there will be a movie night with popcorn at the end of it. In time, you may even notice a Pavlovian response and do the work without needing the treat.

When people begin to notice your achievements or your success becomes public knowledge, you really have to battle the brain. Recently, I participated in the Lake Forest Showhouse. It's a showcase for the top interior designers and firms in Chicago to take over a room and give it a huge makeover. They can spend as much money as they want to trim out their space and deck it to the nines. Many create custom furniture, lighting, paint, wallpaper, carpet and decorate their spaces using every favor they've been owed from every vendor and contractor in their rolodex. I was given a hallway; it's a space that can neither host furniture nor many people. A passageway from one deluxe living room to another swanky, luxury den. Each space around me a thousand times more elaborate than the one I designed, I decided to take a stance as an artist and create a viewing gallery. For my art. It was a simple space with impact. A place to think of as more than just a passageway to the other side of the house.

As people came through the space and complimented me on the color choices, the artworks I hung on the walls, the light fixtures I purchased cheaply online at the last moment, I was tempted to tell them the truth. That I put very little effort into planning what I'd do with the space. That the coronavirus ate my budget for fancy things and that I scrambled to get the paintings framed in time for opening day. I was tempted to out myself and say, "I'm not even a 'real designer' so I'm just incredibly humbled they gave me a space at all." Do you do that? Do you downplay the accomplishments you've made? Do you shrug off compliments and people who are earnestly attempting to celebrate your talent?

No, no and no.

You Know You've Made it When...

What about haters? I like to say that once you have haters or your work is being imitated, then you know you've made it. Before that, no one was responding to your work with praise because it didn't exist. Once someone has negative feedback about your work then you know you've stirred up some emotions about it. When they begin to copy you or rip you off, that's another way of knowing that people are watching. At least you have a following. At least you're taking up space publicly. I've noticed several wallpaper designs that are very similar to mine on the market. I haven't sued anyone or made a stink because I suppose imitation is the highest form of flattery. They liked it so much that they wished they'd invented it first. I invoked that productive type of jealousy.

In my first ever photoshoot of just me, I purchased some clothes from a service called Trunk Club and dolled myself up with makeup. I wanted to empower myself and record the moment in history where I started to feel okay alone (unmarried). I needed some headshots for my social media presence anyway. I was met with much curiosity from my photographer. Also a woman, she asked me questions the entire shoot. I hardly got any good shots because we couldn't stop talking and my mouth was moving. She asked me about how I chose to leave and how I got the courage to get divorced with two small kids. I gave the answers that I thought she could stomach: The marriage wasn't working. It wasn't cultural. We didn't see eye to eye on what the rest of our life should look like. She had two boys that were adults and she recalled having many moments when she wanted to leave her own marriage but she said, "the thought of doing it all on my own forced me to stay." I didn't judge her. She'd probably provided her kids with a very nice lifestyle relying on their dad financially. No one can judge a woman for wanting her kids to have a nice life. Her problem if she let her aspirations go in order to be a parent or never got the love she deserved from her partner. Again, not judging. But I wouldn't have stayed.

When I got the images back, I was so ecstatic that I posted one immediately. She'd done such a nice job capturing my badassery, even if it was staged in a photo studio and I was incognito as a "successful" person and dressed like I *wasn't* a tomboy. I forgot to tag her in the photo because I was seriously posting the image at a red light while driving my car to a job site. Not tagging your photographer in the pictures is a cardinal sin of social media, so I'll be the first to admit that I fucked up. But what happened next was not expected. She blocked me and then she wrote a long paragraph about how I was a fake feminist. She stated that I say I support other women, but I don't even give them credit for their work. It wasn't until my intern notified me that somebody was writing hateful things on my Instagram feed that I noticed it because she'd blocked me, and I couldn't see any of her posts/comments. I even tried to tag her after the fact and couldn't because I'd been blocked.

That experience was a great lesson. I had opened myself up to this woman and told her vulnerable things. I had gone out on a personal limb to hire her and dress up and get my photo taken, which in some cultures can feel like having someone steal your soul. I did that, for the same reason that I am writing this vulnerable book. To tell my own account of how life has been for me as a woman. As an artist, shapeshifter, transformed into a businessperson. I wanted to inspire other women to tell their stories and leave bad marriages and sell their art for the highest dollar amount they could get. To stop discounting their worth. My mind was blown, and I tried really hard not to take her comments to heart. She called me a "Fake Feminist." It gradually stung less and though I tried to reach out to her and explain she never wrote back. I had to come to accept that sometimes I would mess up on social media and sometimes I would be blacklisted. Sometimes I would be criticized for doing what I thought was pretty earnest. That's just part of putting yourself out there, I guess. It leaves you open to "feedback" of all kinds and that feedback isn't always going to be glorious.

Haters and copycats come out to play only when you push your art out into the world. They don't exist if you shove your dream into a drawer, along with your graphite pens and drawing paper. They won't exist if you never photograph yourself and introduce your beautiful face to the world by way of Instagram. They can't hate you if you don't exist or don't have anything to say. Steep price to pay for turning your back on the one thing that always made you happy: creating.

This is How I Meant it to Look

You don't have to tell the truth. The whole truth. And nothing but the truth. If I had told the truth in the post about my "coming out" as a divorced single mom running a business, it would've looked like this: *"Hi World. I don't know what I'm doing. I make mistakes every day. My kids don't have everything they deserve but I spent a lot of money to hire a photographer and buy all these fancy clothes so that you would think I am successful. Do you? I'm trying. But truth is, I will return these clothes tomorrow so that I don't overdraft my checking account. LOL Still learning how to adult. Give me a thumbs up if you think this is what being a hashtag momtrepreneur looks like! Tryin' to be Happy Tuesday"*

That's not very good marketing. What I ended up saying is this, *"Hi World, it's me Erin. I'm the founder of Relativity Textiles, a luxury wallpaper brand located in Chicago. I am the proud mom of two boys and a fine artist. I started this company as a way to share what I love with the world. I hope you enjoy some of our globally inspired patterns. Thumbs up for moms in business. #motivationmonday"*

Writing that took every bit of guts I had.

What I posted was mostly facts. A small and sweet recap of my good intentions when I began my business. The mission statement, if you will. You read very little "real" details about what it looked like for the Wizard of Oz behind the curtain. In business, sometimes vulnerability is a good thing, and sometimes giving away too much about how you're feeling is not good for growth and sales. Again, the shrink, the boyfriend, and the client— you don't use "honesty" literally and unilaterally with everyone.

What I mean is that by overexplaining how your process wasn't exactly how you thought it would be, or how hard it was to get here, you inadvertently discount the finished product. Typically, what we [your audience] are looking for is how it turned out--the finished result or product. We don't have time [nor desire] to hear the backstory or speculate how it could have been done better! You have to assume that we want to buy it already, even without any explanation. Just state, '**This is how I intended it to be.**' And listen to what people say. That little nugget right there I have carried into my business life, my relationships, my art making, etc. The BTS (behind the scenes) is our little secret. You guys are the only ones who are hearing the real BTS of how I got to this place and you're hearing it because *I just put myself on blast by writing a book.*

Between you and me, we are here, looking at your artwork now. Your life, your finances. Stop spewing out all your intentions of what it could have been if only blah blah blah. Don't illuminate the disparities between the vision in your head and how the real thing isn't exactly perfect. You don't have to say that you still need to refine it or build a website or make a series of 10 more... Just advocate for the object that is here right now. If there is praise, say "thanks" and feel good about it. If you strive to improve it, do it. Right after we shred it to pieces with an onion peeler.

One thing might surprise you though. To you, it's not perfect or finished. To someone else, they just took it to the cash register and bought it. They drank your Kool-Aid, bro! And you didn't even have to do much but shut your ego up for a second and list your drawings on Etsy. Suddenly you have money in your bank account because of that momentary lapse of inhibitions, aka bravery.

What if it's less about confidence and perfection and more about courage?

Don't Discount ($) Your Work

While we are on the subject of downplaying your talent, dare I ask you? Do you discount your work? I know you've been discounting your skills, your time investment, your talent and drive. I know you've been posting photos of yourself that are really pretty and saying, "I hate having my picture taken, but here's my new headshots." But, are you also doing this with the price tag on your artwork? Do you charge less because you feel BAD to charge what it's worth? Or if they ask you to knock the price in half? Why? Why do we do that?

Here's s business tip: *You set the value of your work.* If no one is paying, there could be several reasons. First thought is that you aren't reaching enough people. Just because you posted it once on Facebook doesn't mean all 1,500 of your friends saw it! Keep hustling, keep knocking on doors like the girl scouts do. The other thought is that maybe the value you are delivering to the 'consumer' doesn't match up with the price tag. News flash: That doesn't mean you should lower your price; it means you need to target a different audience. Maybe the demographic you are going for is people with MORE money who are WILLING to pay the price you're asking… KPWOOUFF! Did your brain just explode? Mine did when I heard that for the first time.

Here it is again. You set the price for your item or service. If you are doing wedding photography, for example and you want to make $5,000 in a weekend, but everyone you've met only has $2,500 then you need to find customers somewhere else. There are people who pay $10,000 for a wedding photographer. They're just not in your current network. How do you find them? That should be the next big research project your creative mind puts to task. They're out there. You just haven't found them yet. Don't scurry like a mouse after every piece of cheese. There are more than enough clients out there for you to find one that can work with your budget. You just need to get introduced to them somehow. We'll explore all this a lot more later.

Don't downplay your achievements or talent. As artists we are quick to say that we aren't as good as the compliment being paid. "Wow, your floral arrangements are incredible!" You demote yourself by saying "oh, gosh. That old thing? Thanks, but it's just a hobby."

While watching the Michael Phelps documentary about gold medalists who often become suicidal after winning the Olympics, I started to ponder what achievement really means. What talent is worth and what the payoff is to all the hard work and dedication. Success is in the process. It's in the tiny compliments (no matter how backhanded they might seem). Someone is noticing you. Someone took the time to tell you that. Their small congratulations may not be a gold medal, but what athletes work their whole lives for is often over in the blink of an eye. Yes, they might even win the highest award of recognition for their athleticism, but one day later they'll sit in their hotel rooms and wonder, "What now?" Once you reach a goal, the funny thing is… you just have to set some new ones.

Why are we quick to dismiss a compliment, or celebration, or congratulations? I honestly have no answer. I assume that other people in other industries where it takes hard work and personal strength to achieve things will say "Thank you so much!" when they are paid a compliment. Every win, even the silver medal, deserves congratulations. I doubt an athlete will say "shucks, I am not that great at running" after they've just won second place. They might say it wasn't their personal best, but that's a moment of lacking self-esteem! You just ran your best race! Say thank you! Feel proud! No one will shoot you down in the street for accepting a compliment.

When you downplay your success, it is a form of pessimism-- it is the anti-self-esteem. It's rooted again in perfectionism. If you can't win first prize and be the richest and most famous artist alive, then are you just nothing? Are you worthless? Let me phrase it another way. Are you better than the lady down the street who knits blankets? She considers herself 'creative' too. Yah. You are. Just as much as I was asked to do a showcase when plenty of other more talented interior designers in Chicago are not! So, why should I question it?!

The part that drives me crazy about being an artist is that there is no universal standard for how we operate. There's no rubric for success. When I taught high school, I learned to evaluate students on specific criteria: 1) Did they follow the assignment? 2) Had they given their best effort? 3) Was the activity complete? I never assessed their skill and graded them from "A" is for experts and "F" is for fuckups. Art in the real world assumes that the audience is judging you constantly about whether or not the work is good.

Guys, I'm going to point out the obvious and it's going to sound *super judgy:* People will pay for bad art. Lots of people own bad art. Lots of people paid for ugly websites to be built. Lots of people have poorly designed...everything. Listen, there's a market for everything and an audience for every price range. I'm not saying that your art is ugly and it can still sell! Not at all. Hear me when I tell you that if your biggest stumbling block is that you didn't get an A+ in Pat Eddington's high school art class (or never even took an art class) it does not mean you can't call yourself an artist, or draw stuff and sell it. Anyone can do this with the right formula of mindset, network, and tenacity for marketing themselves. So to everyone I've ever met who said, "I can't even draw a stick figure," I'd like to respond now with this: George W. Bush makes paintings and sells them. Google it. He's not 'good' at it but he does it anyway! Maybe your horrible stick figure drawings would be popular in certain circles. You never know until you try.

Sometimes, the artists who I think are not the most talented are wildly successful. In many cases the ones who put in the most effort do not reap the rewards. Many artists start something and never complete it. That said, when and where do we create our own rubric for success? If we are reaching our own goals and doing our own personal best, doesn't that mean that we have succeeded?

If I'm not worried about comparison, then it doesn't matter if you're an artist just like Aunt Suzie who paints horrible watercolor paintings in her spare time. Because you are defining what "artist" means to you and it can look totally different than her definition. The world doesn't have to understand that distinction. Said well by the authors of Art & Fear, "The important point here is not that you have — or don't have —

what other artists have, but rather that it doesn't matter. Whatever they have is something needed to do their work — it wouldn't help you in your work even if you had it. Their magic is theirs. You don't lack it. You don't need it. It has nothing to do with You. Period."

There will always be lots of people better than you and a lot of people better than me! At a lot of things. At everything in life. Fitter. Richer. Better at drawing. Inversely, there are always thousands of people who are worse than you too. You're already winning then. Because when you thrive as an artist, you use your talent on the daily. And you will feel it, too. You'll start to notice you have magic within you. One of the key strategies to really reigning in your magic is to stop negating the celebrations, congratulations, and compliments. Let them love you and your artwork. Let them admire you. Let them think your shit doesn't stink! You're the only one who knows that it does. Hold onto that information as a secret. Lock it in the vault and spend two minutes soaking in the praise. It's good for the soul.

Limiting Beliefs

I want to introduce you to a concept called a "Limiting Belief." It is something that time and time again has been a topic during therapy and life coaching sessions of mine.

A limiting belief is just what it sounds like: a thought which you are holding onto that doesn't help you progress. It holds you back or limits you in some way. Limiting beliefs, I used to think, were built on attitude. My people, or family of origin, are very pessimistic people. Their attitudes are shared openly and sometimes tend to lead to Chicken Little narratives where the sky is falling. We would run around freaking out that the world was about to end, only to find out that it wasn't. Everything was fine. Much of that has to do with my mom also being a hypochondriac, which as a healthcare professional, does happen. But I was raised in this environment where everyone and everything was against me--or so I thought.

A limiting belief is a conclusion you come to in your mind, not on a whim. You've had repeated exposure to events in your life that you captured as "evidence" to support your claim. For example, artists don't get corporate day jobs. That led you so far to a string of freelance work or part-time gigs and you've been scraping together just fine, thanks. But because of your limiting belief that artists can't be _____ (fill in the blank), your brain turned off any receptors that might a) challenge that notion and b) accept new opportunities or information. You're looking at LinkedIn one morning as you sip your $15 hipster coffee at the local cafe where all the corporate people are getting a to go cup before jumping on the "L" Train when you see a job post for "Creative Director." The posted salary is $100,000. Your brain is an old-fashioned piano, you know the ones with the holes in the paper than play on their own? Yah. It's tinking out a tune like this, without your knowledge,

> *"Tink tink tink, the real artist doesn't sell out! Tink tank tank, You could never survive a corporate environment! Tingy tingy tang, The corporate job is not for you! Tang. Bang. Bang. You silly little artist, get back to your coffee!"*

That old fashioned piano isn't as cool as you think it is. It was innovative in the era of the Wild Wild West and it's great for museums. But you've got to get a new technology going if you want to progress in life. How about an electronic keyboard? You know, the ones with pre-programmed jazzy beats? If you reset your mind to a jazzy beat, many doors may open for you. And I know I'm pushing this metaphor to the limits but stick with me.

> *"Untz untz untz, May-bay I can, May-bay I can. Untz untz oontz, What if I try? What if I try? Untz untz untz, That would be great, that would be dope. Oontz oontz oontz, Dammit apply, just go on and apply!"*

The belief is no longer that you can't. That artists can't. That women can't--if you listen to that jazzy beat each time, you're about to second guess or downplay your skills, you are challenging your limiting beliefs. The programmed beat. The scripts.

I'm sure each of you have collected so much data and lived through so many experiences that you could fill volumes about the plight of an artist and all the things they are not appreciated for, how society doesn't value us or our work, how jobs are scarce, how paydays are few and far between. Because I used to believe all those same conclusions--I lived in that reality, suffering and struggling and wondering why I couldn't catch a break. What if, just imagine it with me, what if these scripts were untrue? What if you could fill a balloon with all these limiting beliefs and let it go? Up, up and away it would fly.

What would you have, if not volumes of evidence? You'd have to rely on faith or hope, or collect new information, or try a new approach, or pray to GAWD for help. But you'd have no other choice but to turn on some new tune and let it be the rhythm of your subconscious and roll with it. I'd like you to give that a try. Instead of asking "What if____?" and thinking through all the worst-case scenarios, you just created a new narrative. "This is the part where _____." The part where you got a new line of work. Where you could afford more cool things. Where you set out to meet all new people and they gave you advice and resources you never knew were possible. Where you resolved that credit card debt that's been holding you back from buying a house. Where you decided to listen to your spouse for once and go get some certification you've always wanted. Where you went out on a limb not knowing if you'd fail but trying it anyway. Where you called in support.

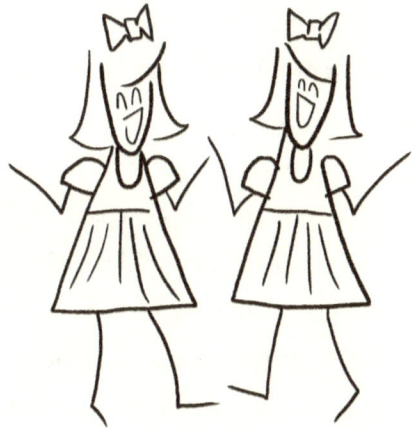

Why the Comparison Model Always Fails

I've shared a face with another human being for 38 years. Contemplate that for a minute. On August 24, 1982 two baby girls were born. My identical twin sister was born first, and she weighed about 1 pound more than me. For the rest of our life stories, life has been one big, fat competition. As we all struggle to maintain a sense of identity and uniqueness, especially in our teenage years filled with angst and rebellion, I had a real life doppelgänger. I was a twin--an EXACT twin. Even our dentist could not tell our teeth impressions apart because they were so incredibly identical, he relayed to my mother, "Even if their remains were found in a fire, I would not be able to determine which child was which based on their teeth alone." Grim, but true. We are basically the same.

Where you told the whole world your goals. Where you stopped giving a fuck.

were so incredibly identical, he relayed to my mother, "Even if their remains were found in a fire, I would not be able to determine which child was which based on their teeth alone." Grim, but true. We are basically the same.

In elementary school our teachers couldn't tell us apart. I remember my PE teacher would call me "Jessica-Erin." She didn't know if I was Jessica or Erin so I guess she assumed that if she called me both names that she would get it right. Still to this day if someone yells "Jessica!" in a crowd I turn around. I prepare myself to say: "I am not her." We ended up going to separate middle schools, separate high schools and separate colleges. I suppose because we wanted our own identity so much or because we really hated each other for most of our teenage years. My sister and I grew up in the same household and we share DNA. That being said, we have very different lived experiences. *We have very different perceptions of the world.*

We had to share everything growing up. Not only did I share my face, but I shared my birthday as well. There were always two presents of the exact same size for birthdays. If one of us opened it first, it killed the surprise for the other. So we would attempt to open gifts at the exact same speed like a race so that we both had the same amount of surprise when we opened our own gift. I got used to being compared to her by everyone I know. By the time we were freshman in high school there were definitely different characteristics about each of us that were known. I tried out for every sport a girl could play. I was such a tomboy that I practically had a unibrow and biceps. I wore a sports bra most days. My clothes never fit my body. I did not notice any attention

---

[4] (He's actually now a very talented comic book writer, author, and plays for an awesome band… should've snached him up).

coming from the male species. Except for Dave Chisholm who was a trumpet player in the school band and sat across from me in art class[4].

My sister on the other hand was taking modeling classes as an extracurricular activity. She would ask for makeup from the MAC counter for gifts. She loved fashion and never tired of looking at Seventeen magazine. She won the affection of many boys in our class and even older boys too. Freshman year, we were asked to a school dance together by two boys for a double date. Instead of being asked individually by two boys, they asked us together.

In Salt Lake City, the way you ask a girl to Homecoming is to be very clever and indirect. This was before Pinterest, so they'd likely ask their moms to help them with a project to creatively "pop the question." A knock at the door one afternoon revealed a bucket of Doublemint gum and a note attached that said: "Double your pleasure, double your fun. Will you go to the dance with *us*?" There must've been 1,000 pieces of Doublemint gum in that bucket and we had to unwrap each one in order to find the name of the person who had asked us. It instructed us that "Erin, your date's name will be on a wrapper and Jessica, your date's name will be on a piece of gum." We unwrapped every piece until we found out who we were going to the Homecoming dance with.

The hotter guy asked my sister. The guy who asked me was his best friend, but he was also on the wrestling team. Turns out they were both kind of dead-end guys, but two crushes formed that day. We began hanging out with the boys and I was always a bit jealous that my sister got the cuter date to Homecoming. She was prettier and more confident though. I understood why my name was thrown into a bucket with hers. They may not have been able to tell us apart. They may have assumed we were both the same. One of the guys might have been too shy to come up with his own Pinterest worthy ask plan. But the way people saw us was as a "unit." Not two individuals. "The Twins" is what we were called most of our lives. We were always at the same developmental stage. We looked so much alike even some of our friends had a hard time differentiating. We could have attended one another's classes and taken tests for each other if we'd corroborated more. But I learned to take on half of an identity, the whole of which was only complete with Jessica nearby.

When you're half an identity, you need to differentiate. People noticed one of us was always *more athletic*. One of us was always prettier. One of us was *smarter*. One of us was *more fun*. And we always aimed to be better than the other; in order to define ourselves as unique or individual. If her hair was long, I cut my hair short; if she dyed hers blonde, I dyed mine black. If she was wearing preppy clothes, I was goth. We did this on purpose to be noticed. To stand out. To give people something to remember. To signal, "Here I am! I am right here! I am not a twin; I am one person-- an individual-- with strengths and talents and dreams that are different from hers!"

Now the story might seem a little far-fetched, if I am to tell you why the comparison model always fails. Because I'm willing to bet you don't have your own doppelganger like I do. But this is just where I honed in on the idea of "the comparison model." There's always going to be someone in this world who has more *money* than you. There's always going to be an artist who can draw 1000 times better than you. There's always going to be someone with more social media followers. There's always going to be someone who got into a magazine for their success, while you sit around self-loathing that you didn't make the cut. Your bestie might have a nicer body, more clothes, a hotter husband than you. And when you think you deserve to have all of those things too, because you are the best, *put your identity in check*. The comparison

CHAPTER 3: SAYING NO TO NEGATIVITY

model always fails.

You're not going to win everything. And it doesn't matter if you do. I could have been the sexiest, the smartest, the most athletic, and deeply unhappy. I could be the wealthiest artist you've ever met in your life, and not even have a sense of self. I learned this lesson early in my life that it was less about trying to *win*, and more about trying to be your *best self.* Because if you spend all your time comparing yourself to others, you will always see your inadequacies before you see your strengths. Like a magnifying mirror in the fancy hotel bathrooms, as soon as you turn the lights on, you're going to notice LOTS of blemishes. You can pick and pop and ruin your face, or you can stop looking for problems. Say, "Hello beautiful." And walk away. Because on the flip side there's also always going to be someone poorer than you. There's always going to be someone in worse shape than you, and that person is probably looking up to you. So please be a role model for them by appreciating where you are. For having some gratitude about what it took to get here. Show some pride in who you are and put some focus on the good parts. Less paranoia that you're not enough.

You are more than enough.

So just because you're not as far along in your career as you want to be, or you haven't acquired fame and fortune yet does not mean that you're not successful. Compare yourself to who you were last year. Ask yourself if you've gotten ahead just a little bit. Ask yourself how much more money do I make this year than I did last year? And the fear should not be that you're not good enough because you're not like so-and-so. If you should be that you're exactly in the same exact space as you were last year or the year before. That means you haven't progressed in comparison to your old self. So if your identical twin and your doppelgänger and your alter ego is your past self, the only comparison you can make right now is to your past self.

If there's something that you are striving to be, it might be an amalgamation of many different people who inspire you. Do you want to have a podcast because Oprah does? Great! Do you want to have a fashion line because Kate Hudson does? Great! Do you want to have a cooking show because Jennifer Garner is bored, and a celebrity and she shows her bread recipe on Instagram stories? Great! But you don't have to be Oprah and you don't have to be Jennifer Garner to be a success. You just have to be yourself.

See the problem with how we've been conditioned as women (and most likely as men too though I've never existed in a male body) is as if there is a goal to achieve in terms of body image or sex appeal. Why do you think so many women are getting boob jobs? And butt implants!? I honestly have no idea why this type of surgery exists. If you were not born with big boobs --and I am the captain of the itty-bitty titty committee so please know that I am speaking about myself here—then you're just shit out of luck I guess.

When I read the chapter about Rachel Hollis's breast implant surgery in the book called "Girl Stop Apologizing," I was laughing hysterically at her account of how insecure she was before she got her implants. She advocates for women doing whatever is necessary to become more confident about themselves. I think that her experience is true for her and she did what was right for herself. So I'm not knocking anyone who wants to surgically upgrade themselves. But there is a moment right here for exploring what it would be like to just come to peace with what you have.

The value that is placed on a woman who is sexy and also

successful-- you have to be both, or you are nothing? Being overweight, having bad acne, and all of the other things that make us hate ourselves are not *who we are*. They are characteristics or identifiers that others see, yes. Self-hatred is invisible. Beauty fades. Tight bodies eventually get saggier and wrinklier. I hate that we have to look at our "flaws" as imperfections or something to *be fixed*. Here's my angle: There is something to revealing oneself in an imperfect state for others to see that is uplifting. I think that if more celebrities were posting pictures of themselves with no makeup on, we would understand that there's a tremendous amount of smoke and mirrors involved with the image portrayed to us by Hollywood. If we all wore bathing suits around postpartum, then we'd collectively feel more comfortable with how disfigured the human form can be once it's been a hotel to a human for 10 months on end. We could normalize these things. Then maybe once we stroll in confidence, it would be that air of loving one's self that would attract the opposite sex. And make other women feel drawn to us, for our sheer attitude of giving less fucks.

When you start to augment reality for yourself with tons of makeup, big name brands, and cosmetic augmentation, you become less and less your true self. Your authentic self. I do believe that feeling pretty is very important. But through which lens are we looking? Are we looking from a male gaze? Are we evaluating the success of our appearance based on who is attracted to us?

In nature it is usually the male animal who is parading with brilliant colors and funny dances to attract the female. In our current human culture, we expect the female species to seduce and lure a man's gaze. Even women look at each other through the male gaze. We evaluate each other's sex appeal and rate one another on how successful you've been at achieving the ideal. The woman who hasn't plucked her eyebrows or shaved her legs; the woman wearing not an ounce of makeup, hasn't dyed her gray hairs is somewhat of a rebel (or a failure). Because she doesn't participate in the normative cycle of primping and grooming, she is confident and comfortable without playing into what magazines show. I am especially talking about being a single woman, because this is the time where you are supposed to be attracting a mate. There is a heightened awareness of your "appeal" and how good you're doing based in if you can find a partner who will stay with you and value you.

I wish there was a way for us to be happy with who we are exactly and how we were made. But there's something here about the comparison model that's never going to die. This competition between you and your idol artist (mine is El Anatsui) mentality is not good for our art. Neither raw talent nor superstar beauty, is something that anyone was *born* with. It requires a daily routine to apply that illusion or maintain the perfect form. It requires mastery, and we will get to that by the end of this book.

I wish I could say that there was a way to end this entire illusion about negativity. But I know as a businesswoman who has more receivables than payables and annual double-digit growth there will have to be an amount of parading in order to project an image to the public or to your colleagues of success. And here's where I'm going to make a little turn in my argument. *There is a time and a place* for smoke and mirrors. When you are going to appear on TV or speak to a large audience, you will want them to perceive you in a certain way. I don't think that there is harm in creating the solution. In fact there are several species in the natural world who are able to morph and camouflage strategically as a defense mechanism and a mode for survival.

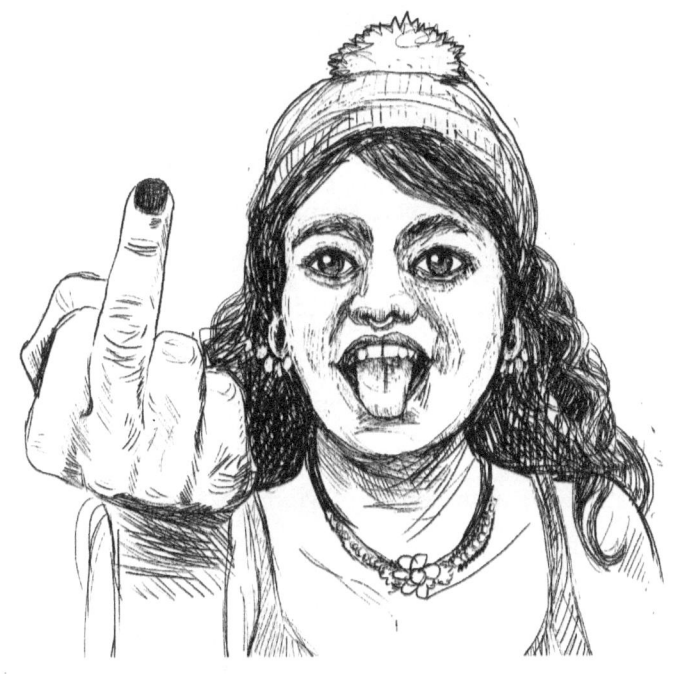

The Artist's Tongue

What if you could make millions doing the thing that you were put on this Earth to do? Would that be okay? No, seriously, answer this question. Would it be okay for you to be rich and do what you are good at and love? Go back to Section 1 and read the part all over again about the Portrait of the Artist as a Millionaire. When you get caught up with all the mental blocks of perfectionism or excuses remember the dream goal. Allowing the possibility means sometimes sitting in your own shit. Like really waiting it out, waiting for someone to come and rescue you or an answer to fall from the sky. You made this mess yourself. You're going to probably have to clean it up. But sometimes "Thriving" is the last thing that feels possible. Keep going and remember to watch your goddamn mouth.

Language is fascinating. Isn't it? How the world is made up of thousands of dialects and none of us can understand one another. That we can learn a new language and open the door to the possibility of communication with so many new people is incredible. I learned Spanish in high school only because my sister was learning French. I went all the way to AP Spanish and eventually used it on trips to Mexico, Spain, and in many food service jobs and construction sites. I studied Farsi, which I never mastered and eventually became fluent in Arabic. It took me 7 years before I started having dreams in Arabic. I could tell several jokes in Arabic and had several aggressive rebuttals for a man's cat calls to me in the streets of Morocco. That's when you know you've gotten good.

Language in our mother tongue is also a tool. It can help or harm you. It can empower or oppress you. It can hurt people. It can excel your career. Language plays a significant role in developing your sense of self. It propels you into the new chapter of your life if you can master it as I mastered Arabic. I am fluent in Arabic.

It wasn't easy but I had an audio tape (yes, a cassette player in college not an iTunes account or any pod or phone tools). I studied abroad in Morocco in 2002 where I lived with a host family who spoke zero English and studied three hours a day. I made it to the advanced class and was talking in two dialects by the end of four months living there. It's a skill I can only practice with cab drivers and shawarma restaurant employees now. But I even began to dream in Arabic. See, my ex-husband is from Morocco and so I went back there every summer from 2006-2016 and related to his family in their language. Without me learning Arabic fluently, seven other people would have had to learn English, so it was only fair for me to be the one to trade my tongue for an Arabian one. I literally had to speak with a different tongue, tone and affect in order to say words like a local.

In the book *The Four Agreements*, by Don Miguel Ruiz, one of the rules is to be impeccable with your word. To speak with integrity and only say what you mean. Avoiding language/speaking against yourself (as well as gossiping about others). If you use words in the direction of love and truth, you will find power. This is a part of the process of growth. In arguments, as well as in proclamations that you make each day, watch how you hold yourself. Watch the values you have subconsciously collected about yourself or about "artists" or "creatives" as they are spoken by you and by others. You may be surprised about the way you are interpreted based on your own definitions of yourself. Your own statements might be making a mockery of your dreams, your career or your talent. You may speak in a demeaning way about yourself. You may be setting yourself up for failure by continuously speaking in a negative way about yourself and others.

Here are some Artist tongue dialogues pulled from my everyday life or imagined scenarios. With our artist tongues we've become prone to cynicism, negativity, downplaying our skills. We allow others to belittle us, and we respond with apathy. We collectively talk as if thriving is not a possibility, as if we are not deserving, as if we simply can't. What dialogues can you notice in your everyday life? Let's name the mean girl or inner cynic. Let's call her Brittany. My new approach and positive inner voice is my authentic, patient, and truthful persona. Just me, Erin, saying what I feel.

<u>Brittany</u>: I just want to go back to bed. I've got nothing going on until 9 AM and the coffee pot is so far away. What if I just take another hour to catch up on much needed sleep? No one will miss me while I'm gone.
<u>Erin</u>: Hey Brain. Thanks for sharing. Although that does sound very

seductive, and we could all say that our time doesn't matter these days because we've got nowhere to be if I really think about it! But you have so much to do! You have a book to write. Your editor is relying on you getting these thoughts out and it's going to take time. Coffee isn't that hard to make, so go do that and I'll let you wake up super slowly until it's done. But once you're caffeinated, you're going to need to get going! The whole world is waiting to read this.

Here's another example: I've just met someone new and told them what I do for a living.

Stranger: "Wow! You are an artist and you also run a business. That's impressive, since typically creative people can't do both."
Brittany: "Yeah. You're right. I guess I have something special to be able to do both. I'm still learning how to do it all well. I'm not even sure I'm doing anything right."
Erin: I hear this so often, but it is not a stereotype that serves me as an artist. It reinforces stereotypes about creative people that are really harmful and limiting. It's challenging to carve out space for art and business, but I'm sure there are more examples of successful artists that you know. I'm sure you know of an architect? Or a graphic designer? Or a wedding photographer? Those are all artists who sell their services and most of them make a pretty good living. Right?

My least favorite use of language is when you are actively selling or showcasing your products at an event or trade show and a stranger approaches your booth pretending to be browsing your wares. Under their breath they chime, "I could make that."

Here's one place where I struggled a lot after school with language. I was feeling so worthless, actually, once I was in the real world because

I'd left the nest. At SAIC we were a community, we all came together each week for a purpose which was shared. We supported each other, even during critique, and we had a sense that what we were doing was valiant or valuable. The pursuit of art was an admirable one. I got my master's degree in Fine Arts. I used to say it was "really expensive therapy" and that I left art school with no marketable skills. Not to mention the student loan debt… "I could have chartered a yacht, bought a couple of cases of champagne, and sailed around the world for

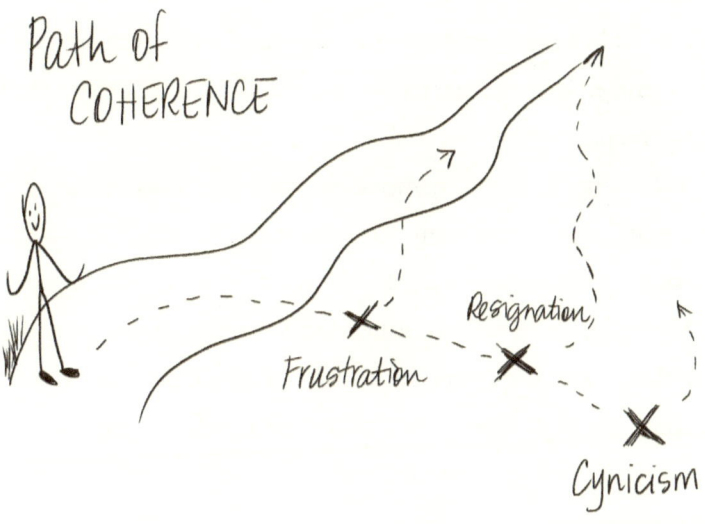

a year instead!!"

Leaving the Path of Coherence

Do you know that cynical inner bitch or bad guy? Do you know why that happens? It's because you strayed off the path towards your greatness. Your goal. You fucked up and you lost your way. You didn't bring the map on your hike and you ended up going in a circle or not knowing where you are.

The first time you leave the path, you get to frustration. You can call yourself mean names, become demeaning, criticize your industry or your employer. Then, you have to find your way back to your path. If you don't maneuver yourself back to coherence, you can actually end up farther away from the trail in no man's land. That is where people resign. They quit. Lastly, once you've made it to cynicism you're pretty much at the point of no return. It would take so much effort to get back onto the Path that you essentially stay in limbo forever… It is just so much easier to collect more evidence for why things suck than it is to make major changes in language, habits and mindset to relieve yourself from playing the position of "failure."

What has been my compass to steer me back to my path, my purpose and my power is my "Standards of Integrity," as it's called by my coaching mentors. I want to change this up a little bit and call it my "Magic." Each of us have little sparkles, magic, light, energy or gifts. Those things are unique and make me one of a kind. They are the parts that shine through when I am at my best self, my highest vibration. When I'm not feeling frustrated and I'm on my way to my goal.

I am:

- Creative
- Family Oriented
- Funny
- Carefree
- A Leader
- Loyal
- Inclusive
- Inspiring
- Fearless
- Genuine
- Honest
- Kind
- Positive
- Intelligent
- Perseverant
- Self-Aware

What is your magic? What are the qualities that you embody when you're happy and feeling good? Take some time to list the pieces of you that others see and applaud, but also the parts that may not get to show through as much. One key to deciding who you are is to look to those you admire. Think about the reasons you look up to them. It could be people who have passed, historical figures, fictional characters or your neighbor Liz, your coach Allison, your college friend Heather. Think about what stands out about them. Once you write those qualities down, and you determine what is so heartwarming about them (the fact that they are prompt and financially responsible may not be the most heartwarming quality so leave that off the list) do you see that you are drawn to them because those qualities are also... your qualities?

To get back on my path from frustration and cynicism I had to hack the Artist's Tongue. The inclination to always bad mouth art, artist, the Art World, the system, the damnation of the economy, etc. I had to focus on what is more interesting and inspiring. I have an MFA. It is the terminal degree in my field. I taught for three years before becoming an entrepreneur, and although I didn't learn business skills in art school, I did refine my *ideas*. The concepts I was challenging in graduate school are funneled into the themes of my wallpapers; cultural inclusion, identity and pattern as a way for foreign cultures to enter our everyday American vernacular. I am *proud* of my education. Going to art school taught me how to speak about my ideas with authority and to be resourceful. I'm entering new conversations now that I wouldn't have if I'd stayed an artist, earnestly working in my studio forever. I am a part of a larger design community, where art is appreciated, and I get paid to sell my work and my products."

There are sometimes subtle shifts or corrections that need to be made. And sometimes you have to be confrontational and expressive. But you don't need to be defensive. Accepting the fact that there are very common stereotypes about artists in our world is a fact of life for you. But you don't have to buy into the language of the Artist as an outcast, Artist in poverty, Artist as lazy, Artist and business owner never being used together in a sentence.

Beginning with being impeccable with your word, Ruiz talks about how to not *gossip* or *slander* and we know this to be true from the Bible up to today. Just because there have been some leaders in our country who have no notion of being impeccable with their word(s), it doesn't give us permission to resort to shaming, blaming, and name

CHAPTER 3: SAYING NO TO NEGATIVITY

calling. Consider thoughts about one's self as "internal words." The way in which we either boost ourselves up or tear ourselves apart with our self-image and self-talk has major consequences for our belief systems.

We've all been there. The moment when you lock yourself out of your car or you run out of gas. (please tell me I'm not the only person who owns three gas cans...okay I know your answer is "Erin, you are the only person who runs out of gas more than three times a year.) That moment is not the nicest. If I were to record the thoughts that ping pong back and forth inside my head. "You idiot!" I tell myself. "What kind of lame-o locks their keys inside the car!?" That type of monologue trips an alarm inside the brain to not trust itself again. To believe that you are horrible and bad and just damn stupid. But those words carry a weight and if repeated enough times they reverberate through other more mundane times of day, like when you oversleep a little or forget to pack the kids' lunch boxes into their backpacks and you literally only notice it when you've returned home and put your slippers on.

Saying only what you mean or what you desire is not what we are taught. My dialogue then should be "Magical gas fairy, please appear and fill my tank." Just kidding. Love letters to the self are the practice of telling yourself the nice stuff that you wish someone would say when you're not fucking up. It's a testament to you trying your best and being noticed for the effort. Like someone giving you a compliment for the invisible progress that's been made; a stranger seeing that you've lost one pound because you've been working out for a couple of days. Those loving words of affirmation need to take precedence over the "You idiot!" conversations you're having with yourself if you want to move ahead in the world.

To Assume Makes an "Ass" Out of "U" and "Me"

By definition, limiting beliefs require tearing down, but the practice is a lifelong one. I'd like you to try visualizing something. This would be more helpful if I was sitting in front of you to guide you while you close your eyes. Vay, my second coach, asked me to close my eyes and think about what's stopping me. What is holding you back from living a life full of ease and grace? What's the one thing that time and time again feels to you like a block? Narrow it down. Narrow it down to a single phrase. What are three to five words that really summarize what's wrong? Why can't you progress?

The phrase I landed on was "It's never going to be easy." It wasn't getting any easier since I had to double time teach kids at home with limited internet, tools and resources whilst running a business. My assistant was quarantining. My ex-husband was flying in airplanes and I asked him not to see the kids until he'd been grounded for 14 days. While talking to my coach Vay, I was finishing up a mural at a daycare (where no children were allowed to be). My two boys were outside the car and antsy. They were playing with plastic swords on the sidewalk outside my car. I was trying my damndest to max out this little 30 minutes of coaching while multitasking, because I had no other choice than to cancel it. So, here I was, closing my eyes and thinking "It's never going to get easier."

Vay asked me to take five deep breaths. She counted the inhale and counted the exhale. She asked me to visualize this phrase as if it was a gas or cloud inside me. She asked me to name this cloud "Never going to be easy" and assign it a color. I thought of an orange, like an orange peel that sat in the sun and started to brown. This disgusting cloud, like a smoke bomb, had gone off inside me and was about to break free. Vay asked me to imagine a bubble or balloon. She prompted me to keep breathing, but as I exhaled, I blew the smokey orange cloud little by little into the balloon. Its noxious appearance was in my imagination, since I'm so visual, I could see it as if it was there. This might take some practice for you. At the end of about ten breaths, I got rid of all of the gas and the balloon was filled twice the size of a watermelon.

Vay told me to let it go. If she'd had the balls that I do, she would've said "Girl! Let that shit go!" I released the imaginary balloon into the air. I kept my eyes closed, as I listened to the sound of Vay on the phone and my kids "Ckshhhing" sounds outside the car window, imitating light sabers. I watched the balloon far longer than I needed to, until it was just a speck in the sky, waiting to make sure it disappeared forever rather than coming back down to me.

These types of visualizations have been very powerful for me. I've tried transcendental meditation, reiki healing, and hypnotherapy. While in a profoundly relaxed state, and being prompted by someone else, I have been able to release a lot of emotional weight off my chest. I've aligned my chakras and all that other hippy dippy voodoo. For me, these techniques work.

See, the possibility of relief was always far more interesting to me than the frontal, logical part of my mind that wanted to dismiss its legitimacy. My curiosity led me to these things, and I tried them like my kids try Brussel sprouts. I knew that if I hated it, I could always just spit it out into the trash.

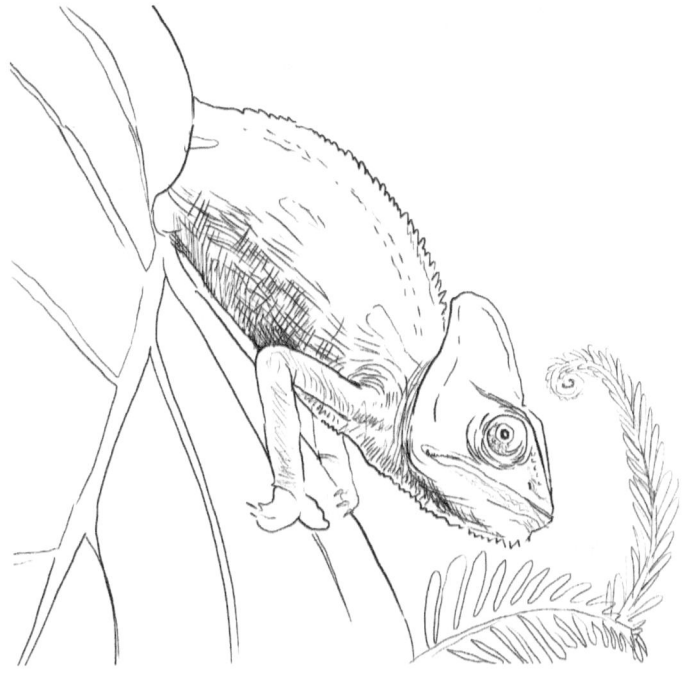

Chapter 4

A Habitat to Thrive In

In talking through all of the ways our mindset is the main driver for how successful we turn out to be, there are so many messages we've been fed that need to be deconstructed and even rejected. There is a rebuilding the identity that takes place, and we get to determine how to project our image out into the world. The way I choose to view this type of skill set is to allow a fluidity of character based on time and place. It's like we each have a collection of hats. Some of you may have been born with many hats, but I have had to purchase or scavenge my urban environment for new hats to wear. I put each hat on as if to embody a new persona. When I'm picking up kids on the school playground, I am a soccer mom. When I am walking into a networking meeting, I have high heels on and perfume, make up and a set of business cards ready. That hat is for the entrepreneur in me. It is silly to think that I wear all of these hats at once, because I can only truly wear one at a time. In a new season in my life, I now wear the hat of an author. It didn't fit at first, but I am getting used to it.

The way to embody all of these new identities, while still remaining true to one's self is to have courage. To be well rooted in your identity but allow flexibility for how others see you. Being afraid to look dumb won't get us anywhere. Being afraid to sell out will keep us broke. Being shy when it's our time to sing will only lose us opportunities for larger stages and more airtime. So we have to see this identity shifting as a self-preservation mechanism. A learned skill to thrive in just about any environment; and why I believe it can work is because I've seen it happen in nature. The mimic octopus, the chameleon, the shark, the deer, they all blend in when they need to in order to survive. Here's a story about the ultimate survivor.

Self-Preservation: The Chameleon

A Chameleon will do whatever it takes to blend in with his surroundings. Why does he do that? Why does he change his skin color to represent the things that are around him? It's called camouflage and it happens in several species across the globe. The chameleon camouflages himself for *self-defense*. Self-preservation. Survival. When they say 'survival of the fittest' they don't necessarily mean the one who is strongest and built like a tank. You could be tiny but fittest and fastest. For survival we all need to come up with different modes of blending in. Depending on our environment we may need to be something different than what we are in our natural habitat. Take a realtor for example.

One of my best friends in Chicago is a realtor for a cutting-edge firm in a trendy neighborhood. Five years ago, she made the transition from being a full-time arts administrator at a community arts center and decided to get her real estate license. She went from working 50 hours a week and barely grossing $55,000 per year to working all day every day and making bank. Before Coronavirus struck, we used to meet up every three weeks and get our nails painted. We'd gossip and talk shop about our careers. Marketing, client issues, but mostly relationship problems.

She once told me that a client and her husband had been looking to buy a home worth $4M. She felt very insecure to take them on a drive around town in her car, so she had them meet her at the property. She guessed that they decided not to work with her because she pulled up in her Subaru. This woman just bought a $1M home and I helped her design and decorate it. She's moved up in the world as an artist in so little time that she completely upgraded her life. It wasn't without a lot of hard work, some stomach problems, and a lot of sleepless nights I'm sure. But I've begun to think of her as The Chameleon, not Clara. This woman has mastered the art of survival too. She is thriving now, and her beginnings were not so glamorous.

Clara grew up lower middle-class Latina in south Texas. A third generation American, her family was clearly just as American as they were Mexican. She played soccer in high school and remembers visiting a town where all the players spoke Spanish. Though she had wanted to be fairer skinned to fit in with her peers, visiting another town closer to the border, she realized that she wasn't Mexican enough. She straddled the two worlds as well as she could.

Clara and I talk about our upbringings while we chat at the nail salon. I programmed a date into my iPhone for every three weeks to get a manicure with her not because I am a nail "froo froo" girl, as my mom and dad say. *I'm not girlie at all and neither is my bestie Clara.* I do it because it's a guilty pleasure to be pampered by another human being. And it's even guiltiest when Clara and I open up about our deepest darkest secrets while our toenails are being critiqued. Massage chairs on- check. Trash talking can begin.

Clara explains how her parents worked hard to make a living. Her father was a macho Latino man who balanced his hobby as a body builder with his career as a car salesman. Jesse "Iron Man" Morales once had his photograph published in her town's newspaper. Her mother was an administrative assistant and eventually went on to be an entrepreneur and CFO of a large car dealership, but Clara faults her for relying on men too much (her father in particular but also her next husband). Her mom became a punching bag for her partners and never let her own dreams or voice stand out. Clara has basically devoted her life to living out the legacy her mother never made for herself.

I like Clara because she is a strong independent woman. Many who know her would say she is "fierce." When I met her, I was a textile artist and graduate student and she was the director of the textile arts program at an uptown arts center in Chicago. She almost accepted me to become the artist in residency, but I had an infant child and she thought someone else may take advantage of the opportunity more whole heartedly. She later hired me to teach screen printing and block printing for fabric classes. We would drink a beer together and chat after class. I learned that her two daughters were the same ages as my own two sons. She was a lady who didn't take any shit from anyone. She was making about $30,000 a year working late nights and long days, running the show at Lillstreet. Training teachers, keeping up the facilities, enrolling students, and generally just answering *everyone's* questions about everything. I didn't envy her.

What was happening simultaneously was her and I met, and I was about to leave my job(s) and start a business. I also confided in her that I was hoping to leave my spouse; she was one of the first people I ever told. Clara was studying at night to complete her real estate license and eventually got hired at a local real estate office in Chicago. She quickly became a legend in the Chicago real estate industry because in the first three months as a realtor, Clara exceeded her entire yearly salary in arts administration. She was just *that good* at being an agent. She was driven and hardworking and generally good at answering *everyone's* questions about everything.

Growing her partnership with another broker, she branched away from the first small boutique firm to establish herself with Compass. New York City tech gurus developed this brokerage to be the most chic and innovative way to buy a home out there and they hand-picked agents to join their Chicago team. Clara now runs the business solo and is in the top 10 in her Bucktown office.

During one of our Mani-Pedi sessions, Clara told me about her experiences working late nights and weekends. She told me how her marriage was being pulled in every direction. Her husband came to work with her for a short time and then he left to pursue his own career. *Clara is a bottler.* The type who bottles everything inside. All the stress of the new job was not equilaterally paid back by the large sums of money that she was bringing in by the time she'd been doing real estate

5 years. It was hard on her mind and her body. She began to experience her arms going numb. Rashes on her body. Digestive problems. Pain with unexplainable sources.

See, a realization that I've had since I've known Clara is that stress and anxiety are no joke. And if you don't seek therapy or some outlet (like crying into multiple boxes of tissues when a client is mean to you) then the technique of "shoving it down" really just represses the emotion. The emotion has to come out somewhere. It will physically manifest as pain because it is pain, but the type of pains of the heart and mind. Those spiritual and emotional grievances need an escape. Her body was signaling to her "Let me out!" and she had to stop everything she was doing to see an acupuncturist. There's a need to relieve those feelings and alleviate the body of doing all the heavy lifting. The vessel can only hold so much water before it begins to spill over and flood out the top.

She has taught me so many lessons, but one is about how to really thrive. Realtors know a lot about hustle and struggle and working overtime. They are on their phones and emails at all hours of the day and any client who beckons or summons them they have to prioritize to make. That. money. But Clara has an analogy. Mom of two girls, everything is a rainbow, a unicorn or covered in sequins. She calls her energy and love "sparkles" and describes it like fairy dust. You sprinkle some on each member of your family, some on the clients and co-workers and some on your neighbors. By the time you get home you are all out of sparkles. I've learned that if you want to not have your work own your soul, you have to keep a little bit of sparkles on reserve for … yourself. You're not stingy, no. You're keeping the bare minimum like you keep your bank account from the number zero. You keep them just in case there's a crisis. You keep them for days you're not strong. And those are the times when you actually need to give some sparkles, some fairy dust, some self-care and love to yourself. Because those sparkles are your lifeline.

If you're a giver of sparkles, or a bottler of all things sad or complicated, consider how shoving it down into your subconscious mind and not dealing with it affects you in the long run. It leaves you seriously deficient of magic. Would you rather let everyone else hold your energy, your time and your goodness? Would you rather fall ill? And have to take medication or seek doctors? To relieve your body of pain, or would you rather do the complex thought work that goes into relieving your heart and mind of trauma or grief or anxiety and depression? Those feelings need to be poked with a needle and flow out too. Consider it. Because it could possibly be the single one thing holding you back from the greatest life you haven't yet lived. Or wealth. Or a better relationship with your spouse. Or a calmer and more composed mommy.

Clearly Clara has mastered the art of fitting in. She's an artist doing the work of a realtor. She's been able to buy a million-dollar single family home in Chicago and renovate it (with the help of me as her interior designer). There's something to be said about her camouflaging herself amongst the rich and famous, wining and dining her $3M buyers. She's been persistent enough to make a name for herself as one of the biggest players in Chicago's best agency. She's a baller. The thing is, she's not enduring all this stress for personal triumph. She's not trying to live an elite life where she only wears brand name clothing and never visits a dive bar. She's still a hipster at heart. And her master plan is to elevate her lifestyle for her kids to grow up better off than she did. She is growing an empire so that soon enough she can step away from the machine she built and let the other agents on her team do the heavy lifting. She's building a brand.

What I think some artists resist is the notion that making money will turn you into an evil person. That you'll get greedy in the face of tons of money and stop caring about your special causes like veganism, arts charities, housing for working class people, screen printing t-shirts for little girl soccer players with uteruses on them to try to get the attention of the coaches so that the girls can be starting lineup… true story. These are things that Clara actually still donates her time and money to. She's a die-hard feminist. She's got insanely hip and outside the box style in her home. She's an avid runner, swimmer, cyclist. She sits on the board of ArtReach and donates her time to the charity when she can. She isn't Scrooge McDuck, swimming in a room full of gold coins. She's wealthy. But, rightfully so. And she's still a good person.

To get here, there was some faking it in order to make it. There were some real long nights, elbow grease and challenging humans to deal with. Nevertheless, she pushed and pushed like a freight train to reach her goal so that she could set up her financial future and work less. Who doesn't want to work less and watch as money keeps coming in? We were together enjoying a glass of wine at the annual benefit gala for ArtReach one year when an older lady walked up to us. She'd been involved at Lillstreet and Clara recognized her. She drew the eighty year old woman into our conversation about motherhood and careers. "Do you ever get tired of hearing things like, 'How do you do it all?!'" I asked her.

The older woman inserted her two cents.

"You know what you tell them? Next time they ask you 'How do you do it all?' you've got to respond by saying 'Watch me.'"

I won't forget the smirk on Clara's face when she said she was going to use that line. I've used it a few times since then. Although we are all in the fight of our life to do it all, this older woman spoke about being the mother to her two boys as the greatest job she'd ever had. All while working full time. That made me reflect that I am not the only woman out there who's got it hard. Every mother and father I know is trying to balance all the plates like a juggling magician in a stage magic show. I am not alone. Neither are you.

There are 5,280 ways to skin a cat. Well, maybe not that many (that's how many feet there are in a mile). But you could become a realtor, a wallpaper designer, or anything else that has nothing to do with your art practice. So long as you follow the three rules of running a successful business. 1- Focus, 2- Focus and 3- Focus. Put your mind to one thing and push it forward with all your might like Clara "the body" Morales. Take no shit. And show them how it's done.

Success isn't for Extroverts

I used to think that I was an extroverted person. Maybe as I've aged, I've become a lot more introverted, or maybe since the Corona virus has locked us all inside our own personal hells, we've all had to be less concerned with friendships and more concerned with ourselves. A common misconception is that when it comes to having a great idea and getting it out there you have to be "good" at it. You have to be a people person or a natural born salesman. Although my grandfather was a traveling salesman, I didn't inherit the gift of loving to sell stuff. What I realized through the journey of becoming the Lead Sales Rep for my wallpaper brand is that I don't have charisma and stage presence. Some of that can be learned. All you have to do is have a good story which you wish to tell. The more heartwarming the better. The more personal, the more people will relate to you.

I walked into a firm of 18-21 designers to basically do a 'show and tell' while they ate $150 worth of boutique pizza and salad I had catered for lunch. It's called a "Lunch and Learn" and I've done it for firms across the country. I traveled one year to NY, Las Vegas, LA, Texas, Atlanta, Denver, Minneapolis. In every city I brought food and beverages and told my story in front of a few, or many, designers. Sometimes their conference room had a projector screen and I hooked up my laptop to show them my website and some slides of the wallpaper installed. I always brought samples spread out around the boardroom style table. I bear it all in 30 minutes flat-- my story. What resonates most with people is not the wallpaper's removability or my short lead times. They are surprised to hear that I am the owner, the artist, and the saleswoman.

People ask me questions about how I started out all the time. They ask me about when it was time to hire people. They ask me, how do I market all over the country? They ask what inspires my drawings. They're genuinely curious how I made this work. Same dumbfounded look on their faces as Marc from the printing press who wished me luck but didn't quite believe I'd make it. These people were wondering how I did it all.

I'm going to tell you how. I did it by getting WAY outside my comfort zone. Like a chameleon needs to blend in, I had to sometimes play the part of the extrovert. The saleswoman. The confident bad ass I thought maybe I was deep down inside but hadn't practiced much. I had to adopt the body language and tone of the people I was presenting to. I had to dress the part. Do you think that all of this parading around as someone I'm not came easily to me? And that is why I am successful? No! I was uncomfortable all the while. But, I did it because I was desperate for my life to change. I needed sales to pick up so I could

CHAPTER 4: A HABITAT TO THRIVE IN

support myself! I needed to prove to all the naysayers that they were wrong. I needed to show my children that Mommy is successful and driven and smart. That's not being extroverted. It's being hungry.

What I mean by habitat for success is not that you stay in your cozy jammies where you feel the most comfortable. I don't mean plaster your room with inspiring images. I don't mean, plant a garden and spend time outdoors. All of those are wonderful things, but I want you to consider that making a dramatic change to the PLACES you insert yourself and trying to maneuver and get comfortable there is key. Getting comfortable comes with practice. You will hate this at first, but it will get easier. Find a sidekick if you have to. Drink a glass of wine as soon as you get there if you need to loosen up a bit. Just try something new.

Shake it 'til You Make it
(a·bun·dance)

I took the advice of my best friend in the world, who I've known since third grade. Sydnee Grace is one of the prettiest mothers of 5 boys you have ever known. She's always dolled up and smiling. She's carefree and her husband is a solid dude with a rock and roll attitude. They're both always positive and fun. I asked them recently to give me their secrets to success as a couple and parents of 5. Their life is controlled chaos and they've definitely overcome much adversity to get here. How can their home possibly be a habitat for thriving?

It wasn't always easy. Sydnee and I were best friends in high school when she got pregnant and had to drop out of school. She was the best soccer player, snowboarder and suddenly she was sewing baby blankets with the other moms getting their GED's. I held tight to our friendship and we only grew closer as the years rolled by. I was her maid of honor at a home wedding to her first husband Dave. Their parents had to sign their marriage certificate because both of them were too young. I painted their basement apartment kitchen yellow with Dave, and he got me to love country music. I was there for the birth of their son Caleb and, in retrospect, so thankful for the opportunity. I watched as my sixteen year old friend-sister pushed a human out of her body. It was the best birth control a sixteen year old girl could ever take. "I don't want to do **THAT**" I thought for many years after.

Sydnee's first marriage fell apart not long after Caleb turned 1. Syd was later remarried to a man I had little rapport with, though I was maid of honor again in their small chapel wedding. A second son was born, Brendan, and I got to hold him when he was only days old. I was in college, traveling back and forth to see her, and I had no clue how much work it was to have two boys. We still made it out for a girls' night on the town and danced and drank flavored shots out of test tubes. Whatever, it was the early 2000's. By the time I was out of college I'd become highly judgmental. Sydnee's newfound career went hand in hand with becoming a single mom again and loving the party lifestyle; she needed to make enough money to pay her mortgage on the house she'd bought after her second divorce. I thought she'd been bartending when I mysteriously found a suitcase she'd been taking to work. It was filled with bikinis and lingerie. A giant tub of body glitter and clear acrylic heels that were 6 or 7" tall…

My world came crashing down as I imagined her on a stage. Everyone watching her. Mom of two. Wallet loaded with $1 bills. She got breast implants and started partying really hard with a bunch of girls *I wouldn't be caught dead with.* And I judged her for it. I even wrote her a letter telling her she should be ashamed of herself. Three days

CHAPTER 4: A HABITAT TO THRIVE IN

later, I called her and said that if she got a letter in the mail, I didn't want her to open it. Throw it away when it comes. She told me she wouldn't. I bet you she read the letter. I bet you she knew all the reasons why I'd told her that good moms don't become exotic dancers. I bet she didn't care. All I know is she forgave me for being so judgmental. In retrospect, I feel like an asshole for disowning her at a time that was probably insanely difficult for her. I didn't know what it was like to be a single mom of two kids or how hard you had to work to pay a mortgage-- though I know all about it now. I was just a dumb college graduate with hardly any life experience. I was reckless and entitled. Who was I to judge her?

Syd later rekindled a friendship with her teenage first love from high school, Paul. He was the love of her life. Now her husband of 12 years, Paul was a friend of ours in high school, but I didn't know him well. He was the son of a polygamist Mormon family and had a brother the same age as him from another mother. They both freaked me out a little bit. Paul was not the typical Mormon kid; he was one of the "jack mormons" who didn't really go to church. He plays in a band and rides a motorcycle. He's a big ass kid at heart. They make each other insanely happy. I was *their* maid of honor too-- third time's a charm-- on the ocean front property of No one. A secluded beach in Cancun was the setting of their wedding. Only about ten people in attendance, Syd's dad officiated her wedding. Her brother and Paul's brother, his dad and moms were there. Two of Sydnee's friends from the stage named Jade or Candy or I don't know what. It's funny to think back on that now. We all had flowers in our hair and white linen dresses on. I didn't cry this time like I did during her first two wedding ceremonies.

She's grown up a lot. Paul and she have a son who's now 11. She likely got pregnant on their wedding night. They waited a few more years to try again and got a BOGO; twins arrived prematurely when Sydnee was out running errands in another city. She rushed to the hospital nearby. The babies stayed for weeks and by the time I met them they'd grown to be 6 months old. Now the mama of 5 boys, she invested in herself and became a top mortgage broker in the city of Heber, outside Salt Lake City. The president of her Business Network International chapter, she dominates the industry. She now owns a huge home equipped with a trampoline, massive outdoor sofa, slip and slide a mile long, and every gaming system the kids could ever ask for. She and Paul go every year or two to Burning Man and other festivals. She participates in the party scene as a thirty something hot mom like she's still 18. Her massive polygamist family-in-law watches her younger kids while her and Paul motorcycle around the country. She's a carefree, spiritual advisor to me. She recommended half the books I've read (If you're listening, thank you Sydnee for always letting me hack into your Audible account and get my fix). She radiates positivity. She has ALWAYS supported me, even in my darkest hours. She's the sister I have always wanted.

I asked Sydnee, as I told her that I was writing a book, what the secret sauce was for her all these years? Through it all, she said, there is a constant need for self-improvement. She reads and listens to audio books. Before Audible, there were CD's and tapes. Her dad raised her on Wayne Dyer and other gurus of self-transformation. "Feeding my brain positive and supportive material," she lists as one of the most important factors to becoming who you want to be. Along with having amazing friends, working out, counting your blessings and "getting fucked up over the weekend once in a while." Jumping on the trampoline was also on the list as well as… orgasms.

[5] https://www.amazon.com/Subtle-Art-Not-Giving-Counterintuitive/dp/0062457713

What advice I've gleaned from her, time and time again is this: other peoples' opinions of you are *none of your business*. It's called feedback. People are going to judge you. They may disagree with you or look down on you. I'm sure most of the people that know Sydnee in her professional life now have no idea what her past was like. I'm sure most of her family has come to accept her for everything she is. They can't hate her. She's the kindest, most beautiful spirited person alive. Through it all, she never gave a fuck what other people would think. "Don't let other people tell you who you are, Erin Minckley. You are strong and sweet and beautiful." No one's opinion of me can define me, and I can't take it to heart. She taught me that.

See, like the wise words from Mark Manson, *"In my life, I have given a fuck about many people and many things. I have also not given a fuck about many people and many things. And like the road not taken, it was the fucks not given that made all the difference."* [5] What a coy way to riff on Robert Frost's "The Road Not Taken." It was all the things you didn't pay mind to, those opinions that you ignored and didn't let get in your way, that made all the difference.

It's rare to hear of a stripper who made it to millionaire, even ones who shook their booties all the way to the top. She just might make it there in her lifetime but that's likely not her goal. But she has mastered abundance. Really, she mastered joy and good fortune, through all her divorces and stumbling blocks. What I admire most about her is her tenacity. She's on the journey of life to enjoy every moment.

The thing I love about telling her story is that Sydnee was always striving for something better. She was always working on herself. She was determined to be free and have fun and express herself in every way she wanted to. She didn't give an F what others thought. She singled out the friends who could meet her at her level of energy, her specific vibration, and everyone else fell away naturally.

My past, judgy self, could easily have looked at her situation and said that I have it better off. Now, I am a single mom with bills to pay hustling wallpaper and trying to thrive. At least I don't have five kids and two ex-husbands! Truthfully though I know I've got nothing on her. She has lived every square inch of her life with as much passion and pleasure and perseverance as she could. She is the loyalist of friends and an inspiration to me. She has zero regrets in her life, and I hope to be just like her in many regards someday.

So take some advice from my best friend "The Stripper" about abundance. How do you squeeze every ounce out of life? If you want to manifest more positive things in your life? That's called "a-bun-dance" ha! Literally shake it 'til you make it. Get paid more. Get laid more. Get happy. Be grateful. Grow your mind. Feed your heart and soul. Get drunk sometimes. Love your kids. Sleep in as much as you can afford to. Who cares? So what if you fuck up from time to time? *Life is short.* It better be artfully lived.

Actress Helen Bonham Carter puts it this way: *"I think everything in life is art. What you do. How you dress. The way you love someone, and how you talk. Your smile and your personality. What you believe in, and all your dreams. The way you drink your tea. How you decorate your home. Or party. Your grocery list. The food you make. How your writing looks. And the way you feel. Life is art."* [6]

---

[6] https://www.goodreads.com/quotes/911380-i-think-everything-in-life-is-art-what-you-do

Now let's go make our life's work. Make art or make a beautiful life, which is an art form in and of itself. You can truly live out your greatness when you channel your creative magic and start using it instead of shoving it under the bed. We have to be brave superheroes, not only for ourselves and to prove to our kids that we are mighty. We need to lift up the community of artists we belong to and show others how it's done. There will be a fair amount of shifting your point of view involved and a lot of trying to mimic your new surroundings. That is survival of the fittest.

Part Two

Creating New Relationships

In order to become accountable for our lives we have to build ourselves some new skill sets. Remember the canoe that is going to allow us not to drown in the Art World Ocean? Yah, raise your hand if you're a master carpenter and know how to steam bend wood. Okay, great. That's a rare f'ing skill, though a few friends of mine can actually do it. If you want to build a canoe you have to buy some new tools, make a workshop in your basement and read the directions.

The two relationships you already have but aren't benefiting from are your relationships with Money and Time. Repeatedly, I hear artists say that their number one stumbling block is either not having enough time or not being able to fund their projects.

Well, let's wake up and smell the coffee. You get to be in whatever relationship you want with these two things. If you're in a dysfunctional relationship with either Money or Time (or both, you two timin'...) then we need to make it into a functional relationship. If you want to truly thrive, you've got to become excellent with these two things. I know, I know, it sounds boring and hard and who gives? *Right?* That's totally fine, Polly PussyPants. Dig your left hand back into that bag of Cheetos and scan Netflix for some comedy show to take you back to your comfort zone then. If your work here is done, you can resume a life of mediocrity.

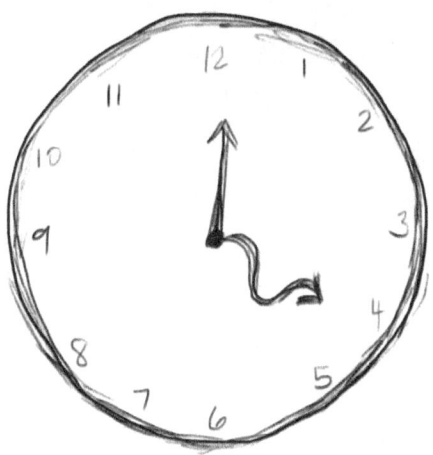

Chapter 5

Your Dysfunctional Relationship with Time

Time is of the essence. Time flies when we're having fun. Time is on my side, but time is a cruel thief. Time and time again, time is money. We are strapped for time, we are out of time, we are up against the clock. Time is like sand through the hourglass, and so are the days of our lives. Had to insert that for anyone else who watched in their peripheral view the Guiding Light on TV in the late 80's while their mother vegged out. Benjamin Franklin, Einstein, Mick Jagger, all passed on wisdom about time but still somehow, we lose it. Is it because our lives are busier than in the time of Confucius? I live in an ever-increasing frenetic western world not with monastic simplicity. Fast food, co-working spaces, online dating, e-commerce all are our attempts to bundle, package, sell, ease, and display at a quantum rate making us rush to our untimely demise. Even audible books are read at 1.5x the speed now. How has time been manipulated to our advantage and how has that rapid acceleration of life prevented us from productivity, enlightenment, or even sheer contentment?

I was diagnosed with ADHD at the age of 34. I have always been known to be flakey, flighty, miss important deadlines or events because I simply forgot. Anyone who knows me well as a fast talker, big idea generator, white tornado of energy! I never stop thinking, dreaming, doing. I don't even watch TV because I consider it a waste of time. I am frantic, frenetic, manic. It's how I can do all of what I do. I just got used to this buzzzzzzzzing bee of a lifestyle always flying from one flower to another. But when I step back to really assess time as a "relationship" I wonder what this character is like and how I treat them. I wonder what role Time plays in my life and how I could nurture the relationship a little more.

I'm in this co-dependent relationship with Time like a lover who relies on me and I rely on him, but I know it's deeply dysfunctional. We are deeply enmeshed and codependent. He's a narcissist and he thinks his way of doing things is better than mine. I ignore him sometimes and deeply disagree with his rigid rules for how to live. I shit-talk him behind his back. I love him when he helps me beat the odds, but otherwise I'm blaming him for all of my problems. Wouldn't that be great? If we could just call Time a person and label him the bad guy? What happens in toxic relationships is that nobody takes responsibility for their own shit. Starting now, we're going to have to break up with the idea of Time and come to terms with some of the lies you've gotten used to.

Time is as universally true as the law of gravity. Being on *time* isn't something that humans are born with, and honestly, since I know you're a Fringe Person, I know you resist with all your power talking about your own dysfunctional relationship with time. It's why women with abusive husbands don't leave. But you aren't the victim in this case. You have been abusing this scientific law way too long and it's catching up with you.

Before I help you create a new relationship with Time, let's just be honest about something: Lateness is a chronic *lying to oneself*. Here are the top four lies I learned to believe and then fall back on as a crutch:

Lie #1- I'm Flaky

I was on the freeway after a client presentation went way over schedule when I realized the Google maps was putting me down in front of my kid's school at 40 minutes after the bell rang to pick him up. I was late-- always fucking late -- but I never missed the 3:30 school bell. I panicked and between gently hitting the gas and brakes, I imagined a world where my car could levitate directly upwards , hover over traffic for a short second, and blast off with a plume of smoke like Michael J. Fox. I'd screech into the parking lot in 2 minutes flat and be there with a tiny bead of sweat on my forehead. The stress would dissipate, and my first grader would come trotting out with his art project and backpack and sweater and lunchbox, fumbling with all his shenanigans as I hug him and take all ten items.

Instead, I curse and grip the steering wheel. I flip channels on the radio trying to find a song that doesn't suck. I'm looking for the word of God to come on and say, "It will all be okay," in a loud booming voice like James Earl Jones. It's not fucking okay and I'm less mad about traffic than I am about my own shortcomings. I'm silently listing all the ways I suck as a human and a mother. I'm snotty in noting that none of the other moms have to travel to the suburbs to talk about wallpaper at noon and end up jabbering for over an hour before realizing they need to cut off the conversation RIGHT NOW and get your ass in the car.

The other moms. Yes! Brilliant. I look up Julie, I dial her number. She's always there. She has two kids with their million backpacks and things and her kids are so sweet they always hug her first. She is the parent of the year. Maybe she can adopt my child for 40 minutes until my dumb ass can arrive to get my kid from school. We arrange that I will pick him up at her house. I get there sweating profusely. Exhausted from all the excuses and name calling that just flew around like ping pong balls in my brain. Katy Perry was the only thing on the radio, and it was hot and my thighs were sticking together.

I walked into her place like a zombie and she has to run to swim lessons, so I collect my child who'd rather not leave. He asks if he can play Legos five more minutes but what I think he wants to stay forever. Maybe Julie can make him a bedroom in her basement and he can enjoy organic orange juice every morning before they all skip to school smiling.

I'm just the worst. *Right?*

I'm always late. I have a bad relationship with time. I'm a flake. No one can rely on me. I'm just late wherever I go. The text message that needs to be auto programmed into my phone: "Hey Girl, running 15 minutes behind, as usual. Ugh. I hope you can wait for me?" When in doubt... I'll say I lost the parking garage ticket and maybe they'll let me out without paying the extra fee. All this negative self-talk and negotiating happens offline without you even monitoring it. Your brain is like a seismometer charting the ups and downs of the earth's movements in the moments leading up to an earthquake.

At the core, what is the real problem? Let's break it down.

The problem is that you've been making up your own rules. The posted signage that says No Dogs in the Dog Park after 9 PM? It's 8:55 and you're like *"meh*, who will mind?" The light that is yellow, but you think you can make it? *Eh*, well it was more orange than red by the time the red-light camera caught you rushing through the intersection. The movie theater is the worst! Who watches the previews!? "Excuse me, *sorry*, oh gosh...I'm sorry." It was so dark I stepped on their feet as I ruined the first two minutes of the flick for showing up at exactly 7:01.

Being on time is a figment of the imagination. Albert Einstein said, "Time is an illusion," and he is a genius, so I believe him. We created time as a way for all things to pass by us. But humans base their day on this elusive thing.

Time is static. 8:00 means 8:00. Aside from Chicago city buses, most things happen when they say they're going to. Most people show up when they arrange a meeting at a certain time. Most employees arrive *before* their shift starts so that they can clock in on time. Most moms come to pick up their kids 20 minutes prior because parking in Bucktown is wicked difficult by 3:10. So why have I been cheating the clock for so long? Why do my rules and law of time always fail me? Why do people judge me so much when I just barely go over by a few? Why are "normal" people doing this with ease, and you are locking the car door at the exact time you need to be somewhere, rushing across the street with your work uniform half on half off? Why are my clocks and watches always my enemy?

It's about integrity and accountability. If you don't have it with yourself, you sure aren't going to have it with Tim the Time Clock. Or your friends. Or your family. Why is it that artists get a bad rap for flaking out on their obligations or always being late?

I've got a hypothesis. Creativity pollutes the mind. A very well working mind has internal timers and alarms that go off when it's time to leave a certain place. They check their watch; they track about how many minutes or hours they've been somewhere. And as they're parking their car, they make a marker in their internal system to watch out for the meter's expiration time. They know that they'll have to put 5 or 10 minutes ahead to grab their coat, walk to the parking lot… Our creative minds have so much work to do and so much excess noise inside our brains that our alarm system is broken.

If creativity pollutes the mind, you ask, then why is it also the greatest gift we've ever been given?

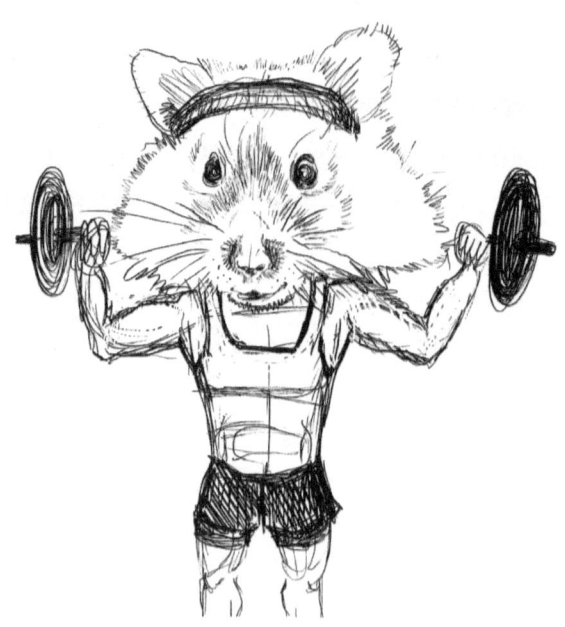

CHAPTER 5: YOUR DYSFUNCTIONAL RELATIONSHIP WITH TIME

The truth is, I am unstoppable because of this same creativity that makes me lose track of time. I don't know about you, but my mind never shuts off. I have so many ideas and a *fairly functional* filtration process that helps me weed out the bizarre or unrealistic ones. However, being artistic and having a diagnosis for ADHD, I just have a brain that's like a hamster on a wheel, kicking it into overdrive. My hamster chugs a Red Bull and eats a whole box of Hot Tamales every morning around 5:30 AM. He's ready to rock that wheel as hard as possible from the minute I open my eyes. Sometimes he crashes at 4:30 PM and is in bed by 9. He's wearing a sweatband like Richard Simmons and he just wants to rock life with a smile on. He cannot be bothered by alarms chiming "Hey! Reality awaits! Get off the treadmill and stop what you're doing!"

This is why when my phone pings me that it's stopping time, I chance the clock. My hamster on the wheel inside my brain is so determined to knock out the last two minutes of his workout that he convinces you there are two minutes left to draw or finish an email. *There aren't two more minutes* and truthfully you know you'll email for three minutes, then search for your keys for another five. That's what makes you get in the car eight minutes late and get to the gas station as you are literally running out of gas. You think you can *chance* it, but the reality is there's no teleporting to your kids' school. There's no quicker route through Bucktown either. You are late from the time your hamster decided to finish doodling in illustrator on a project that took you hours; and you just wanted to finish before transitioning to the next thing!

Instead, a few minutes before it is time to go, you ought to slam the laptop shut so that you can't even make a single other adjustment. Start looking for your keys and get in the car. This is where the hamster needs to be okay going from full sprint to water break. Full stop. Also, if you wanted to set yourself up for success, an hour before it's time to stop, you can set your keys right next to your work station so you'll be ready to literally GO, in the instance that you do take two more minutes to finish.

We all need to find a way to transition more gracefully into the next activity. How to come out of the creative fog and focus on the next task at hand. I'm not sure what it is that sucks us into the vortex, but it's a strong magnetic pull that we must work against. Alarms help me. They snap me out of my haze. They bring me back to the real world.

Lie #2- I'm Lazy

In the book *The 5 Second Rule*, author Mel Robbins explains that she was in a rut in her life financially and morally. She was avoiding reality by hitting the snooze button every morning. She would get up late or procrastinate doing things, because making an impulse decision or action felt too bold or scary. As she watched the nightly news one evening, she watched the NASA rocket launch into orbit with 5 seconds on the clock. The tremendous energy that it took to get thousands of pounds into space only took a fraction of one minute and she decided then and there to make more profound, split second decisions. It transformed her life.

Now, prior to reading her book I thought the 5 second rule was where my kids scooped a popsicle off the floor, picked the dog hair off and put it in their mouth, because someone somewhere told them that the germs couldn't latch on to their food in time to make them sick. As long as they picked it up before 5 seconds had ticked on the clock... That's kind of a metaphor, in and of itself, right? The ability to say,

CHAPTER 5: YOUR DYSFUNCTIONAL RELATIONSHIP WITH TIME

"Who cares" and eat it anyway, because it's still good. It still tastes the same, just a little "added protein" as my dad would say if he discovered a tiny fly in his food. He'd pick it out and keep eating (yes, I come from a hillbilly household).

Rather than re-coin Robbins's phrase the 5 second rule, I guess what I'm aiming at is doing things with a 3-2-1 blast off mentality. This concept might not stick right away. Trust me though, it is a very important component to being successful at running a business, running a household and a damn necessity if you're going to become the CEO of your own life. When your brain thinks about something that you need to do, ex.: pack the kids' lunch boxes before bed so that they're ready in the morning, your mind has about 5 seconds to convince you that you *can do it later.* Or that you're just going to give them money for hot lunch. Or that tomorrow morning you'll have a fresh, new energy to make lunches, so you'll watch some tv because you're pooped.

It's hard at first, but it's going to get easier. In fact, it becomes a *habit.* If you sort of embody a rocket ship, as Robbins explains, and 3-2-1 launch your brain into full gear you can just make the damn lunches and get it over with! It will take you ten minutes. At most 15? The best part about doing it now is... wait for it... you don't have to do it later! Guys, I didn't do a lot of heady research on Cognitive Psychology in order to make this seem believable, okay? I left that data collection up to the experts. I just put it into practice in my own life and it has worked thus far. Fingers crossed.

Being an entrepreneur, I've learned that you begin to have a "who gives a crap" attitude. What's the worst thing that could happen? You start job searching and come across a lead. You send your resume to the biggest firm in town and the *worst* thing they could do is *never write you back* to acknowledge that they got your job application. The second worst thing that could happen is that you get a courteous email from them saying (essentially) "thanks, but no thanks." I have hundreds of rejection emails form all sorts of things I've tried to apply for and gotten denied. But at least I tried. When you do the 3-2-1 with a higher stakes item like auditioning for a part in a play, submitting your portfolio for an exhibition or getting down on one knee to ask a pretty woman to marry you, how many seconds do you think your brain takes to decide if the decision is a good one? Do you think that because it's heavier on the importance scale that the human brain can give more time? No. It's also still a 5 second process. The human brain will say "risk! No! Don't do it!" and you'll talk yourself out of it in myriad ways.

The problem is procrastination. Procrastination (quoting Robbins) is the putting off of the thing that causes you anxiety. Whether big or small. You choose to do something that causes you pleasure instead. Usually time wasting, brain cell depleting, moronic, nonsensical shit like trolling Instagram for memes about being a "boss babe" so you can feel like the productive CEO that you want to believe you are. Sometimes you clean the house though, in an effort to avoid work stuff. Sometimes you work out in an effort to avoid the personal growth or relationship growth stuff. Sometimes your habits get in the way of progress. Sometimes you use your kids as an excuse for why you can't lead the life you want. Look, I am also guilty. But if you want to not be a flake, you have to start acting like a rocket ship. Launch. Like, right now.

Don't be a flake. Don't put stuff off. Don't say someday you'll get around to it. Don't live like that. Be a little impulsive and just do the thing. Go for a run instead of talking yourself out of it, because the weather is gray. Do it anyway. The rewarding satisfaction of checking it off your to-do list awaits you.

Lie #3- I'm Forgetful

It wasn't until I reached a certain level of success in my business that I had too much to do, too much to remember. I needed help. I kept missing important meetings and deadlines. I had wallpaper orders coming in from several showrooms across the country and samples to cut and label and mail out. I had kids' functions at school and court dates to attend for my divorce proceedings. I was a hot mess.

I finally got clear one day when I noticed that the things that I forgot had typically never been written down. I usually had the intention to remember them, but sometimes I even said at the moment where a new date and time was introduced into my agenda "Yah, I am never going to remember that." So two things were taking place.

1) I was committing to things that I had no intention of following through with (or committing time to things that were a drag!)
2) I was delusional if I thought that my flighty brain was going to dog ear the day with all these things to remember and I'd magically be reminded after the kids went to sleep to actually *program them into my phone* or write them into my calendar.

So I did what any visual person would do. I went to the office supply store and I purchased an old school paper calendar. I picked a bright fuchsia one so that it would be obnoxious and unforgettable. I went home and started writing down the things that I could remember off the top of my head. Then, with no intention or being redundant, I went into my phone and looked at this week and next week for appointments, and I wrote those down in ink on paper. *Something critical happens when my mind watches my hand write something out.* It's at least 70% more likely to make a mental note for some reason when I write it on paper. I went into my emails and found all the emails tagged with "TO DO" or "TO ATTEND" labels. (Yes, I color code my emails with labels and file them all away under specific categories, never deleting anything. That might be weird to some people but do a brief search on Google about what it's like to really have ADHD and you will know that this is a ninja tactic to outsmart my own brain.) I also have a few highlighter markers that I use to put anything really IMPORTANT in pink or orange. I circle the times so that even if I barely glance at tomorrow, I know I have a meeting on Zoom at 9! I need to be ready by 9, my brain says. Ready for what? I don't actually remember.

Giving dates and time a physical form. Having a place on the calendar sets aside time for an important thing. I started waking up each morning (normally I'd wake up in a panic wondering what I could possibly be missing) and looked at the paper calendar. Sometimes I would even screenshot my paper calendar using my phone so that I had it in my Photos folder just in case I was away from my desk (say on my way home from dropping off the kids) and needed to see a quick look at the crucial times for the day. Now, this practice is a holy practice for me. My paper agenda/calendar doesn't leave my desk. It's next to my computer and always staring at me. I fill up each week with goals and appointments and sometimes I even schedule in the mundane. Like haircuts or laundry. Because then I won't overbook myself or double book that time of day with something else that seems super important. It also signals the hamster to take a water break so I can do brainless shit like grocery shopping.

Eventually this practice will get easier. Another trick I've used for four or five years since things got really busy is to carry a pen and a Moleskine notebook around with me wherever I go. I write down notes at every meeting and I doodle when I listen to other people talk. Usually, when it's a speaker on a panel or a consultant/coach giving me advice over the phone. I don't doodle in front of people anymore because I've learned that it's considered rude. They may think I'm not paying attention. Little do they know, I am actually creating a carbon copy rubbing of our exact conversation, so that when my visual brain sees the doodle again, my gray matter reacts by saying "Oh! I know this conversation! We were talking about the sales pipeline for November. That's why I drew a bunch of pipes weaving in a geometric grid pattern…" My brain actually retains information better when I draw. Some people have a kinesthetic intelligence and they remember better if they're moving their body. Others are musical and can remember the Table of Elements if only it's put into a song. I… just need to see it. Write it. And revisit the site of the writing.

Jim Kwik was just a grade school kid when his teacher leaned over to a colleague and whispered, "That's the kid with the broken brain," while subtly pointing her finger at him. He had a learning disability due to a brain injury as a child and wasn't able to remember things as other children could. He developed a fascinating system for retaining information and learning faster. He also claims to help people forget less. In his masterclass, he name drops famous people he's done workshops for like Barack Obama and Elon Musk, as well as massive corporations like Google. I recommend reading his book Limitless or watching his many Ted Talks if you want to get clever about remembering things.

My brain wasn't broken, though it felt like it was. Managing my creative, idea-generating hamster on a wheel was a full-time job. However, being visual turned out to be the key to remembering things in my own weird way. You may have a different approach, but so long as you're aware of what works and what doesn't work you can make some course corrections. The thing is, we are hooked up to our phones all the time. We are easily distracted. Our brain has ten tabs open at any given moment. This way of being isn't the clearest path to an agile memory. We rely so heavily on Siri and Google and reminders and our iPhones/earbuds/smartwatch/Echo devices that we have lost old techniques for getting shit done.

That's not to say that I denounce apps on an iPhone. I for one will always be an advocate for as many backups as possible. I carry a gas can around in the back of my car for reasons we discussed earlier. I have, however, become fond of using both the paper calendar and the iCal app. It gets confusing when someone sends a Google Calendar invite so maybe I have both apps going. But, the most key usage for remembering things isn't the calendar. It's an alarm.

You're at the coffee shop and you only put 30 minutes on the parking meter. It's been 40 because you were having such a nice time talking to your friend that you didn't want to interrupt by pulling out your phone and recharging the app payment. So you go to your car and find a $150 ticket for going over the time by seven minutes. That was the most expensive coffee you ever drank. Here's the deal. Try it for a week, and like everything I have told you thus far, if it doesn't work for you then trash it. I want you to set an alarm on your phone for practically everything. An alarm twenty minutes before you need to leave to go get your kids from school, so that you can wrap up what you're doing. Then, I have another alarm for "You need to leave at this exact moment or you'll be that crap mom who sucks at life and can't find a parking spot so she is double parked Chicago-style with her flashers waiving and mouthing "sorry" in pantomime to all the good

CHAPTER 5: YOUR DYSFUNCTIONAL RELATIONSHIP WITH TIME

moms and dads as she shuffles her kids into their car seat.

Set an alarm for waking up. Set an alarm at lunch time if you work for yourself so that you take a break and eat. Take your medicine. Set an alarm for when you need to start dinner. Set a thousand of them, for anything of varying importance. Just as a cue for your overworked and underpaid brain so it doesn't have to do so much heavy lifting. Pretty soon you'll sink into the routine and you can delete some of those cues.

Set aside fifteen extra minutes for everything. I even set my clocks in my house, car and watch to ten minutes ahead to trick myself into thinking I am late. Just so I arrive on time. I plan to be there fifteen minutes early. I set doctor's appointments for 1:15 when it's actually scheduled for 1:30. This way you can't dick around and try to scam the clock and bargain, "I've got a few more minutes to wrap up this Photoshop file..." and then you're suddenly leaving the house 5 minutes after you were supposed to be somewhere.

You see, what I realized when I had a super diligent, practical, and prompt boyfriend is that successful people aren't late. They don't constantly forget shit. Not only are they not those things which describe me, they are early. For everything. They also consider people who are late to stuff (within reason. Five minutes late is human. Fifteen is…) rude. By all accounts they believe that the people who are forgetting their appointments and showing up late and running out of gas are not just unfortunate in the way PigPen the Peanuts character is just a little off. They judge us. They think we don't care about their time.

I remember trying to wrap my mind around that when James asked me to be at the movie theater at 6:30 but the movie wasn't starting until 7:00. I figured I'd be parking at 6:55 and have plenty of time… no? He told me that he thought I was underappreciating everyone else's schedule. That the things he had to do were unimportant in my mind if

I was always running late to meetings and stuff. He took that to mean that I was disrespectful. It was at that moment that my bubble was truly burst. I thought people were just giving me the benefit of the doubt and letting me off the hook. But truly they may have viewed me with dismay. What a shocking realization that time was valued differently by others and that my image would be tarnished if I didn't get my act together.

Mindfulness is something to note here as we end this section about being flaky. Sometimes we are flaky because we are trying to do too much at the same time. We overload ourselves and aim to be productive as possible. It's counterintuitive to real productivity, which is doing something as efficiently and completely as possible. Then, you move on to the next task. Being mindful is devoting your whole entire mind to one thing. It's also allowing your mind some rest and breaks.

Transcendental meditation is something that I was urged to look into when I sought a psychiatrist to help me manage my ADHD. She didn't just quickly write up a prescription and send me packing. She asked me a lot of questions about my life and as I began to tell her all the hats I wear, she noticed I was prone to stress because I am doing A LOT. It's hard to focus when you're the only parent. It's hard to be present when you also own a business. It's hard to write when you are doing those two things on top of creating a unique manuscript from thin air. So she asked me to find time for nothing.

I beg your pardon. Find time for nothing? That sounds very anti-productive. But what she made me confess is that if I scheduled every fuckin second from the time I woke up until the time I closed my eyes at bedtime, there wasn't any dead space. No single moment for reflection and quiet. My life had become a triathlon each day of "go, go, go!" and I was burning out at a rapid rate because I had no silence in my life. Mindfulness and meditation can assist you in being productive in the times that you are working. Because your mind is allowed to do one thing instead of twenty. I encourage you to download a free app from the app store and practice some five-ten minute meditations. Breathing, calming down and letting the hamster just take a power nap is good for both stressful situations and neutral ones alike.

The antidote to forgetting is being mindful. Setting appointments at the exact time you create them, in your phone, on your calendar. Example: I am having coffee with a friend. She asks if we can get our nails done next week. I say "yah, sure, let me know after the weekend what time would be good." We leave it at that and then our nails never get done or we scramble to call and make an appointment. See, having two artists in a relationship makes this even more challenging! But the inverse is to say, hold on. Get out my phone. Set a reminder for Monday to call the salon. Make it an alarm. Then book a tentative time with Clara that works for her schedule. If we both book an hour for it next week, the likelihood of us setting too many appointments and not having enough time for nails is way decreased. Beyond setting reminders, I like to set my calendar appointments for ten minutes before it actually occurs so that you can "trick" your mind into being on time, if I am ten minutes late. So if my pediatrician says 10:30 sometimes I will put my calendar event in my phone for 10:00. Giving me ample time to be an asshole and run late. Worst case scenario, I will arrive twenty minutes early and have to entertain the kids with looking for Nemo in the fish tank or doing crossword puzzles in a Highlights magazine.

I sometimes have a hard time cutting off a conversation because I need to get in the car and get to my next appointment. I linger until the other person has said everything they need to and I have tended to their needs. For this reason, meetings always go over. But what I have realized is that if there's an alarm in my purse it gives me a great excuse to cut things short, because it feels like an important thing I need to tend to. It gives me an out. I can say, "I am so sorry, but I must get going". Images of the rabbit from Alice in Wonderland just flashed through my mind. "I'm late! I'm late! For a very important date!" If only the rabbit had an iPhone…I set reminders for my parking expiring-- TEN MINUTES before they will expire, not at the time of. I set a reminder for ten minutes before a really important meeting so that I can be in front of my computer, have make up on, coffee, the dog is put away, and I ate something. That gives me time to sit and "get clear." Getting clear looks like reviewing emails from our past conversations. Or if it's giving me anxiety, I like to ask myself this: "How do I want to show up to this meeting?" I can assert myself however I want. I can be a "listener" and collect information. I can be the leader and create an introduction to myself and what I hope to get out of the meeting, before I start. I can ask people involved to please take notes. I can ask people to put their questions in the Chat box instead of asking them out loud. Etc.

The true problem, I have come to accept, is that I am babysitting those who I'm in a conversation with. I am caring about their feelings and I want them to feel heard. I want them to find our exchange endearing and not rushed. I want them to see me favorably and find joy in talking with me. In essence though I am valuing their time, feelings, and needs above my own. I have done much work to unearth the worms that are my own issues. They're buried in the dirt. The fattest one is codependency. Another worm is gross and wiggling around, trying to get away: Insecurity. If I just rush out of a meeting because I literally need to go pick up my kids, am I rude?! No. But I don't want to be seen as such and so I give my time away for free or I let people rob me of my time. Working on boundaries with one's self will be reflected back as boundaries with others. When I enter a meeting saying, "Hey, I'm so excited to meet with you today to show you my wallpaper, but I need to head out at 3:00. I have something important right after our meeting." Then the other will see that it's 2:50 and start to wrap up. They may even tell me "Hey, don't you need to go? Don't let me keep you."

Lie #4- There's Not Enough Time

I wish I could say something funny here like, "There's never enough time for anything, ever. The end" but the truth is, we all feel like we are running out of time. In truth, it is likely for the reason that we are overbooking ourselves. We are committing to lots of things that we probably aren't really that passionate about. We are giving our time away instead of reserving some time for doing nothing or being with those who we love.

Many a dramatic TV show starts with a family split apart because the dad works late nights and the mom is always taking on the brunt of the household work all by herself. Or at least I think there are shows like that... There are those of us who marry our jobs because we think that our identity is linked to the profession or title that we hold. We allow it to fill up more than eight hours of our day and we ask those we love to give us permission to work that hard because we really want validation. We want our boss to say, "Good job!" or we want our bank account to grow. We want to know that our labor pays off. We want to feel important. We want praise. We want to identify as hard working. We want to accumulate wealth and think overworking is the only way to earn money.

The problem is, *you are not your work.* You aren't your job. I am not Relativity Textiles. I am an artist and a mother who happens to own a wallpaper company that is open only from 9-3. The hours that my kids are in school. I decidedly made those the hours because after-school programs are a racket and I am the single parent who is their only consistent force in their lives. Their dad comes and goes as a flight attendant and he sees them about eight days a month. I am the one who will be teaching them the majority of life's lessons and setting the tone for their home life. With this comes: Routines. I always had guilt about leaving them at school until 6 PM while I was home working. I'd rather stop and go get them and bring them home for a snack and quit work at 3:00 and I purposely designed my business to have those hours because of my oldest son.

He was in first grade when I was the busiest. I didn't have a full time assistant yet. I was on my laptop and he'd been watching a TV show after school when he approached my desk where I was staring at the screen. "Mommy, can you stop working?" he said.

"No, buddy, I have to write this email." I said in an 'I'm sorry bud' tone.

He gently slammed the top portion of my laptop closed and replied "Do the email later."

This one simple line stuck with me for the rest of my career. It can wait. He was right. There were more important things in life than checking emails. And the clients can wait. So if you feel like the important people in your life need you and you can't seem to find time for them, you just have to MAKE time. That might look like ending work early, if you are self-employed and you can do that. Or it might mean working late one night a week to store some hours for an early ending time one day so that you can get ice cream with

CHAPTER 5: YOUR DYSFUNCTIONAL RELATIONSHIP WITH TIME

your kids after school. If you don't have children and you're not in a domestic partnership (and even if you are) you might want to consider slamming your laptop closed each day to just take a walk or go for a run or meditate or take a nap. Doing something for yourself will, in the end, make a better mommy. A better partner. A better person.

So sorry if that's uneventful news. You have been telling the lie to yourself that everything you're doing is really f-ing important. But something's gotta give. You can't do it all and you don't want to burnout trying. So take some of the less important things off your plate. Schedule into that pretty paper calendar of yours some "me" time and learn how to relax. This will result in you no longer feeling overwhelmed or out of time.

Do you think I have time to write a book? I am a single mother of two boys. It's summer of 2020 and there's a global pandemic. I've been afraid since this virus made its landing on our continent that I'd lose my business. On top of trying to run a company by myself, I'm raising humans by myself at the same time. I have no time to write a book. I will offer you this morsel of wisdom however: There's never enough time for anything. If you really care about something, if you really want something bad enough, you'll work for it. Lose some sleep. Give up your hobbies for two or three weeks. Hell, I haven't watched television since Dexter was airing a new episode each week. Stop hanging out with friends or online dating or trolling Instagram. In the thirty minutes I spent sitting in the parking lot outside my wallpaper manufacturer's loading dock waiting for them to find my order I wrote the first 5,000 words to this book. I'm not kidding. I wrote it on my phone. In the Google Docs app. Everything happens five words at a time. Little digestible chunks at a time. Small baby steps. Slow and steady wins the race.

You see, when I was late, I'd say, "I'm bad with time." When I was cursing myself about forgetting something, I'd say I was just "forgetful." I believed those things to be truths, not lies. In believing those things, I never had to face the reality that: If I continued to live with these statements as truths, I would never break free from being late, being forgetful and being seen as a flake. It took me a very long time to "get clear" about these truths putting my inner artist into a major time-out. It starts with taking a look at your life, noticing what's wrong and telling the truth. The truth is, my sense of time needs major improvement. From there, I created an action plan to be on time more and forget less.

Here are the main life hacks you can try if this sounds a lot like your own life:

1) Write everything down. In a paper calendar
2) Back up all dates on your phone calendar
3) Use alarms and reminder apps to notify you of everything. (I have alarms set for the exact time that I need to stop working in order to get my kids from school on time. Every day, M-F, that alarm sounds at 3:15 and that's the ultimate cut off time for focusing on an email or artwork file, chatting with a client, or dilly dallying. It's not a last call, 'you have about five minutes left before you need to go' type of an alarm. It's a 'get your keys and get out the door right now' type of alarm.
4) Trick your brain. If you are the person who chances the clock a lot, how can you set yourself up for success? What if you trick the clock itself? I have all of my clocks set for ten to fifteen minutes ahead. That way, if I see it's 7:00 AM I tell myself, 'I have an hour until the kids start school. Hurry up with breakfast because you still need to do x,y and z before

you head out the door.' Setting all your clocks ahead might drive your family crazy but it's a foolproof way to accidentally show up ten minutes early everywhere you go. Or... on time, because normally you're ten minutes late.

5) Go over your calendar the night before (or take pictures of it). I've found that I need to glance at my calendar every morning so that I know what I've got on my plate for the day. It prepares me mentally for a slow, coffee sipping morning, or a sit down at the computer morning, or a load the dish washer morning, or a dress fancy and grab your presentation materials kind of morning. Having forgotten instantly what I had for the day, I've missed important meetings because something more interesting caught my eye after I dropped off the kids at school. This is why I take a photo of my paper calendar. If I haven't entered every little task into my phone, at least I know I have it in my paper calendar. I see a photo of it, and it reminds me I need to be by my computer by noon or call my coach at a certain time.

A good relationship with time gives you, Thriving Artist, something a Starving Artist will never have: Freedom.

A Note on Invisible Labor

I want you to try and actually pencil in everything you do, not just for your creative practice and/or work. Not just kids' important school dates. What if you started actually writing down EVERYTHING you do on a daily basis, short of penciling in your bathroom breaks? If you humor me and actually make this agenda full, you might begin to notice why you have no time. You're doing a lot.

If you attempt this activity, which I hope all of you dare to do, you've scoured your brain for every single thing you can fill your schedule up with, take a step back. Look at all of the things you do. To all the moms. Bravo. I am clapping a slow, loud, irritated clap for you because I know how much "invisible labor" there is. The podcast "Dear Sugars" once had a husband and wife make lists of all the things they did in a day and the results were shocking. The stay-at-home mother's list was so long she covered the front and the back of her paper. The man's list went like this:

Wake up. Go to work. Come home. Eat dinner. Watch TV. Go to sleep.

I'm being a little angsty towards the male species right now. Mostly because I am raising kids in a one parent household so I'm lucky if I accomplish half of what's on the mom's list and the dad's list. I'm snarky but I'm also very *lucky* in some ways too. I don't have the resentment that builds when the other parent has time to work out but I don't. I don't have to iron anyone's shirts anymore except my own.

So write your list (for a week or so?). Then prepare to be amazed. You can't jam a hundred things into a day and expect to make art, let alone thrive at it. What you need to focus on for this exercise is to include everything. It's going to feel very Big Brother to be accountable to your own schedule and I know you're going to want to say "Damn the Man." I know this because I am not a rule follower either and I hated clocking in and out. I haven't had a "real job" since 2006, okay? What you might learn from this though is what is achievable in an hour. How efficient you are (or aren't). How much time is caught up in dilly dallying? The secret sauce for entrepreneurs is sometimes just efficiency, precision, and routines. The boring stuff. The spreadsheets and sticking to a schedule. I'm not asking you to wholeheartedly change everything you do. But, for the love of God, just try it.

The Administration of Life

The minutiae of the everyday is what I like to call "The Administration of Life." That if you were to assign a ten person staff to do all of these things, I am almost certain you could fill an eight hour day for the following personnel:

> Personal Chef (research the Keto diet for women and put together a 30-day meal plan and four weekly shopping lists).
> Housekeeper (please get the area under the toilet where the landlord never caulked because that's where the boys' pee puddles and it's impossible to reach with a mop)
> Appointment Manager (oil changes, pets nails clipped, change air filter in furnace, dental cleanings)
> Kids' Activities Manager (part Nanny and part chauffeur, moonlights as a baseball coach and homework coordinator) Note: during global pandemics this person just sits next to the child for six hours and makes sure they're not playing Candy Crush when they're supposed to be doing Google Meet or Zoom.
> Physical Fitness Coach (the obvious is that they'd be there at all times to make sure you weren't slouching in your chair or eating the cookies you smuggled in that aren't on the Keto meal plan)
> Financial Advisor (keeps a spreadsheet of credit cards, student loans, bank accounts, paid subscriptions, credit score, mortgage rates, and gives each adult a latte allowance for the week)

And the list goes on. Those would be your trusted advisors and highly paid staff. If you were the president or God. But you're not, so you do all of those jobs part-time.

Generally speaking, in the 21st century in modern America, the household is still a gendered zone when it comes to labor. Most moms are writing down the grocery list. Most moms are Spray-n-Washing the grass stains out of multiple pairs of jeans (or skid marks from the whole family's underpants!) Sorry I'm a boy mom so my mind goes to a dark, dark place. Laundry is a real labor of love for me, ha! Most moms are either cutting their kids' hair or scheduling the haircuts. Most moms are helping with homework or taking the kids to karate. Most moms make sure their kids are thriving well before they're applying for a new promotion or carving out time for the workout routine. But, even if you are a unicorn mom and you're putting yourself first, there are still a lot of things that are invisible on your calendar.

When you make your priorities visible, it's impossible to ignore. Do you follow what I'm saying here? *Put it on the calendar.* Make a post-it note wall. Write it on your hand if you need to like the days of Hillside Middle School. Jot it down on a big To-Do list. Just make it visible. Sounds stupid, but it works. Then let's see what transpires when you follow your own routine for one week. Just see what happens.

Our spaces and priorities are cluttered as fuck because we don't realize all what we are keeping. We don't use half of our own brain. We don't write things down and we surely can't remember all the invisible stuff. We can't find the hammer because there are six places in the house where it could be. We don't want to sit in the living room because there are stacks of bills in there, so we avoid entering that room altogether! When things are disorganized, it leads to a massive snowballing effect of avoidance. And then we have nowhere for peace or imagination or to get centered. So, in short, we need to get rid of all the things that aren't serving us. We need to stop tolerating piles and baskets full of stuff we have no intention of organizing. And we need to stop those habits that created the mess in the first place. The new system will leave you feeling secure, that you know what's ahead of you. It's not going to be comfortable. It may take a LOT of work, depending on how much of a hoarder you are and what emotions are tied up in your shit.

But if you can get through it in one week, that's progress. And if it takes a month, don't beat yourself up about it. The antidote to not having enough time is to schedule in time for the administration of life. If you work from home, please put a one-hour lunch break on your calendar. Workout at this time, fold laundry at this time, and stop eating your salad over your keyboard and multitasking through the lunch hour. It sounds counterintuitive but trust me; you need the break. Your mind needs the break. You need to put an hour a day aside for the not-so-monumental important stuff. Like making sure your pill box is full of seven day's worth of medication, the coffee has been ground for tomorrow's pot, the roller-skates are not on the staircase. Because heaven forbid, tomorrow when you wake up in a rush because you snoozed three times, you will be rushing to take your vitamins, cursing the coffee beans for not grinding themselves, and potentially breaking your neck as you run with hot coffee down the stairs for your first Zoom meeting of the day.

Cosmic Timing

In order to reverse the lies you tell about Time and all his wrongdoings you must be clear about the natural evolution of things. Cosmic timing is at play. You had a one in one million chance of becoming a human. That's how many sperms were released when you were conceived. And here you are, right on time. You met the people you met because of cosmic timing. They came onto your stage from behind the scenes and caused drama or perished or made the narrative even sweeter. They stayed forever or they exited Stage Left. But those things were meant to be. You got certain jobs or went to a certain school as a steppingstone to the next stage in your life. Even if you failed at something, you learned along the way. Time, being the elusive character that he is, has been lurking in the background as all of the events of your life have unfolded. Explained by Lama Surya Das in his book called, *Buddha Standard Time*,

> *"Each moment is intersected by a realm of infinite spaciousness and timelessness, known as Tibetan shicha, the Eternal Now. This is the precious awakened dimension that I call Buddha Standard Time, and it is available to us every instant. 'Let go the past,' the Buddha said, 'let go the future, and let go what is in between, transcending the things of time. With your mind free in every direction, you will not return to birth and aging.' When we are in touch with being only in the present moment, only with what is, instead of what we regret, fear, or anticipate, our sense of limits in time will no longer have negative power over our lives. This is ancient, timeless wisdom."*

To be free from the limitations of time, we need to try and live in the right now. Doing work on the past is good for reflection. But coming to peace with how things are is crucial. You have all the time you need to do all the things that are important. You have all the years in your life to accomplish what you were meant to accomplish. You are right where you are supposed to be. Everything is on time. It might not

CHAPTER 5: YOUR DYSFUNCTIONAL RELATIONSHIP WITH TIME

be where you want it to be, grasshopper. But *timing* is different than time.

If you believe in God, you can see it as someone having a plan for you. If you don't then have faith in the fact that you are on the right path, even if it's the path least taken. Focusing on time passing or the time passed is like being at the SAT tests and staring at the stop clock. It's hard to be calm under pressure of a looming timer going off. Life isn't like that, thank God, but when we work to channel our own magic, it's not because we have only a certain amount of time before we shrivel up and die. It's to be the best we can be in this exact moment or minute or hour. Using our time wisely, on things that matter. Rather than letting our past inform our level of confidence to move forward, or our fear of the future restrict our potential.

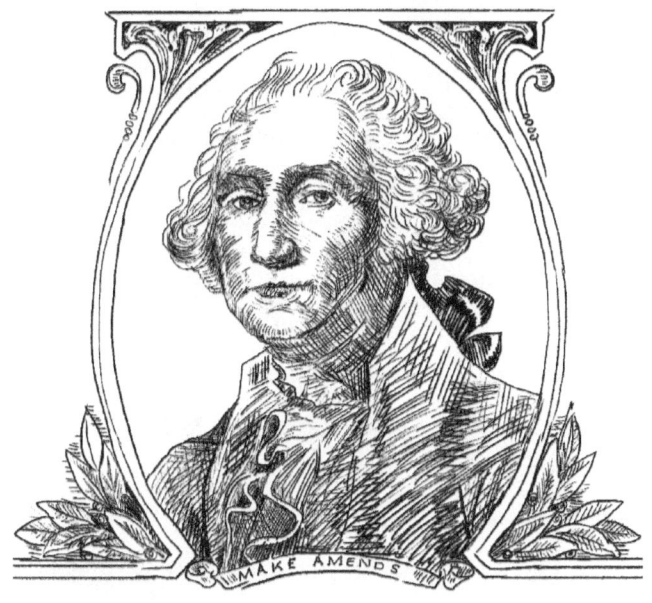

Chapter 6

You and Money Need to Make Amends

Money is a man you found on Bumble. He's got scraggly hair and you've been letting him crash at your place for years. He is a deadbeat, darlin' and it's time to kick him out. You can do better. There's another man out there that I am about to introduce you to. Consider me the

Millionaire matchmaker and you can thank me later. "_____ (Your name here), meet Wealth." He's a little out of your league. What do you do to impress him? How do you behave so that he sees your good side? How do you win him over? You stop saying he's too good for you.

Wealthy people operate differently than poor people. Raise your hand if you were raised by poor people. I was. I never learned important techniques for how to earn money, save money and spend money. I surely never learned how to invest in the stock market or acquire massive passive income. Let's do a little brief therapizing about how all of this is our parents' fault but let's give them an ounce of compassion as we do (since they were flawed human beings just like you and me, chugging along and doing the best with what they had too). Let's take this moment to make amends with your PigPen money role models and pursue a more creative and joyful idea: Money is yours to be had. Like time, you need to figure out what you're doing wrong and make some course corrections.

Your Money Attitude

There are two types of money attitudes out there: The Spenders and the Savers. Typically, you fall into one of these categories. Raise your hand if you're a spender. Your Amazon cart usually has some things in it that you're waiting to buy until your paycheck drops into your checking account. You're a generous gift giver because spending money on people you love gives you a warm, fuzzy feeling. You have a hard time understanding why your checking account is always so low, because no matter how much you are making, it seems to magically disappear at the same rate. You believe that money is meant to be spent, since YOLO.

CHAPTER 6: YOU AND MONEY NEED TO MAKE AMENDS

Savers are shaking their head at those folks right now. They're waving a disapproving finger at you. Savers are tightwads. They split the check at dinner. They don't have an iTunes subscription; they use Spotify because it's free. They have an account full of money which they monitor. They are saving for a vacation or a new computer. They love it when things go on sale. They rarely let their checking account hit a certain dollar amount threshold because it makes them nervous. Zero is not a number that they can handle as a balance.

The real odd balls come from two other subcategories and aren't true Savers or Spenders. They're the Avoiders (usually stemming from the Spender persuasion) and the Monks (strong thread of Saver running through). Think of this as the Meyers Briggs of money personalities. I am a Spender-Avoider. You might be a Saver-Monk.

Avoiders don't want to open their bills because they don't want to see the truth about how much they owe on their credit cards. They think that they're not good at money, so they don't try to get better... they have so much other stuff to focus on in their busy lives. They usually check out at the register by handing over their debit card and closing their eyes, so they don't have to see the total. Avoiders can't process 401ks or wills or other types of insurance because they don't want to think about the bad stuff happening. They also just spend everything until it's gone and act like "How did this happen!?"

Monks are holier than thou. They do not need Earthly possessions nor does wealth seem an admirable goal. They donate excess cash to charity even if they could've spent it on something they've truly wanted. They either feel guilty to have more than others or they're truly uninterested. They're not the humblest though. They're silently judging everyone else for letting money dictate politics, global warming, and they may blame capitalism for the world's problems. They're on

Facebook posting rants about the failures of commerce, the defunding of the Arts, and they might've been seen five years ago striking with non-union employees for the Fight for Fifteen. They resent money and see wealth as a meaningless, vain pursuit. They have no interest in trying to make money lest they be associated with all the evils of capitalism.

Miriam Webster dictionary defines "making amends" like this: *to do something to correct a mistake that one has made or a bad situation that one has caused.* If you want to level up in your life, you're going to have to admit which money profile you have and figure out what habits and patterns it's caused. Most likely the way you've been thinking about money, treating your money and using money has not been in your best interest. When you look at your bank account, you'll see what I mean. If I ask you to tell me the God's honest truth, you know that you're doing it. How do we make amends?

In Alcoholics Anonymous, making amends is the ninth step in a twelve-step program to recovering from addiction. It is an important position to take as the alcoholic begins to admit the damage they've done to their family and close friends. There are three tiers of amends: those that need to be made right away, then "there will be those to whom we can make only partial restitution, lest complete disclosures to them more harm than good ,"[8] and the third tier is reserved for deferment. The last bit is for people that you aren't in direct contact with and don't want to reconnect with. Admitting that one's drinking made them hard to live with is to announce one's deficit. Acknowledging it before saying, "I'm sorry" lets the receiver of the apology know that one is aware that they have done harm in the first place and is making a conscious effort to stop the behavior.

---

[8] https://www.aa.org/assets/en_us/en_step9.pdf

CHAPTER 6: YOU AND MONEY NEED TO MAKE AMENDS

I know about AA peripherally as the niece, sister, granddaughter, and cousin of people in recovery. I am the daughter to two humans who were not alcoholics themselves but were raised by raging alcoholics. The damage and abandonment that formed my mother and father's early childhood has a ripple effect into their parenting techniques. Al-Anon was created for the family of alcoholics because AA believes that alcoholism is a family illness. Adult children of alcoholics exhibit traits such as arguing, inconsistency, unreliability, and a tendency for chaos. This is because they were never given the attention and emotional support they needed during their early development. Trusting others is difficult which effects interpersonal relationships[9] . Denying their own feelings of fear, sadness and anger is a survival mechanism and later in life those repressed emotions eventually surface.

My analogy falls short of giving you a twelve-step program to overcome your dysfunctional relationship with money. I don't think you're an addict. I think you're likely the byproduct of your parents' dysfunctional relationship(s) with money though. Thus, my advice will be the al-anon approach rather than AA. You learned from someone who had incomplete information, bad strategies for dealing with money and attitudes that allowed negative spending patterns. Whether your parents charged up their credit cards, took out tons of student loans for college, went bankrupt or pinched all the pennies and made you drink powdered milk, you were not taught about money by experts. Am I right?

Let's first address the elephant in the room. MONEY is tied to EMOTIONS.

---

[9] https://www.verywellmind.com/common-traits-of-adult-children-of-alcoholics-66557

Feelings + Thoughts = Actions

Money has many connotations and those are different for everyone, but the way we deal with money is nine times out of ten representative of our feelings. Feelings about wealth- either greed or guilt. Feelings about worth- either low self-worth or egotistical. Feelings about poverty vs. abundance. Feelings about saving. Feelings about spending. Feelings, feelings, feelings.

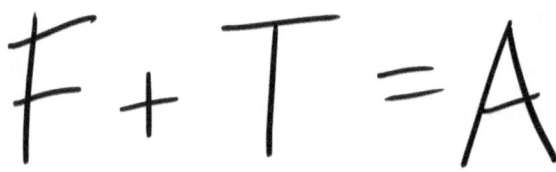

I learned this along the way, from many a guru and self-help author, so I'll spare you all the titles and you can read my annotated bibliography if you want to research all the instances where this is true. Feelings lead to Thoughts. Thoughts lead to Actions. So your spending habits aren't going to change unless you tackle the emotions that are tied to them.

Would you be willing to try something new? First, we are going to reflect on our thoughts and feelings. Then we'll come up with new mantras that make moving forward a little easier. We'll use our artist superpowers to make magical things happen, because we are creators after all. And we have vivid imaginations to invent a future for ourselves.

Take out a piece of paper. Yes. I am making you do an activity. Pretend you just spent $44K to be in college again and you're sitting in

CHAPTER 6: YOU AND MONEY NEED TO MAKE AMENDS

my class. I'm going to teach you some skills you never learned in school. These are the life lessons your parents didn't teach you otherwise you wouldn't need to read my book. You'd already be thriving. These are the secrets of the thriving artist.

Write down the following phrases five times:

Money is _____ (five times with five separate spaces).
Wealth is _____ (you get the picture)
Rich people are _____.

Now, you're going to write these statements once but give yourself a few lines of blank space to answer in a longer sentence or bullet point multiple answers:

The reasons I can't (or may not) become extremely wealthy are: (list as many reasons as you can)

Some of the possible negatives about being rich are:
The process of becoming rich would be:
My greatest fear about being wealthy is:
My greatest fear about money is:
The worst thing about money is:

Break time. I'm eating a peanut butter and banana sandwich while you record your answers. Back in January of 2020 before the virus shut down all life as we know it, I attended a three-day seminar. It was called the Millionaire Mind Intensive and was derived from a book by T. Harv Ecker with a similar title. It was full of about 150 people who were tired of working hard and not getting ahead. Tired of being broke and undervalued. Tired of living with lies and excuses and not knowing how to dig themselves out of debt or a bad relationship.

You see, I was above all this. The exercises. The mantras. The standing up in the air and shouting, "I have a millionaire mind!" and high fiving my neighbor. But I met some interesting people during the course of three days. I entered the seminar downtrodden. I'd recently become single again after dating post-divorce finally worked out. I'd moved back out on my own again. I was grappling with whether or not my business actually was going to succeed or if I was even passionate about wallpaper anymore. I was tired of being broke. They taught very finite terms for how you should stash your money in seven different bank accounts and I never followed through with the tactics because I'm (again) born of the Clan of Skeptics. I never finished the book *Getting Things Done* either, for God's Sake.

By the time I left the workshop, I had clarity for the things I needed to work on if I wanted to achieve my goal. I had a dream that seemed impossible. I wanted to buy a house. I'd always thought that it took two to buy a home; two incomes, those of a husband and wife. I'd never gotten a chance to do that with my husband because I was in grad school and raising small babies. The entire time we were married, come to think of it, I hadn't had a full- time job. We were barely breaking even. In the aftermath of my second attempt at love I broke up with my boyfriend who I'd lived with one year and moved out of his house to "start all over" again as a one income household and single mother. I was convinced that I'd rent apartments and homes forever. The ecosystem I belonged to was a landlord/tenant agreement and I'd never be able to knock down walls or wallpaper a bathroom without permission.

If I wanted so badly to own a home, first I'd have to stop feeling guilty about money. If I wanted to make shit tons of money, I'd have to stop thinking things like "Money is something I never learned to

CHAPTER 6: YOU AND MONEY NEED TO MAKE AMENDS

use." I wrote things in my workbook like "Wealth is something other people have and understand," and "Rich people are not ashamed to use money to their advantage." The answers that I scribbled down revealed clues about how I viewed money and wealth and whether or not I was deserving of it. I was forced to have a hard conversation with my beliefs and what became clear was that my tenant persona was the victim in a sad story about mommies who don't own anything. There were layers of grief and abandonment, loneliness and still a faint crying out of "It's not fair!" Whilst friends who were married purchased homes and posted photos of their keys on closing day, I was signing yet another twelve month agreement to give all my money away to the landlord. But that was a choice in some way. If I wanted to break the cycle it was going to be like anything else. Being a victim to obesity is something that has to be changed by the overeater. There are steps towards repairing my credit and saving money that I'd need to complete if I was ever to move into my "Forever Home" and do a jump in the air for the camera to capture! I was in charge of directing this course, not the self-driving car I'd been riding in thus far...

When I was filling out my workbook that you just also detailed, I realized that I worried about dying poor. I worried that my kids would never learn how to be wealthy, just like I hadn't. I even blamed parenthood as a reason why I couldn't become wealthy, because I had really trained my head to think that either I am a good mom OR I am a wealthy mom. Like I needed to choose one or the other! Those are fear-based thoughts and they limited my perspective. They put blinders on potential and possibility and therefor the answers to getting out of my rut weren't clear! Because I couldn't see anything but the "facts" and the sorrow of my own victimhood.

Look, we've all got our issues which I truly hope you'll consider delving into at length with a professional. I don't know what your unique form of excuse is for why you haven't allowed yourself or trained yourself to become rich yet. All that bullshit is your own secret to keep or burn like the dumpster fire that is your credit score and savings account balance. But I'm going to give you a very Minckley family, hard knocks rebuttal: "Excuses are like assholes. Everyone has one and they all stink." The limiting beliefs you hold about yourself likely inform your limiting beliefs about wealth. That he's too good for you and you should continue to suffer by dating losers like "broke" and "Starving." Those are personas that you identify with right now, but they don't define you.

Our beliefs inform our actions. If money is the root of all evil, then surely you won't want to have it play a part in your life. If wealth is for harmful, egotistical and ungodly people you surely will not want to picture yourself as such a person. If you think that it is all a lottery, and that your luck/fate was not in the cards then you can throw your hands up in the air and never become rich. But, I'm here to challenge you with some statements that might seem so far-fetched you'll begin to create awesomely distracting rationale for why I am not an expert, I am wrong, I am too lofty and I don't possibly know you or people like you. But you're not immune to the system of capitalism just because you're an artist. You know why?

Because you're not. Ha! You still have to pay rent/mortgage just like the rest of us. You still need to eat food and clothe your body. You still have bills. Let's figure out a way to make paying those a little easier and on top of that, let's produce some extra income for you to do whatever-the-fuck-you-want with. Like buy art supplies. Or take your girlfriend to Tahiti for a five-night vacation. What?! Artists can't vacation? Give me a break, friend. We are looking to make massive change, remember? We want all artists to thrive and to shift the paradigm about what we deserve. Maybe we deserve cleaning ladies. Maybe we deserve new underwear. Set the bar high or low, that's up to you but just please, dear god, make it an improvement on what you have now. And now, a word from a real contemporary artist.

Making Something from Nothing

Chicago-based sculptor and performance artist Theaster Gates said in his TedX talk that one of the most exciting things about being a ceramicist (he calls himself a "potter") is that "you very quickly learn how to make great things from nothing;" I am the first to admit that in graduate school when I passed an ally behind an architecture firm to find hundreds of old blue prints in the dumpster, I pulled them out and took them back to my studio and made collages from these free materials. They already had an aura, so the paper was imprinted with someone else's history. I've taken dressers from alleys and turned them into swanky baby's changing tables. I've got an arsenal of tools in my basement to construct just about anything or paint it. I love watching something that was once underappreciated become valuable just by the labor and ingenuity of my own two hands finessing the object. Care and time are free, and thus improving something is "easy." Or making a pot out of clay just requires a wheel, some water and a little know-how.

There is a resourcefulness about us as artists that does not happen in the non-creative world as much. And if you don't consider yourself an artist but you've taken seventeen panels of old reclaimed wood from a house renovation to create a standing planter bed for your backyard this spring, then I'd ask you to define it again. Whether or not you are an "Artist" with a capital "A" or an artist in the broader definition. From my definition, anyone who can take wood or clay or plain white paper and make it into something is an artist for all intents and purposes.

Gates goes on to explain the larger implications that him being an artist has on the world, "The limitations of my capacity and my ability is limited to my imagination… The process of learning has been very helpful to my life." He explains that it's the repetitive action of trying to make something that he learned a key strategy about how to make a place for himself in the world. As a potter, he explains, he began using the mentality of someone who shapes clay to begin to shape the world. He started to use materials to make art that carry a social significance to a black man, like fire hoses and tar. And he shaped them into works of art with tremendous meaning.

Like a potter at the wheel or a carpenter in the wood shop, it requires a significant amount of vision and ingenuity to manipulate materials into a given form. Especially, if you have a thread of perfectionism running through your veins. What creative people have that other types of people do not have is the imagination and ideas before the finished form has ever even been verbalized or explained to others! It exists only between your two ears at first.

If you can't tell, I like sports analogies. Wayne Gretzky the famous hockey player once said, "You miss 100% of the shots you don't take." This makes me think about all the ideas that are lying dormant in the brain of an artist or creator. The objects or inventions that never came to life because you never made them manifest! Consider the fact that "everything that is, was once imagined." Einstein quoted this to illustrate that none of our modern conveniences would exist if it wasn't for an inventor, a scientist, a designer, or an artist. Flushing toilets we use every day were invented to solve a problem. The keyless ignition in a Prius. Bluetooth speakers and headphones. All of these things never would have been possible if the inventor (aka artist) would have kept that "stupid idea" inside their head. None of the art hanging in the museum downtown would exist either! Do you stop, as I have done, to consider that even Elon Musk must have had so many people along the way who told him, "E. Seriously. There's no way you can make that happen." The Tesla founder would be even more loaded I'm sure if he had a dollar for every person who ever doubted him.

So if we can take raw materials like wood and form it into anything we want… why can't we take something like Money and use it to our own advantage as well? Why can't we work within the limitations of our imaginations and the confines of how money works and … make it work for us? How can we create something of value with very little to begin with? So there are limitations with everything. Money doesn't grow on trees, this we know. It also cannot duplicate itself like a science experiment where you grow crystals. But there are probably a lot of things that money can do that you just aren't trained at doing. Fair? If you were to learn how to use money like you learned InDesign for making your catalog for the handcrafted earrings you made out of playdough… Couldn't you get better at creating more money too? Like you got better at all the other things you do? What if you stopped working for dollars and put your dollars to work for you?

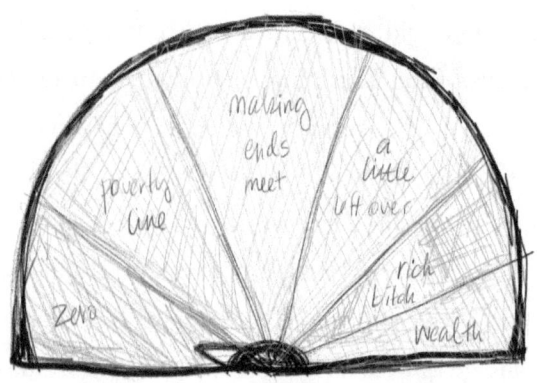

The Zero to Wealth Spectrum Explained

For how long have you been living without financial security? Savings. Retirement. Money left over at the end of the day. I have never really felt like I had this component of my life mastered. I didn't know how. I didn't do anything to change that either. But as I sit here now trying to think up a way for everyone reading this book to relate to the concept of "zero" I know that all of you are at different places in your financial lives. That said, we could all stand to get better and have more money. Think of all the things you could do with it! For many artists I know, the mentality of breaking even is real. If you added up your rent, your costs of living, your student loan payments and credit card payments and totaled the monthly amount of money that you absolutely need to survive, that is your goal. Whether you collect a paycheck or you're self-employed, the incoming funds better equal that number, right?

Wrong. That equals zero and zero is the enemy. What happens here is simple math, but we confuse ourselves. I only barely started to understand that I was doing this wrong when I calculated my monthly expenses. I see how much I'd been bringing in and discovered that it was usually always close. ALWAYS. Sometimes a little over, normally about exactly as much, and sometimes less. I was relying on child support payments to help offset the costs of feeding and housing my kids. But even without that I was trying to just cover the costs. The problem with this logic is that by the time you pay all your bills you are still at zero!

Zero is thus, the enemy. Not only are you fighting to earn what you need to survive, but you need to be earning that amount AND THEN SOME. The larger the "and then some" the more freedom you'll have. Not to dick around for a month because the following month is "paid for," no. You need to be putting it aside for specific things. And eventually you need to be planning for wealth. But right now, we are seeking minor upgrades to our life, like new undies or organic carrot sticks.

How do you get from the negative to zero to skirting by to wealth?

Types of Income

Did you know that wealthy people have multiple streams of income? I know that will not surprise you because you are smart, and you know things. But what sounded like a no-brainer to me during the money conference was not being applied to my life. I'd been skirting zero and eligible for food stamps so long that I hadn't thought to rearrange the way money worked in my life. The cool thing is as they began detailing for me and the other students in the course what types of income a person could make, their examples were very boring and drab. Passive income can come from owning a laundromat, but because I could never in a million years see myself doing that I wanted to define what it could possibly be for an artist. Here's a brief breakdown of the types of income one can make:

Earned Income/Working Income: This is where you get a job and you trade your time for money. Most of us have this type of job. It has set hours, set tasks, and there is a ceiling to how much you can make doing it.

Profit Income: From high profit selling. This is when you trade goods for money. Commissions, or selling stuff with a set price. You still have to work for these things to be produced but the price is set, so if you go over the number of hours you estimate, the amount you earn isn't changing.

Interest Income: This is money paid to you for lending your money or letting another entity use your funds. You may have an interest checking account and you earn 1% on your money in the bank. On a larger scale, interest income is the amount earned by an investor's money that he places in an investment or project (once the project is sold or completed).

Residual Income: This money comes as a result of doing something once, and then being paid multiple times or on an ongoing basis for that initial work.

Dividend Income: This is money made from stocks or mutual funds you own. This could be held in an IRA account. It could also be a little more complicated where there are two types of dividends or distributions: ordinary dividends -- is as it sounds -- classified for tax purposes as ordinary income. Qualified dividends may meet certain requirements and are taxed at lower capital gain rates.

Royalty Income: This is income received from allowing someone to use your artworks or intellectual property. Royalty payments for the use of patents, copyrighted works, natural resources, or franchises are most common. Most often the person using the property does so to generate revenue (they'll quickly make their money back). Royalties are usually legally binding with an Artist Licensing Agreement.

What type of income do you make? Would you like to have more passive income? Where you can work once and collect money multiple times? I discovered that making wallpaper afforded me this luxury, because I wasn't painting walls for every client. But there has been a significant trade off to becoming my own boss and owning a company. There are several other ways I could have used my drawing skills to make wallpaper, most of them involve me giving my art away to someone else and knowing they'll make a LOT of money off of it. That said, of their "LOT" I would receive a royalty of 10-30%. Not bad.

I could also make art and post it online available for download, where many people can buy the same image. Stock photography and graphics websites are abundant. Check out www.creativemarket.com or www.society6.com. You can make royalties on sites like www.minted.com if you are lucky to be chosen as a featured artist. You could also list your services for hire on websites like www.upwork.com or freelancing sites, because the internet has come a long way since I graduated from college and we found jobs in the newspaper or in the "Gigs" column on Craigslist.

Each of us will do it differently. If you were to give each artist $25 and ask them to make it into $100, they'd do something completely different. Maybe they'd buy some micron pens and arches paper and draw something. Maybe they'd invest it in the stock market and wait. Maybe they'd purchase an online course and generate a new skill. It's always a little bit of a 'roll the dice' but there are some pretty easy ways to start making income that we will discuss in Section 3.

The money has to go somewhere. Right? I'd like to remind you that Donald Trump is super wealthy. His kids are wealthy, and his parents likely handed him money to start every business he has. He's been on TV. He's a household name, and he was well before becoming the president of the United States of America. However, he is not the smartest person alive. He is not well spoken. He is not deserving of his own fame. He is not skilled at any one thing, especially not a craft. But he is rich. Think of another person. Kim Kardashian. Miley Cyrus. Thomas Kincade, painter of light. Jeff Koonz. Anyone. Think of someone rich and ask yourself "Are they the most skilled? Are they the greatest model human? Are they the smartest?"

To me, the sheer fact that some people who are wealthy are not the most talented or the most deserving are the richest. Do you think that's just? You are earnest and pious and skilled and just plain *good human*. And *you are not rich*. But someone else is richer than you with less skill. Or less common sense. Or less purpose. No. It's not fair. So why are they rich and not you? Seriously. Think about it. Why do they deserve that ease, that they can sit in a chair overlooking the ocean and write or read or do yoga or play guitar and drink a beer or sleep all day and contribute nothing to the planet? And you have to be struggling and hustling and slaving away to have that two bedroom in Avondale with no A/C. You can't afford wine that costs more than $9. You ride the bus or the train sometimes and you ride your bike when the weather is good. Because you don't want to pay for the car stickers and the insurance and the gas. It's all too much.

Your Ideal Life: Start with the End in Mind

Another activity has come your way. Please get out your notebook and favorite number two pencil. The second chapter is all about *doing* sorry. If you're trying to read this book on an airplane and don't have a notebook handy, you can come back to this, but please make sure that you do. It's an important part of progressing forward. If you like analytical or organized ways of thinking, by all means, please feel free to pop open your laptop and start a new Excel document. Knock yourself out (I also have a free template for the Ideal Life worksheet on my website: www.profitableartist.org/worksheets).

What does your *ideal life* look like? Think about it. Not the Ferrari speeding down Hwy 1 to Malibu with your Ken Doll husband in the passenger seat. No, I mean right now. Where do you want to live if you upgrade from your current place? Start with that. I thought this exercise was dumb when I first tried it. At the time, I didn't see much point in daydreaming or being lofty about a lifestyle upgrade when I was just here trying to survive. But there was a key shift that needed to take place and it's stuck with me ever since.

How much is that dream apartment in the more refined neighborhood? You may have to spend some time going down the rabbit hole of Zillow or Redfin to search houses in the neighborhood you'd prefer to reside in order to see what the cost of your dream home is. See what the mortgage payment is. See what the property taxes are for that home. And calculate what the monthly cost would be for that house. Add in utilities. Then think about the vehicle you want. It may lead you to doing more research, but I'm not asking you to go and test drive cars! I've read a book and I can't remember which one it was where someone went out and test drove her dream car. Just to feel the sensation of what it would be like to drive a Lexus or a Range Rover. *Just to imagine that it was hers.* To see the view of the world from inside that car. And that's *valiant.* But right now, we're trying to build out a rough skeleton frame for what your upgraded life might cost.

Here are a few other things to consider:

Will you have a nanny?

A housekeeper?

Will you go to therapy more or the gym more?

Would you have a physical trainer?

Would you get that fancy Rodan + Fields face soap your friend from college is always selling on Facebook?

Will you get your nails done?

Will you get a boob job?

Will you send your kids to private school?

Will you enroll in art camps each summer?

Will you take lavish vacations?

Will you pay off your student loan debt in 5 years instead of 50 years?

All the way down to what kind of coffee you buy from the grocery store. That Dark Matter coffee is supposed to be amazing, but it's $25 fucking dollars a bag. So if you're now spending $100 a week on groceries, just double that and add it into your monthly expenses spreadsheet.

When I did this activity, I was searching online for two bedroom condos in the bougie neighborhood near my kids' school in Bucktown. I realized something. Bucktown wasn't that far off from where I was living in Ukrainian Village/Humboldt Park. The residents weren't as diverse in Bucktown and thus I did love U.V. but there were sirens all hours of the day and rats and many people still walked home with their groceries in a granny cart. In Bucktown, everyone has their own garage and a BMW inside it. That said, when I looked at some numbers, I was

CHAPTER 6: YOU AND MONEY NEED TO MAKE AMENDS

surprised to find that renting in that neighborhood wasn't that much more expensive than where I was.

It was about $2,100 to rent a super nice apartment with an elevator and a parking spot in the secure garage. I was at the time paying $1,200 for a three bedroom in a broken-down house that the lights didn't come on unless you turned a switch on the far side of the room. Everything was a little janky. The yard was unkempt and I did my best to take pride in my home but when you're renting you have a mentality of "It's not mine" that prevents you from wanting to sink in energy, effort, time or money into a place because at the end of the day, you will just move out and someone else will move in. (I always still painted the walls or installed some wallpaper in one of the rooms so that I could have a pretty living environment. But as for major fixes or yard work, I usually let the landlords take care of those things because it's a common expectation that that is their duty).

I was about $1,800 away from being able to upgrade my life. And if I could make that much more money doing what I was doing, I'd be able to move up in the world and cover a few more costs of living. That was six rolls of wallpaper. Everything in my life now gets measured by the cost of one roll of wallpaper. Three rolls are the average sale, and so I'd need to make two sales to get to the new lifestyle. It wasn't for a year or so that I finally started selling enough wallpaper to upgrade my lifestyle and I landed an interior design client who helped me pay some bills too. Our new coach house was perfect because we had no upstairs or downstairs neighbors to complain about. My kids could run free and wild and make noises or make messes (I was usually the one making the messes with art projects and the like). But, we did it. We made it to the upgraded version of our life. The following year we moved again and upgraded to a new school. I sit here today in a completely different home, four homes after my initial discovery.

When you're done filling in the spreadsheet or homemade table with total, we are going to just sit with these numbers for a moment. We're attempting to do something nuts. You know that, right? We are actively creating a new habit and imagining a new future for ourselves. Your old way was to break even. To pay for everything and be at zero. That was the goal, but we've just created a new goal… and it's going to be a bit of mental gymnastics to train your brain to be on board with this new lofty way of thinking.

The Squirrels in the Attic

One year into being a single mother and an entrepreneur I had made my way somewhat in the interior design scene of Chicago. I had a few close friends who were coming up as blogger/designers at the same time as me, which helped boost my audience. I got featured in Luxe magazine, and for no required ad spend I got a four-page spread called "Meet the Maker" followed by multiple luxury showrooms around the country asking me to rep my brand. I paid to be a part of a network of designers all around the country called IVY. I had access to over 5,000 designers in one place. Yep. Facebook. I didn't do much advertising and I didn't pay a PR company, but slowly I got a few more magazine features.

The boys and I moved out of the house where my second son was born and into a small coach house. It was a tiny house where a garage should have been behind a brownstone Chicago three flat. We had a cement pad out front where the kids could throw a ball- not a yard. We lived right up against the alley where the trash was kept for the whole neighbors; in essence it was a rat buffet. The week we moved in I spotted a shirtless man hiding in the bushes in front of my house and had to call 9-11. Turns out he was responsible for a shooting a few blocks over. The weeks rolled by and I hired some interns to keep me company. I was still sharing a car with my ex-husband. I could barely make ends meet and I sometimes negotiated with my staff to take a paycheck a few days or weeks late.

I was skirting it, barely skimming the positive numbers close to zero...sometimes dipping into the negative. Sometimes borrowing money from my parents, though usually when I asked, they'd send me a whopping $80. I'd collect on any unpaid invoices and I'd reach the positive dollar amount again. Phew! Business was such hard work and such a struggle for me during those times. I felt like every other textile designer I'd met was married and their husband was successful enough to pay all their bills. Their company's profits were their spending money. Some also worked part-time for larger textile companies doing rug design or bedding mockups. I'd wished many times I could have a part-time job to help me pay my way, but I knew that time was precious. Every hour I wasn't shaking the Relativity Textiles money tree, I would be putting energy into something else, then it was an investment in the wrong direction.

It was a revelation for me a few months earlier when a man I'd been on a few dates with posited an idea to me I hadn't ever considered. What if I was doing all of this backwards? Covering my expenses was my main goal. I had this number in my mind that I needed to reach and every sale of $900 got me closer to the goal. Once I reached it, let's say it was $5,000, I would breathe a sigh of relief and hustle a little less until rent was due again. Each month was exactly the same. I had no idea where my sales pipeline was coming from. I had no security and no guaranteed income but the child support I'd fought tirelessly in court to receive from my ex-husband. I was paying a few people to help me, and their checks got cut just as soon as my bills were paid. It was a frantic time.

A business acquaintance named Carl Blando came to visit my home office (my dining room table) one afternoon and he heard the tell-tale sign of a Logan Square coach house. He had recently been laid off as one of the lead sales reps for a reputable wallpaper company and I think he was looking for work. He asked to meet, and I obliged, though I wasn't sure what his interests were. Unfortunately, in the middle of our meeting something horrifying happened. The squirrels who'd bore a hole in our roof were running back and forth in the rafters of the attic. Squealing as they played, the rascals stopped our conversation dead in its tracks. As Carl looked at me to ask *"What the heck is that noise?"* I shyly explained that the landlord was coming to fix the roof soon, but in the meantime, we'd become the play space for Tom and Jerry, the squirrels. He laughed for a whole minute. After we adjourned, I walked him out to his car, and he told me a wise nugget of wisdom.

"Take pleasure in being small. You'll look back on this moment and say 'Remember when we lived in Logan Square?' The place where you may feel frantic and uncertain, as my life did at that time. You may be wondering "when is this going to get easier?" You may be working a 'real job' and wondering what it would be like to give up the certainty and guaranteed income; and to this end I've just literally scared the shit out of you! I apologize. Not every leap into entrepreneurship is so bleak. That said, you wonder how to make the step from where you are and where you want to be and sometimes (most of the time) it feels unattainable. Keep positive, my friend, and enjoy this place where you are. Bookmark this page in your life so that you can come back to it someday and say, "Remember when…" and reminisce about how you've made it so far. It's been three years since I lived in the coach house with squirrels in the ceiling and it's a funny joke now to me. It wasn't funny when I lived there but take pleasure in the place where you are and embrace the wanting better. It won't come just because you want it, but feeling that emotion and staying patient while in that holding pattern is a hard earned skill.

Carl also offered this advice, "To become a huge company overnight would overwhelm your staff and resources. So, don't wish for that. Just grow slowly and eventually you'll make it." Sage advice, my friend Carl gave me. I think back to that now as I'm renting a real house in the northern part of the city. It's safer here and no rats or squirrels live in my home. We rarely hear a siren. My kids bike around the block while I sit inside and I don't worry about them getting abducted. I haven't called the police once since I moved in a year ago. I wonder when it will be for me to look back on this moment and say "Remember when I wasn't even an author yet? When I rented that cute little house in North Mayfair?" Every stage we're at we wish to be further ahead. Revel in the moment you're in for the grit of what you've survived is what establishes your strength and tolerance for new experiences.

As you draft the budget for your upgraded life, don't jump from $1,800/month to $5,500. Find a way to fold new expenses into your normal expenses like the beaten egg whites in a Belgian waffle recipe. Slowly, gently, strategically. And if you find that the income of your Etsy shop starts to really pick up and you have lots of money to spare, maybe don't go buy a new power suit for $400. Put some money aside in savings. Hold onto some of it for a change. Or if you're a Saver, maybe let go of some of it. Donate it to charity or buy something for a neighbor as a gift. Letting go of control and giving it to the universe says, "I choose what I do with my money." Make wise decisions and build up to the millionaire future self slowly, like Carl said, embrace where you are. Remember where you came from because, when you become a thriving artist, you will move to a different level and a bigger life.

Growing slowly, incrementally, inching towards your dream life sometimes looks like a live ice sculpture artist with a chainsaw hacking away at the ice from a cube, bits at a time. No one knows what the hell he's doing. It looks kinda pointless, kinda intriguing, and also pretty dangerous. They'd never expect to see a swan once an hour has passed. Precise details carved into the wings. A quiet, crystal clear rendition of this graceful natural creature that evolved from a huge cube shaped piece of frozen water. Forming your vision may only make sense to you for a while. You don't have to stop and explain what you're doing either. Just keep carving, and wait for the "ooh"s and "ahh"s when you're done. Nobody can see what's inside your head, your dreams shouldn't need to be explained before they've even come into physical reality, but with a few close confidants. Just as you wouldn't judge a chef whose cake hasn't even gone into the oven yet, "That cake doesn't look quite right... Are you sure you added the right ingredients?" Don't apologize for making a mess or slow down your process. Just, stick with your intuition that you're doing the right thing and it will be beautiful in the end.

The Struggle is Real... or Is It in Your Mind?

"The Struggle is Real" is a phrase I hear a lot. And from artists, I hear it because they're constantly in a battle with their objectives. On the one hand, they want to spend time in the studio adapting their work, mastering their medium, taking ideas and putting them into motion on paper or in physical form. They're following their heart in this moment and they are in some ways ignoring other obligations to sustain themselves or their family by doing work that is profitable. And I don't fault them, because when I talk about 'them' I am talking about myself. Every moment spent thinking, making, procrastinating, etc. in the studio is 100% necessary to the life of an artist.

But that struggle is a choice.

I chose to be an artist. I chose to run a business. I chose to get a divorce. I chose to not teach at another school or get a job at Starbucks so I could have health insurance and a stream of income. I chose the riskiest path there is, but it was my own choice. No one forced a gun to my head and said, "Become an entrepreneur." I jumped off the deep end of the pool and just started swimming for dear life.

There is a secret to finding that freedom. To be your own boss or make your own rules. There's a carrot on a string, for me. It's this. The freedom. Freedom that comes with doing something that makes you money is: Ease. Life gets easier when you have some cash. Am I right?

When you can afford all the things that you want in your life, and you don't have to worry about bills and how you're going to pay them. It makes the rest of your time a little sweeter. Time spent making a mess in the studio and then cleaning it up is well earned. All the countless hours of thinking and jotting down ideas and then painting just to hate what you see and cover it up with white gesso again is not a waste of time anymore. Because it's like a luxury to even have that time. It's leisure time. It's the celebration at the end of the hard work. It's the reward. It's called "freedom" or "ease."

If you want a different outcome, you have to do things differently. If you want a better life, you need to be making more money. I know that some of us have such hatred about money that we reject this notion with every ounce of our being! But we can all agree that freedom of how we spend our time isn't free. And I hate to break it to you but sometimes, that means a little less time dicking around in your art studio and a little more practical pedal to the metal. Or a little less time contemplating cleaning up your house and a LOT more time actually DOING it. So that you can basically buy yourself some ease. And buy yourself some space and time for your creative play/work, whatever that is. You have to work hard to make this shift and I'm going to give you some real tips now on how to do that.

Please note: That as I give you this pep talk or hard knocks real talk, please know that I am also still speaking to myself. I'm championing myself doing these same things as I cheer you on. I'm trying to also walk the walk not just talk the talk. Because my goal is to make my first million. So that I can sit near the ocean somewhere with this man I love and my kids (who might be fully grown by the time it happens) and have bought myself a lifetime of ease and free time. That's my goal for me. You have to think about what the goal is for you. And dream big. Because the things you can imagine are possible.

Albert Einstein said, *"Everything that is, was once imagined."* So if you think that all the rich people of the world were handed a check for one million dollars and that's how they started out being successful, you are right about only a very small percentage of people. Most of them worked their ass off to get there. And I'm not writing this to convince you that you should all be millionaires. But you can surely be a little better off than you are now. Am I right? You could surely buy yourself a little ease, no matter WHERE you are in your life right now. No matter how much money you're making. We could all use a little more money.

Because the "monkey mind" will have many opinions about this.

CHAPTER 6: YOU AND MONEY NEED TO MAKE AMENDS

And instead of closing your laptop or putting this paper aside and saying, "That's just plain unrealistic." I need you to meditate on a few thoughts.

You deserve this life. You can achieve this life. You are closer to getting there than you think.

They say, "You've got to spend money to make money." How would your ideas about money have to change to allow money to leave your pocketbook as quickly as it enters? I know it's hard to imagine spending money when you don't have any to spare, but the whole idea is that every dollar you invest in yourself or your business is going to pay itself back tenfold.

Do the simple math. Clara says that she broke down her real estate license into how many homes she'd had to sell before it paid itself off. If the first year was going to cost her $4,000 in licensure, she'd either need to sell one home for $250,000 or two houses for $125,000. Likewise, if she sold only one house that was worth $500,000, she'd cover her expenses with that commission and have $4,000 left over to play with, save, spend on marijuana, or give to charity. I bet she'd choose to reinvest it in herself.

The smartest thing you can do with your money is invest it in yourself. Let me repeat that in another way. I know a woman named Shana. She's got a son about my older son's age. She became a reiki master healer though she currently has a day job as an art teacher. What is one thing that Shana could put some money into that would yield her one new reiki client? How many reiki clients would Shana need in order to completely leave your day job? (This sounds like a word problem on a multiple-choice quiz in the handbook of Artist's Who Thrive workbook).

I know Shana loves her day job because it provides her with the financial security she "needs" as well as a sense of meaning. She loves to have a purpose and her parent community truly adores her. Those kids need her. The trouble is, as she described it to me, her son can't have kids from his school over to play because her apartment is tiny. The kid's friends all live in single family, million-dollar homes with cleaning ladies and fancy light fixtures. She is insecure about how she lives because she is comparing herself to someone who makes more money than she does. Of course, she feels inadequate. The wealthy parents of her son's classmates likely work as hard as Shana. Possibly more. They have a staff of one or two to help them keep up the Administration of Life. They've got a financial advantage and higher monthly expenses. But what's the main difference between Shana and the other moms?

Those moms aren't artists. They think about money as a tool to help them have the lifestyle they want. They don't feel guilty about making money. They feel proud about being able to have the huge home, the landscaper, the fancy hoverboard for their kid to try out and injure himself on. Those bragging rights are the thing that Shana is jealous of because Shana thinks artists aren't deserving of those things. She has ultimately limited herself from being open and receptive to Wealth and a healthy love affair with him. She, Master Healer of other humans, confessed she heals people… for free.

If Shana were to make some effort to do some financial housekeeping (she also confessed to have a living space that stresses her out because it's disorganized) she'd do the following things:

1) **Invest in herself.** Make a business card or flyer about her services and pass them out to the parents at the school. Her network already exists and isn't limited to her role as "Art Teacher" just like a neighbor offering to mow lawns for $25 a

month, and you gladly pay them.

2) **Ask for Money.** Start charging $198 dollars for her one-hour reiki sessions. Not only because her time and literal cosmic energy is donated to each client but because any service a person provides ought to be compensated. Something magical happens when you ask the universe to bring you money! It occurs in weird ways, things that you don't expect sometimes.

3) **Learn something business-y.** She should take a course on Instagram basics or pay for a membership to a health professionals networking seminar. In doing so, she can meet others doing what she wants to be doing and learn from those who came before her. They don't have to be ancient ancestors to have wisdom. Remember, you don't know what you don't know. Learn something new. Anything.

4) **Clean up her house.** Like Shana, even if your home is humble, someone is bound to allow their child to come over for a Pokémon card match and organic Goldfish snacks. If you aren't proud of where you live, then you won't want people over. So, do what it takes to clean up or hire someone to clean up. That buys you one more hour of whatever-it-is-you-do time and the clean house will be worth $100.

I can consistently create ideas for how someone can leave the realm of poverty and skirting Zero. But they're ultimately the only ones who can follow through with the homework. The undeniable truth is that everyone who got ahead had to spend money and time to get there. If you're afraid to spend a single dollar and too stingy to donate an hour to achieving your next level life, then for sure it's not going to happen. If you're a money monk like Shana and you simply don't want to level up for fear you'll burn in hell or never reach nirvana, then fair enough. You don't need money, you're right. But then you absolutely, whole heartedly, 1,000% have to stop complaining that you don't have the life you want (or that other people have fancier things). Because, your lifestyle is a reflection of your earnings, full stop. In Section three, I am going to give you a bunch of ideas to kick start your new life into full gear.

The Portrait of the Artist as a Young Millionaire

I am not yet a millionaire, but I hope to be someday. I am actually quite determined to prove to myself that I can do it. I want you to know that five years ago, if you were to tell me that I'd be doing half a million dollars in business by year five of my wallpaper company I would stop smiling, sit in shock for 0.5 seconds and then tell you *"You're full of shit."* I would never have believed that. But that is what 2019 looked like. 2018 was half as good. The year before that, I was broke AF. And so, in the spirit of just using our imaginations, I want you to pull out a pad of paper again.

Take a few minutes to imagine yourself as a millionaire. We'd all be doing something different. Some of us would be swimming in an infinity pool overlooking the ocean. Others of us would have established a mission in Uganda to provide healthcare to babies with cleft palates. What would you be doing if you were a millionaire? Not saying you won the lottery. I am asking you to imagine an empire that you built, with your own to hands, just like Theaster Gates took a hunk of clay and made it into a pot. If you were to sculpt your dream life, what would it look like?

Chapter 7

The Humans in Your Life

We've talked about Time. We've talked about Money. These are two evils that restrict our access to fame and fortune. We have so much to blame on them, and since they are not real people, we can do that without too much trouble. But the next one is going to be a shocker. It's the people that surround you, and this time we can't slash and trash our attitudes towards them. In fact, we need to tread lightly and do a little damage control. "Successful people surround themselves with great people-- people that are positive, supportive, inspiring, talented, knowledgeable and successful."[10] We're about to take a look at the humans in your life and whether they're helping or hindering your progress.

I say this a lot. When I was in graduate school and my flight attendant husband was somewhere over the Atlantic Ocean on his way to Dubai, I was usually at an art opening. Followed by a cab ride to a dive bar like the Rainbo Club in Wicker Park. We'd drink the cheapest beer there was, leave the smallest tip and save a dollar for the photo booth.

---

[10] https://www.besthealthmag.ca/best-you/wellness/7-habits-of-successful-people/

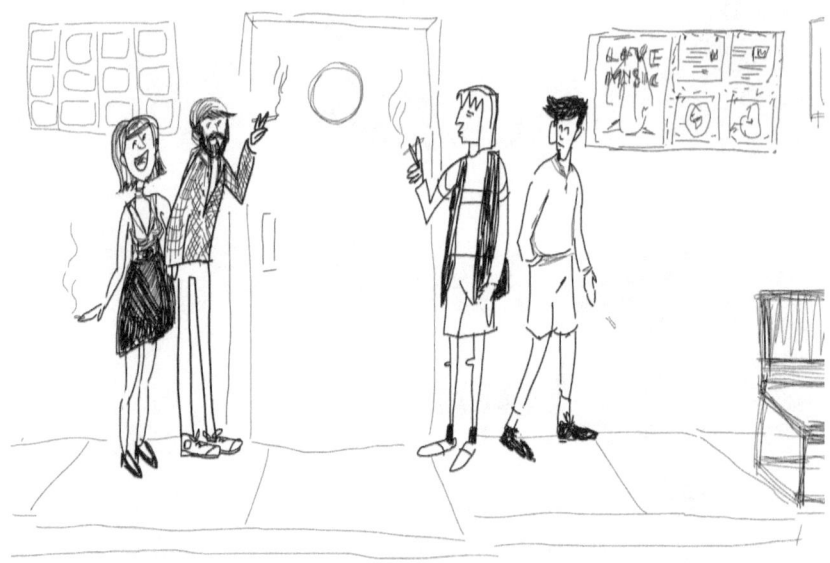

All of the men and women wore skinny jeans with a few splotches of paint on them. We chain smoked cigarettes on Damen Avenue wanting so badly to be picked up by a gallerist. We earnestly worked during the day in our studios like servants to our craft. We spent a lot of time together in art school. We were all so passionate and devoted to art that even our social lives were attending art events and lectures. If it wasn't for getting pregnant in 2010 mid-way through my two-year MFA program, I would potentially still be standing outside the Rainbo Club on any given Friday night around midnight. I'd be wherever is cool now. Talking to whoever was important in the art world now.

Having a child in graduate school is like friend repellant. It started with everyone placing bets on whether or not I had just gotten fat or there was an announcement coming. During our department slide presentation, I asked to go last and included a slide with my ultrasound photo. "This is my latest artwork. It's a collaboration between myself and my husband Karim. It's launching in February 2011." The crowd went wild and David Harper said, "You owe me five bucks, Steve!" They'd continue to go out drinking and smoke breaks and I was so tired I'd lay down in my studio on the floor and nap. I left one semester from the finish line and had my son, Anwar. We stayed home together for three months and I enjoyed that time with him so much even though my persona as an artist was completely lost. I tried going to art openings but with a stroller and diaper bag it just wasn't a good look. I dropped out of the art scene and began a lonely journey into the stay at home mom world. Once summer had passed, I returned to school, though only part time and it took me another year to finish the credits of one semester. I was a mom and a student and an artist. My cohort had graduated, and I was left to mingle with new students and mostly aligned with faculty members who were working mothers.

The humans in my life have routinely been recycled. From the friends I had in high school, to college, to the teachers on the Indian Reservation, grad school colleagues, and then fellow faculty. I feel like I had to don a different persona or wear a different hat for each group. Once I decided on becoming a businessperson I bought a black blazer and asked a friend to shoot a headshot of me. I edited my LinkedIn profile. Later, I joined the realm of the interior world, an off shoot of the art and design world that is more vapid than academic, though they successfully support themselves so who is to judge? I had to again renegotiate my identity like a chameleon changing the business suit into a red floral sun dress with mustard colored tassel earrings so that I could be seen from across the room as a textile lady. I've come a long way from the days of skinny jeans or maternity pants. And the crowd I traveled with changed just as much as the Emperor's clothes.

Let's dial in to your crowd. In accordance with other parts of this book, we want to imagine the crowd of people that you'd like to call comrades. I want to hang out with Brene Brown and AOC. I want to be a boss and a well-known author, not an instafamous designer of luxury thingies that made it momentarily into a magazine. I want to be an intellectual influencer or activist or academic. I want my brain to shine as far as my brass earrings. Who are you hanging out with right now and how are they supporting your vision of who you want to be? Are you seen as you want to be seen? Are there some subtle shifts that need to take place so that you can be in the right place at the right time? Are there venues and events you want to be included in? If there were a stage of expert panelists giving a talk about something, what would you be up there for?

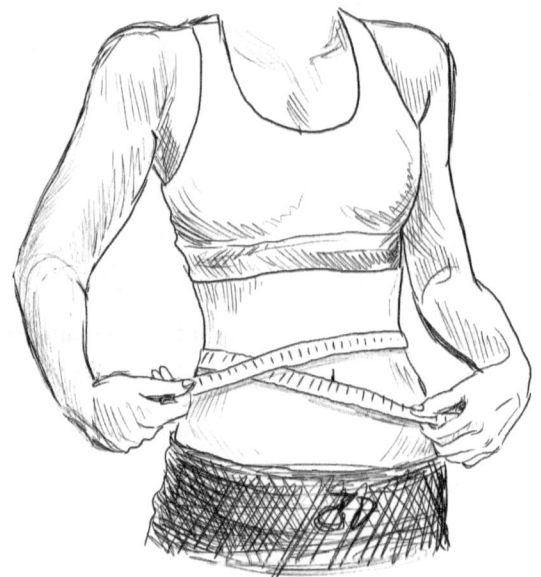

Go on a Diet

Here's a piece of advice: Sometimes you need to go on a diet; A friend diet. A family diet. Just cold turkey quit a person, but just for a while until you learn how to reintroduce them back in (with healthy boundaries this time). If it doesn't feel right to do this because of your specific situation, then don't but, for me, I was at a boiling point-- My mother, my twin sister, and my separated husband were all telling me things that were so negative and so unsupportive that *I had to literally just stop talking to all of them.*

I had to rid my life of negative voices. I have enough negative voices in my own head! I don't need a reality check from a crowd of non-believers. I don't need you to tell me how I've been since I was two, "Super independent but sometimes wore her pants backwards" which I know embarrassed my mother. I don't need to be told that I'm "stubborn" because that is not helpful to me. I'm taking cues now from Tina Fey. "Don't waste your energy trying to educate or change opinions; go over, under, through, and opinions will change organically when you're the boss. Or they won't. Who cares? Do your thing, and don't care if they like it."

I would rather believe that I am persistent, resilient, and determined. Kurt Cobain blares this quote, "I'd rather be hated for who I am than loved for what I'm not." Is there something you're doing that others are trying to talk you out of? Are there dreams that you've shared that others have dismissed? How has that felt for you? Are you able to authentically jump into your new life if these voices are raining down their criticism?

I had to literally go on a diet and eliminate my mother from my life or else every time I'd take one step forward, her judgements would cause me to take two steps back. I did the same with my husband right before we divorced. Can you imagine that? It was the only way to stop caring so much about their opinion. My husband said, "You tried art school, you tried teaching. Neither of those worked. What makes you think you can do this?" So I just plugged my fingers into my ear holes and said "lalalalalala" and stopped listening to them. I stopped calling my own mom. Almost a year after my husband and I separated, my sister told me, "I'm sorry for not supporting you when you left your husband or when you started a business. I was afraid for you," she said, *"and I didn't think you could do it."* My husband said, "You tried art school, you tried teaching. Neither of those worked. What makes you think you can do this?"

Mic Drop. Da what? I mean, it was nice to know that these family members felt sorry in retrospect. But those types of things that people say to you are so deeply hurtful and so incredibly destructive they don't even know that they're doing that to you. They think they're just speaking the truth and they think they're helping you out. What I wanted to hear is "You're doing awesome. Keep going. I support you." Forever. Nothing else. Just that. What they are doing subconsciously is barfing their own insecurities onto your shirt. It smells. They are projecting their fear onto you. They are limiting your potential, your drive and your powerful imagination by reducing you to a "what if" statement. What if you fail? What if people laugh at you? What if you can't raise the money? What if your art doesn't sell?... Look, I have enough monkeys in my own damn mind, I don't need to know your fears for me also!

Starting Over

After my husband moved out I kind of did a "Moms Gone Wild" tour de force. I had a year of being stupid and single. I met my husband in the age before smartphones were invented so there were no dating apps or photo text messaging. Certainly, no Instagram or TikTok. Once

I figured out how to talk to suitors online, I crafted a speech, a persona, and a method for screening douchebags before the inevitable bad first date. I wasn't about to pay $15/hour for a babysitter so that I could meet someone uninteresting. But it all started to sound the same. I'd tell them about my life, my kids, my business… It was like networking for love. I learned not to open up my trench coat too soon or show all my cards. I was reckless sometimes though I also met a dozen very decent people. I fell in love and had my heart broken. Time and time again figuring out that those people weren't for me. No one I dated in the first year would have made a good stepdad anyway, so what the hell was the point? In 2017, one week before my thirty-fifth birthday I fell into the lap of a very handsome politician who brought me flowers and wrote me love notes. We dated for two years and lived with each other for a short time. Our Brady Bunch consisted of my two kids and his lovely son, Dan. During our tenure, this logical, law abiding man never quite understood how I had such a propensity for risk. He looked at me sometimes as if my career was like jumping out of an airplane with a parachute that maybe worked?

I had such a hard time convincing my boyfriend that my lifestyle was on the up and up. Year after year, though he couldn't see the progress, I had doubled my revenue. I tried to show him the dizzying projections I'd made of just how many wallpaper rolls I needed to sell to make it to my dream life. He wasn't familiar with the lifestyle of an entrepreneur. His job in politics was fast paced and always changing but his paycheck stayed more or less the same. There was very little uncertainty in his cost of living. We helped each other in so many ways when we joined households only six months into our relationship since now we functioned as a family. All three kids went to boy scouts at the same time, they played little league, I picked them up from school, he took them to get haircuts. It was always a meeting of the minds to compare notes on stability and goals. He was on the side of safety, calm, and certainty. I was up for adventure, risk and huge rewards (with a lot of elbow grease and determination along the way).

Our fast and furious romance ended two years in. When I broke up with him my mother told me, "Your boys were just starting to get used to life again with a man in it." She told me, "Don't leave him." Even though she had no idea how deeply unhappy I was in that relationship and how he stunted my creativity and zest for life. How many tears had she witnessed from across the country? How much did she actually know about me since our relationship was tense at best? My kids had witnessed my boyfriend and I fighting. They were growing more and more attached to him and Dan. My ex-husband made remarks about how 'that lasted for five minutes' or 'I'm not surprised.' Those hurtful remarks made me feel like more of a failure than I already did. I'd later forgive those people for how little they knew about my feelings, my life, and my story.

I learned a valuable lesson in this season of my life about relationships and how they're not like Kickstarter. You can't set a goal or draft a vision for a marriage and expect that day by day you can hustle towards the finish line. You can't just inch your way to good, stumbling a bunch along the way. It's better to lose sight of the title "wife," and all that comes along with it, almost as an exact opposite of the crowdfunding mentality. The more important goal is to be open, loving, kind and keep your cool every day with no timeline or deadline. Every moment counts in relationships. The way you keep your home and show up, the language you use to talk about yourself and about each other, how much you stare at your phone when they're talking to you... The varying degrees of emotional distress that you convey. All of those things that are stressing you out about work or the kids, the suffering you've sustained before that partner ever walked into your life. All of that has tremendous bearing on whether or not your relationship can succeed. You need to constantly put yourself in check and honestly, you need to let go of the outcome. Wishing to be married, I had set it in my mind to just make it to the finish line. I lost track of any and all boundaries and self-work in order to make my dream of being a wife again come true.

I poured so much energy into my lover when I should've been focusing on my children, my business, myself instead. I didn't realize that 'devotion' was a double-edged sword which I fell onto and cost me my heart. No one had any clue that I was a servant to the new family structure. I had no security in pretending to be the 'wife' to a man with no intentions of marrying me. We neglected to talk about a lot of those things because he harbored his own rolling cart stacked high with baggage from the past. He had grief, trauma, loss, resentment, depression, anxiety, and loss of identity paired with a heaping serving of parenting dilemmas and job instability. Our issues were like cheap enchiladas, just waiting to explode from the back end of our partnership.

Dating is a necessary evil. When you are looking for love at the same time as a major life change like starting a business or changing jobs, it's not advisable to leap into the deep end of the pool. Serious relationships, at best, are a distraction. Using the diet analogy, they are foods high in saturated fats, corn syrup or fructose. I'm telling you not to overdo it when you're working towards a career shift or building your empire. That sounds fairly pessimistic, but from what I have learned in my own trials, if you are to do the hard work of writing a book or pivoting to a new pursuit or career it might not be the right time to be fiendishly swiping and looking for Mr. or Mrs. Right. The immediate gratification that you seek in a partnership is a feeble attempt to soothe the hurt of the past. Gaining validation in the form of a compliment may seem like the exact thing you need to know you are worthy of love and attention. But it's a vast abyss of time suckage. You need to cut this from your diet if you are to create, pivot, pursue an idea as if it's your next best relationship; because it is the only thing that will motivate you or propel you into your future. Not that date with a hot girl that's going to get you one step closer to liking yourself. Being accomplished as a writer will make you love yourself. Having hot sex and waking up in a stranger's bed was nice, but it took you twelve hours further from your goal of becoming someone that Mr. Right might want to marry. Yes, you. You'll be more eligible if you're the type who finishes shit. Who doesn't let your own boundaries down for a quick thrill. Who doesn't lose sight of the prize.

The Lion's Mind

This meditation is helpful to me for focusing. Imagine there is a dog in front of you and you are holding a bone. The dog's eyes watch and follow the bone as you wave it from side to side. When you throw the bone in the corner of the room the dog does what? He runs after the bone, as if he doesn't even have a choice. It's impulse and instinct. Now picture a lion. You're standing in a room with this beast and king of the natural world. You have a bone in your hand again and you're waving it around slowly, taunting him. A lion has his eyes on the bone, but he also has his eyes on you. You're a big bag of bones. A tasty treat for a lion that size. As you chuck the same bone into the corner of the room, hoping for the lion to chase it, what does he do? He takes a look at it. Then sets his sights back on you.

This metaphor is not my own, but it illustrates so clearly the two states of mind. The dog mind is one to chase every little bone that is waved in front of its face. It's not stupid. He is following the thing that looks fun to play with or tasty. Bones in this metaphor represent distractions in our lives, right? It could be sexy humans we're after or it could be seductive part-time career posts on Indeed.com when you're unemployed and trying to find work. The dog mind keeps us unfocused on what we need to be focused on. The lion sees the distraction. He has a choice. He notices it, he keeps his eye on it, but he maintains focus on the bigger picture. Learning how to work with distractions and not follow every impulse is an important state of mind. Your bone could just be thoughts racing through your mind. If you were to follow every thought, it would be like a monkey swinging through the jungle, from tree to tree he would swiftly shift and dart back and forth.

Awareness of the distractions in your life in the form of relationships of any kind is key. Meditations like this one are super helpful to checking in with your body as if you are the Lion. Even when you're still, focusing on the movement of your breath instead of the racing thoughts, is a way to bring quiet and calm and clarity to your life. The constant swiping left and right is a dog's mind practice. The point of meditation is to actually clear your mind out altogether. Having an empty brain is really complicated for someone like me who is always manic and always making a plan. For that reason, if you are constantly hunting for the next solution and searching tirelessly for homes to buy or clothes to wear or other things to fill the void, it might behoove you to stop and put away your phone and just settle into an empty mind once a day. A few minutes of quiet is like a stretch break for my Richard Simmons hamster in my mind. He may go right back to the spinning wheel, but a pause is definitely needed.

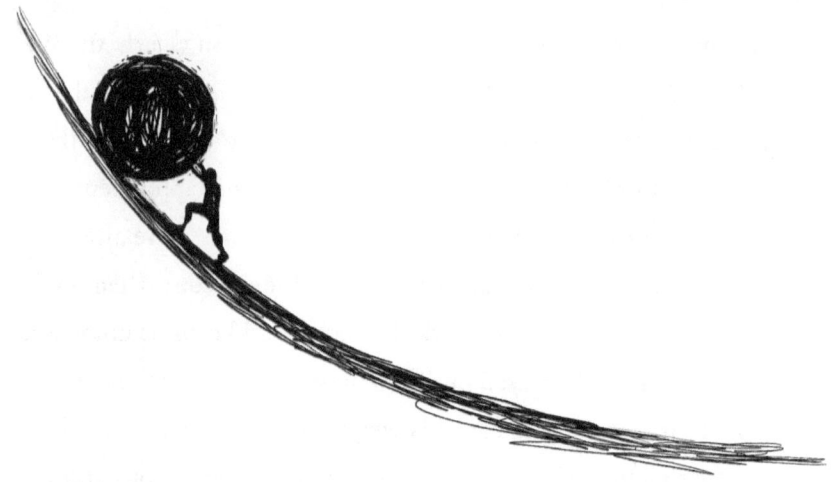

Resistance to New Boundaries

I will warn you. When you go on a diet or limit the interactions with those who aren't supportive of you, those people will take notice. They will clue in to the fact that you aren't excited to hear their perspective anymore. They'll notice you don't call or want to hangout as much. Here's what happened in my situation. Those human beings had a full-on collapse. Catastrophic, toddler-style, grown up tantrums ensued. They did everything they could to pull me back into the vortex of negativity. I wasn't having it. I had to put up a Sue Storm, Marvel's Invisible Woman, force field around me to reject their magnetism. They wanted to make me feel like I was abandoning them or neglecting their feelings. They said, "Now that you have money you don't need me anymore?" or "I guess your new business friends are more important." It was damn tough to not give in. That resistance is their way of protesting your new boundaries. It's typical, so expect the chaos that will come with setting new limitations for those people and stay strong. Don't give in, no matter how good they are at guilting you into having no boundaries.

My mother noticed I didn't want to talk about what was going wrong anymore because I was focused on forward momentum and reaching my goals. She and a few other friends and family kept asking "What's wrong? Why don't you want to talk to me?" I had to make my life sound very boring. Your people can't argue with you being busy. You are busy. You're busy working on your own growth and don't have time to try to heal everyone else's trauma. You're busy building up the walls of your fortress that blocks out all their fears that have been projected onto you and held you back. That construction project is lots of work. They'll wail and kick their arms in the middle of the supermarket practically to get your attention. You have to remain strong in your assertion that what you are doing is important self-work and it has to be priority number one. Be understanding that you have been their sounding board for so long and having you gone leaves them without the affirmations they need. The magnetic pull to apologize and re-devote yourself to their sad story is as strong as being on a real diet and walking into the bakery full of treats you'd normally allow yourself to eat. You must resist the urge.

They say those things to protect you. But they may also be ostracizing you because they're jealous. I believe my ex-husband wished he could see himself conquering life and tackling all the obstacles as I was doing. You'll be inclined to offer these friends and family advice for how they too can thrive, to inject your newfound wisdom when they didn't ask for it. You'll be inclined to want to take them with you. This backfired for me time and time again because unsolicited advice is implied criticism. They interpret you giving them advice as 'they aren't good enough as they are.' People literally can't hear the good place you come from, especially when you are still imperfect yourself! "Who are you to be telling me how to live!?" they might say, "As if you have all the answers!" If your purpose is clear, you stay on track, and you just do your best to stay in your lane. You keep moving yourself forward and eventually they'll become proud and praise you. Once you've made it, they'll act as if they believed in you all along. Just wait out the storm.

I am writing these vulnerable words with a matter of fact tone because I've done a lot of forgiveness rituals trying to move past my family's hurtful words. I write this section for those of you that don't have the loving embrace of a spouse who says your ideas are incredibly inspiring. For those who don't have the undying support of parents and siblings who ask, "How can I support you?" or "What resources can I provide?" For those who don't have children who find ways to get involved or cheer you on. This piece is for you because I know that it's often really hard to muster the courage to do all of this on your own. To be hopeful, to be strong, to be resilient and creative and tirelessly push forward without a single loving embrace. We tend to want to blame our shortcoming on a lot of things, like circumstance or the way we were raised. But where I've come to accept all the past and people who made me who I am the only nugget of wisdom I know now is that I am the only one who can make the choices moving forward. The future is mine to design. If I end up doing it alone, but I have no one to doubt me or convince me I can't, then so be it. Each person's path forward, unfortunately, happens when it's the right time for them-- cosmic timing. This isn't something we have any control over.

Folks, if you're like me and you don't have that family embrace when you jump out into the unknown, you will end up working 33% harder than the rest of the people who read this book. If you're like me, you're not going to complain about it or dwell on the sad fact that you lack support. I'm living proof that there is a thread of hope yet. You will find a tribe. A gaggle. A network or a commune of like-minded creative people who can *see your magic*. These new family members will replace that void to some degree, though maybe never completely. So, if you don't have people who are saying these glorious affirmations to you, or offering to pick up the tab on your startup costs, please keep some faith. You're not going to do this alone. You need to find your net as quickly as possible and stop using the lack of support as a reason to not get started.

Get a New Network

How are you going to learn a new way of being? How are you going to embrace uncertainty and pain, while continuing to push through the tough ideas in your work, struggle with the medium and grow? You think you're going to find an oasis in the desert that is the perfect climate to thrive. Where is this mystical land? Well, I'm not sure where you are living and what the art scene is. If you're not in Chinatown in LA or Manhattan, sorry. I say "sorry" sarcastically because being in traffic for an hour and a half to get anywhere in LA blows. As does the struggle that most artists endure to live in Manhattan- Dust Bowl era poverty with an Instagram appeal. It's not for me. Just because you're not living in one of the thriving art capitals of America doesn't mean that you won't have an art career and make money. You can do that pretty much anywhere thanks to this amazing magical place called "the internet."

First, it starts with a new network. Think of them as a well-planned, deeply dug down into the earth, irrigation system that helps bring water to your desert oasis. They're the ones who will bring you leads, advise you and inspire you. They're all around you. But, they're not your current friend group. Unfortunately, if they were, you wouldn't need to read this book because you'd already be thriving. You don't have to become best friends with these new connections, you don't need to tell them your deepest secrets or share clothing. Not everyone is your proverbial twin sister. But they are going to be your "business" advisors. Mentors. And you will learn to model their behavior much like the chameleon does to survive being eaten. Copy them. "Fake it", in a way. You will begin to emulate them and if they're successful people, you will begin to "make it."

Let's face it, you need to ask for help more often. We all need a web designer, a photographer to document our work, an intern to cut wallpaper samples or stuff envelopes for course credit. We all need an intellectual property attorney once a year to file our LLC to the correct address, since face it, you move a lot. You need a consultant and a coach and an acupuncturist to make sure your limbs don't fall off. And where do you find this diverse group of professionals? In the land of Networking.

Beyond needing help, you may want to try surrounding yourself with people who are prompt, professional, and have prestige. You may want to upgrade your wardrobe to don the attire of a successful person, whatever that means to you. You might want to find a group of people who you can ask questions about business from who aren't going to charge you for advice. You can ask them, not because they've all done the same thing you want to be doing, but because they started down their own path at some point and have the perspective of time and incremental growth that you don't have yet. I don't remember who told me about BNI but it was probably a neighbor who is a realtor. She suggested that I come to one of her meetings and just introduce myself to some new folks. Bring some business cards. See what happens. I had some beautifully hand letterpress cards that always wowed. So, why not?

CHAPTER 7: THE HUMANS IN YOUR LIFE

I attended a BNI meeting in the West Loop neighborhood of Chicago on a Tuesday morning at 7 AM. I remember that because after the meeting I left so invigorated that I joined the group. For about $500 a year, your membership granted you access to one meeting a week. No free coffee or anything else but a CD and book to introduce you to the mission of BNI and a pin to wear (which I promptly tossed). The point of this type of meeting is to pass leads to one another and give each other business referrals.

Not all referrals are created equal. Sometimes you get a lead that leads to nowhere. But, of the leads that generate business, you would write down the amount you received from that customer or client and turn it in to the president of the BNI chapter. At the end of each week, the group will announce how much business was passed. By the end of the year we had passed $1M between 20-25 members! That's crazy but it averaged about $4,000 each month.

Many of the members were from opposite fields as me, in fact the majority were male. There were many attorneys, insurance brokers, realtors, mortgage lenders, estate planners, and a dentist. The women in the group were myself, a PR agent, a chiropractor and a gym owner. Everyone was very professional and had a kind demeanor. It never felt like a fraternity meeting. They mostly wore suits and I invested in a black blazer from H&M so that I could camouflage myself. I sometimes bought coffee because that's all I could afford. Others bought breakfast.

Here's how each meeting went. We went around the room and each of us talked for one minute. That's all you got. They even timed it and moved on when you hit 60 seconds, even if you weren't done talking. 25 minutes later we had all given our elevator pitch. Here's my sample one-minute speech:

"Hi, I'm Erin Minckley the founder of Relativity Textiles. I design and

manufacture hand screen printed wallpaper here in Chicago. We are devoted to bringing foreign cultures into your everyday life by way of wallpaper. My ask this week is for any pregnant women, especially in their third trimester. The reason they are great clients for me is that they are impulsive shoppers. If they like it, they buy it. Also, they're likely decorating their nursery-- but also their entire home. And they need it done in the next three months. So please send me leads for pregnant women that you know! Thank you!"

Then the president would talk about weekly news, referral totals and other relevant information. The next thirty minutes were given to one member to expand on what they do for a living. When it came my turn to talk, I bought in wallpaper samples and showed my wares to the audience. People were awed by my talent, the knowledge I had about my product and the passion I'd put into my business. They asked questions and it was done.

For the next year, whenever someone said, "I'm looking for a good dentist," I would know a guy. Or an internet/audio installer. Or a mortgage broker. I had referrals for people. And I passed as much business as possible to try to prove my contribution to the group. I didn't get tons of leads. The likelihood that someone says this during a conversation, "ugh! I just need to find a good wallpaper in Chicago. Who do you look at?" is slim to none. It's not like a dentist. Everyone needs an OBGYN or a dentist. But I also think that many potential clients were not ready to buy. This is why your ideal client or "ask" needs to be specific. And I learned this through reading the silly book that they gave me when I joined BNI.

When you ask someone for a lead, it is generally someone who is not expecting your call. Like if my dentist gave me his sister's phone number just because she is pregnant, I would have to cold call her and explain how I got her number. She might be put off by my sales-y approach.

"A referral, on the other hand, is a true opportunity to sell your product. These are people that a friend or associate told about your services and they expressed interest. When you call a referral, they will already know who you are, what you do, and in the best cases, may be expecting your call already."[11] This is why most of my BNI contacts would do an email introduction to their interior designer bestie and sing my praises a little. Especially once they had heard my thirty minute pitch and knew more about me and my brand.

Networking is helping you out in a lot of ways. It's increasing your visibility. You are staging yourself in an environment where people know about you and respect you. They are free advice givers because you'll build a rapport with them. They also may bring you business leads and sales. There is a sense of belonging, which is a human desire to be a part of something. Don't get me wrong, these folks may not become "friends." And you may have zero things in common other than this goal of meeting to share business once a week. But, in any event, you are practicing the art of being a professional. You are increasing your chances of making it. You are pretending at first, maybe but you are learning to mimic the rest of the world who aren't artists. And participate in some mainstream ways of dealing with colleagues. It might feel yucky and you might have major anxiety about going. I used to get so nervous to stand up and give my one-minute speech that I'd shake and couldn't eat. My palms would sweat. But I did it anyways.

---

[11] https://www.bni.com/the-latest/blog-news/the-difference-between-referrals-and-leads

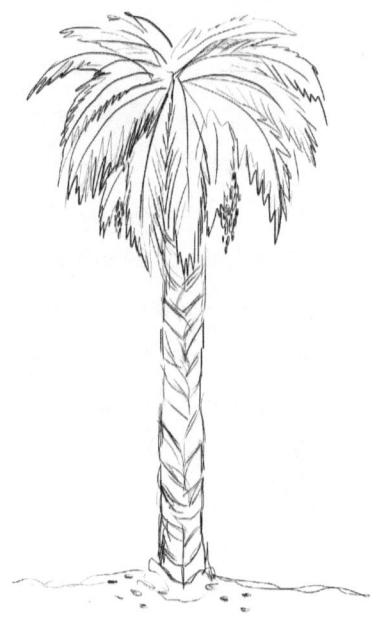

Your Ecosystem Must Rely on You (and You on Them)

You need to begin seeking advice and mentorship; this we know about being coachable. You also need to ask for help, which we're going to talk about soon. This is a food chain, so to speak. It's a natural system like an ecosystem that we learn about in fourth grade social studies or science. You are somewhere floating in the middle, even if you're not yet considering yourself an entrepreneur. There are people who look up to you. You are a teacher and an inspiration to those at work, or church, or to your own kids. Hiring a team of qualified staff will be one of the greatest ways to alleviate stress and give yourself more time, but that means that you need to become an effective leader. Some people don't want to do that. Even still, let's say you remain a one-man or one-woman show forever. Who will you look to for advice? Ask pertinent questions to? Who will you model your art practice on?

Likewise, as you refine your process (or just straight up grow old) there will be people coming to you asking you how you did it. "Can I pick your brain?" they'll ask you. You need to be ready to donate your time to becoming a mentor. Once you've mastered something, share your experience for free. Even though it takes an hour or two from your already limited work week, be generous with your advice to those who come after you. Your flame will not be extinguished if you light someone else's candle from your own.

In the Sahara Desert and other hot climates throughout the Middle East date palms grow in large oases like pine trees grow in mountainous regions of North America. But typically, they need a water source. So they're clustered around villages who have industriously irrigated the arid landscape by digging wells far down into the earth. The sprawling palm forests provide shade and protection for these rural communities but also grow seasonal fruits which are significant to the Muslim religion. Dates are traditionally eaten during Ramadan when breaking the fast in the evening. For this reason, dates are a commodity that is highly valuable to these cultures and can be sold to those who do not live near palm forests.

The people of these regions grow palm trees for food, but the fruits are impossible to reach once the trees reach heights above 10'. They use sticks to beat the treetops and harvest the fruit. Tarps laid out at the base of the tree catch the bounty. Once the tree is 20' tall, they throw stones at the skinny branches that hold the bundles of dates, and the fruit will drop from the treetop easily.

There is an Arabic proverb about a date palm. (I may be butchering it, so please don't quote me.) **Be a date palm.** If life throws you stones and beats you with a stick, you have to just keep giving your fruits. Bear the fruit because that is what you do, not because the people need it. It's your gift. That relationship is one where the villagers need you but in order to reach your dates, they must throw rocks at you. This type of abuse is part of the natural ecosystem, though it may seem to harm the tree. The tree never says, "I'm done with this! I don't want to give you any more fruit. You've been mean to me! I can't take it any longer! I am fruitless now, so leave me alone!"

Or, "when life throws you lemons"? *Make art about it.* Keep giving the world your gifts. Keep growing. Keep learning from the experiences you've had and keep providing juicy inspiration for the world to benefit from. They are grateful for your art, even if they seldom come to thank you. And honestly, sometimes the best work comes at a time of tragedy, pandemic, trauma or otherwise uncomfortable state. The work is your way to process through the hard stuff and find the silver lining. It resonates with others because they too have endured pain and grief and uncertainty. They get to see through your eyes albeit with their own perspective.

CHAPTER 7: THE HUMANS IN YOUR LIFE

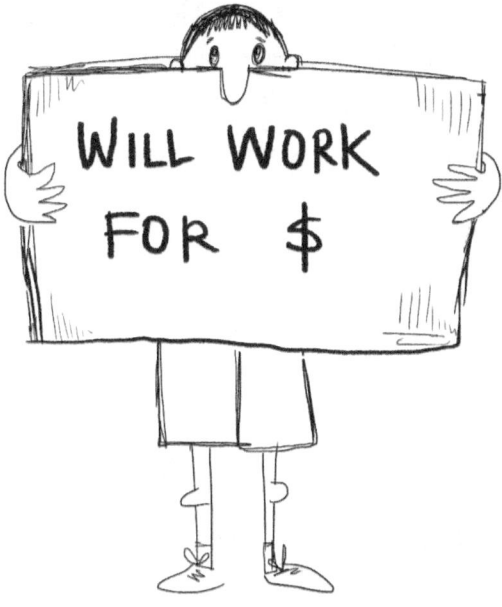

Asking for Help is Not a Handout

At one point and time I wanted to do a conceptual performative artwork. It was time based and caught on video. I would be standing with a cardboard sign at the freeway off ramp. The sign would read "MFA = $125,000 in student loan debt. Career as an artist is uncertain. Will Draw for Money." As people zoomed by maybe they'd give me $1.00. I wanted to see how long it would take standing out there to get the assistance I needed to pay my bills. I wondered if panhandlers made a decent living, because you know, sometimes you hear that these guys make $100/hour. And I was desperate. I felt like everyone I knew was in the same boat after grad school. Many of them were bartending or working at Starbucks because at least baristas got health benefits and a retirement package if they signed up for one.

It didn't occur to me to ask for help. Nowhere along the way did

I think I could do this by myself though. My family situation was very shaky; I felt like an orphan actually since I lost my marriage in the same month that I established my wallpaper business's LLC. My parents are poor and in bad health and always in and out of jobs, so I couldn't rely on them. So I just felt like I was going to have to "hustle" harder and make ends meet the only way I knew how.

As I began digesting every book and seminar I could about how to run a business, I realized that everyone in business had so many resources. So many people hire things out to. So many auxiliary staff that were not full-time employees, but that made their machine run. It occurred to me that I was not going to be able to do this all on my own. But there was some friction around this idea. I was really causing the friction myself and I didn't know how or why, since I was just praying for things to get a little bit easier. I was hoping for one order that would change the curve of my success and launch me to the next level. But that came so gradually and in increments that it never felt like a jet pack had kicked me into high gear.

Do you ever wonder why artists have such a hard time asking for help? I bet you're sitting there nodding with a sort of disdain that separates me from you. Like, I'm sure you're saying "Erin, you're a businessperson. I am just an artist." Right? Well, I'm going to clue you into something that just might save you from starvation. Here's the deal: You are not going to be able to thrive on your own. You are not going to become wealthy on your own. You are not going to maintain sanity if you try to keep doing everything all by yourself. So why are we still so stubborn about this?

Here's my hypothesis. In art school, we are taught that we are the divine creator of our Art. That our genius is the currency that propels our unique visions and creation of sacred art objects. Our process, the

CHAPTER 7: THE HUMANS IN YOUR LIFE

way we make stuff, is almost as important as the THING itself. And therefore, the process becomes part of the story. When explaining how Jasper Johns created his "Bed" piece[12] don't you imagine him standing over his quilt with a bucket of paint?

---

[12] https://www.moma.org/collection/works/78712

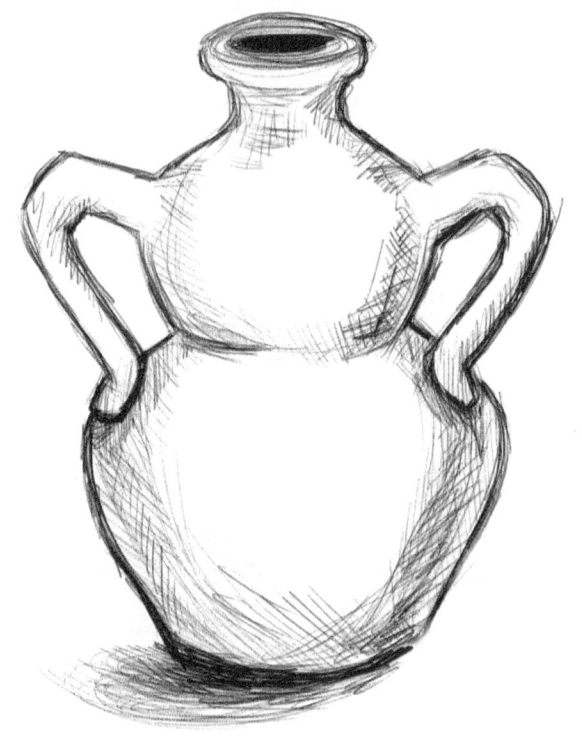

Chapter 8

The New Love Affair

Your Relationship with Your Body

Your body is just a container. Like a modern-day Tupperware bowl or an ancient urn, it holds all of your creative magic, your energy and spirit. It is also the vehicle that gets those ideas onto paper. Your hands working tirelessly to build things, your legs and arms dancing or acting out stories. The power of your mind is strong. We've talked all about the mind in Section 1. But this my friends is one of the simplest and most powerful ideas of all. The body is the vessel that holds your soul. It is therefore as precious as the museum that houses a famous and valuable painting. We need to care for it, maintain it, keep it locked and secured. We need to have an intimate relationship with our own vessel, one of love and care, if we are to allow our soul's longevity to flourish.

Now this may sound hokey pokey to some of you who don't like to believe in spiritual ideas. Fine, skip ahead. But for the rest of us, there's been a nagging suspicion for some time (and especially as we've grown older) that our bodies are important. They can eventually fail us if we aren't careful. They can fill with disease. They can function less as we enter harmful chemicals through our lungs, our eyes, our mouths, etc. We can be susceptible to disease. We can put ourselves in harm's way and by simply not wearing a seatbelt risk our life completely. One huge lesson for artists is to take care with our bodies because we routinely overexert ourselves, diminish the need for self-care and poison ourselves with drugs, drinking and smoking cigarettes.

As you have dug a little deeper to determine the way in which you think about money, time, relationships, the last relationship you might want to consider working through is that with your Self. The self is deserving of love and care. For each of us that means something different. For me, I want to be strong and fit. I want to exercise every day. I want to practice lots of self-care and for me that means yoga, meditation, writing, biking, walking the dog, painting my nails, massages, etc. Anything that I can do to take care of myself five to twenty minutes a day. Naps. Singing loudly in the car when no one is with me. Hugging my puppy.

Dopamine is the reward chemical in our brain. When we complete a task or do some self-care, dopamine is released. When we eat food we like or celebrate little victories, our brain sends us a "hooray!" signal with dopamine. Oxytocin is the love hormone. When we play with a cute animal or baby, when we hold hands with a lover, when we receive hugs. Giving and receiving compliments is also a way to release oxytocin. Family therapist Virginia Satir once said, "We need four hugs a day for survival. We need 8 hugs a day for maintenance. We need 12 hugs a day for growth." While that may sound like a lot of hugs, I'd like to stand as living proof that hugging my kids and friends is addictive and gives a pleasure sensor in the brain a squeeze. Serotonin is a mood stabilizer chemical in the brain. The types of activities that release serotonin are meditating, running or exercising, being exposed to sunshine, swimming or cycling. Those little bursts of energy remind us that our bodies work and even five minutes can be like plugging in your phone to recharge when it's running low on battery. Endorphins are the brain's chemical for killing pain. Watching comedy shows on Netflix and laughing can be an essential daily routine for letting some endorphins enter the brain. Some people believe in essential oils to stimulate the brain to release endorphins. Dark chocolate is also a way.

Self-care can be done alone, and it can be social. During a global pandemic, we have no choice but to participate in a yoga class virtually, or air hug. It's a sorry substitute for the real thing. But remember that there are several different types of self-care and you don't have to practice each one every day. Physical, Emotional, Social, Spiritual, Personal, Spatial, Financial, and Work/Career related self-care are all ways. Try to maintain a balanced giving in all of these areas, rather than thinking that just one area will satisfy the Self's endless need for care. They are all plants in your greenhouse and they'll all need watering. Alone time can be a great way to schedule in these practices, if you are introverted or consumed by caring for others most of the time, AKA parenting. Just being in nature is a spiritual practice or journaling. Getting enough sleep at night and rest during the day is crucial to a healthy brain and body.

What I think many artists and creative people lack is a sense that this stuff needs to be prioritized to the top of the hierarchy of your daily to-do's. It may feel selfish or like a waste of time when you're always on the go, busy, energized and making things. When it all feels really overwhelming and starting is the hard part, I like to do lazy practices like writing that can happen in my bed or on my phone. The basis of looking after yourself is self-love. Not the narcissistic kind where you stare into the mirror saying, "who is the fairest of them all?" That is false self-admiration. Having love and compassion for yourself defines you as a precious human being who deserves to be treated with respect and care and who has the right to be who they really are. It is a spiritually based ideology, but in all a generous attitude towards your Self. It is essential to know that if you look after You on every level of your being that living the best life you can will be the outcome. Thus, in order to thrive, you have to pay homage to the vessel and everything it holds.

CHAPTER 8: THE NEW LOVE AFFAIR

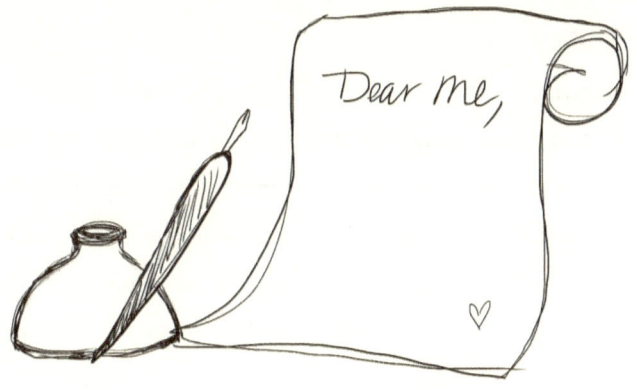

Writing a Love Letters to Yourself

The week that Corona virus hit I was in Orlando at a three-day business conference. The topic was to learn how to master your idea and get it out to the world as quickly and effectively as possible. The focus was to MAKE MONEY doing it. Much of the principles they were teaching to the 150 people in the room were pretty rudimentary to me since I had already started a business. But on the second to last night of the conference the last speaker of the evening was a hypnotist. He was accompanied by his wife, his lovely stage sidekick. He spoke about his own personal story of not being able to read and getting kicked out of Catholic school about halfway through grade school.

He saw a hypnotist perform at a carnival one summer and was fascinated by the show. He later learned how to hypnotize people and as he asked for volunteers to come up on stage, we all knew we were about to be entertained. Several volunteers ended up being put to sleep and performed all kinds of silly tricks like playing the air guitar or patty cake with the person sitting next to them. But, as he spoke, he told the story of all of us. We are trapped in a state of fear and inhibitions.

241

We don't allow our dreams to rise to the top because we are nervous to speak our truths.

He captivated the audience and brought me to tears when he stated that "Someone along the way in your own life may have told you that you can't. That you weren't worthy. That you didn't have the brains or bravery. And you believed them." This guy was a grade school dropout and a millionaire. He instructed those who'd been on stage that they needed to immediately start living up to their potential. They needed to love harder, earn more and dream as big as possible. And achieve all of their goals in life. He demanded it. He told them to stop believing outside voices who criticize and tell them they can't. That resonated with me so much because I'd been carrying those voices around in my emotional baggage and it had gotten so heavy. He gave me permission to let it go.

Who knows what the people from the stage performance ended up doing with their lives! To this day, I wonder what has been holding me back? Who had told me I couldn't? And where did I go wrong in believing them? It motivated me to take the place of those naysayers, the voices in my head or the real live people in my life and replace their scripts with the one I wished they'd tell me. I began to write. I started writing a letter to Erin from someone who's voice had been telling me "you can't." It was remarkable how easy it was to allow someone to tell me they love me. That fictitious character turned out not to be my ex-husband, ex-boyfriend, mom or dad. The letter was written from me. To me. About me. Here's what it said verbatim:

Day One:

"A love letter to myself.

I am committed to your success because I love you. You are the most special human I know. You are kind and caring beyond belief. Thank you for being loyal to me all these years. I've got big plans for us. Don't you ever listen to those nasty people who don't believe in you. Do not let them get you down. Their grief is not your problem. I give you permission to be the best and shine forever like the bright star that you are. Go out into the world and tell your story because it is worth telling-- so many people will value your honesty, your humor, your sense of wanderlust and you Just. Might. Change. the world; one person at a time.

I will always be with you, cheering you on. Much love and gratitude, <3 Me"

Day Two:

Good Morning, Beautiful.

You are beautiful today as always. Thank you for taking care of me in the past few days with enough water, good food and restful sleep! It makes a huge difference. You are doing great. People need your inspiration. In this lifetime, there is no reason not to share your story with as many people as possible. You have been so brave. So passionate. So daring and bold of character. So generous and compassionate. So selfless. Don't forget that all of the love you gave away was not a waste, even if it did not come back to you in the form that you desired. Something wonderful is headed your way. Keep pushing-- full steam ahead-- towards your dreams. You will make it. The world will be yours and your children will learn from you how to dream big, pursue what they are destined to be and help people to live a bold life -- by your example.

I stopped writing to myself after two days because I got on a plane from my fancy hotel and stepped out into a world filled with panic and fear. School closed down the following day for good and my kids ended up at home for the rest of the school year. An invisible pandemic swept my city and our country. It shut us out from the rest of the world, and we began to do some rearranging of priorities. I for one was not accustomed to this much introspection and isolation. I wonder what would have happened if I had kept up the habit of writing a letter to myself every day.

At once, it felt very self indulgent and narcissistic to be telling myself "I love you" and "You're amazing." But those words were the things I'd been yearning to hear from my lovers and family and friends for thirty seven years of my life. Sometimes I would hear little bits and pieces of pride or love. But, unfortunately, there was never one person who was able to honor me as much as I thought I deserved to be honored. No one who stood by me, even through my crazy ideas and late-night artistic adventures; my messes that lead to innovation or my spontaneous travel trips to get inspired by new lands. There was never anyone who consistently showed up at the finish line to cheer me on. There was never anyone who said "Flaws? Nah. You're perfect." Except me. I was the only person who stuck with me through all the up's and downs. I was the only one who kept forgiving myself time and time again for arguing or getting upset when things didn't go my way. I was literally the only one who looked at me in the mirror and said, *"just keep going."*

And it dawned on me that I would be the only one to do that

forever. So if I gave up on myself as a friend and as an inspiration, my flame would just *go out?* I realized I have a duty to support myself in the way that I'd been searching to be cared for by someone else all along. And in fact, what I learned when I wrote myself that letter was that it was time to let go of all the grief I'd carried about why no one talked to me that way. All the disappointment about how I'd chosen the wrong husband, or my boss didn't keep me on staff, or my students could care less what knowledge I'd brought to the table that day... I needed to let it go and focus on giving myself that support that I needed so much. Because I may never be able to find it in the external world and *that was okay.*

Put very succinctly by blogger and coach Kara Loewentheil, "Radical self-love as a woman is a radical political act – and especially as a woman of color, or a fat woman, or a disabled woman, or an immigrant woman, or or or, and and and. The more identities you live in, the more radical it is to love and accept them all."

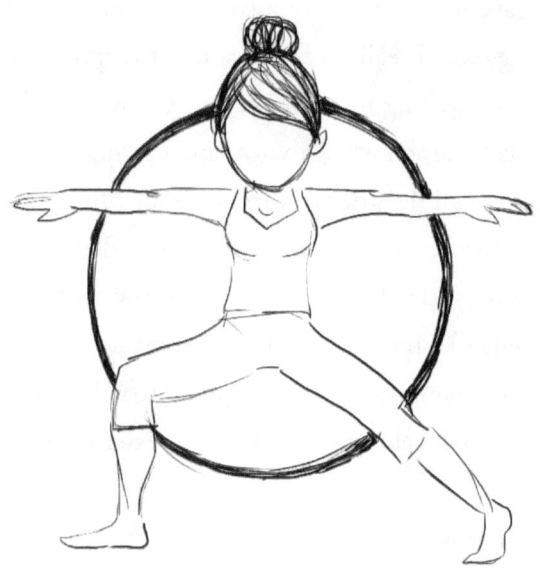

Exercise is Legit

One thing that separates my experience from many other artists is that I was an athlete in high school and college. I used to run two hours a day in college and was in the best shape of my life. As my life has gotten busier and busier, my stress levels heightened with work and life, one thing that I can say for myself is that personal physical health is seriously important to staying balanced emotionally and mentally. I no longer run sprints or exercise in one hundred degree weather, but I do try to move my body in the morning when I wake up and during the day several times. Being an active mom has kept me pretty thin, that and a healthy diet. But I will say that I noticed a very dramatic shift in my mood when I stopped exercising for a period of time.

I am not a doctor. I am a sister and daughter to women with mental health challenges. Being a witness to the emotional ups and downs of the internal world, I can't help but wonder what might change in my family's lives if they were to practice daily exercise. How it might regulate moods. I can cite several texts that prove exercise can reduce stress levels and anxiety. The risk of depression is significantly reduced by a daily exercise routine. Social well-being is an added bonus if you are doing gym programs or team sports. The human brain is also dramatically boosted by exercise including improved cognitive functioning (which includes decision making and learning).

What I think is lacking from books about how to be an artist is that we need to participate in some more mainstream ideologies. It's rare to find artists exercising together, though there are volleyball leagues for insurance brokers and running groups for financial advisors. Team sports have historically been diabolically opposed by the art kids in high school, since their black mohawk or chain wallet didn't match the mesh shorts provided as a PE uniform. So many artists think they can sit this one out, but I urge you to take one for the team.

You don't have to become an Olympic disc thrower or a triathlete to be moving your body and raising your heart rate. You could do jumping jacks in your underwear at 5:45 AM or bike around the park two times after your Life Drawing class. Yoga and swimming are great low impact ways to start moving and getting in touch with the integration between mind and body. It's a powerful advantage to be that coordinated, to overcome difficulty and to reach personal goals. My goal is to do ten push-ups. I've always sucked at doing push-ups. But if I were to be able to do that I might feel on top of the world because I was at my personal best. Some of you may laugh! But that's what it is for me.

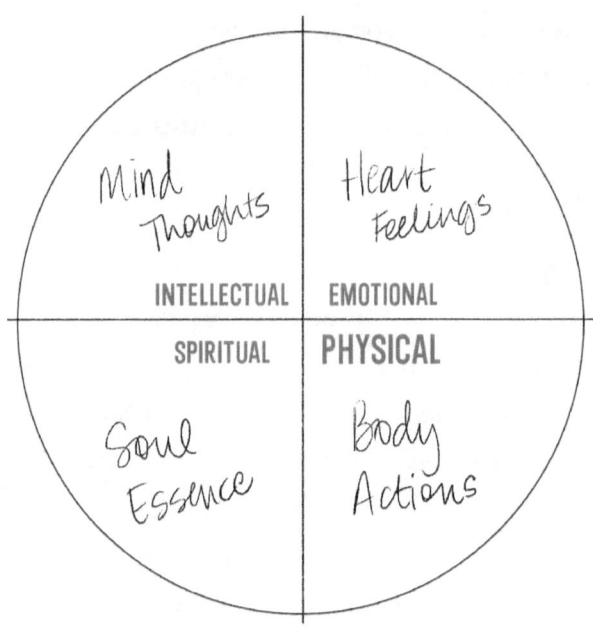

The Quad's (Not Your Leg Muscles)

In the midst of writing this book I was able to take several online Zoom courses. I was recommended something called "the Hoffman Process" by an old friend from middle school. She'd learned to leave her childhood trauma behind and went on to live a more vibrant life because of the teachings that she gained from the Hoffman Institute. Their core belief is, as I came to find out, that we all have four parts to ourselves, otherwise known as the "Quadrinities."

These four parts of ourselves assume different roles, different periods of time in our lives and different responses to life. In simple terms, it put my F + T = A conclusion to the test. Because it disproved that Action is always the result of our Thoughts and Feelings. That only accounted for three out of four of the quadrants of their model. What we are going to get into later in the book is the fourth, missing piece.

But, for now, imagine that you have been neglecting your physical body. Your mind is working on overdrive to process all of the data you're giving it. It's smart as hell and proving itself. Your heart is an earnest little machine, which comes from an earlier stage in your life, maybe age 7. When you had come to many of your basic conclusions about how life is, from a feelings standpoint. Your Emotional self is just as important as your mind and mindset and it has often been neglected too. We're rarely patient with it because-ugh, feelings are hard. It's easier to ignore them or drown them out, that's why grown-ups invented drinking and Netflix, to numb the inner child.

But lastly, let's talk about this vessel that actually is a container for your many selves. It's the only physically concrete part of the Quad model. We see it and we judge it. We judge other peoples' vessels. We shame them if they're not skinny enough and we applaud them if they're supreme athletes, even if they're emotional self is quietly sucking his/her thumb and their intellect is a door nail. Our bodies are representing us a lot of the time. So as artists, why do we dismiss them? Why do we value creativity more than health?

If you're in the midst of considering changing some of your habits after reading this book, I don't want to fool you into thinking that changing just one part of your life is going to make you into a successful person or a millionaire. Most successful people do not neglect their bodies. They don't dress in garments that look like they belong on a scarecrow. We need to start engaging in a conversation with ourselves about habits in all of the arenas, and physical fitness is just one place where we as artists fall on our faces. If we are to improve the perception of artists (or simply of ourself first) then we'd need to begin to care for our body as if it is an antique Grecian urn circa 600 AD. It's precious. It's valuable. It could be on auction at Sotheby's for a pretty penny (or on Tinder for free!) but it's not. It's in the private collection of you. Don't toss it around like a Tupperware container from the Chinese food place. Treat it with respect and dignity and put it on a pedestal.

Madame C.J. Walker once said about her hair products that if she can make it easy for one black woman to have good hair then she just helped her become more confident. One more confident black woman in this world lifts up all black women. It makes slow shifts in the public's perspective of black women to see one business owner or one beautiful example of a woman who is valuable. Madame CJ Walker was the first self-made millionaire in America. She was also the first female millionaire. She was also the first black millionaire. The fact of the matter is, she won the gold medal in three different categories with her homemade hair cream. She ran it like a business. She saw herself as worthy and valuable. She came from nothing. She watched as people told her she couldn't do it. She waited for the right place and the right time to expand her business and start a factory, a salon, and she sadly saw the end of her marriage when her husband's greed and pride interrupted her growth. She endured so many obstacles and hardships as she grew. But she persisted. And, if you haven't watched the Netflix show about her, I strongly recommend it. Her integrity as a "creative" person is inspiring but her appearance was as important as her grit and her heart.

You may think that there are some coincidences here about the way I talk about being coachable, setting goals, becoming persistent, and learning to fail and then get back up again. However, the analogies that are littered throughout this book about sports and working out aren't a mistake. The way we keep our finances or establish a business is mostly out of habit. When we change our habits it's because we are unhappy with the outcomes. We want more. Just as you might be staring in the mirror at your naked body and blaming Corona Virus for the extra roll around your midsection (is that just me?) you can whole heartedly explore a solution (AKA a goal) for that. If you set your mind to it. If you stop talking trash to yourself and letting pessimism get the best of you. If you find like-minded people to walk with for exercise. You can literally use every principle in this book and apply it to your Vessel. Give it a try.

My Body is _____ (list five things you think right now).
Physical Fitness is _____ (list as many as you can).
The biggest obstacle(s) for me getting into the best shape of my life is/are _____
(give some space for multiple answers)

Let those answers sit with you for a moment and see if any of them are serving you. See if any of the attitudes you hold about your own human frame are as depleting and sabotaging as the attitudes you had earlier in this book about Wealth. Health and Wealth are not out of reach. Unless… you choose to think of them as impossibilities. The thought of changing your routine is brutal, I know. I've had two babies. My vessel got big and then small again. Twice. I had to learn how to use it all over again. It was full of babies and then milk and then empty again. All that stretching and contracting does weird things to a female figure. Most of them are not Instagrammable, though recently there have been more ad campaigns depicting new moms as beautiful. I am happy for that. But no matter your gender orientation or age, your body is going to warp and grow and shrink and change. That is a fact of life.

The part that we have not usually considered is that You are NOT Your Body.

You are not fat. You are a magical soul who lives in a 'fat' frame. If you think that frame is too chubby, then you are judging yourself based on appearance. You are rating a whiskey barrel in comparison to an antique Chinoiserie vase seen in museums (or a Kardashian woman from a magazine). Those are made of porcelain and spun on a wheel (The Kar-disaster-ian butts and tits are made on a surgeon's table from synthetic materials which shall not be compared to your God given, imperfect flesh). Or maybe your vessel is more like a pinch pot that was made by hand. See, we can't compare our bodies to anyone else's because that devalues our own form. You are a vibrant soul that lives inside that form and you cannot be defined by your hair, or loss of hair, your skin or stretch marked skin. Your eye shape, your brows, or any other attribute. *The comparison model always fails.*

Love the form you're in. If you want to change it, change your routine. Research the form you want and how to get it. Maybe even hire a coach to help you achieve it and hopefully, you'll build confidence once you do that work. When you achieve the "perfect" body, I hope you can come to a place of loving yourself. Regardless of if your waist is two inches thinner, your butt two inches plumper, etc. you just might be able to love yourself anyway. When we body shame, we eliminate the importance of the deep magical essence of the person. The hero in all of us is inside. Sometimes, the most beautiful and fit people are not happy. Sometimes they are not even successful. We wonder why they have drinking problems or marital affairs. It's because even with the perfect vessel, the inside is empty.

CHAPTER 8: THE NEW LOVE AFFAIR

> *"Perfectionism is a particularly evil lure for women, who, I believe, hold themselves to an even higher standard of performance than do men. There are many reasons why women's voices and visions are not more widely represented today in creative fields. Some of that exclusion is due to regular old misogyny, but it's also true that—all too often—women are the ones holding themselves back from participating in the first place. Holding back their ideas, holding back their contributions, holding back their leadership and their talents. Too many women still seem to believe that they are not allowed to put themselves forward at all, until both they and their work are perfect and beyond criticism.[14]"*

Do a little reflection on what it would be like to just be whole and complete, just as you are. If you loved your body every single time you saw it reflected in a mirror. Are there new scripts to try and follow? I have a post-it note on the mirror in my bathroom that says "YOU ARE GRACEFUL," because someone once told me "You are many things, Erin Minckley, but graceful is not one of them." I let that haunt me and hurt me for way too long. So I needed a reminder that I'm not a klutz or a Tasmanian devil. When I see that note, I say to myself, "Damn straight. I'm a freakin' ballerina." I'm not the most poised but I can treat myself as a ballerina would. I can't dance for shit but I know what grace is. Grace is underneath the skin. It doesn't count the swear words I use, it doesn't mind the many times you left the car door open. I prance out of the bathroom when I see that note, even if my tutu is imaginary.

---

[14] https://www.goodreads.com/work/quotes/44044797-big-magic

"Compassion wears Saturn's rings on the fingers of her left hand. She is intimate with the life force. She understands the meaning of sacrifice. She is not afraid to die. There is nothing you cannot tell her. Compassion speaks with a slight accent. She was a vulnerable child, miserable in school, cold, shy, alert to the pain in the eyes of her sturdier classmates. The other kids teased her about being too sentimental, and for a long time she believed them. In ninth grade she was befriended by Courage. Courage lent Compassion bright sweaters, explained the slang, showed her how to play volleyball, taught her you can love people and not care about what they think of you. In many ways Compassion is still the stranger, neither wonderful, or terrible, herself, utterly, always.[15] "

What would be so wrong with you making friends with Compassion? Let her borrow one of your sweaters. Let her be your friend too. We all keep Compassion at bay because we are afraid that if we make friends with her that other people will laugh at us. If we are nice to ourselves we'll be ridiculed. We shame ourselves because we think that it's what we're supposed to do. We say jokes about our weight or our size or our shape because we're trying to be relatable though we may not know that not everyone hates their vessel. Don't think for a second that you're going to *make it* to the big leagues and shine like a bright star while constantly staring in the mirror and insulting the body who looks back at you. This area of your life requires some work. Hard, introspective work about what it would take to love your form.

---

[15] The Book of Qualities, by J Ruth Gendler. 1984 Harper & Row. page 23

CHAPTER 8: THE NEW LOVE AFFAIR

The Whitest I've Ever Felt

A note on Skin Color: While we're on the topic of seeing people for who they are as opposed to what they look like, it comes to mind that race in America has reached a peak presence in our consciousness. More so than ever, we are beginning to see people, hear people, and allow for their lives to matter just as much as our own. When we say that we don't see skin, sometimes BIPOC, Black Indigenous & People of Color are not impressed. In fact, they want you to see their color. They want you to see their color and value them. Each of us presents ourselves in the way that allows self-expression and beauty to be seen by others. It is imperative that we have conversations with people who look different than us about what their lived experience has been. We need to ask them how they feel about things. We need to listen to what is in their hearts without assuming we know. We need to make space to share our friend Compassion with them.

It hasn't been easy, this 243-year journey as a country. We've made a lot of mistakes. We've taken advantage of many human beings in the short time that we spent dominating this land. White people especially have some reparations to make. Bodies of color need more love and support and care than ever. Let's lead with compassion for how the black, indigenous and various colors of bodies have been undervalued for a long time. Let's try to fill our hearts and minds and lives with pictures and people of every color. What white people often lack is a diverse visual palette of friends and coworkers and classmates. Staying with the pack, they rarely venture out of their comfort zone. To place yourself in the midst of the unknown can feel scary or alarming, but people of color assimilate on a daily basis in order to thrive.

What about sending our children to the school nearest our house even though white kids are a minority? What about hiring someone who is on an F-1 visa and needs the job more than anyone in order to stay in this amazing country and live out their manifest destiny? What about including models of color in your fashion shows or Instagram posts? What about illustrating black girls in your children's book pitch about mermaids? Let's begin to be more open minded and open hearted about where we position ourselves in our daily lives. Let's be more inclusive about who we imagine or depict so that voices of all people can be heard, admired and our work can resonate with children of mixed identities.

Before I was ever married or went to art school or became a mother I knew I wanted to teach. I had graduated college and worked a variety of dead end jobs including painting houses and bartending. When I entered the teaching credential program at my alma mater, I wasn't 100% sure I wanted to teach art, but my dad had been a teacher and, to some degree, I thought I knew what to expect. Summers off and some school politics. I got hired as I was leaving the parking lot from my first interview and suddenly, though I wasn't even finished with taking night classes, I was going to be a teacher.

At the wise age of 23, I became the new art teacher on an Indian Reservation in southern California. What I didn't know was as soon as they'd hired me, they gave me only thirty days until I quit; they were hedging their bets on whether or not I'd be able to handle the job. My students, grades seventh to twelfth, came from twelve different tribes and were bussed in from many cities in the Inland Empire and Orange County. Much to the bewilderment of many of my white college town friends, I did not say "How" to greet the principal. He was a loud boisterous man who passed as white; Donovan Post swore more than he said intelligent words. He was popular amongst the kids, because even though he looked white he was from the tribe. With a small percentage of Native American blood, Mr. Post was still an "Indian."

One month into teaching I went away to a national education conference for Native American students. I learned from many Native scholars and educators. I was refining my ability to teach within a specific cultural landscape as a white person. The students hated me for the most part. Not only because I was regimented and by the book (I didn't know anything better since I was literally going to school at night still to learn how to be a teacher). We learned about the color wheel and pointillism and Frida Kahlo. Often my kids would say things to me like "Why aren't there any Native artists you can teach us about?" and I felt dumb for not having any relevant curriculum.

When I got back from the conference there was some bad news. A former student of the school passed away. As information became clearer, I learned that the school had been shut down the day before due to it being a crime scene. The student, Nadine, was stabbed to death on the baseball field at our campus. She was involved in a knife fight with her cousin. She dragged herself from the baseball diamond to the field house where she had performed as an all-star basketball and volleyball player. Her lifeless body was found in the early hours as well as her cousin who was still breathing on the baseball field.

We were all told to attend Nadine's funeral. Nadine's younger sister Yolanda was in my art class and she despised me. I didn't know what to do to support her family and since I was one of the only white staff members I tried to stay in the back of the small white Catholic church on the reservation and blend in. As the funeral procession ended, the teachers were asked to carry the floral arrangements from the chapel to the gravesite.

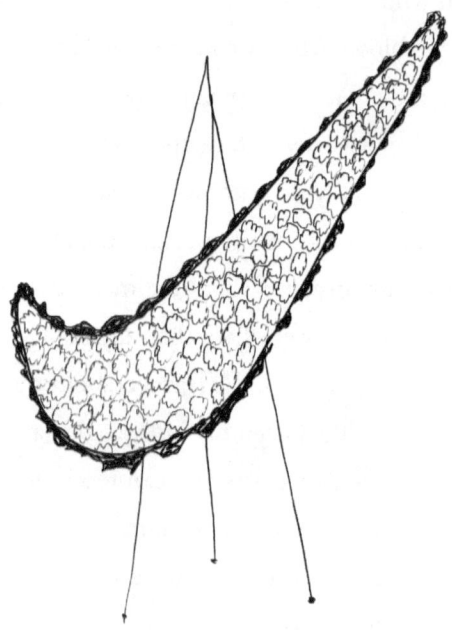

My job was to carry a Nike swoosh shaped arrangement, made of white carnations; it was about 5' high and was taller than me with the metal stand.

The irony for me as a white person attending a Native American funeral is that the last thing, I thought I'd see was something so "American" as the Nike swoosh. The graves were marked with white crosses which also felt inauthentic, since it was how Christian graves would be marked. But it was as Native as it was American, seeing as how Nadine was an athlete and an *American*. The funeral was brief and there wasn't any Indian dancing or chanting or prayers in languages that I can't understand. We left in silence and I began to reflect on the symbols that summarize our lives.

What we often fail to remember is that some people carry the heaviest burdens. BIPOC (Black Indigenous and People of Color) carry generational trauma, stories from their ancestors that are forming their everyday modern reality. I became acutely aware of how to treat others, as Native kids don't like to make eye contact. I began to take notice of how every "body" I came into contact with was a vessel, carrying precious cargo. They are host to a seven year old (Emotional), a highly skeptical brain (Intellectual), and an essence that you won't know unless you put in effort to meet them (Spiritual). Each of us holds the quadrinities inside of us and the body is just the physical shape that carries our sensitive pieces around. Being as Gentle and Kind to others, even those I don't know, as I am with your own body was a reframing that was necessary.

On the "res," life was very, very different from where I'd grown up. Each home had its own plot of land where the trailer was at some time converted from a portable home to a permanent home. Some homes were built like ones I recognized. The front lawns were dead or just dirt and some people had fences around their property. Some homes had driveways. Some had pit bulls as their alarm system. Many homes had large expensive cars parked in the driveway like F150's or even Hummers. The disparity between poverty and wealth existed in one yard. Most of my students were first generation wealthy people. Their parents had grown up receiving "commodes" or public food donations for indigenous populations who ranked as some of the highest poverty communities in southern California.

That was until the Japanese investors started arriving with big plans and blueprints. They built a casino on every reservation and the names of the casino's normally corresponded to the name of the tribe. Pechanga. Marengo. Saboba. Every single person who belonged (on paper) to the tribe and could prove their heritage was given a check each month for a percentage of the profits from gaming. As people from all around the area would drive onto the res to throw away their money on gambling, the Native populations finally had a chance to experience some of the finer things in life.

My students had dog tags in 24K gold engraved with Tupac Shakur's face. They owned brass knuckles and designer clothing. They drove Hummers and other expensive cars even though they were not able to pass their driver's license test. Many of my students read at the third grade level. Our school, and other Indian Schools existed to push Native kids through the education system even if they weren't always reaching state standards. Many students had a 'D' average and read well below their grade level, but they had to graduate if they wanted to continue to receive their checks from the casino. A few of my students were addicted to drugs, a few of them raised by addicts. A few whose parents were in jail.

As an art teacher, I had lofty dreams to inspire my students and instill a love of creating things by giving them new skills and techniques to create. Quickly I realized that I wasn't going to become anyone's hero or friend or role model. My students looked at me first as a white person, secondly as a teacher/authority figure. They had no desire to connect with me because they held some deeply rooted beliefs that I was their enemy. They had strong reasons why, and I understand on a deep level how much impact the white community at large has had on the daily lives of Native people. It's not just a historical atrocity that occurred in the past, it's a current and ever-present hierarchy happening on the land inherited by these peoples' ancestors. Some of my students really hated me. I had students who threatened to beat me up or slash my tires. I had a student write "slut" on one of my charcoal drawings at the front of the room. It was a struggle to reach my Toyota Prius before I'd start crying. I'd cry all the way home sometimes. I felt helpless to do anything about the large problems these kids faced.

CHAPTER 8: THE NEW LOVE AFFAIR

I remained friends with a few of my students from 2005-2006 and I hold tightly to my memories of my first year in teaching. The good and the bad, and yes, I made it to graduation day before I resigned. What has stuck with me the most is the ability to look from another set of eyes. I am not saying that I know what it's like to be Native American because I taught art on the res. I have no idea what struggles they have or the pride they hold in their hearts about their culture and their place in society. What I do know is that it's a tangled and interconnected web that's more complicated than a TedTalk about colonialism or diversity.

History has a funny way of being framed by whatever textbook we discover in school. Culture is more layered than a fictitious narrative like those found in the movies "Smoke Signals" or "Coming to America." The only way I would have ever been confronted with the complex reality of race and its role in our country's fabric was to be sleeping under the quilt of my experience on Soboba. Each night tucked in, contemplating where I would be if I were my student. I was confronted with my whiteness. My fragility, my helplessness, my guilt. I was asked to see all white people for what they'd done and to monitor myself. I had to look in the mirror for the first time. Many of my actions were flippant in a way only white people can act, like the rules don't apply to them or they can anything. I had to change my language, lower my eyes and talk to the space next to a student's chin, rather than looking them directly in the eye.

I experienced prejudice for the first time and I almost wish that every person who's never been hated for their skin color could walk a day on the reservation. I now know what some people see when they look at me sitting in the front of the bus. I make eye contact in 2020 with a person of color who is sitting in the back and I wish that I could Airdrop them my thoughts.

"I understand. More than you know."

I wish to differentiate myself from other white people, but I cannot escape pigment or skin. So, I have to stand up and be an ally, I have to seek ways to be a co-conspirator. I have to insist on equality in situations, microaggressions towards people who are not white because I feel a sense of duty to do so. For my Native kids and for my half-Moroccan sons. Sometimes it takes someone who looks like me to chant the battle hymn in order for people who look like me to listen, as if it's not enough that our whole BIPOC population is trying to push and propel the mass consciousness forward. Sometimes you have to stand up for the bodies and the voices who don't have a stage or a microphone to speak into.

This note is for white folks: If you want to learn, you should seek any opportunity to teach or serve a community that you are unfamiliar with. Giving back usually begets some of the best lessons about the self. Choose something totally foreign. Learn a new language, maybe not literally, but metaphorically. Invest part of yourself in understanding what it's like to see yourself from the other side. Teach, volunteer or become an ally. Examine your whiteness and ask hard questions like "How has my life been easier because I was raised by white parents? In a white neighborhood? With a white pastor, boss, teacher, idols…" Engage in dialogue with your white friends about what life is like in other places and confront them when their entitlement shows. Interfere with the notion that we all have the same opportunities because it's simply not true. Disrupt spaces that are not inclusive. If asking these hard questions doesn't make you feel grateful and at the same time sickened about the place where you come from, the skin you wear each day and the advantages you've been given I don't know what will.

We all happen to be the same color on the inside. Our human organs are relatively alike. We all breathe and love and dream, even if about different things. We all deserve to take up space.

In closing out this chapter about Relationships, I want to highlight the agency that you have to make a shift in your narrative. Our relationship with time, money, people, our beliefs, our bodies is the single most political move you can make. To take charge of your life is to draft a plan for moving forward. You are limited only by your imagination and the physical limitations of time and labor. Within these restraints, which are different during each season of your life, you can make a big or small impact on your life starting right now. Depending on how supported you feel, the tasks seem easier. The more you support yourself with positive encouragement and healthy lifestyle choices, the restraints seem to lift to ease your daily struggle. It's as if the universe is giving you the gift of ease and grace, when truthfully, you've chosen to give it to yourself. Care is key.

Care for yourself might mean establishing healthier boundaries with others and it might mean showering yourself with acts of love. Getting help might mean surrounding yourself with new friends or hiring some professional advisors and personnel to streamline your work. All of these actions can combine and coalesce to construct an organized system that works towards your mission statement. People who believe in what you're doing will be drawn towards you and you will find joy and pride in the work you're doing. Most of all, as your following grows, don't forget to place value on bodies/vessels other than your own. Treat others as if they are a true friend, when maybe they're a complete stranger. It takes courage to change your own habits. Be courageous in your interfacing with others and you may discover the world is full of lots of magic.

Part Three

How to Achieve Results

Now that we've dissected Resilience and how to overcome mindset challenges as well as the Relationships we need for a thriving ecosystem, let's put our money where our mouth is. Let's make the changes needed to insist on a better life. Let's think big, work small, start where we are, and work with what we have until the you-as-a-thriving-artist vision comes to light. Let's rally together our resources, dig deep to find our true calling and get out our tools.

It's time to build the canoe.

TV host and author, Mel Robbins, states in an interview that she is the survivor of sexual assault. For this reason, she purposely stays constantly busy and on the go. "Can't catch me" is her go-to mentality. I relate to her survival mechanism because distraction is my frenemy, allowing all types of bad behavior to arise.

Here's where the ADHD tactics that my brain spins me into turns against me. I have created an alternate world to live in sometimes. I've become so focused and distracted with the wrong things sometimes that I look up to reality and I'm late for the meeting I really didn't want to attend. I'm constantly staying less accountable to my own obligations because drawing or doodling or taking a walk after eating a THC gummy is just way more awesome than reconciling last year's taxes.

Are you purposely distracting yourself so much so that you are avoiding the important or hard stuff? Results come when there are responses like Action or Curiosity or Commitment. Results don't ever come as an outcome of avoidance. Being present to your life is hard. Checking in with your four parts of YOU is also hard because you might be afraid of what they say. Sometimes, as I do, artists fall back on excuses like "Oh I just have a hard time focusing, because of my ADHD." However, maybe the naked truth is I'm just focusing on things that have NOTHING to do with what needs attention most.

That's my "catch me" type of thinking. When I set my email inbox to a vacation response saying "So sorry, we are out of the office..." but I'm in town and delaying responsibility, I'm not on vacation. What I needed was an emotional vacation. My emotional self is thirteen years old. She is listening to her first CD in the closet of her bedroom, hiding from her mom. Adulting will have to wait. Responsibility is on hold until I can get ahold of my four different personalities and rise to the occasion of adulting.

Robbins articulates this well when she aptly describes "discipline" as an ugly word and instead she prefers to call it manipulation. That word has such a sour taste for me but let me explain what I think she means by it. To be disciplined is to have all kinds of power and control over your body, your habits, your day-to-day routine. It feels like Boot Camp. I considered writing this book as an artist's "boot camp." If you felt like so many other people were simultaneously earning their rank as artists then all you needed was a step-by-step system to go from zero to hero. The problem with that type of framework is that it assumes a lot. It assumes we are all defined as needing help, that we are all starting from scratch or that we all lack discipline. It assumes that I am a coach or teacher or sergeant ready to whoop your butt if you don't complete the obstacle course in under 4 minutes flat. Boot camps are for herding lazy people into formulaic workouts and ropes courses and there's a certificate at the end or a Biggest Loser weigh in where we figure out who the Most Improved Player is.

The distinction I'd like to make is that I'm not teaching you how to run a business. I'm teaching you how to be the boss. I'm not here to give you the plan, I'm here to coerce you into coming up with your own plan. I'm here to open the closet door, rip off your headphones, pause the rock music playing on the WalkMan and ask you politely to stand up and come to the dinner table. *Life is waiting.* [My hand outstretched waiting for you to accept].

Discipline is required (if you want to see results) and a desire to manipulate your future is a plus. There is no money back guarantee because you're in charge of doing the reps and fighting the dragons yourself. Failure might even be the outcome. But it's progress. It's being on the path that was designed for you. Don't drag your feet. Don't cause everyone around you to be held up by your childish tantrums.

Manipulation has many meanings. I don't want you to play mind games with yourself, or bribe yourself, though I did mention rewards as a way to entice your spirit into doing the work. Manipulation is what Theaster Gates does to clay. It's what Joan Miro did to thin metal wire to make the mobile you can find in the Museum of Contemporary Art in Chicago. It's what jewelry designers do to turquoise and silver, and black and white film photographers do with aperture settings and stop bath regimens. Manipulation is to *mold*, to *manage*, to *bend* until it's almost about to break. To manipulate words (as a writer) is to arrange the page, the sentences themselves, so that the meaning rises up and takes hold of your reader's heart and mind. Writers manipulate words so that the meaning sticks, and every word is useful in achieving that goal. Required: refinement and editing. Writing is spewing and then organizing. Sound, strategic manipulation ramps us as artists up for the betterment of You, Inc. Robbins says "You can learn how to manipulate yourself into the person you want… I see my own bullshit and I push through it."

Results don't come easy.

I wish I had better advice than that. It seems a little limp as I sit back and stare at those four words. Like, 'no, duhhhhh, Erin, I kinda knew that." But did you? Because, for a long time, I did but never pushed through my own bullshit excuses and mental barf.

No lie, I thought this book would take about eight weeks to deliver hot off my fingertips and onto Amazon's library. Instead, I have gone through waves of self-congratulation and self-annihilation. I've procrastinated, though I'd like to think it was the healthy kind where thoughts brew in a witch's cauldron until they're ready. I've conquered every obstacle, including a global pandemic that left me and my editor reading together on Google Docs and meeting via Zoom. As my children run amuck, they now know that I am writing and need to be left alone. My 38th birthday coffee mug says, "Fuck off, I'm Writing," which makes my six-year old laugh hysterically. I quarantine my own guilt about being a negligent mother into a remote place in the basement of my subconscious and opened the door to creativity long enough to spew out a few pages at a time.

Financially, I can't afford to take this "break" from my everyday work of running a business, but somehow, I found a way. And as I approached my 38th year around the sun, the universe has conspired against me. All my bullshit showed up on my doorstep like the dead bird a cat caught as her trophy and left for me. It's dead and stinky and I want to dispose of it, but I also may hold a silent one-person memorial for it. Salt to an open wound: I lost the co-dependent relationship I was in and now I'm cold turkey manipulating my future, whilst trying to give advice to a bunch of people about how to be rich and famous and free.

Results don't come easy. For anyone.

I wish I had a magical key to unlock the mysteries of the universe for you or a ship like the Milano in *Guardians of the Galaxy* where I whisk you away to a place where you can safely and joyfully practice your art and thrive. I wish I could teach you how to manifest it all, as if imagining could magnetically draw the dream life to your bed where you sit in your jammies and read. I wish I could give you a twelve-step program or a boot camp that was so concise that all you had to do was accomplish one homework assignment each day and at the end of three weeks—POOF!—you'd have it all whipped.

But like Chapter two said, there are a lot of things that you're going to have to do that aren't that much fun, aren't intellectually stimulating and are painstakingly repetitive. I can tell you what you need to do in vagaries: Make more art. Make more money. Find more time for these two things. Make excuses to talk about your art more. Stop feeling bad when those things become successful. Rinse. Repeat.

Becoming an Artist Who Thrives is not Jillian Michaels' workout DVD (which is covered in dust in my top drawer) called "21 Day Fix." Her body is a chiseled specimen of what happens when you discipline yourself enough to do the reps. In three weeks, I really did have abs once. That's why I kept the DVD. Because it works. Only problem is... I no longer own a DVD player. I'm holding onto an old plan for the perfect body and my excuse/obstacle is the absence of outdated technology. The excuse stops me, makes me freeze because guess what? If I powered through the excuse, I could get creative and go to the gym or run outside or cue up a number of apps on my phone that could generate workouts based on the day of the week instead.

Do you have excuses that no longer serve you? Outdated plans for outdated forms? What's a new plan? What's the easiest way forward? What's one step you could take right now towards the new plan?

In this section, you will walk you through a few areas that likely need work. 1) Channeling your magic, 2) Focusing on launching one thing at a time, 3) Expressing your unique worldview, 4) Instating some critical structure, 5) Using your time well, 6) Learn to delegate and dump, 7) Make lots of lists and 8) Putting all goals on a timeline.

If you've already mastered all of these areas, consider yourself lucky. If you half-ass mastered them, level up. If you have no hope of ever achieving mastery… I give you thirty seconds to pause and feel sorry for yourself. Okay, time's up. Get your big girl or big boy panties on. It's time to work. The life of your dreams is out there. All that is required is courage. Confidence is an acquired taste, like a fine wine or a French cheese. Right now, just try. See what you can do. Build up your tolerance to achievement of little goals and then go for some Big Hairy Audacious ones. Here we go.

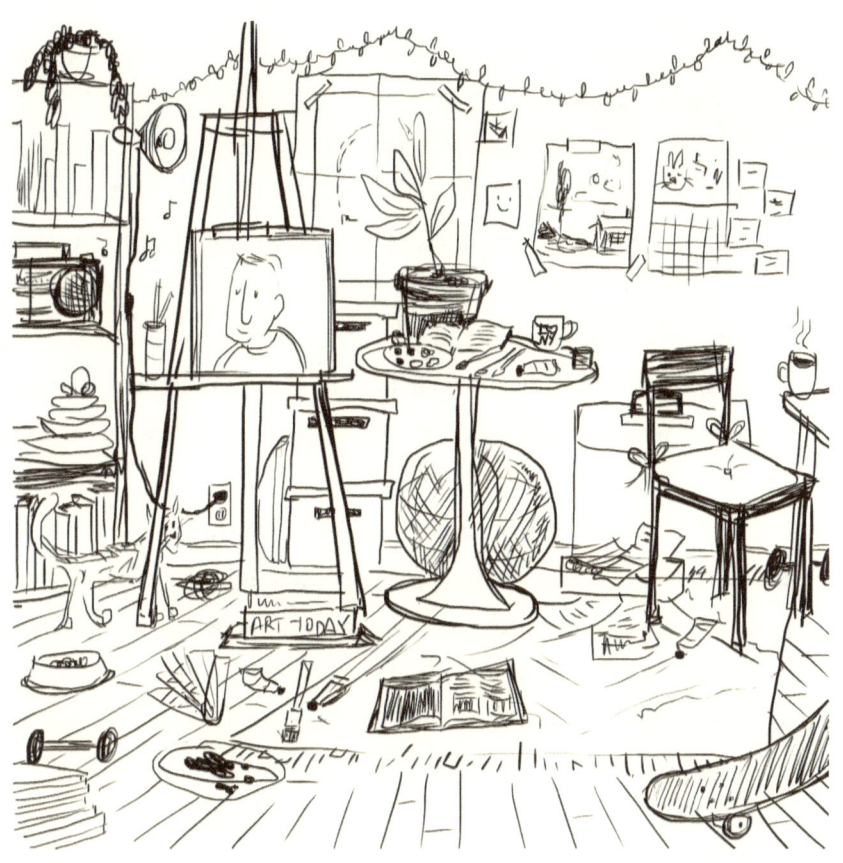

Chapter 9

The Studio Mess Conundrum

During the pandemic, we were confined to our homes and many people lost the luxury of working in a studio space where exciting innovation occurred. Many lost access to co-working spaces or gyms where the energy of improvement and growth and community vibrates them out of the ordinary and closer to greatness.

Where we work wraps us in an energy field, catapulting us this way and that. Artists. What is your unique situation? Where are you working and what are you working on? When was the last time you looked around and whispered: "This is where I create."

If you're working a day job, let's focus on busting out your side hustle. If you're earnestly creating with no intention of monetizing it, and this book gives you an itch to see what could happen?... Scratch that itch. Because we want to see you thriving through your artful revolution of self. Be demanding, insistent, vigilant. Habits are everything, goals are the outcome towards which we are working. And your studio....? *Your studio is the sacred place where your magic and creativity and dreaming takes physical form.* Aside from your tools and your two hands, your studio is the most important variable in the equation.

Let's get real. Does your beautiful mess help your creativity? Some creatives firmly believe that their chaos is organized. That's what they call it: "organized chaos." They claim they know where everything is. They need to make a mess in their studio in order to let the art ideas run free like butterflies at a nature center (or dung beetles who are going to take all the poop lying around and roll it up into something useful).

We all need to splatter paint sometimes and get it out of our systems. We need to make saw dust in order to build the stretcher bars from scratch. That makes a mess, yes. We need to crumple up drawings over and over again until the waste basket is full. Then progress has a real profile that others can see. We need to fill pages with writing and sketches and then stack the full Moleskin notebooks like soldiers waiting for their orders on a shelf. We collect the tools of our trade in the corner of the room to establish a physical representation of failure, or progress, or accomplishment.

But, what of the things that were made? Where are those finished works of art? Productivity in the studio ebbs and flows. There are times when we get super busy because there's an exhibition coming up or a client coming to visit the studio. There's a flurry of excitement and the studio takes a toll. The mess piles up and the pencil shavings cover the floor. And then? Like the tree in my front yard spent all spring growing and protecting its buds, all summer sprouting leaves that absorbed all the sunlight they could to nourish the tree. In this season, autumn, the leaves expire and wilt and fall. Littering my yard. As the respectful tenant that I am, I recently visited the hardware store in anticipation of all the weekend raking I'll be doing. Disposing of the evidence that that tree created for months to just go back to being bare and naked, paring down for the inevitable winter.

What is the seasonal calendar like in your studio? What is the life cycle of your trash bin? Does it fill every day? Every week? Only once a year? Would the space deserve a weekly routine cleaning? Should your desk be cleared of debris every morning so that you can start fresh? Is the disorganization leading you to be more creative or the opposite?

Have you considered that stack of bills on your desk to actually be *prohibiting* you from getting work done? Is your creative space also your kitchen table; your studio and home have no beginning or end and the mess just sprawls from the front door to the back? In that type of environment, are you allowed to keep projects in a state of completion ranging from "done" to "horrible mess that is in progress?" Or do you need to just pile it into some plastic Tupperware or wicker basket that you'll never get around to organizing? You do need to use the ironing board for pressing work shirts, but instead you're using it as a Heat 'n' Bond Station for the felt samurai costume you're crafting for your first grader, three days before Halloween. Let's talk about your spaces, the emotional landscapes there, your bad habits and an actionable plan for getting it cleaned up. I'm not as cute or calm as Marie Kondo, so apologies now for kicking your ass into high gear.

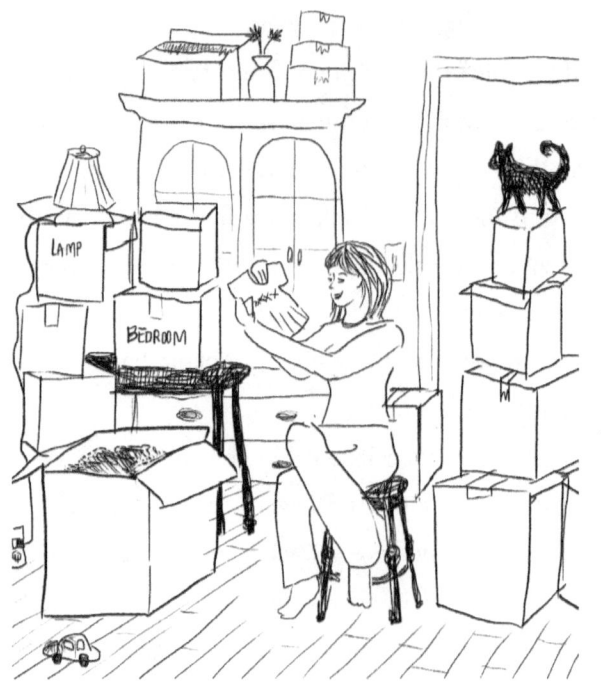

Hoarders Need Love Too

I was helping a friend named Sandy move from her tiny one-bedroom apartment this spring—before Covid-19 banished all my friendships into isolation. Her daughter is the same age as my oldest son, and they were in the same kindergarten class. We went trick or treating together and when I learned that she was a single parent also, I invited her over for a glass of wine. Sometimes mothers host play dates so they themselves can have adult friendship jam sessions. We confided in one another about online dating, the trials and tribulations of finding the right career and parenting solo. I felt an immediate connection with her because she is a very humble, caring and funny person. We both secretly love country music and wouldn't dare tell anyone else that fact.

Sandy *is not a hoarder.* She's an artist like you and me. She would not consider herself an artist, at all, but she is as creative as they come. Sandy has worked all different kinds of jobs since I've known her. Property management, elementary school teacher. But what I found out after talking to her long enough is that she's a certified massage therapist. In return for me helping her sort through her closets of stuff and pack to move, Sandy promised me a free massage. I've had massages. Sandy's are by far the best. Her hands are so skilled at human touch that I left feeling loved. That might sound creepy, but I could physically feel her love of her craft coming through during the hour-long ritual. Massage can be an art form can't it? Again, I define artistry loosely as anything one creates with their own two hands. Massage is ephemeral, there is no product left behind. But what Sandy left with me was a level of relaxation that was almost divine.

Sandy never practiced the 3-2-1 blast off mentality of "do it now or not at all." She had saved little scrapbooking elements hoping to someday make a photo album of her daughter's different stages. She'd collected CDs and DVDs to watch for later, though her daughter was already in third grade and wouldn't ever want to see the Elmo ABC's movies her mom had sentimentally saved. She had a thousand art supplies for her child, but my guess is she is holding onto her own artistic dreams by superimposing a love of crayons onto her offspring.

Her craft, her artistry, had fallen by the wayside as her primary concern was parenting and bringing home enough money to survive. She's had two clients that she massaged for the past twenty years. She even admitted to once giving a massage to Grace Jones in a hotel in Chicago, who afterwards exclaimed, "That was spiritual." Grace Jones insisted that Sandy come upstairs to her room to meet her son. That was her moment to grab an opportunity, to have a celebrity client for life. What if Grace Jones had flown Sandy out to NYC once a month to massage her or taken her out on the road!? It would only take that one client to potentially set her up for word of mouth referrals to wealthy clients who are friends with Grace Jones. I prodded her a bit about why she never followed through with her. "She gave me her number on a scrap of paper. It's probably around here somewhere." We both scanned the room at the boxes of stuff knowing it would quite possibly take Sandy a lifetime to hunt that number down.

Why do we, as artists, hold on to things? Sometimes creative people have a vision for something but there is a moment that blocks them from following through because . . . . wait for it: there's less risk when you put things on pause. You can't fail if you don't try.

Helping Sandy sort through her belongings brought up emotions and thoughts in me that caused a tidal wave of questions. How much stuff we collect might be an indicator of how much struggle we've had.

The important stuff gets put on the back burner when we are surrounded by our own junk. The junk, albeit a reminder of the past, is a distraction from the present. It's a constant nagging parent bugging us everywhere we turn. It's towering over short statured humans like Sandy. It's bad feng shui. It's soul sucking. It affects us not only on the physical level by taking up space or collecting dust, it inhibits the emotional freedom we all seek. It bogs us down spiritually too. We are not our highest selves in rooms full of clutter. So maybe, and this could be a stretch, we avoid cleaning up because we are afraid of what we will find. Without our belongings, like on a retreat at a Buddhist monastery (where we can't even look at our emails or phones, read or write) all we have are our feelings, thoughts and actions. All we have are our hearts, our brains, and our bodies. It's pretty much all we need (except we're American so we also probably need toilet paper, a bar of soap, and a toothbrush. Oh, and the cooling pillow we've become accustomed to and our Apple watch? $F + T = A$ is the equation of dealing with your emotions and intellect with dedication towards action. Action of any kind is good action. One step forward is action, and so are two steps back.

Single moms are likely the strongest, bravest and most resourceful creatures on planet Earth. Single dads, you are also unicorn ponies. I'm not knocking anyone else's situation, but when you are responsible for another human and also trying to take care of your own "Administration of Life," it's really tough to make split second decisions or take action when it comes to parting with the stuff. We don't always have money for new clothes, bikes, sleds, etc. When the time comes for the next size up in clothes, will we be broke? I have kept clothing, books and toys not knowing where we'll live in a year or if I'll have the means to afford it again.

Do I keep this? Is it sentimental? Will I use this for another child (even when you don't have a sexual partner yet to help you create that child)? These psychological traps often debilitate us from making decisions about what to keep and what to let go of. Yet, if you want to create a life that is new—like becoming a thriving artist after years of letting others ride that boat—then you'll have to make SPACE to create something new. Making space and sometimes letting go. Getting rid of things. Decluttering. Pairing down. As if you were packing to go to the monastery. Ask yourself, "Do I really need this? Will I use it in the next six days? Have I even looked at it in the last six months?" If the answer is no, it's time to let go.

Myself, I will admit to having tremendous guilt about waste. Throwing something away when it is "still good" seems grief inducing. When "there are babies starving in China" and I discard a whole box of Chewy bars that got melted in the back seat of the car, I feel an emotional weight. I keep old cans of house paint because I am the rescuer of materials that don't belong in landfills.

That fantasy has flashed through my mind time and time again: The fantasy life where I will have room for all of this stuff. A garage. A basement to store things. I keep bins of stuff so that someday if I have a "Sewing Room" I can set up my grandmother's machine and keep fabric on shelves. What fantasy life are you keeping things for? The one where you fit your jeans from high school? The one where you have a huge studio? How far away in the future is that? Is it ever really going to happen? Are you keeping stuff in vain? Is it weighing you down in the meantime?

I believe all artists are nostalgic. We don't have a *purge* bone in our bodies. A true artist holds onto things for a surface to draw on, a "project" that they want to complete, or "materials" to paint with. The clutter is the ego's way of proving we are failures, starving artists, incapable of organization. When we are surrounded, confined, strangled by all this STUFF it stands in our way of creating! Less stuff = more focus on what is important. The real tools of our craft are usually quite limited. For me as a writer, my computer and reading glasses. As a textile designer I need a new sharpie and a pad of tracing paper. Some scotch tape and scissors.

I can't fail at painting pictures that sell if I never paint them. Wayne Gretsky can't miss a goal if he never shoots it. It's easier to clutter up our spaces and erect obstacles to getting it done than it is to DO IT. Write, draw, sing, sew, create. This stubbornness, this hoarding is self-induced, and our studio is self-made. Hey! You! You could create something someone wants to look at! Or read! Or buy! Or enjoy! If only you had the space to create in.

Our computer desktops become the venue for business to happen, especially in a world plagued by a pandemic or a crashing air travel industry. Teachers are teaching online, artists are selling work online, galleries are opening exhibitions virtually, coaches are coaching online. Entertainment and commerce found a new platform to call its home, and our screens are intimate stages for our wildest dreams to perform. Your computer desktop is also jammed with eight million files, endless garbage of yesteryear. Your 'Folders' and cloud is a sea of disorganization. You can't find anything and there are always seven tabs open. Parse through it. Dedicate one hour a week to just weed through it all, making room for flowers to grow. Make folders with easy labels to remember and dump things en masse. Approach the computer like a Virgo would with a bunch of sticky notes or a label maker. Section things off and organize because your experience sitting at your desk will be more calm and relaxed, perhaps even enjoyable once you know where things are and the junk is in the trash.

My ex-boyfriend saved everything his son wore before he turned 4 just to remind him of his kid's childhood. As if keeping the items will instill the memories better. As if the memories and the objects are linked. *But they aren't.* Memories exist in your subconscious mind. Feelings you had about your child live there in your brain and are resurrected not when you see a tiny baseball glove but when you think about your kid in the outfield. The little pants or dress Sandy held onto for lamenting the days that are gone, but the stuff isn't gone. It's a constant reminder of the past because the past *won't ever happen again*. You hopefully will keep your memory for a lot longer than the shelf life of the stuff. Prepare for the now. Boxes of clothing hamper your freedom to create because they literally *take up space* and, worse, the past takes up space. Memories and things are two different spaces. Memories can't be wiped like a hard drive from an ancient laptop. Things were meant to be used and someone tiny, somewhere in your town, can benefit from tiny pants. So be generous in releasing them to a new owner.

Marie Kondo's TV show and book "Tidying Up" gained glorious applause with her simple (yet ironically totally *foreign*) techniques to getting rid of ***stuff***. She asks homeowners to take their entire clothing closet and put it in a big pile in the middle of the room. We watch in awe as the closets are emptied and wonder if we'd need a bigger room than them to pile our own stuff in. We see old band t-shirts from the era when we were thin. You've kept a similar one because it's tied to the memory of college parties or your glory days as an athlete. What Marie Kondo adds to her mission is to give thanks to those clothing items that held a place in our life's timeline. Tell them "thank you" and then wish them farewell. Those items served you once, but you no longer need them. She urges people to get rid of things and then teaches them how to fold their undies into an origami crane, thus maximizing the capacity of your stupid American dresser drawers.

How does this manifest for you?

Are you a food hoarder? Is your pantry full of items that you are scared to check the date on? Do you have five Tupperware tubs so large that a human body could fit inside, filled with kids toys that you intend to list on Craigslist but never will? Does your kid even play with Thomas the Tank engine anymore? Or are you holding onto them because you wish he did and you're not ready to release the memories of his early childhood and come to grips with the fact that he ONLY plays with his iPad, three plastic hero guns and the Black Panther costume you bought him for Halloween? I am literally pulling from my *real life* here for these examples and I'm guilty on every single count.

Perhaps you keep stuff because you feel guilty about the money you spent. *Was it expensive?* That treadmill in your basement that acts as a clothing rack for the things that haven't made it upstairs from the laundry room. Or the motorcycle you never ride Or the film camera from 2000 that took splendid photos on film that you haven't used since they invented a camera that fits in your pocket and holds everything on a tiny chip. Those things cost money (past tense). *That money is now gone.* The investment was made and whether you lost ten pounds running each day on the treadmill or rode across the country on that motorcycle, *those days are over too.* The "use value" of those things is now $0. You're no longer using it. Hold those memories in your internal hard drive and empty your desktop. Trash or recycle or upcycle or drop it off at a thrift store and donate it to the Sandy's of the world. They need it more than you do.

We tie emotions to **things**. But, in truth, they're *just things*. To anyone else they hold no value. Or maybe they do, but *that's why God invented eBay.* Take some horrible pictures with your iPhone and post those things on Craigslist. If no one follows through, and they nine times out of ten will never show up when they say they will, then donate it. *Ugh! My car isn't big enough.* Fine. Call a service. Do whatever it takes. Have them come and retrieve it. You know the Salvation Army will come pick things up? If you approach this as you approach the other household chores on your Administration of Life list, you will need to put aside an hour a week or an hour a day or thirty hours once a year to make this event happen. Write it on your calendar if you have to. Make it a micro goal. Take small actionable steps to finish the chore.

And for heaven's sake, if you are in need of those things down the road and you find that you're really feeling regretful about getting rid of them because they were so useful, then there's a magical, mystical place to find them again called Amazon.com. *You're welcome.*

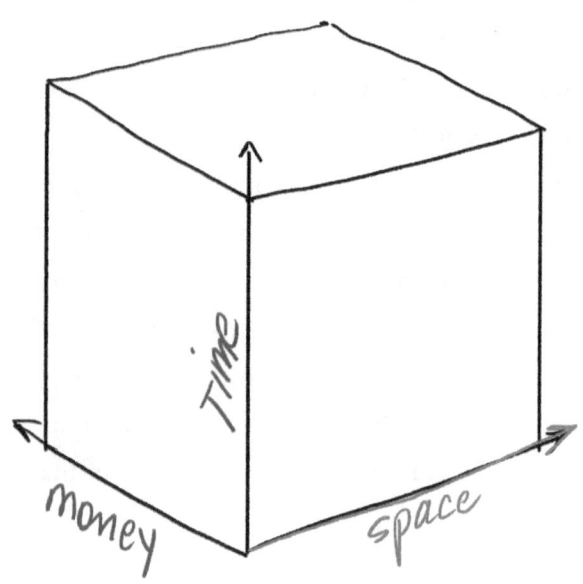

New Daily Habits & Organization

If you expect to practice new habits with regards to money and time, but you think your space can stay the same, you are wrong. There is a concept I've come to know while writing this book of a

3-Dimensional shape, like a cube in Two Point Perspective[16]. The height, width and depth are these skills we're coming to know as universal. Amongst successful people, the habits they keep are grown in every direction, not just one. You can't expect to begin manifesting your best life while sitting in a pigpen. You can't get rich if you don't make amends with money and train your sense of time as you would train a wild horse. We are aiming for equilibrium and balance, not perfection. There is no right way to do this, but I can tell you that it gets easier. The more you focus on all areas, little by little things improve.

In reading *Atomic Habits,* one of the hilarious things I learned was that you can trick your brain into thinking that you will start by just doing *two minutes* of work. Anyone can do two minutes of habit formation. Even you. Let's say you are having friction about getting your office cleaned up. Or working out. The best way to begin is to just allot two minutes of your time to it. Tell yourself, I am going to go to the gym. Get on the treadmill and run for *only two* minutes. The nice thing is here, you are giving yourself permission to suck. You're not a pro. You're not efficient. You're not excelling. But you are *trying*. And two minutes of running would legitimately be better than none, right? So, commit to two.

Once you're there, the likelihood of you doing two sit ups and then packing your gym bag back up and leaving are pretty low. You'll likely run for ten minutes and feel that you exceeded your own expectations! Yay! You'll likely do three minutes of ab exercises because that's where the hot girls are using foam rollers on their hamstrings. You might even spend a whole hour there if you buy a protein shake and shower. You'll likely get a mental high from the endorphins released and feel empowered by the raise in your heart rate, which will motivate you to

---

[16]Ask a high school art teacher to explain.

do it again the next day. These are the ways to really manipulate your own brain into beginning something new. Creating new habits two minutes at a time is the gentlest approach and may be all it takes to turn two minutes into thirty or sixty.

My web designer, Nate, is an artist too. He created himself a day job that pays his bills and he's got multiple passive income streams. He posts his vector art online in marketplaces, and designs typefaces that he licenses online too. He built a team with freelancers in the Philippines. He's got a knack for note taking and curiosity. He loves solving problems and it makes him a great asset to a business like mine. Nate is sweet and creative and kind and so I trust his advice. We never met in person, but we became good friends after meeting on a social media application. I hired him to transform my e-commerce website from WordPress to Shopify, to which he was delighted to do. He did an amazing job and as we spoke about this book and my vision, I realized that he *gets me* because he's an artist too. He gets the artist's stumbling blocks. He is also a divorcee and he gets the shift to "Life 2.0" when you have to reinvent yourself and create a new future all by yourself. Nate also struggles with ADD. Nate asks me all types of questions, some about business but some about life. We have shared so much with one another about the creative process. His is different from mine because he has a very stable income and totally different type of clientele. He mostly provides a 'service' and I sell a 'product.'

Nate sits down at his desk each morning to get ready for work. He goes through the tasks he'd like to accomplish for that day. He makes a list; he revisits notes from the day before and writes down three things he is grateful for. This is his Starting Ritual. It's how he gets centered and focused. It's his way of compiling his tasks and his thoughts into one place and limits other distractions. I thought it was a brilliant method to get clear and kick your workday's ass. What I didn't have at the time was a Starting Ritual. I didn't have an Ending Ritual either. I had a chaotic system of organization that really was not working all that well, because I never had enough time in a day to do everything I'd wanted to do. I just sat in front of my computer and tried to fight all the fires at once.

I realized I needed to schedule in time to eat, relax, take bathroom breaks, stand up and walk around a little, play guitar, eat a burrito, whatever. Nate taught me to do that. Now, if I want to do stuff, I schedule them onto my paper calendar. Set aside time for them. Stop putting it off or expecting the day to have an extra hour.

After hearing Nate's strategies, which I will detail in the next pages, I finally had to come to terms with the fact that *I have a problem.* I stood up (to the non-existent AA meeting), cleared my throat and admitted my faults. "Hi. My name is Erin and I am a pile-aholic." It wasn't easy to come to terms with the fact that I am someone who was failing in the art of habit-making. And even my inner Virgo winced as I admitted that I lack organization in a few key areas.

I pile things. I assemble neat little piles all over the house and procrastinate putting them where they go. I have a pile at the top of the stairs for things that need to get put away in the basement. I have a pile at the bottom of the stairs for things that need to go up. I have a pile of bills. I have a pile of business cards that need to be entered into my CRM software. I have a pile of earrings. I have a pile of pens. I have a junk drawer that is a mildly organized pile. I like piles. Scratch that- piles are *my vice.* Battling procrastination is a full-time workload. Starting is always the hard part like quitting for an addict. I needed new skills to stop the putting off, piling and procrastinating.

Let's tackle the disorganization of your workspace (and maybe even home life too!) We are going to do this together and as I take my own advice, you will be with me following the motions. Here's what is already working for me. Designate one area of your home to art supplies. If you're baking cakes, you'll need to designate sacred space to all the baking stuff. If this space is the farthest, most remote corner of your house, for sure you're not going to use it. Pick some place where your materials and supplies are in your view. If you can see those supplies, you will have no other choice than to use them-- they'll be calling your name. I want you to get some cheap boxes from the dollar store and a label machine. I don't normally advocate for buying new stuff and throwing out stuff all in one page but, we are about to get organized. This is one of those 'Invest in Yourself' moments where it's okay to purchase something.

Label each box for one category of stuff. Colored Pencils. Markers. Tape and other Adhesives. You can group all the materials together if you don't have that many. If it's sewing supplies, you can put all the pins in a small baggie, the threads in a small baggie, the bobbins in a small baggie. Snack sized zip locks are great for getting compulsively organized. I don't know about you but it's deeply satisfying for me to go nuts categorizing all the nails and screws on my workbench. I got an organizer from the hardware store for this and it has twenty-five compartments. Now I know where the safety pins are. The paper clips. The push pins, etc. If you exceed twenty tubs of "Keep" bins, then you know you and Sandy have more in common than you'd like to admit.

Efficiency is key when running a household; even a one-person household. If needed, borrow some Adderall from a friend and get to task. When you categorize things and you designate **This is the Place** for things, you basically stamp them into your brain. When you need them, you know where to find them because they have a home in your house and also a label that can be seen from afar. When you park in the seven tier parking garage, remembering which level you're on can be a mad scramble. More than once I have had to walk the lot until I found my car because I failed to note which color or number floor, I left my vehicle on. Spend less time looking and more time creating. If your art supplies or equipment is strewn all over the place, in ten different drawers, it's easy to get overwhelmed. It's easy to start the negative self-talk like, "You idiot. Where'd you leave the hammer this time…?!" This is sometimes an area of contention with your spouse, partner, or roommates. "Who moved the fuckin' hammer!?" Umm.. Yah, it's under your bed. Or in the laundry hamper. Or in the freezer. *Why?* Who knows!

What's insane about my pile situation is that if I just set aside ten minutes a day to PUT SHIT AWAY, I actually wouldn't have piles anymore. Here's the most annoying part about being creative and having ADHD. On my way to put away the one pile I just got to the laundry room and realized I needed to fold some sheets! Then I fold the sheets and put them in the basket, take them upstairs and I see some shoes on the floor. Since the dog could easily chew them up, I put them in a drawer designated for shoes. In the drawer, I notice the shoes are all messed up and out of order so I line them up, close the drawer and head to the kitchen for a nice, refreshing LaCroix to celebrate that I just moved two piles to two other places and basically put away nothing! The laundry is sitting by the shoe drawer, not put away in the linen closet. The pile of shit I took downstairs is… God knows where…

Things that you use every day need to be out. Where you can see them. Things you use once a year can go away. Like, basement, garage, attic, closet in the guest bedroom. Go! Away. You might need to make a note to yourself where you're putting crap so you don't end up like a guy

I know who owns three shovels because he couldn't find the first one so he just goes to the hardware store and buys another one!

Being disorganized wastes time. LOTS of time. With that time, you could be doing 5,280 other things like having sex or eating a burrito or smoking a cigarette or learning your craft or any number of other pleasurable activities! Let that motivate you to become organized. You'll

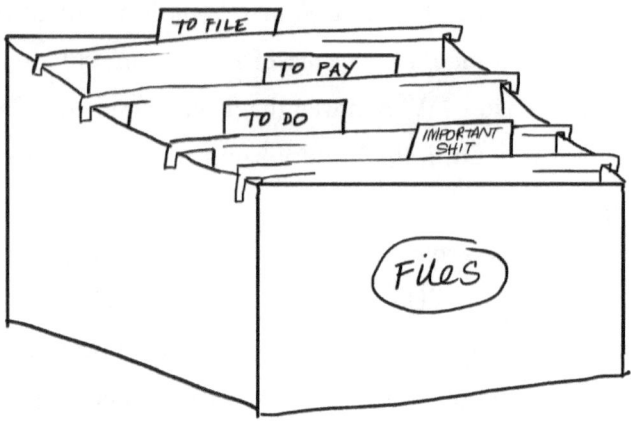

give the gift of burrito hours back to your life. I want you to make an actionable plan for yourself. Organizing takes as long as meal planning, balancing your checkbook, crimping your hair, whatever. If you do it ten minutes a day, you won't have to devote thirty hours to cleaning your home properly once a year. You can also sleep easier knowing you put all your piles away in their rightful destinations. Your shoes are lined up and your laundry is folded (and put away).

You have to begin a ritual, whether it's first thing in the morning, twenty minutes before you end work for the day, or after the kids go to bed. Find time; and don't do it once in a while. Do it every day. Write it down on your calendar if you have to and stick to it. If you don't write it down, you know you will avoid things like this. James Clear wrote a riveting thriller about habits called Atomic Habits (I am being facetious. The book was pretty boring, but I finished it in order to summarize it here for you) which outlines an interesting strategy for making the drab habits you'd like to avoid easier. It's called Habit Stacking. If you already have a ritual when you leave the office, like shutting down your computer and putting all your pencils back in the "I Can Haz" cat mug on your desk, you can stack an undesirable habit on top of it. If putting away papers is the bane of your existence, it's likely because you have six weeks of papers on top of your desk. Would it be okay if you never had to deal with that again? You'd need to file everything on your desk away before you shut down your computer and put the pens in the mug. If you spend three minutes filing away paper in a neat little folder every day before you exit your studio/office, you wouldn't have piles anymore.

The file system I recommend after five years running a business from home is this: To Do. Done (need to be filed). And to Be Paid. Three folders. You can have them in a desk top filing shelf, hanging folders in your top drawer or in a pile on your floor covered in cat hair. The nice thing about a system like this is you are partially deferring the chore of filing until later. The two sections "To Do" and "To Pay" don't require you to take action right now. But at least you know where things are and have a dedicated place to store them until you're ready to take action. The ones that are "To Do" papers should be looked at every day. The ones that are "To Pay" can wait until the first and the fifteenth of the month if that's when you get paid. But I like to take out a highlighter and circle the Due Date on accounts that are NET 30 or more so I won't forget to pay them on time. And guess what else?... I write those dates in my... Paper Calendar. Yep, so you can see it. That's when it becomes a thing you stay accountable to. You backup your memory this way, like an external hard drive. And the joy of crossing it off the list ought to motivate you.

I like to see my papers "pile" like this. Makes me feel very organized and accomplished and in control.

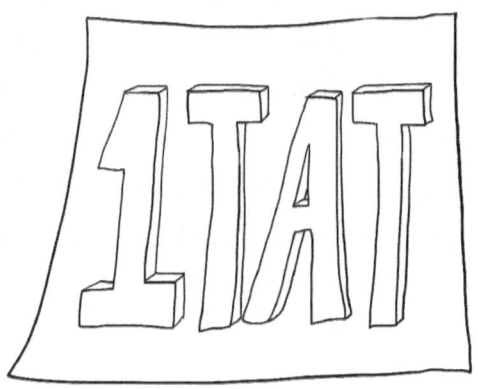

1TAT (One Thing at a Time)

Back to Nate, my awesome web designer and his daily practice for success. I spoke to him about how he starts his day. One text message exchange was enlightening. I am going to share his keys to success with you now in the hopes that if my weird system of organizing doesn't make sense to you personally, that you will go for Nate's creative solution to battling hamster brain.

Nate's morning routine looks like this: Wake up. No scrolling in bed! Put down the phone. Get up immediately after waking up, drink a glass of water. Exercise and shower which takes an hour. Eat a healthy breakfast that will fuel your brain. Meditate fifteen minutes. This is where Nate sets his intentions for the day. Then he finally sits down to his desk. Everything he does is on the computer, so he is going to be there for a while. His morning practice is my end-of- day practice. Nate calls it "Clearing Debris." He said that junk or garbage or shit is a negative way to look at the stuff on your desk. Because it's important but it's flung around like dust settles in nature. To sweep it all up and get tidy is a gentler approach. So he clears his desk off. It likely also reminds him of all the work that was not finished yesterday, so it acts like a refresher for the mind. He also looks at clearing debris as a way to get rid of mental and emotional debris AKA stress. The act of tidying his office relieves stress because to have a clear desk is to have a clear mind.

Want to know what his mantra is? Damn, *this is genius*. It's 1TAT. He explained that he calms his impulse to multi-task by trying to accomplish only one thing at a time. 1TAT = 1 Thing At a Time. Choose ONE specific task. Giving himself specific permission to FOCUS on that ONE thing makes him feel free. He even goes to the point of opening the notepad app (I use Stickies) on his computer desktop and writes out the task at hand and writes himself a reminder of the task at hand, i.e. "Create Logo for Artists Who Thrive." He keeps that reminder at the top of his screen until the task is done. He limits all other distractions and puts away his phone.

Limiting distractions is key because the phone provides endless beeps and buzzes for you to steal attention away from your task, ADHD or not. It gives you an excuse to NOT do the thing that is time-sensitive, perhaps boring or repetitive. The Instagram banner saying that an influencer you follow is going LIVE is a great way to not stay FOCUSED. You can turn off notifications for a set period of time too. But here's what I think is great about how Nate determines the hierarchy of tasks, since he creates the day he wants to have. He says, "If you really want to browse Facebook, put "Facebook" [in the Notepad] on your screen." He is allowing himself a timed participation in the meaningless blather of social media. He is giving himself permission to make it part of his day 1TAT-style. Planned scrolling and only scrolling, and only for a short time. Not endless.

If there is "wait time" in the midst of your task—such as a videographer who is encrypting large files or compressing (or whatever the technical terminology is for what secret magical things you do!)— Nate suggests using that time for letting the mind go blank. Instead of filling that void with something attention grabbing, he admits to meditating, reflection or just sitting with that time. "Not switching to another task, no matter how small" is Nate's own way to battle the hamster's desire to keep running on the wheel. My hamster jumps off the spin cycle and hops onto the treadmill. It's good for little hamsters to take water breaks and stretch. Literally you can take a water break and stretch, do yoga, or lift some dumbbells into bicep curls while you stare at the screen and wait. *There is peace to be found in the waiting.* Nate's 'serenity now' approach might make you want to barf. But this is how he battles the attention deficit we all have become super accustomed to. It works and I urge you to try it.

In art class, we learn about negative space—that which is not used. Nate applies this to his computer desktop. He maximizes the success rate of his work by closing out all the other windows and customizes his workspace for the specific task at hand, i.e. if he's designing my logo he only has email (with my feedback) and Adobe Illustrator open. If he has other windows open, he could be tempted to bounce around. He works efficiently by breaking the task down into smaller parts and then writes out a step-by-step guide for what he is going to do. He also… some of you will cringe… puts a timer on his screen. It's a Macintosh app called Red Hot Timer. He uses this to time block and when the hour is over, he can move on to the next item on his agenda and save his work or keep going! He masters the moment. He does not allow the moment to master him.

Nate was initially embarrassed to share his technique with me and I was blown away by how detailed he is. For Nate, the 1TAT system isn't just a nice way to get things done. It's the marked difference between success and failure for him. He *enjoys* his work more because 1TAT eliminates chaos and efficiency means true productivity. I guess his job is to be detail-oriented and nail down every aspect of a website, making sure it's pretty but also *functional*. I could never be a web designer because my attention span is literally so short, I could not manage all the details. Hearing his perspective makes me consider putting into action some new habits or adapting someone else's genius routine. Not because I like structure or rules! I actually hate them and it's why I resist anything as precise as 1TAT! That said, I admit that becoming a professional who really thrives by their creative talents might require reinventing the structure of how we work in order to enjoy it more and get things done easier.

Here's the thing: *Starting is the hard part.* Beginning a new task or beginning the day takes disciplined effort and stamina and mental clarity. Having that mental clarity might require medication, as it does for me. It could also come from refining what is not working for you and putting restrictions and systems in place to help your hamster brain thrive. These are details that only you know. Lean into why you're unproductive and maybe test some of Nate's theories out. See what works.

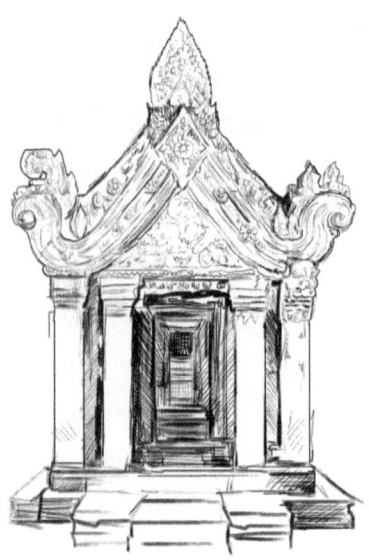

The Studio as a Temple

There have been so many dysfunctional relationships we've explored in this book. Money. Time. Your friendships and family. The artwork itself. But the one that smacks with the most importance is the studio. Think about your office right now. You have the power to control your space. Or your garage where you work. Or your basement where your painting supplies are tucked into a corner. I ask you: Do you get an "ugh!" feeling or an "ahh!" feeling when you think about this space? How important is that emotion to your overall goal of getting into the studio more? How could the feeling be improved, if like me, you get overwhelmed with seeing piles of dust and piles of crap in your studio? Do you even call it a studio or is it a dreaded office with kid's toys and yellow pads of paper dotting the carpet? Your studio/workspace/creative sanctuary/office is where the magic is supposed to happen, no?

In Buddhist teachings there is an idea called Vedana. It is an ancient Sanskrit word which involves, literally, any feeling state that we experience. There are three feeling tones that all of our experiences fall into. The categories are: pleasant, unpleasant or neutral.

Thinking through this approach I thought about people that I consider pleasant, foods I consider pleasant, and activities I consider pleasant. I look forward to these things and I perhaps even overindulge from time to time. I wish there were more of them. I want to only experience pleasant feelings. Then, the vast majority of people I could care less about. I don't love them, I don't hate them, but when I'm making a list for who to invite to a dinner party, they slip my mind. There are foods I don't even see when I'm strolling in the grocery store, but when they appear mixed in with a dinner at a restaurant I neither avoid them nor get excited to see them. Sometimes I eat those foods and I have no great emotion about it. Lastly, there is a shit list. If you've made it to this short set of humans, you have really done something or said something to piss me off. I've had multiple encounters with you that I'd like to pretend never happened. I may have said things that were unnecessary, but these people really push my buttons. I don't want to run into them, I don't like receiving a phone call from them and I surely don't want them over for cocktails. Foods I hate: green olives, shrimp cocktail and black licorice. I can tell you the exact time I either got sick from or discovered I hated the taste of these items. I remember the taste of them coming back up. It prevents me from ever wanting to touch them again and I pick them out of food if they're involved in a salad. Smelling them ruins my day.

Mindfulness is required to have balance in your experience of good and bad tonalities. We all want to feel more good sensations, sensory experiences, and feelings. Expecting to never have negative experiences would not be realistic. We all encounter things like Brussel sprouts or spreadsheets, which normally make us react with disgust. Our aversions to experiences involving those things make us sigh deeply "ugh!" or you may avoid anything on the menu of life with Brussel sprouts or spreadsheets. Author Martine Batchelor, a French nun who lived in Korea for ten years, taught me this by way of an interview she gave. It got me thinking about the studio. This concept made perfect sense with people or foods… but what about space?

Why the White Cube?

I am drawn to the field of interior design for several reasons. Mostly because I feel a deep commitment to our living spaces being beautiful. Our homes, in some way, define us. Our four walls can be decorated in a way that is exciting or calming, or cozy or minimal. In thinking through space with Buddhist tonalities in mind, what types of spaces are you drawn to? Modern and open? Organic and earthy? Converted vans? I want to encourage you to really think about the space that would make you feel the most creative. Lord knows my piles of papers and tools all over the house doesn't bring me ease or grace, but I'm working towards a home that's clear of clutter too. What could a coat of paint do for your office? What about a throw rug? I'm not saying hire a designer and spend $10,000 on your office redesign. I'm talking about simple feng shui and calming things down with design. Don't go down the rabbit hole with Pinterest boards and DIY projects unless you have the time and the means to do it.

Anything that has a pleasant tonality will elicit a similar response in the brain. "Ahhh" is the outward expression. Even if it's a postcard you put on your bulletin board (or computer desktop) of fields of tulips in Holland. Happiness may be evoked from that one image of the landscape striped with vibrant colors. Why are you purposely depriving yourself of that feeling of pleasure? You don't deserve it? A studio or office should be a White Cube[17] ?

Now that you've had a quick yogi lesson, look at your space again. Does your space take you fluidly to the act of creating, dreaming, thinking, conceiving, giving birth to the ideas that will express what is in your heart and head, ideas that will garner the attention of others and be valued so much that people show their appreciation with platitudes AND moola in exchange for your artistry? Is this where someone successful could work? Is this the laboratory for the million-dollar idea?

Let me impart the truth to you here. Let me tell you something no one else in your life is ever going to say.

The studio is your temple. If it is truly a holy place, a place of worship where the magic happens, then we must treat it as such. You are not praying to deities there, though you might channel creative sprites to invigorate your creative practice. However, there are no studio fairies, gnomes or elves who are going to come and clean that shit up for you. So let's take a pause and channel in on the vedanā, or sensation you get when you are in the zone. Close your eyes and imagine you at your creative prime. Start in the middle of the process when you are deep in a project: paint is flying, or scissors are cutting, or depending on your art endeavors, you are probably making a big mess and loving it.

Take a moment to jot down some ideas for the work you'd love to make. Think about how long it might take, what materials you'd need, and any specific equipment, tools, or facilities required for the project to be completed. What in the equation is missing? The art, obviously. But are you lacking a chop saw, a convection oven, a welding tool? How about just a place to sit and some electricity, a laptop, and your favorite

---

[17] https://www.tate.org.uk/art/art-terms/w/white-cube

coffee mug?

What is the sensation you feel in those moments? Is it bliss? Isn't it pleasant? Notice your energy when you begin to brainstorm in this way. Notice how excitable you are when you get some time to sit with these imaginary things you've yet to create. See how jittery your fingertips get to just do the damn thing. Feel that buzzing in your veins, that "can't wait" antsy-ness that lures you into the studio in the first place.

Entering the studio and exiting the studio might feel different depending upon your chosen medium. If you run a creative business or work predominantly on the computer, the desk is your studio, the desktop of your computer is your studio. When you sit down to do the work and get going, you get into the groove, but I'm concerned more with that physical space and how it makes you feel. I have a generic image on my desktop, the same one that was there when I bought the Mac and took it out of the box and plugged it in for the first time. Could I have something that makes me feel more at ease, relaxed or joyful? Yes! Why don't I have puppies romping in a field of daisies as my background image?! For those of you who are writers: You've got an office. It's taupe or tan or gray. What would happen if you transformed it with fern wallpaper? From the gardens of England where you visited in college. The smell. You can almost smell the ferns. What if you had light bulbs that soothe your senses? What if you had a eucalyptus vaporizer machine with soothing colors in your office? Have you ever been to a therapist who has a sound machine to drown out the patients in the room next door? What if you had white noise? Everything from the chair you sit in to the window treatments could probably use an upgrade. If not an upgrade, definitely your undivided attention.

Here's where my privilege rains supreme. I work in the interior design industry. I have countless vendors who sell fabric and furniture

CHAPTER 9: THE STUDIO MESS CONUNDRUM

at my disposal. I know upholstery workrooms and drapery fabricators. And if I had an unlimited budget, I could be working in a luxury office like those I save in my Someday folder on Instagram. But, alas, I have an IKEA desk. I have some plants. I have organizational drawers. I have IKEA drawer sets that all match and are labeled with the name of every wallpaper pattern so I can easily find it. I have a swing arm sconce and a bunch of photos torn out of magazines taped on the walls. It's not a luxury environment but it's functional. I rarely have clients here so I can make a mess with samples or drawings materials. The problem is, the chair I sit on is three inches too short for me and my arms always feel distressed when I've been typing all day long. The chair needs wheels to roll back and forth, but instead I pick it up and put it back down, because I have a cute carpet in here. But I remember the days of a "real" studio.

Gray floors layered thick with paint from decades of art students splattering. White walls with 5,280 push pin holes in them. Track lighting and a canvas curtain. Walls only went ¾ of the way up. You could hear each other making, spraying, singing along to the music in their headphones. You could smell turpentine. It wasn't a temple for professionalism, and it wasn't a showroom. It was a haven for messiness and loud noises. It was a space no one gave a fuck about because it would get turned over to someone new next year in the studio lottery. It wasn't a home and no clients would ever come in. It was a laboratory for ideas.

I've grown up since then and I'm adulting harder than ever before. I've realized that I like clean spaces too. Offices with so much storage space that nothing has an excuse to be left in a pile on the floor. Everything has a home. I want my office to feel like a design firm that could be featured on a blog or in a magazine. The current office is set in the living room of my house, overlooking my front yard. Dogs currently serenading me from around the neighborhood. But my basement is the lab, the floor with a million layers of paint, where no one cares it's messy. I now have the best of both worlds.

Creating a space that is pleasing and joyful is important. Having a space that functions, for me, is an always evolving stream of furniture, paint colors and (re)arrangement of things. If you don't have the luxuries that I speak of, what if you create a small space in your home or even a section of your artist space that is for you to sit and do work stuff? What if you hang some pictures of your family there? What if you tape up some inspirational quotes? Or a fortune from a cookie you got that spoke to you. What if you paint the walls a new color? What if you moved your desk from one side of the room to the other? Would it feel "new"? Would having some shelves be a good investment? Or a big ass file cabinet? Are you trying to pay taxes in the same space as you are writing novels? No wonder each time you sit down to write your body feels overwhelmed with icky tonalities. It's why 2/3rds of the way through this book I stopped writing. My desk was jumbled, and I was tempted to run my wallpaper business even though I'd set aside one whole day to write.

I simply shut down my computer. Moved my entire desk into the middle of the room. Shifted everything that was on top of the desk to some pile in a corner of the room. And turned the computer towards the wall. Instead of facing the wall I am now facing the middle of the room. I can't say I am lighter, nor is my tonality totally at ease. But I am looking from a different perspective. I now have a two-point perspective in front of me: a view of outside and a view of inside. I am resting in both worlds and my width and depth is more expansive than when I'm staring at a wall. That feels too two dimensional and my existence has a

CHAPTER 9: THE STUDIO MESS CONUNDRUM

depth of field of only twelve inches between my eyes and the computer screen. A subtle shift made a big difference. I advocate for giving thought to the space where you create. Don't just tidy up or rid the desk of debris one paper at a time. That's good for everyday maintenance, but holistic change can take place when you upend your old ways. Paint the walls a soothing color. Sit on the floor on a yoga cushion. Light a candle. Do something new to get fresh eyes.

In working with an editor, I met a remarkable Italian woman named Michelle. She is an author, an editor, a mother of three, and founder to an organization for young writers. She gave me months of support and feedback about my writing, but mostly encouragement to shuffle through my shit and fears and just write the damn book. She asked me many questions and I answered with every honest thread of my being. We laugh and cry and think together. We workshop the manuscript together. But she confided in me that her office was a dismal pit of despair. The piles of paper prohibited her from getting creativity out and onto the page. She had no system of organization and lacked an administrative assistant to manage the minutiae of running her busy life. She had to, in turn, become the boss of her own practice when she met me. I didn't kick her ass so much as I pointed a finger at this issue which plagues every creative person I know. The studio is rarely a temple. In a text message she writes to me, "I took my son to the University of Tennessee this weekend and I just about cried myself a river. End of day Monday I looked around and inspired by your book, I took every shred of paper, every pile, and I tore through them. It was like I was in a war oath to reclaim my creative space. That would never have happened if it wasn't for your BOOK." Arivaderci mess. Goodbye.

What Michele learned from this book, before it even went to publication, is that her "creative mess" was not lending to a feeling of "ahh" when she entered her office. Even calling it an "office" needed her attention. An office is where the secretary goes to work and makes minimum wage. She's got a rolodex and a landline phone with five lines. This was not an ideal way to think of her creative temple! She began to call her third-floor converted attic space her "Writing Studio" and she put away all the papers. She then had an aha moment and confided in me that it was a dramatic change. The outer world reflects the inner world. If your studio needs attention, it's usually because there is chaos within. The less business left unattended to in the exterior world, the more peace and calm you can find in your home and office life, the more time you may have to devote to matters of the spirit, the heart, or the magical unicorn pony resting deep inside your chest, waiting to spread it's joy and sparkles onto the page or canvas. Clean up and wait for the change to happen.

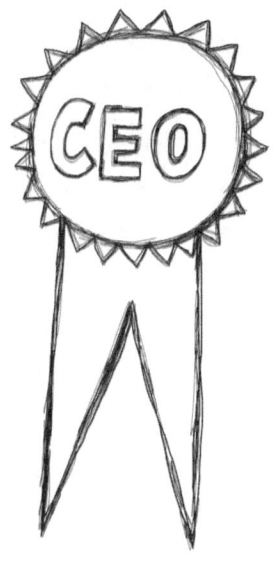

Chapter 10

Become the CEO of Your Life

If you want to take charge of your life, you are going to have to refine your resume. The job title you're going to insert at the top of the document is CEO. You are the Chief Executive Officer of the company/business called *"your life."* You're not only responsible for hiring all the staff that will make the company run, but you're in charge of finances, marketing and operations. This sounds like a LOT to someone who's never stepped foot inside a corporate setting. But, even for those of you who have, it is a lot of work. It's the only way to change around your life is to reframe yourself as the boss. The freedom and positive outcome of all the work in store for you is this: You can run your business however you want. If you want to only work three days a week, fine. If you want to work only 4 hours a week, there's a book for that. But the reframing we've been scaffolding up to in the first two sections of this book are going to come to a head. And it starts, like any fairy tale does, with a little magic.

I have never been the CEO of a large company. I am the CEO of a one-person company. I am also the Lead Designer, Director of Operations, Sales and Marketing Manager for all territories including the USA, Canada, and Australia. I am the bookkeeper, the administrative assistant, and the janitor. So I will not tell you (who might be working in corporate America) what a CEO's job is. I will define for you what I mean by becoming the CEO of your life. You're not the boss. It's not your job to boss yourself around or others. In fact, to the contrary, you might need someone else to boss you around and that's why I asked you earlier to get a coach or consultant. No, you are going to become the leader. The one who decides things, has a vision and makes those goals come true. You are about to determine the path and push with all your might to the finish line. You're about to involve other people in your plans and vet them. You're going to have to orient many people to your mission and perhaps even write out procedures and protocol. This, in my terms, is what it's like to be the CEO; Chief Decision Maker and Chief Message Spreader; Organizer of People; Controller of Standards; Manager of Expectations.

Start with Your Why

The Mission Statement of every business is written earnestly in the early days of developing a business plan and perhaps posted on a website or a physical plaque in the office. If a visual artist writes their Artist Statement, it is usually as a cover letter or addendum to a resume. It shows the breadth of the ideas behind the work and gives a brief bio of their life's path. In some cases, it may divulge the process by which their artwork is made, but only if that is a central focus of the conceptual thrust of their work. This allows the viewer to interpret your work knowing all the facts and details behind the work. Those details inform the *meaning* you hope the viewer receives.

Contrary to that of a visual artist's statement, a mission statement states: 1) A company's goals, 2) What the company does for its customers 3) Explains how the company does that thing, i.e. how it's made 4) Elaborates why.

When I told you earlier to start with the why, this is how you can reverse engineer your creative pursuit. Think about *why* you aim to create, which many lead you to what you want to create and lastly who it's for and the name of the brand. Like a formal business plan, writing this can help you understand what ideas and themes you want to come across when you're building the new identity of yourself and your art form. Maybe you want to make patches for socks, since you keep busting holes in yours. You assume that other people also want to stop throwing away good socks. You are looking for customers who have longer second toes than their big toe, therefore geniuses. You want to call it "Polly Sock It" because you played with Polly Pockets as a kid. You really just want to help geniuses with their footwear longevity.

It's a little tricky to think about yourself as a business when you may not have launched your art under a company name with a defined brand (yet). For example, my business is Relativity Textiles. My brand "brings the world home" through original, hand-made wallpaper. As an artist, I am Erin Minckley and I make paintings. I purposely didn't call my wallpaper company Erin M. Textiles. (I was sneaky and used my then initials EMC and likened it to E=mc2, Albert Einstein's theory of Relativity). I didn't want to link the two things because even in the beginning I had a hunch… "What if this takes off and gets really huge?" I didn't want to be the face of the brand, per se. I was happy to keep my art life and my company separate.

In my art practice, which I still sometimes find time for, I paint. I am interested in illustrating themes of cultural identity through pattern and portraiture. My paintings are painstakingly created with tiny brush strokes and gouache paint on paper and panel. I make pictures to illustrate a narrative of belonging and translation of the foreign. I want people to connect to places they've never been, fall in love with something different and open their hearts to others by way of curiosity. Each painting is like opening a music box and hearing a short song. I want my viewer to look deeper, stay longer and ask more questions.

I decidedly started a company because I could tell that there was a gap in the wallpaper industry in 2015. There weren't a lot of super artistic and creative or avante garde wallpaper brands out there. A lot of stuff was boring or kitschy or traditional. My business was an extension of my art practice because I used the same themes in my *artwork* as I embedded into the collections of Relativity Textiles's wallpaper patterns. I thought that having an income from a business would allow me tons of free time to just paint and take the phone off the hook. But that was a farce. It created twenty times more work than I've ever had in my studio and I became the CEO of a real live brand that breathes. I thought I'd go back to be an artist someday, and I just might. For now, what's the most interesting to me is that I spent five years building a massive audience on Instagram that I never could have if I was "just" a painter working anonymously in my studio. I was able to do that because I thought of my "work" as a "brand." I now get to insert my artwork into Relativity Textiles's menu of items for sale and it works because it's all under the umbrella of Wall Decor. Art, Wallpaper, prints. I can only do that now that I have a soap box to stand on now and a foundation for legitimacy.

I'm not a revolutionary. Andy Warhol is famous for doing commission-based work in his factory of artists that operated like a sweatshop selling screen printed posters and doing corporate ad work. Warhol called this his "Business Work" and it turned out to be some of the most important work he ever made. Salvador Dalí also famously took many commissions, including designing the infamous Chupa Chups sucker logo/label. Dalí was not above capitalizing on his works and earned a nickname "Avida Dollars" or eager for cash.

If it wasn't for starting my brand, I don't think I'd have made it to Thriving Artist status. I realize in retrospect that if I had applied to my art practice the principles that seemed so much easier and more appropriate for Relativity that perhaps I could have scaled my revenue with my art just as easily. But I would not go back and do everything differently. There was something in trying out being a "real" company that gave me confidence. Enough so that I now am able to do consulting with other brands, coaching with individual artists and I'm writing the book on the topic. Thriving for me had to happen separately. I saw what I was capable of. I saw that hard work paid off. Now I get to choose how I approach my art making, whether it's a hobby, free therapy, or a money maker. The nice thing is that we get to choose.

Not every creative pursuit needs to be monetized.

I want my following to view me as an artist first and foremost. My brand, the defining pillar of my brand, is an artist-owned brand. The artworks are transformed into wallpapers. The finished product is a work of art. It goes into someone's home and becomes a part of their collection. The themes I explore through my art, the emotions I hope to evoke are tied to my artist identity. Just as I look for a higher purpose in my painting, I know I must find a higher purpose with my full-time, pay-the-bills creative work. Your mission as an artist is enough to define yourself and drive you, motivate you, and establish your personal brand.

In creating a mission statement, you can then find your audience because your audience is the *recipient* of your mission. You can figure out how to reach them (marketing). You can determine your market and price your work. You can find ingenious ways to enter those domains and dominate. But the real work happens way before all of this strategy that you can find in any online course or basic business book. I'm not here to teach you business basics because there are so many other books out there that do that. I'm here to catch you as you sneakily try to follow my advice but with the wrong type of "business."

In creating a mission statement, you can find your audience because your audience is the *recipient* of your mission. You can figure out how to reach them (marketing). You can determine your market and price your work. You can find ingenious ways to enter those domains and dominate. But, the real work happens way before all of this strategy found in any online course or basic business book. I'm not here to teach you business basics because there are so many other books out there that do that. I'm here to catch you as you sneakily try to follow my advice but with the wrong type of "business."

What happens sometimes is that we don't allow or honor our REAL magical superpower. Talent is one thing. I rock at Adobe Illustrator. I crush it at drawing. I could be a home organizer because I'm good at cleaning and throwing things away and stacking neat piles of towels in the closet. But who cares?! I want to paint portraits and patterns. I have refined over time this notion that I could create just about anything and make it into a successful business. I could design websites or logos. I could create patterns for swimwear or baby pajamas and have a day job at Macy's. That said, I figured that pattern has a place on the walls, and I love decorating interior spaces. I figure that wallpaper is the best way to talk about culture and there's a market for it. I figured out how to make money selling wallpaper because I am a girl scout at heart. I want to sell lots of stuff and win a trip to London for being the Top Selling girl.

My editor Michele confided in me when she read this chapter that all she really wants to do is write fiction. She's an excellent writer and generates content for clients and consumers which supports her life with a generous income. But her dream is to be a *novelist*. She once wrote a volume of short stories which were sitting at the tiny desk she reserves for her real love, Fiction. She left the notebook near a window in the guest bedroom and when it rained through the open window her stories bleed through the pages and onto the tiny desk. The words were washed away. She was depressed and defeated and knew it was her duty to start again. But the nagging suspicion is "Am I a thriving artist?" She uses writing on a daily basis and her bills are paid. But her God given gift of writing fiction, her voice, her mark is left to be made on this Earth.

If you focus less on what's going to *generate lots* of cash flow and more about where your true passion lies you might avoid some of the backlash, I've had in realizing that I'm not tapping my best resources. I'm not sharing my drawings with the world! I am using drawing as a skill as a means to an end. My bills are paid and so are Michele's. For all intents and purposes, our peers see us as successful since we are being "creative", and we are getting paid. But are we pursuing our gifts? What if we pursued those gifts as shamelessly as we pursue selling wallpaper or writing content for clients? Forget about the money for a second. Think about what you were put on this earth to do. Some skill or some message that you have to share that no one else has quite like you. If you're going to go through all the stress of really forming a business, do you want it to bore you in a few years? Do you want it to suck the joy out of your life to the point you don't even like your hobbies anymore? Let's get crystal clear about WHAT we are monetizing and IF that's the answer to all of your problems.

Before I go on to tell you how to channel all of your magical unicorn powers and make money doing it, I'd like to make note that we have just written a mission statement about what we do. But WHY we do it is just as important. "The primary stance must be 'What can I give?' not 'What can I get?'" That quote stays with me from a training I did to become a Life Coach with ACE, Academy for Coaching Excellence. The founder Maria Nemeth is mentioned many times in this book because she's indirectly taught me many life lessons through her academic work and coaching program. Her point is a nice aside to the idea of Starting with your Why. "What can I give?" is equally important. I do this for my kids. I do this for my community. I wrote this book so that it could benefit many others. Think about those you serve with this work and remember to focus on those future contributions with as much ease and grace as possible. It could be simply a donation at the end of the year to a charity of your choice. But, doing so is designed to help you grow into your authentic self (or the fourth quadrant of the Quadrinities, your Spiritual self).

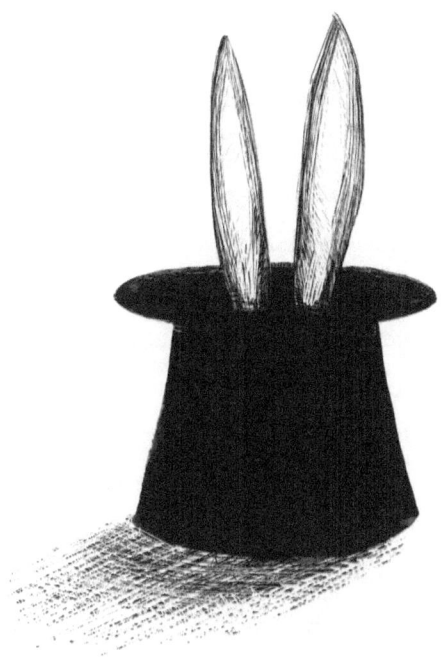

Channeling Your Magic

I know that your onion has been peeled back by this point in the book, leaving you feeling a little vulnerable and a little tired. It's daunting to do the transformation stuff. It's exhausting. That said, what's about to take place is a rebuilding and it will be courageous and valiant. It has to start with a little bit of whimsy and faith because otherwise we'd need money to fall from the sky and more than twenty-four hours a day, right? Flying can feel impossible without some fairy dust. Shat is that magic that I am alluding to? Where can I find some? Does it grow on trees? Is it packaged on Amazon and can it ship Prime because I need it now?! Nope.

It's already deep inside you.

There is something special deep inside you that you were born with. Your kindergartner self-embraced it and your parents applauded you for it. You did it without much effort and it brought you joy. You spent zero time doubting yourself when you were in your creative prime (yes, you were 5 so it's been a long time). This magic is different for all of us. Some of us were born to play soccer like Mia Hamm. Some of us were born to play the guitar like Lenny Kravitz. Some of us were born to draw, like Picasso. Some were born to sew and design clothes like Diane von Furstenburg. Some were born to marry rich, and for those of you that were, darling eat a bon bon for me. The rest of us have work to do.

I can't make this shit up, guys. Your magic should not be confused for talent. It's not what you're good at. Some people can draw but it's not their unique magic. It should not be compared to the thing that you are passionate about, because you're passionate about helping save the starving puppies of the third world. I am not asking you to turn that into a day job. Your magic shouldn't be the thing that will makes you money quickly, like designing websites for other people. You're moderately good at that and you've heard people charge unbelievable amounts of money for that. But, you know what? Doing that is a "creative" day job and a pursuit, but it's not the reason why you were put on this planet! You need to find your true calling.

You have gifts that no one else has.

Those gifts are the tiniest sliver of onion at the center. It's the sweet, frail, white little guy left over when everything else was peeled back. It's the tootsie roll center of the lollipop. It's the thing that most

CHAPTER 10: BECOME THE CEO OF YOUR LIFE

people don't spend time getting down to. They just bite the top off and crush it. Because they're impatient. Because they don't have the care and time required to count how many licks it took to get there. Or maybe they're just scared they'd have to work THAT long and THAT hard to get to the center again and it's easier to just lick and lick and lick . . .

This magic? Is where we start. You could create a get rich scheme for creating a business with your art, but over time you will burn out or grow less excited about it. Take it from me. I am a painter. I created a thriving wallpaper business using my own drawings to manufacture wallpaper for the luxury interior design market. I sold almost half a million dollar's worth of wallcoverings and services last year, and it wasn't as fulfilling or rewarding as you'd think. It paid my bills. But I am the CEO of Relativity Textiles, when really, I'd prefer to be an artist. I want to be the CEO of my art practice but I am the CEO of a company. I'm also the Office Manager, the Receptionist, the Janitor, and the Bookkeeper.

I thought running a business would give me "free time" to draw and paint but really, I just gave myself a job and became a slave to my own brand. I am the Wizard of Oz and I've acquired a fair amount of clout in my industry, been featured in top magazines, and for what? To chop down trees to decorate your walls? To run around like a chicken with her head cut off, dropping things off at FedEx, shipping high end homeowners their paper so their powder rooms would be ready in time for their in-laws to visit.

It's not feeding my soul.

That's why I decided to pivot and write a book. So like you, I have to take my own advice and redirect my life a little bit. I was put on this

Earth to make pictures. I tell stories and I am funny, and I can sell dog poop if you ask me to. I am good at telling the truth and sometimes that gets me in trouble and sometimes it works to my advantage. But, literally, the one thing that makes me the happiest and puts a pep in my step is to finish a painting. And signing it.

Hone in/Dig Deep

Chances are you're not doing the most magical thing you are capable of. Chances are, you know the one thing in this lifetime you are not maximizing your fullest superpower. So let's cut to the chase here and make some lists. Take out three pieces of paper.

LIST ONE: Make a list of all of the things you are good at-- all of your potential magical superpowers that you could share with the world. Prioritize the stuff you are GREAT at near the top of the list. Keep going until you've seriously thought of everything you've ever excelled at doing, from school to talents. Even add in here things that other people have told you "you'd be a great _____." I've been told since I draw in a certain style that I'd be a good tattoo artist. I've never tried it, but this would go on the first list.

LIST TWO: Make a new list on a new sheet of paper. This list is for the things you feel called to do. Serving your community, becoming a published author, being a spiritual advisor, being a mentor to youth, saving the environment. List out all of the things that nag at you and you've never started. Think through the ones that make you feel warm and fuzzy and the ones you feel guilty about. Maybe take cues from those who you admire; what are these folks committed to that you wish you were involved in as well?

LIST THREE: Make the last sheet of paper fun. You ought

to color this one with crayons or colored pencils. This list is going to potentially be very short in comparison to all of the others. These are the things that are your lifeline; the things that really make you bounce out of bed. Like dancing. Or the idea of one day owning a successful business. The stuff on this list makes your heart sing. It could look more like qualities than an inventory. Humor. Leadership. Fearlessness.

What do you see about these lists? Take a careful consideration when making them, and feel free to add to them over time. I like to really parse through all the myriad options for all three lists before I go back with a fine-tooth comb. It will hopefully become crystal clear that what you're doing in your life right now lacks a few fundamental embellishments. Maybe you need more comedy in your life. Maybe you need to look up a charity to volunteer for. Maybe the sore thumb sticking out is that you love to paint but you left all of your art supplies in Canada last time you moved so you've been using crappy brushes or not making art at all. Something is likely missing from your life and it's right here in front of you.

List One is "Your Gifts." You likely came to the Earth with them embedded in your DNA. Otherwise you studied or practiced very diligently to acquire a talent at them. However, they don't all hold the same amount of *magic*. You aren't equally talented at all of them, but when we are homing in on the thing that we want to pursue as a means to making more money, it has to have elements of all three categories. Not every hobby needs to turn into revenue. Not every talent can be capitalized on. Which is the one that you can bet on?

List Two is an inventory of "Your Life's Intentions." These are the areas where you want to make a difference. By making your life's work about your gifts alone, you may burn out. You may tire of making money from your gifts as I did. Though, if you are appreciating where you are, that is the first point of mastery. To decide how you will have an impact. The second point of mastery is to establish integrity with this list. Doing what you said you'd do consistently with clarity, focus, ease, and grace.

List Three is your "Standards of Integrity " and harken back to section one of the book when we talked about taking inventory of the qualities that you admire in others. Mine were: Creative, Family-Oriented, Funny, Carefree, Leadership, Loyalty, Inclusivity, Inspirational, Fearless, Genuine, Honest, Kind, Positive, Intelligent, Perseverant, and Self-Aware. Without these qualities my life would feel "blah." They might seem "blah" to someone else, but that doesn't matter to me. These are who I am, who I want to be, and my core values. *This is my magic.* My special sauce.

Here's the AHA moment I had when I took an inventory of my life's intentions and narrowed down my standards of integrity. Was I doing that one big thing, the center of my Happy Place, my gift to the world as my *main gig?* My day job? What about you? Are you supporting yourself 100% while channeling your magic? No. And if you were, my friend, you wouldn't be reading this book right now because you would be doing that work instead.

You've been printing zines for the past three years since you got out of art school but also have a day job as a server at a local restaurant. What you REALLY want to do is screen print art and posters but there isn't a studio space large enough for that set up. Or you are doing styling for the real estate market because the pay is good. But really, you want to be a traveling photojournalist full time. You're in school to become an interior designer or you're teaching interior design at the local community college, but truth be told you want to be a textile designer and block print fabric all day long. You're a muralist and every pair of clothing you own is covered in spray paint, but your background is as an award-winning fashion designer. You're studying art therapy hoping to lock in a day job, but if you were to spend as much time drawing and posting your work on the internet as you do reading psychology textbooks, you'd have gotten a dozen freelance illustration jobs by now. But after you had a kid and moved, you lost your network connections and gave up on that career. You are incredibly talented at drawing portraits in charcoal but you're a painting contractor and part-time real estate agent. WHAT IN THE HELL?

Those are actually stories of people I know. All of them. If those people read this book, they will say "Huh!? That's me!" and they might feel indignant about me calling them out for a two-faced approach to their career. They may also read it bashfully and say, "Wow, I made it into her book!" But, most of all, I'm hoping that their stories resonate with you, my reader, the person feeling a little uncomfortable right now holding this book and staring at the truth wondering how the heck they can possibly channel the magic within. Because you and I both know it's there. Someday soon I hope you reach out to me and share your story (not so I can use you as a case study for my next book) but because I want to help you home in on your magic.

Let's say for a moment that you are not one of the people who is starting from scratch. You're already deep into your art practice and a devoted studio rat. You're even selling paintings sometimes or making work for commission. Now is the time to step back and ask yourself what the lovely intake advisor from the Women's Business Development Center (WBDC) in Chicago asked me several years ago when I was about to start a cultural tourism business with my ex-husband. I told her I'd already owned a business. She replied curiously, "Oh yah? What kind of business do you own?" I explained to her that I am an artist.

That I'd been selling work while I was in Chicago and that I was doing pretty well this year. She asked a more diffuse question. "How much money have you earned doing that?" I paused. Proudly, I told her I'd sold two large paintings and a few smaller ones and the total sales of all of them was $3,000.00. Her face did not waver in appreciation of that number nor was she discouraging, but she prodded deeper. "Does $3,000 cover your cost of living for the year?" Confused, I gasped and then laughed and said "No!?!"

"Well, then that's not a business," she responded coldly, "that's called a hobby." My inner teenage brat started to creep up into my throat and I wanted to call her names. I wanted to exclaim that I am a legitimate artist with goals and dreams, and I am working day and night to finish my MFA so that I can support myself someday with my artworks. But I also logically understood what she was telling me. From a tax perspective, and for all intents and purposes, when you are making less money than it costs to live, it can't be considered "Profitable."

A light bulb went off for me in that moment. I begrudgingly mulled it over for days and weeks, still pissed off at her for calling me out. She'd soon explain that a business has to cover all your rent, all your bills, all your living expenses and then have a little left over after that to be considered profitable year to year. I'd been claiming "Artist" on my taxes but really, I was a "student" and no one expected me to be profitable while I was in grad school. The only one profiting on me going to SAIC was the institution and Sallie Mae. But, if my living expenses before children were super low and I was living lean, I'd still need to make about $30k to break even. So, I'd need to be selling anything over that number to survive and have something left in the bank at the end of the day.

Artists generally keep up with their taxes by having a day job.

Have you been filing as "Artist" or "barista"? Maybe you are an artist in your own mind but you don't make a living doing it yet. Listen, there is nothing better in the world than being able to quit your day job and do what you love. But, let's get some facts straight. Is your art a hobby or are you being supported by your art as a career? When we compare our field to other professions it's simply not a parallel universe but humor me in trying. Think about it this way, if a doctor was making $100,000 a year but his lifestyle cost him $200k would that career suit him? Or would he need additional income to keep his life going? He'd need a spouse, or a trust fund, or a second job... So even if you're telling yourself 'I'm living very lean, I don't need it to make tons of money..." you're probably grossly underestimating what you'd have to sell in order to go above the break even point and support yourself in by our Thriving definition. Not only on your taxes, but morally speaking let's transition to thriving instead of getting by. In order to do that, we need to elevate the career title and bank accounts to "Career Artist" not "Hobby Artist."

How the Knight Became the Servant

My friend Tony is the least likely reader of this book because he's doing twenty things right now as *we speak*. He has no time for books. But he is the perfect example of an artist who will time and time again fail to be a true CEO of his own life because he's pursuing all the wrong things. Tony works about ten to twelve hour days. He's got two small kids at home and a stay-at-home wife who probably puts him under a lot of pressure. He chain smokes and drinks coffee instead of medicating his ADD. That's fine, because it gives him momentary release from the stress of running three businesses by himself. Tony is a painting contractor, and he didn't quite know his own worth when I met him.

He was a referral from the realtor who visited my BNI networking group. Vance told Tony that I install wallpaper (which I've since stopped doing because it's difficult and time consuming, and frankly I don't enjoy it enough to hone my skills at it). So, Tony asked me if I wanted to install some paper on a job site where he was painting. I needed money so I said yes. We ended up chatting for hours while he painted walls and I hung paper in three rooms. We've been friends ever since.

He has seen general contractors (GC's) become the boss of the job site without much manual labor. So, he decided to become a GC too. It's a relatively simple process to fill out a form at City Hall and pay $500. He now manages a team of drywall installers, painters and carpenters. In fact, he also just opened his own wood shop so that he can be a carpenter too. Oh, and he is a real estate agent in his non-existent spare time. I guess he figured that working on renovations, he could be the agent to sell the home, the GC to renovate it, and make twice as much money. He tested to get his licensure for that as well. Tony is one human doing the job of six. And guess what? He's burnt out and feeling deflated.

See, Tony is a prime example of the **"Broken Magic Detector."** He is looking for his magic like that guy on the beach with a metal detector looking for an engagement ring. He spends his time with a machine that may or may not work, hoping for something...*anything* to make a proper living and change his fate. Tony's magic detector has led him astray many times. He thought he'd get rich with one thing, but it turned out to be a lot of time and labor. So he pivoted to the next thing, but was still doing the first thing at the same time. It left him little time to get good at real estate because he was painting houses. Now he hired three or four employees and took on seven job sites, which is a full-time management job (poke my eye out). And he doesn't even have time to do his bookkeeping so his bank account is in the negative and he's asking for cash payments from clients so he can cover his workers' salaries for the week. It's a vicious fucking cycle.

What Tony confided in me recently is that he is an artist. I kind of knew he was an artist from the way he runs his life. But I didn't know he could REALLY draw. He makes beautiful oil paintings and portraits in charcoal. His work is undeniably good, but he hides his talent from the world. See, there are not many people on Earth with that skill. I'm sure if I could dig up a statistic on that it would be about 7% of the population who can draw in a photorealistic style. He inspires shock, wonder, and awe from anyone who sees his true art form. *He has magic.* And you know where he keeps it? In a box under his bed.

This guy, bless his soul, is working his ass off to barely break even. He has a massive truck full of thousands of dollars of tools. Overhead of insurance and worker's comp. Potential injury on construction sites. Headaches and insomnia from his high-end clients' demands and a lot of pressure on himself to succeed. And why do you think he hasn't thus far? Besides the fact that he took on too much, he isn't doing what he was put on this Earth to do. He never sat down to write a mission statement, he never started with his "Why?"

Knowing Tony is from a small conservative town, I assume his parents told him in high school "Honey, that's great that you like art but you need to pursue a 'real job.'" Truth be told, our society doesn't see "Painter" as a manly profession. Or he wanted to get the girl, so he channeled Thor and summoned a massive, manly hammer. Unfortunately, Tony's weapon hasn't slayed any dragons or won any wars. He lives to serve his clients and he's never going to live at their level of lifestyle with a job in the service industry; this is the dilemma of every person who offers a service. We are always cobblers with no shoes. Tony became a servant instead of a knight.

Anyone can dip a brush in a bucket a few times and learn how to "cut in." They can learn about lacquer finishes, roller fuzz, and color matching. But not many people have Tony's talent. Truthfully then, it is a sin that he *isn't* using his God given talent. At the end of his life, the people closest to Tony might say "he was an amazing artist who piddled all his time away making everyone else's homes just right, except his own" even if Tony thinks his efforts are valiant.

What Tony is missing is his *magic*. He needs to quit all of his day jobs and get CLEAR about what is important. If he wanted to support his family, could he do it painting portraits?! Yes. Could he make as much money as he is now with one fraction of the stress and running around? Maybe. Would it take a shit load of mental conditioning to talk him into this? Yes. Would he have to change his habits and routines dramatically to get focused and make this work? Yes. Would he have to hustle to find clients and market himself and tell his story as loud as he could to everyone he can? Yes. And trust me, I know how scary that is.

Here's the issue for MOST of the talented artists I know. *Doing what you're already doing is **easier** than starting over.* For Tony, reinventing the wheel all the time because he loses passion or steam on something is now part of his self-sabotage routine. Struggling and being stressed and complaining about his job to everyone is his script for the screenplay of his life. Because what he chose isn't in line with his magical powers. It's not serving him. It's serving everyone else, but with no mojo and no charisma of an artist. It's just… work.

Know what a CEO would do?

They'd write out a plan. What are we doing? (Mission Statement).

Who is performing those jobs? (Personnel) Who do we serve? (Customer Avatar) What are our values and core beliefs? (Branding 101) What are our sales goals? (Yearly Projections or Pipeline) How can I step away? (Your team, training and employee handbook)

They'd also abide by the rules my consultants so wisely advised me on. The three rules of business are 1) Focus 2) Focus 3) Focus.

If Tony is constantly expanding into new territory, he can't master the first job. So, you have to refine and refine until the system is so good that it's bringing in money and doesn't require you as the CEO to physically be there doing the work anymore.

Here's another example. Let's say you write cute sayings. You love calligraphy and you have some catchy slogans like "Go Slow and Caffeinate." You could make coffee mugs and sell them on Etsy and chic local shops. You could also make shirts and calendars and greeting cards and…. Stop. Just do one thing. For now, just FOCUS on one thing. Just write out one phrase and scan it! Just do a quick internet search on "How does dye sublimation work?"

I make wallpaper. Do you have any idea how long I've been itching to design fabric? Not to mention furniture and light fixtures and all kinds of other things? I didn't do it because I didn't want purchase orders from seven different mills and vendors. I didn't want to add those new accounts in my bookkeeping software. I didn't want to make another spreadsheet with sales projections or inventory. I didn't want to have to photograph them all and pay $1,800 for professional images. I didn't want to add them to my website or pay my web designer to do it. I stuck to wallpaper because it was simpler, and I wanted to get good at it. Guess what? It's still tricky to balance just the wallpaper, the mills, the inventory, the shipping labels, etc. But I focused on one thing.

Leave your sketchbook behind. Leave your servant clothes at the door. Put on your Sunday best because you're about to become a knight.

Expression of Your Worldview

You might be saying, "Great advice, Erin, but how long does knighting take? I kind of have to make the car payment by Tuesday." Gotcha. As the CEO of your own life or creative enterprise, once you've decided on your magical superpower stick to it long enough to figure out if you can make it work. Sometimes that's a year or more. So choose wisely. Next, you want to make sure that you're not just chasing the thing that someone else has done well. Just because your girl pal Claire has become a successful interior designer and seems to love her job and make tons of money, does not mean that you have to do that. That's her magic. Being the CEO for a business is different than becoming the CEO of your own magical life. You need to find the outward expression of your own world view. A knighthood, and the female equivalent, a damehood, is an award given by the queen to an individual for a major, long-term, contribution in any activity, usually at a national or international level. Copying your friends doesn't count as this type of contribution.

Here is how I found the outward expression of my world view. There is an important intersection between my mission statement and how I view the world from my very specific perspective. I had to bundle all of my life experiences into a singular package to sell to others. I had to make them want to drink my Kool-Aid. I'm singing the wallpaper gospel, but I didn't want to change the world by chopping down trees to make pretty walls. What I wanted to do, *conceptually*, was to connect people. I wanted to introduce American homeowners to rich cultural histories from around the world, by way of wallpaper. I wanted to be Leo Africanus[18].

I'd married a man from a foreign culture [Morocco to be exact], converted to his religion [Islam] and learned his language [Arabic].

---

[18] Joannes Leo Africanus was born al-Hasan ibn Muhammad al-Wazzan al- Fasi, who wrote a geographical description of North Africa in 1550 *Descrittione dell'Africa*

I became fluent to the point that I could articulate feelings and have deep conversations with people, make jokes, and tell a street harasser to go back to his mama. I realize I am quite the anomaly. Most people never leave their comfort zones. Most never meet someone who doesn't speak their language, and by way of charades or drawing pictures, come to know more about them and their life without having a language to ask them direct questions. I wanted to see what it was like to put on another person's shoes. I wanted to become a chameleon and straddle both cultures, adapting or assimilating when necessary.

In Morocco, I was called "Hayat" which means "life." In ten years traveling back and forth to my husband's small home town in the north of Morocco, I learned to bake bread from scratch, I slept on the floor, I lived like locals do. I stood out like a sore thumb, but I tried my best to blend in. Adopting many Moroccan ways so that I could assimilate quickly. Once a cockroach fell from the rafters in the middle of the night and landed on my face. I screamed and woke the whole family. With all the lights on and enough yelling to wake the whole neighborhood, they began to laugh at me for all the commotion over a 'little bug.' I got used to showering with no running water. Washing myself with a small cup and a bucket, I learned how to conserve most of the warm water for rinsing out the shampoo otherwise the alternative was to turn on cold water and complete my bathing ritual with the frigid spigot on the wall. I adapted to survive.

Hayat didn't need Wi-Fi everywhere she went. She knew how to say, "fuck off!" to a persistent street harasser in his own language; it usually was so jarring and drew so much attention that he'd leave me alone immediately. Hayat knew how much things cost and wouldn't let the shop owners rip her off. Hayat mastered Moroccan way of life not as an anthropologist who is studying a culture. She did it to push her sense of self to the limit and see how far it would stretch.

My world view was that when most of the people I serve in my industry would never dare to step into the shoes of another person because it wasn't comfortable or easy, I wanted to act as the translator or excavator of culture. I aim to adorn peoples' walls with artifacts of foreign places. They may not even know it, but they traveled to Sudan and lived among the Nuba people, whose bodies are tattooed with small permanent scars or markings. The Nuba people live with pattern permanently and would laugh at people here discerning over removability of a pattern that only touches their walls. My customers learn to love Sudanese or Moroccan or Japanese culture and people and accept them as they would their own family. They welcomed them into their everyday life-- even if only symbolically-- by way of wallpaper. My worldview was to try something different on for size and live with it long enough to say, "It's not so different anymore. I actually love it."

Take your beliefs—the very core of what you stand for—and amplify your worldview through your magic. Like: If you are vegan and passionate about it, make posters about animals. Make pleather messenger bags to fill a gap in the leather marketplace. Make dog toys culled from recycled plastic. Make a protest sign and stand outside a fur shop (I literally did this in 1999 when I was a rebellious teen).

Monetize your magic through the expression of your worldview. This is how to thrive inwardly and outwardly. If you feel a sense of guilt or shame because you're earning an income off of someone else's culture or an animal's suffering, then the CEO of your company gets to make an executive decision. A percentage of my profits are donated each year to an organization serving human rights, women's literacy or humanitarian aid. This is the completion of the full circuit. Get inspired by a place, make things, earn money, and give back to that origin point.

When you donate to charity powerful things can happen, but most importantly dear friend, you can let go of the guilt. You've now shared your earnings and wealth with those who helped you make it here.

Your world view is as specific as your magic. You have interests, ideals, dreamy political values, and a message to share with the world. Shouldn't your "ART" or creative widget that you're going to make be in line with your particular philosophy? Hone in on your magic and make sure that your product or service is running parallel to that magic. Trust your art. Let what you make speak for itself.

Do you think that everyone who looks at my wallpaper is interested in the backstory? Do you think that scarification rituals in Sudan are really a *selling point* when pitching luxury wallpaper to a design firm? No. Does a consumer need to know the entire life cycle of my passion or idea or purpose? No. Is it on my branding where I got my idea and who I donated money to as a company? Nope. So I'm holding the aura of my ideas and worldview a little closer to my heart and a little more sacred than any of the other differentiating factors that we discussed earlier.

Instead, let them choose the wallpaper because they're drawn to its symmetry or all-over texture, or because they love gold or because it matches their fucking sofa. Seriously, those are the reasons why people like things for their home. Your product (or service) needs to stand alone without me there to offer a sample at the grocery store. People don't buy my products because I'm rescuing babies in Africa. Even if I was, I want you to consider that it's not as much a "selling point" as it is a feel-good moment where you get to say to yourself, "I am making a difference." It doesn't have to matter to everyone why you do what you do, but I guarantee that if your worldview is embedded in a secret coat pocket of every suit jacket you construct that it will heal your heart and fuel your fire. It just might give you the willpower to keep chopping down trees to print pretty wallpaper. It just might settle the uneasy feeling of the fact that all of your consumers really don't need your product to make their life any better. They're probably already living a great life under your definition of thriving. But you can sleep easier at night knowing you made an impact on an issue that is near and dear to YOU.

Critical Structure

As CEO of your life, making a clear path forward is a given. You will not only need to hone in on your magical gifts and create a mission statement, you will have to assign tasks to yourself and some other crucial people. You will have to master your time in a new way, especially if you are currently already working a day job. This is what we call critical structure.

The next few sections have critical planning methods that worked for me. Without these things I would never have left my pajamas or made a dent in my student loan debt. I never would've moved out of that apartment with the neighbor whose fan kept me awake. I would've remained grumpy and stubbing my toe and broke. The new CEO of Erin Minckley esquire has the following advice. Take it or leave it. If you're already doing it, great. Maybe even improve on it and drop me a line on how you've added to this regimen. Each person has their own obstacles and situational anxiety. But we're here to power through and move mountains one little sweet step at a time so Thriving Artist becomes your jam.

CHAPTER 10: BECOME THE CEO OF YOUR LIFE

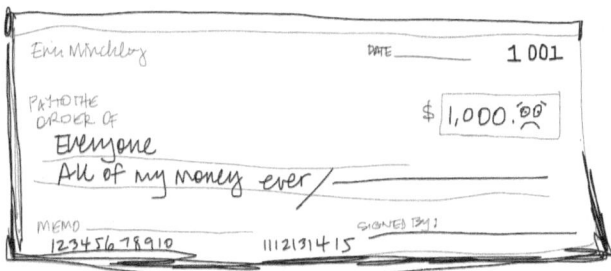

One day, I looked around and suddenly realized that everyone that was in my universe was *being paid*. Everyone who was there to support me was doing it because they were on salary; it was their job to support me! I was paying for the lifestyle of so many people and barely paying for my own life! My point is that even if you've got 20 support personnel assisting you on the journey of adulthood, so long as you can afford it, it's fine. This is what a CEO does. They see the need for someone to do the things that:

1. They aren't good at
2. They don't have time for
3. They don't like doing

It's not possible in the beginning, but as a CEO, you work on a plan to hire all of these people. You don't need to put them on salary. You don't need to offer them full time work and benefits and paid time off. It was a shell shocking admittance to just see how many other bodies it required to do what I thought I could do on my own. Parenting alone required support personnel. Goal setting required a coach. Everything after that that was being delegated and running smoother because I'd found someone qualified and skilled to do it—or at least available and warm blooded—to do the tasks I didn't have time for.

I openly admit that if it weren't for hiring a slew of interns from SAIC to volunteer their time in return for school credit, my business never would have made it to this point.

Every semester, for the first three years in business, I would hire anywhere from one to three young, talented artists to work one day a week. Sometimes they'd work two days. They were my accountability partners. I would have to get out of bed, brush my teeth and make sure the toilet seat wasn't covered in toddler pee before 9 AM. It was truly a feat. I hired them because I needed their help with various tasks that were mundane and boring but things that they could do without much effort and without my help. Like labeling samples. (So many samples were screwed up, let's be honest. But I do truly appreciate their time spent doing the remedial tasks I don't have the patience for).

They'd also research interior designers and send canned emails to them introducing the brand as if they were me. They'd stage photos for Instagram. They'd help me cart boxes of stuff from here to there. I'd buy them lunch or make them coffee or give them advice and life tips since they were still young and in school. Most of the interns I had were go-getters and would someday graduate and become entrepreneurial wonders. They were collecting valuable information for their case study about whether or not they wanted to work for themselves as I was doing, and I'm sure I turned a few interns off with my chaotic lifestyle and studio mess. They'd likely say "Yah, I don't want to run a business because it looks like blood, sweat and lots of tears. So, I'll work at a real company instead!" That's good, because it's not for the weak of heart.

Where could you find help? Could you hire someone who would in return receive school credit? Could you offer them something that would be very little cost for you? Like, could they use the printer at your office? Sometimes the tradeoff is small. Sometimes they want to pick your brain for hours on end, and in this case it's more trouble than it's worth to hire someone. I needed them to show up and get a specific job done, not come ready for me to teach them something they wanted to learn. What small tasks could you give away? What things are you not very good at that are simple enough to do one day a week or one hour a day? What are the things that you need help with that suck your time? Truth be told, I learned to screen applicants and warn them in advance that their job would be boring and their tasks remedial. Several interns quit because they thought they'd learn to screen print or design in Illustrator. If they wanted to work in an upper level job, they were going to have to learn the hard way like I did: on the job training. Title: CEO of your own damn life. This wasn't the place because I simply could not afford to pay them a salary and there surely wasn't enough time for me to teach them everything I know to have them leave four months later and start over with someone new.

A year into running my business, I was able to afford paying an assistant part-time. Kelsey was a former student of mine from the School of the Art Institute of Chicago (one of the students who didn't write a nasty review). She had been an intern the summer before and was now working one day a week while finishing up school. She did some managerial tasks and some design for me. I was feeling very proud for having hired her, and I loved her company even though she was quiet. She'd smile and offer some advice or comradery and she kept us organized. She had a way of making our systems a little better and liked to challenge me when I wanted to keep a written record and also a spreadsheet on the cloud. The teamwork aspect was the part that made it really feel *real* for me, and I had to grow up to become an effective Manager. Like children who believe their parents are perfect until they mature and then realize they're totally flawed, I think Kelsey was starting to see that small businesses are mainly led by flawed grown up's who are scrapping it all together on the fly. A lot of times I felt like she would be annoyed that I didn't have better answers for things. So, I grew to include her in major decisions and invited her to a trade show in NYC with me near the end of her tenure.

In the year I started Relativity, I hired a life coach and I was paying her more than I could afford. I had two financial consultants helping with my books. We talked about the pipeline for sales for a couple of months ahead. I should've been paying them, but when they looked at the back end of my accounting software, they realized that I was in a pretty-much-poverty state of affairs. I couldn't afford them. So they offered to work pro-bono for almost a year and a half. I had a therapist. I had a babysitter... or two or three...who were also artists. I had an attorney who I was paying an exorbitant amount of money to try and get child support or the use of our family vehicle. I had an accountant. A photographer. An IP attorney. A graphic designer, a web designer. I had sales reps in seven cities across America and Canada and all of them were taking a 25% commission of sales in their region.

I am going to teach you how to find and hire these people. I will also advise you not to buy your stick before you buy your herd of sheep (assuming in this metaphor that you'd like to become a shepherd.) It wouldn't make any sense to buy a $20,000 digital printing machine before you have the wallpaper company bringing in revenue to justify that expense. You are going to end up being more like a shepherd to your flock of helpers. Part manager of humans you will need to get better at project management. I adopted some routines, daily guidelines, and eventually an Employee Handbook so that I didn't need to constantly re-teach the same skills to my interns. When it comes to having advisors and mentors, you are reverting to the role of the student. You will need to take notes, do your homework and ask lots of questions when you need clarity. This is where you become the manager of all things.

The danger I fell into was filling the void of teaching with becoming a mentor to all of the artists who wanted to start businesses but didn't know how. Many students would apply to intern with me and they really wanted to learn software programs. I would blatantly tell them that they needed to enroll in a course designed to teach them these skills, because their job would consist of very mundane and "unfun" tasks like sticking labels on samples of wallpaper. What I wanted was creative energy in the room with me and hired mostly females who had an interest in business. Many of them had Etsy shops or were working towards a booth at the Holiday Art Sale that SAIC held every winter. They thought that by just working near me they'd absorb the entrepreneurial gene by osmosis.

I did my best to mentor them, but I had to admit, I'm not the Pied Piper. I wouldn't be able to play my flute and skip through Chicago luring all the Thrivers into the streets to follow me towards Success. If those young artists wanted to run their own business someday, my formula might not even work for them. They'd need to encounter all their own mistakes along the way like I did. I gave advice where applicable and helped them price their wares. I always tried to calm their hysteria about life after school and convince them not to get the first job that they could unless it supported their vision and desired lifestyle. Alas, I could not guide them forever, but I tried to manage the team and foster an easygoing and fun work environment since their labor was crucial to the business progressing. I appreciated them and desired to give something back in return.

I know what you're thinking right now, "Erin, I am not a manager, or a boss and I don't have a company." I know that! Owning your own business can be much like putting on a dinner party for your children and their friends when you haven't gone to the grocery store in a week. You have to kind of wing it. You tell the kids to look in the pantry, look in the fridge and you take inventory. You come up with a menu based on only what you have on hand. You make the most of it. You tell the kids what it will take to pull this off: A little bit of me bossing you around, a little bit of teamwork, a little ingenuity because we've never done this before and most of all, let's have fun doing it. By the time each kid has a chore peeling carrots or boiling some water, the work is getting done. You're going to help out if anyone needs you, but overall you are the one who needs to orchestrate the master plan. The vision. You are going to make it look as if you'd meant for all of this to happen, and act like it was all meant to be. And if you still struggle, I implore you to read more about leadership (a phenomenal book is Dare to Lead by Brenee Brown).

Highest and Best Use of Time

Where are you spending your time? If you recount the last week and you tally up all the time you were working, what types of stuff do you do? How much "free time" do you have? Where is the energy mostly? Tally how much you're just 'farting around' in the studio if you're a visual artist. Tally how many hours of Netflix are you logging in, if you're working a full-time job, but can't figure out how to get a business off the ground. Tally the fifteen minutes a few times a day that you spend trolling Instagram or Bumble or Redfin. You're guilty of wasting time somewhere. We know why this happens, right? We wanted that momentary relief from reality. That little escape. But in the amount of time you spend in the bathroom each day you could be building your social media presence. You should not be spending hours on there interacting with influencers. I repeat. While you're pooping you can be growing a business! So many people tell me they lack the time to get things done but the root of the problem is that you might be working your ass of on the lowest and worst use of your own time instead of your highest and best.

The highest and best use of your time is illustrated above. This is a key concept if you want to become profitable whilst being creative. If you want to stay poor and dick around, please toss this text under your door as a doorstop or use it to light bonfires to roast marshmallows. Please recycle me. Otherwise, if you think that extra cash in your bank account could possibly improve your life, look at the pyramid drawing. You, artist, have been doing all four jobs up until now. You're all of these:

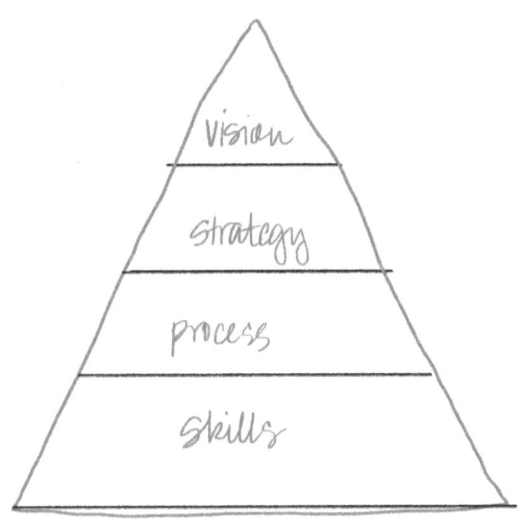

1) **<u>Visionary</u>** - The person with the dreams, goals, and vision is the creative force behind any idea. This is sometimes the "easy" part for artists, but for those of you reading that don't yet think your creativity is your special sauce maybe this is harder. Either way, the top of the pyramid is where imagination is king. It's where the highest paying jobs are too. When you are Steve Jobs, you get to determine the trajectory of Apple. You're not inventing the computer; you're imagining the computer fitting in someone's pocket. Then you find the team to assemble small parts in an airtight room until the working "iPhone" is invented. The visionary is not the "Do-er." He or she or they are the Idea Person.

2) **<u>Strategists</u>** - These are the communicators. These are the people who move their mouths and communicate the message, the vision, the ideas to others. They are salespeople, marketing people, writers, and critics, and influencers. They are the ones spreading the gospel. They are the kid at the Kool Aid stand waving to all the cars who drive by, ready to tell them it's Sugar Free and 50 cents a cup. "How many do you want?" These people are not usually as highly paid as the Visionaries. It's not their Kool Aid after all. But they aren't doing the hard work of mixing it either.

3) **<u>Processors</u>** The person in charge of many is the person who unifies those below him towards the goal or vision. They are crucial because they manage and watch over the system to make sure everyone is doing their job. They ought to have expertise in their field, and likely they moved into this role

by working in the lower tier of the pyramid or the SKILLS category. There is usually a ceiling to this type of role and how much money can be earned. Their job is to unify the team not to implement any new techniques. They might train or teach skills.

4) **Skills** - These guys and gals and folks are the muscles and are the most important role in any business or social system. They are the garbage truck drivers, the Amazon delivery person, the grocery clerk, the automobile assembler, or the plumbers. They Implement a given skill set and their range is usually pretty narrow. It's their job to just get things done, make things, and do it in a timely manner so that all the other people above them can do their jobs and be accountable to their own timelines. If the muscles of the operation fall ill, don't show up to work or leave town with $5,000, and don't install plumbing in the house then everyone else's jobs fall apart. Nothing can be done without them, but their skill set is usually the lowest paid on the totem pole.

This hierarchy of skills and time is an illustration of the many types of "work" there are in any given business-- it is not an illustration of the most "important" jobs there are. As I said in #4, the Implementers actually play the most fundamental role there is for getting a product to market. But their compensation is determined by the marketplace. The Visionary's salary has no limit. Everyone else has a maximum rate of pay. In the equation of Relativity Textiles, the Implementers are the screen printers that hand screen print my wallpaper. If it wasn't for their expertise, time and care I would not be able to sell luxury wallpaper.

Inversely, if I were to have to screen print all of my wallpaper myself, how could I meet clients and sell that product? Or check any emails? Or update my website? I wouldn't have time! This is why I have sales reps in all regions of the USA, to sell my Kool Aid, I mean wallpaper, for me. They are the Communicators. The Unifier is still me, to some degree, but could be an Office Manager or fulfillment center who dropships things out once they're printed.

If you are a one-person business and expect to do everything yourself, the number of products or services you can render are limited only by time and money. You will remain in the role of all four jobs at once. If you create a team of people (even if they are freelance and only work a few hours a week) where you are the top of the pyramid, you will not only have the ability to earn the most in the marketplace but you can maximize profits. This harkens back to one of the first business books I ever read called *The E Myth Revisited: Why Most Small Businesses Don't Work and What to Do About It*[19]. The author explained that most people spend time working in their business instead of working on their business.

I saw that in the wallpaper factory where I once worked. The owner, Murray P., was nearing the age of retirement then. He would say, "I'm just fighting fires," about how his day-in-the-life tasks were organized as the owner of the print shop. He started the business in 1974 as a twenty-something washed up gymnast. His father owned a paint store and when Sears closed down their printing operation, Murray's dad bought their wooden tables, half the length of a football field, to print his own wallpaper. Murray would run that factory for the

---

[19] https://www.amazon.com/Myth-Revisited-Small-Businesses-About/dp/0887307280

next fifty years.

What Murray wasn't doing was working "on" the business. He had essentially created himself a position as "boss" at the company and worked at the shop. He was one of the only people who knew how to expose a screen, stretch the mesh, etc. He had a monopoly of skills and most of the employees had set tasks and skill sets and a high school education. Murray wasn't working on marketing his business. He wasn't improving the facility with proper ventilation for workers. He wasn't researching new ink technology for eco-friendly printing processes. He was making screens and emailing current clients about their lead times. He did the books. He kept the materials stocked. He hired a disabled woman who lived nearby to scrub the toilets. He was the first to arrive and the last to leave.

Had Murray worked on the business, he could've grown his revenue, spent more time golfing, and trusted that his system was working without him. He hired me to help with marketing, bookkeeping, and client management. I did digital art for him and he taught me much of what I know in Illustrator. See, with Murray's degree in exercise physiology Murray might have felt that he didn't have the expertise to work on the business. He was just trying to maintain things. Make sure nothing caught on fire. Make sure the electrical bill was paid and the Flood Brothers didn't come knocking on his door from the trash collector mafia of Chicago. Murray was just muddling along minding his own business. He was just making a living and trying to make good products on time.

This, dear reader, is not thriving. This is surviving.

The highest and best use of an entrepreneur's time is to work ON the business, not IN the business. If you are making earrings out of plexiglass, at some point, you will need to outsource those designs to a fabricator. This will inevitably keep your costs lower and allow you to scale even though an initial investment for manufacturing is daunting. That is called a "barrier to entry." It's why a lot of people haven't started a business yet. For each of us, the barrier to entry is something different. Finding the SKILLS persons to make your products instead of you making it yourself is figuring out the highest and best use of your time.

If you want to sell your earrings to wholesale customers, like a retail shop especially, you'll have to make sales calls to potential clients. You'll have to create a social media following or amass a newsletter group. But those aren't necessarily all tasks that YOU need to be doing on your own. That's where you might consider brand partnerships or e-commerce platforms and marketplaces that already have significant traffic (plus they'll provide you with demographics of your customers' buying habits, how they found you, their age, and location on the planet). This allows you to spend your time designing new earrings or items. You become the Visionary, and someone else takes on the Strategy. Even if it's a website not a human. An Etsy site costs less than sales representatives do. I learned this lesson the hard way, which leads me to one of the most important lessons of this book.

Artist. Friend. Whether you went to art school or not, you have a skill at making something. You have refined it and you deserve to be successful doing it. But, your two hands do not need to be involved in EVERY single aspect of getting that art into the world. In fact, as this pyramid shows, what you need to focus on to create a thriving life is more of the tippy top or "Vision" section of the pyramid. If you can relieve yourself from having your two hands on stuff, you just might be able to last as the CEO and not the employee of your "business."

At first you are the only one who knows the process. You teach others to do it or you hire someone who's already doing similar work. They are now a service provider so that you can focus on the strategy: Who am I going to sell this to? Where can I find them? How much are they willing to pay?

The alternative is that you will remain an indentured servant to your four tiers of the pyramid. You'll wear all the hats and never get ahead financially.

This is illustrated by a friend of mine who would not consider himself an artist, per se. In college, he was a swimmer and water polo player who moonlighted as a rapper (he was actually pretty good). A meathead, yep, he was even in a fraternity. Gasp! He majored in Economics and went on to find success in real estate development, aka flipping houses. In southern California the market is very different from Chicago and you can buy houses rather cheaply. Do you think he got out his hammer and started pulling out cabinets? No. Remember I said he is not an artist and he's successful? He hired contractors and made very close relationships with real estate agents and private lenders. He is spending OPM instead of smoking Hopium. Other. People's. Money. That's how he buys the house, pays the contractors, and he does this all remotely. Each time he flips a house he makes about $30,000 after he pays back the investor. That was twice my salary as a teacher. He does one or two of these a *month*. The reason why he's good at it is not because he's a meathead. He's really fucking clever actually, because he's not doing ANY of the work himself. He now has a system that works, many people under him who do their job well. Not without some bumps in the road, but he's doing really well for himself. Let's hope after reading this book he goes back to rhyming and gets himself a TikTok channel.

I repeat. You don't have to have a hand in making it at all. What I have come to know about my species-- artists-- is that we believe it inauthentic to write poems. To just buy a notepad and No. 2 pencil, sit down, and write poetry is too simple. WE ARTISTS like to go out to the remote area of an enchanted forest in Canada. Take an ax to a small tree. Spend three days in agony as we whittle down the trunk of a tree to a small enough tool and install a fine lead point. Tired, hands rough and bleeding with exertion, we sit down to our paper. And we write. It belongs to us *then*. The *entire* creative process. We did it all with our own two hands and no one can take that away from us. We claim every piece of it as our own intellectual property; our own genius. We win the Agony Award and our poem never gets read by anyone. But we bled just to write it, and that's what counts. We triumph in our authenticity. Alone. Why

Because we spent all our time being a lumberjack when we were a poet from the start. The idea didn't even need a pencil. We could have dictated it into our iPhone on the subway train while hipsters standing nearby in flannel shirts and beards reminded us of the woods.

The 4 D's

1) **Do:** These are the tasks you add to your long-as-it-ever-was to-do list. If you are creating a thriving practice, there are always millions of things you could be doing. But where is the hierarchy of how you decide what can be done now? What fire urgently needs to be put out? What can be done later? And,

most importantly, what can someone else do?

Using time blocking, estimate how much time it would take to do each thing on your list. Find space on the calendar for these tasks. Put aside the time allotted, like one hour. If the task takes longer and you don't really have more than an hour, you may need to spread the task out to multiple sittings, days, weeks, depending. Also, tasks and goals are always needing to be parsed out into easy, actionable steps. Something as easy as "Call Lawyer" requires putting aside 15 minutes. From there you might have an hour-long research ahead of you or a trip to the Small Business Administration Office or City Hall. Those will be added to the weekly calendar as soon as you know what is required. Don't get too far ahead of yourself. Just focus on what needs to be done NOW.

2) **Dump:** These are the tasks you are going to let go of. If you've had "Design a greeting card" on your To-Do list for two months, maybe you're not that into designing greeting cards. Maybe you thought it would bring in some money, but it's a side hustle that makes your skin crawl to think about. The amount of work that goes in? Just to maybe make a buck? You don't want to become Rifle Paper Co. but you also know that she makes tons of money. You can't quite commit to it. You don't have the energy. You keep avoiding it. That is when you know it's time to dump that "dream" because it's not really inspiring or important to you!

True story: Getting my vintage Moroccan rugs cleaned has been on my DO list in the far back corner of my hamster brain for three years. However, none of them smell so badly they need attention right this second. If someone, by an act of miracle, would actually purchase them on Chairish.com, I would need to get them cleaned right away. But I am going to dump that task for now because it's just not urgent, and I can do it later or never. Dump it.

How do I know when something is DUMP or DO? If it keeps me up at night. If every time I pass that pile of stuff I am subliminally reminded, bothered, guilty or otherwise perturbed by that task. If it reoccurs in my thoughts. Then I will shift it to "Do." But if you go three weeks without ever thinking about it again, you have full permission to Dump it forever.

3) **Delegate:** These are the tasks which are not your highest and best use of time. Here's how I determine if I should give a task to someone else. Does it bring me joy to do? If the answer is no, consider giving it to someone else. Of course, in this model, everyone would have a cleaning lady. Do you have time to clean your own toilet bowl? Yes. Does it take less than one minute and thirty seconds? Yes. So do it, cross it off the list, and save yourself some money!

Another criterion: Am I skilled at this? Social media is one of the things that seems to require very little strategy, skill or intellectual prowess. But those who are doing it successfully and using it to grow tremendous followings have a very, very tightly planned strategy. I can recommend several resources for how to grow your social media following. I've sat in on a lot of panels where the same things are said. I came to the conclusion that I have two options. I could continue at an organic pace, posting sporadically. My followers will grow gradually. Or I could hire someone with a really good plan, but an agency costs a lot of money. That's where I decide: Roll up my sleeves and hum "slow and steady wins the race"? Or bite the bullet and invest, hoping that a few wallpaper sales will cover the bill each month.

Along the way you have to make some hard decisions. Just like getting a PR agent, you might be looking at shelling out $3,500/month in expenses to have the pros take over. That, or you could enroll in an online course that takes half a day and only $100 to complete. That might make you better at what you do. Until $3,500 feels like it's not a huge leap or investment, I'd say *don't pay anyone to do anything for that amount*. Unless there is a guarantee that paying that amount will win you back that much in revenue or more (which is kind of impossible). Throwing money into advertising, press, social media, etc. is kind of like throwing spaghetti at a wall sometimes. It can be a waste, until something sticks. So do a little research on your own time. Ask around and see what things cost. Ask for estimates. Ask peers what they pay for stuff. And weigh out if it's worth it to pay for things like virtual assistants, networking groups, etc.

4) **Defer:** These are tasks which are not a priority right now. They are sometimes more of your big picture goals. They're things you might not afford or daunting tasks like writing a book or shooting a video that eventually won't be able to be deferred any longer. Your creative itch will finally make those things a priority, or the direct opposite may happen. You might get a year into running your own business and realize that the things you set out to do in the beginning aren't important anymore or you were missing the mark somehow when you

conceived of them.

I suggest writing a big list of all the things you want to do, hope to do, urgently need to do, regret not doing, etc. The act of writing your list—a brain dump unlike any other—is a cathartic release, a visual person's strategy to untying the ball of necklaces that are tangled up in your jewelry drawer so to speak.

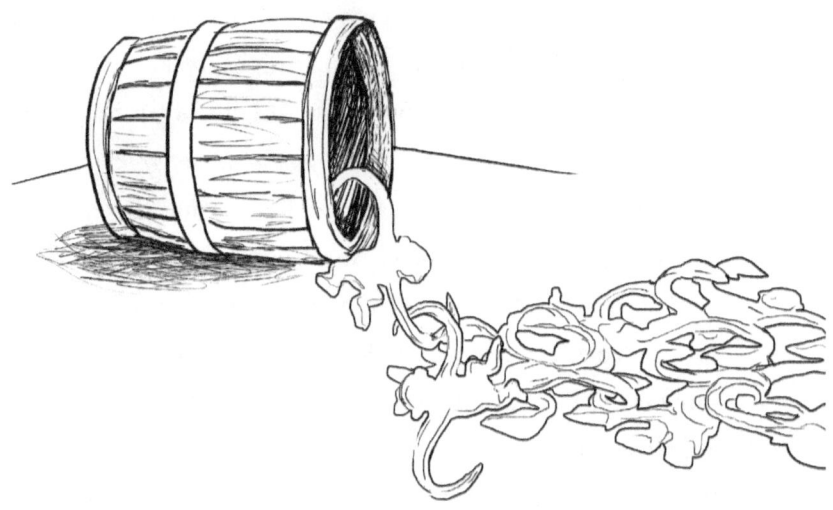

Dumping Out the Incompletions

This activity is a list-making technique and a cathartic act which has no scientific research backing its legitimacy. I call it Dumping the To-Do's or "Incompletions." Like a barrel of monkeys game, I want you to dump out all the tasks left incomplete in your brain, hoping to organize them into categories. You have to see them splayed out on the floor first before you can group them like Marie Kondo makes her participants dump their closets into the center of the room. When we observe the contents of our own cluttered minds, we see those damn monkeys swinging from tree to tree. I find it hard to chase the monkeys around-- I can't possibly write down all of the 60-80,000 thoughts I have each day. I want you to begin to detangle them and count them and then we will sort them out. Dump the barrel out onto one or more sheets of paper. The first time I tried this "technique" I just kinda started listing things.

Step One: Make a list for "Personal" tasks like plucking my eyebrows all the way to taking the car in for oil change. In a separate column or bubble on the paper, I started making piles for "Business" tasks like re-order packing tape on Amazon and revamp website. These things range from .25 hours to 25 hours' worth of work. They involve so many people and small steps to get to the end goal, but all I need you to do right now is try to focus up on just how many things your brain is trying to juggle at once. We will organize the mess later.

Step Two: Use the 4 D's method to figure out what can be tasked out to someone else. It may have a price tag, and yes, that will cost you money to not do it yourself. But, we are moving away from chopping down trees just to write a poem and trying to embody the "Highest and Best" use rule. Delegate whenever possible. It might cost you more to hire a graphic designer to put together a PDF, but that document will be ready quickly and look best when done by a pro. You could learn how to use InDesign and scramble some free fonts together from dafont.com but the time involved is more than one hour. Usually, your time is worth as much as the web designer's time, so you in essence have bought back an hour of your own free time to do what is the Highest and Best use for you. Let others help you. Pay what it costs and consider that an investment in yourself not money out the door.

Step Three: The things that you decide to Defer, try putting a date to them. Like "January" of the next calendar year. You can even write it in your planner. I find that putting dates to things not only allows me to feel like I am accountable to the task, even though it is well in the future, but I also am able to let go of thinking about it. The constant preoccupation with things left undone is like a faint, high pitched noise in another room. It's not loud enough to bug you to death, but it's an annoyance that would bring you peace if it wasn't there. So get it out of your brain by writing it down. And send it into the future to worry about it later.

When it comes to life during a pandemic, I realized that so many things that normally could be so easy, like filling up my five gallon water bottle at the grocery store have become affairs, ordeals, and burdens. Luckily, in many urban areas, outsourcing these chores is common. Uber, Drizly, Instacart, Dolly, or TaskRabbit to name a few will deliver almost anything, put furniture together, or bring you booze. My water can be delivered for a small charge, but I buy back a whole hour of my time to just go to Whole Foods, park in the parking lot and fill my jug with water and get it home.

Step Four: Think about efficiency when you begin to make a plan for getting shit done that's on your list. This is somewhere in between "Do" and "Delegate" because you've given an app or a stranger the power to do a task for you! Bundle as many things as you can on that app. Like windshield washer fluid for that car wash you needed, packing tape for boxing up wallpaper, and also wine for later when you are rewarding yourself for being such a badass. I highly recommend grocery delivery, dog walkers, drive up pick ups at Target, etc. if your town offers these luxuries. You should absolutely pay the extra little amount to buy your time back.

Step Five: Put every task on the calendar. If you are compulsive, like me, you will want to stop everything you're doing right now, including finishing this chapter and get to work. That's fine and great, but life will indefinitely interrupt you and make it hard to accomplish everything in one fell swoop. That is literally the only thing you can count on in life: here will never be enough time to finish one thing all in one sitting. Unless your goals are to eat a burrito. Check. Complete. So you might have to separate out the things you can actually do today, and start putting the other things one or two or five at a time on the list for the next day, the day after that, etc. Don't pull an all-nighter and accomplish it all. You have to schedule in time for real life. Eating meals, sleep, working out or socializing with other adults. These things are important, because after all you are not a machine. If you burn out on my super cool advice, you may start to dislike it and not want to follow my activities anymore! This is what leads to burnout! Trying to do too much all at the same time. And, hopefully, once you do the task and cross it off the list, it won't be a recurring event. Writing monthly email newsletters must be built into the plan/calendar and written down every month for the next twelve.

Step Six: As you parse through tasks, some may lead to more tasks-- dissecting each big task into small reasonable bits takes attention to detail and some reality checking. If you think you'll do five steps in one day, but you only have an hour, then you might be biting off more than you can chew. Resist the urge to do this. Example: When you're trying to set up a business bank account, they will ask for a FEIN Number, or a federal business ID. That takes time to register. So slate seven to ten days on your calendar and then go back to the bank to set up your account. Likewise, if you are trying to hire someone, and you want to post "We're Hiring" on social media, you need to first write a job description. One task sometimes turns into a few. But that's OK because you are ON it. You are patiently writing it all down, calendar blocking, taking time for each task, and staying calm.

Exercise your CEO brain power, systematize stuff, and take it easy on yourself. If it takes two weeks or three weeks to accomplish all the teeny tiny goals your list, so be it. Don't forget to reward yourself for the accomplishment. Even if it's just a burrito. Eating a burrito was something you were probably going to enjoy anyway, but if you tell yourself "Chores Then Burritos," you will have a carrot dangling in front of you as you work.

You don't realize it now, but the little incompletions are preventing you from getting on to the good stuff. Just as hoarding boxes of stuff takes up space. Just as your loser friends are taking up a seat at the table when someone else [who could possibly make your life more joyous] would be a better dinner guest. What you might not be aware of yet is that if you are going to get to BIG goals and major success, you need to clear up all of these little items FIRST. Your mind only has so many gigs of RAM and this little stuff is taking up space on the hard drive and slowing down functionality for 'highest and best use' tasks.

Chapter 11

Eliminating Obstacles & Having Courage

There will always be obstacles on your journey. Money and time are huge obstacles, and the people you love and care about are also reasons why you can't do things sometimes. We've talked about the mental and emotional gymnastics you're going to have to conquer in order to achieve your goal of becoming an artist who thrives. But what about the real world reasons for why you, Artist, cannot get things done?

Tip: The obstacles will make themselves known, and then you tackle them.

I've come so far in five years of business (even if at a snail's pace) from where I was when I first quit all of my jobs. If it wasn't for my coach always calling my bluff, I think I would've gotten stuck many times in the maze of entrepreneurship. The symptoms of a tricky mind are what she refers to as Monkey Mind. Defined by the Chinese in late Qin Dynasty (384-487 CE), the mind was hard to train[20]. It was therefore primitive like an ape, and needed proper conditioning

---

[20] https://en.wikipedia.org/wiki/Monkey_mind#:~:text=Monkey%20mind%20or%20 20%20mind%20monkey,confused%3B%20indecisive%3B%20uncontrollable%22.

to become more civilized. Whereas the heart was thought to be like a horse, it had the willpower to love and was the epicenter for feelings, the Mind was the origin of thoughts and ideas.

The upshot: Both the mind and heart need training.

There are certain universal truths about designing our dream lives that all humans must face. In other words, they are excuses. It is the monkey disguised as an obstacle. Here are my top five excuses that I've been in communion with for five years.

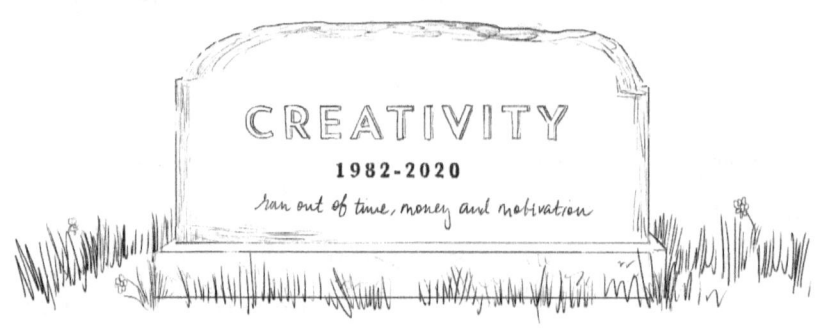

Excuses:
The Leading Cause of Death to Creativity

All excuses suck. So let's say they're like vacuums. How many vacuums do you own? How many reasons do you have for why you aren't living a great, vibrant, successful life where you are joyfully pursuing your art form [and making a living doing it]? How many circumstances are you blaming? How many other people are getting in your way? How many reasons do you have for why shit sucks right now? We all do. Welcome to being human.

I remember the days of graduate school when it was all we could do to try and assimilate into the real world during the last months of our studies. Doctors get internships, and bankers get jobs post-graduation. What do fine artists do? They look for exhibition opportunities or artist residencies. Preferably ones with amazing facilities or located somewhere with a temperate climate. The best ones pay for you to come, rather than you paying to participate. So, I was looking into a couple of residency programs and was also applying for teaching jobs and exhibitions. There was a really important application due and I shared it with my life coach.

She followed her routine of asking me about the actionable steps required to make this application happen. I told her I needed to upload slides to an online database, edit my CV and type a cover letter. She made me choose a calendar date to write it down on, and I promised to keep my word. I was working on integrity with myself and my own promises at the time so I would usually say "yes, I promise" without really knowing if I could pull something off by the deadline. I was also looking at Thursday and writing down "Work on CV. One Hour." but seeing that Friday was open, knew I had some wiggle room for being late to accomplish my goal. The application was due at midnight that night.

On Saturday, she checked in with me to hold me accountable and support me, as a good life coach does. She asked how the application went. I paused. I told her I didn't submit it on time. I felt a real sense of shame and disappointment. I regretted to admit that this thing I was really excited about wasn't going to be an option for me anymore because I fucked up and didn't do the thing I said I would do on time.

The next part is the real kicker. And I wish I could be in a room full of people like you who are all reading the next paragraph at the same time and just wait for all the heads in the room to start bobbing up and down in agreement.

"I just got so busy…I had laundry to do and then my kid needed to nap. I forgot about grocery shopping, since it wasn't on my calendar. My day escaped me…I thought I'd finally get around to it once my son went to sleep, but I woke up around 11 PM in a toddler bed and didn't have the energy to get on the computer and rush to submit it all on time. So….I just gave up and didn't apply."

My coach was quiet on the other end of the phone. I could sense that she was disappointed. Not in me, but for me. Like I could have won the ArtPrize, but I did laundry instead. That was my real reason?

Allison is a gentle creature. She laughs with me and supports me, but she is the force that I am channeling when I call her bluff. She sat me down (even though we talk on the phone) in this moment and got me to see something I'd been trying not to see for as long as I can remember.

"What would it be like for you to talk about why this happened?"

Oooookay…? Umm, sure.

What was parsed out in the next few minutes is this. There are things in life that are always going to be on my to-do list. Like mowing the lawn. They're not something that stops. Until the snow comes and then shoveling snow is on the to-do list. Those things don't go away. I had allowed the administration of life to pile up, so much so that if I didn't do laundry that day, the whole family would have been walking around free Willy while I was applying for an art opportunity. I had allowed laundry to take precedence but not because I was a good mom who was taking care of business and serving her family members. Not because it was a life or death situation. I was choosing to do the laundry as a self-sabotage tactic.

Let me say that again, loud and clear: I SELF-SABOTAGED MY ONE OPPORTUNITY AT BEING SEEN (both me and my artwork) AND MY ONE BIG SHOT AT BEING RECOGNIZED IN THIS WORLD.

What would've actually taken one hour, max, I put off until the last possible moment. I waited and procrastinated and deliberated and delayed until the clock was ticking and time was up. I let the sand run out of the hour glass. I made excuses for all the other things that needed to be done with an unconscious effort to put myself last. To put my priorities at the bottom of the list. And to tell myself, your goals are not as important as meeting everyone else's needs RIGHT NOW. I let this be not urgent, though in the scheme of things, it was urgent. It was time sensitive because it had a deadline. And I should've cleared my calendar to do the damned application before anything else. Because truth be told, there is always time for laundry! And, I'd probably been procrastinating going to the laundromat for at least seven days anyway, which is why we were all out of underwear at the same time!

"So, what would it take to have made this happen?" she asked me.

"Well, I could've done laundry one day earlier?"

"Yes."

"Now, I want to ask you something. What do you think successful people do?" They likely have a housekeeper who comes on Tuesdays or Fridays and does the laundry. He is paid to arrive at a certain time and do certain tasks. So if you're not rich, like I am not, and if you don't have a housekeeper, which I do not, then you will likely have to be your own housekeeper and put laundry in your calendar. In fact, it would behoove you to get on a schedule with regards to your entire administration of life. So that your electric bill getting paid on auto pay doesn't overdraft your checking account and your laundry day doesn't coincide with an important work/career/creative dream deadline.

Stop thinking that your creative dream doesn't matter. That's degrading to the power your talent VIBRATES into the world. Treat your art with the same commitment and reverence as a job that depends on you. Or a person. If you treated your dreams like a client, you'd be catering to them and dressing up for them and showing up on time. If you treated yourself like a close friend, you'd be encouraging yourself to cast a large net, accomplish small tasks with a fearless persistence and spread the message of your amazingness in as many ways as possible. Shit, you'd probably even promote your friend! On social media and in real life.

So, why aren't you putting your creative self on a fucking throne?

Your Job Doesn't Define You

I worked for a year and a half at the wallpaper manufacturer who later became my print shop for Relativity Textiles. It was a stinky warehouse on the north west side of Chicago. The owner was ready to retire and didn't keep up the shop. The wallpaper was from the 1970's when he opened his doors. He had two dogs that roamed around the office. All of the employees there had a high school diploma. That's it. They were the hired labor, and though the mythology of screen printed wallpaper needs to illuminate these characters as artisans and craftspeople, they really weren't making a working wage. One guy was released from jail and had five kids who he supported. He needed the work because the government was garnishing his wages and cutting checks to five different mothers. He barely had any money when all of that was gone. He admitted to being homeless before he got the job. He was a veteran and proudly sang R&B music loudly while listening to his music with headphones in. His singing voice was terrible but always made me laugh.

Chester was my buddy. This sixty-five year-old Polish immigrant had left high school to work in this career path. He had only missed two days of work since 1975, the day his mother passed away and the day his father died. Chester combed his hair for photos that I would post on Instagram with a small black comb he carried in his pocket. He smoked one cigarette a day and enjoyed a can of Pepsi. He rode the bus to and from work. He had a separate outfit for work, in case he spilled ink on himself. He always had a smile. He spoke five languages and liked talking politics. He was always abreast of the latest news and listened religiously to NPR. Chester taught me how he mixed colors without a formula. His eye was so precise that he could add a bit of yellow the size of a pencil eraser and get the perfect color match.

Although I did not fit in with the crowd at the factory, I took the job to subsidize my teaching salary. I got pregnant while I was working there and I made OSHA come to test the air. The fumes from the ink and solvents they cleaned the screens with was so potent I would go home and even my bra smelled like screen printing ink. I wanted to change so many things when I worked there and give the workers a better environment. OSHA determined that the information on our chemicals were inconclusive, so I always had a hunch that my child would be born with deformities. Luckily I had a healthy baby boy.

At that job I worked thirty hours a week. I made $12.50 per hour. I could have worked ANYWHERE else for more money. I would have been appreciated more. My skills would have been utilized in more effective ways. But I considered it my "internship." At that factory, I learned all the things that other girls [who think they want to design wallpaper for a living] will never know about. I learned where the paper came from, how to mix ink, how screens were made and how to edit them in the dark room if there was a mistake. I learned how to bill people and create purchase orders. I learned how to print checks and keep track of inventory. I learned digital printing technology and even went to trade shows with my boss to sell his label of licensed sports peel and stick decals. That show was a bust but I learned from it.

I illustrate this for you because at the time I was super unhappy and frankly it was a very unhealthy working environment. But I was obsessed with the print process and the friendships I had there made it more tolerable. I was there to learn. It was a stepping stone and well worth the suffering I went through to be able to know everything there was about making wallpaper. To the point I considered opening my own print manufacturing business a year after I'd quit. That was actually the only time I ever wrote a professional business plan and met with potential investors to help me get the operation off the ground.

I want you to think about the job you are in now. How is this leading you to becoming an expert? Is this the field where you want to become an expert? Then think about a potential job you could take that would enable you to learn everything there is to know about a topic you do want to be an expert in. Where is that job? What role would you have? How can you move up to the position where you want to be? Do you absolutely have to start at the bottom of the ladder?

I knew I didn't want to start at the bottom and I couldn't afford to work for entry level wages with two kids and a butt load of debt. That's why I eventually created my own job. But, when I was working in a dirty old factory it wasn't clear to me what my next move was. There were other factories but they weren't in my city. I could start my own factory. I couldn't fathom that type of overhead when I didn't even have a pot to piss in. Starting my own business felt so scary and I felt totally underqualified.

My job as Office Manager at a factory didn't define me. I had time to consider that in fact, though I was underpaid and suffered a little, I was kinda sneaky in figuring out the one place to work if I wanted to design wallpaper for a living. Yes, I took less pay, but want to know how I made up for it? I took away some extra knowledge as the proverbial currency, because sometimes you can't read about this stuff in a book. You can't figure out how wallpaper is made by watching a YouTube video or doing a short field trip. You have to actually work there before it all clicks and makes sense. Then you can use that to your advantage later. I'm saying that if you're somewhere being underpaid, instead of complaining or moping or sulking about how there are no good jobs for artists, instead try to reframe it as an "internship." Because even doctors do residencies where they're overworked and underpaid for a period of time. But after that they use that experience to go off and do great work, sometimes with a great big paycheck.

If you want to create custom stationary, you could work at Paper Source or Hallmark, yes, but you could also go work for Rohner Press and see how cards are made. The nice part about understanding (as only an artist is interested in knowing) how things are made is that you have a very well rounded approach to design or sales after that. The process becomes part of the form, meaning you design knowing the paper is thirty inches wide and the installer can't carry anything wider than fifty-two inches without a helper. Having a broad knowledge of an industry or a product or a service will allow you to hear some of the break room conversations at an interior design firm. Literally, all they do is complain about their clients. And all the general contractors do is complain about the designers. So, you might want to know that going in!

Is this job you're in really going to help you do what you've always dreamed of? Or are you working visual display at Anthropologie so you can get the discount on clothes? If you're not going to be a set designer for the rest of your life, you might want to get an "internship" somewhere a little closer to the goal. What if the goal is to make enough money that you can afford the Anthro shopping spree without having an employee discount? Let's set the bar high enough that having that type of life isn't so far out of reach.

I worked as a high school art teacher on the Indian reservation. Before that I painted houses for a summer and bartended. I later worked in an art framing shop, was a substitute teacher, and worked at an arts supply store. In grad school I answered phones in the Career Development office and assisted other artists for peanut wages. I later taught college art and taught night classes to adults at indie print studios. I started a tourism company with my [then] husband and took high school kids to Morocco. I had a short stint assisting a Ukrainian seamstress who taught me work ethic and etiquette with wealthy clientele. I went on to work in a wallpaper factory, then freelanced as a textile design assistant for Hygge & West. I learned all about the industry of wallpaper. I started a business and had some side hustles like consulting other brands, and doing rare interior design projects. I helped friends with social media marketing. I created custom artwork for interior designers I met along the way, even though they just wanted me to replicate Cy Twombly—I did anything for money, to get by, and to refine my plan. (I told her "never tell anyone who made this" because I didn't want to be known as the copycat painter).

My work history is less like a path of small stepping stones leading to the Secret Garden and more like a frog on a deep pond filled with lily pads. I just jumped from one to another trying not to get soaked. I had no idea where I was headed, but in hindsight it all seems to make sense.

So many jobs in the realm of "helping" and "interior space." Whether I was learning to 'cut-in' with the painting contractors or hemming a Roman shade with Oksana, I was developing an understanding of what it meant to solve problems for people in their interior spaces. While teaching, the interior space was a college student's brain. Those are mystical, messy environments that often are untamable. I did my best to decorate them with propaganda posters of Rosie the Riveter.

Your job doesn't define you. You're not a title. You're not a "Photographer;" Photography as a medium doesn't even define you! You define your title. I am a momtrepreneur. Sounds vague but it's everything in one word that is made up. I am a textile enthusiast. I travel the world scouring souks and bazaars for the next inspiration and then come home to design things! I want to be an adventurer, explorer or anthropologist.

A Title Versus a Pursuit

On a trip to Mexico City in 2018, I had this epiphany about the titles. We went to visit the studio and showroom of Esrawe, a furniture designer. He's actually an architect. His firm does interior design also. So that's when they started their furniture company, in order to furnish the homes he'd built and the interiors he'd designed. Why not have every piece, like a dollhouse, created by one brilliant mind?! In Mexico, so many things are possible. In Mexico, people have been making things with their hands for 3,000 years! So there are fabricators, decorators, facilitators of all kinds. There are raw materials coming out of the earth. Granite and steel and everything are so cheap in comparison. So this guy's work is beautiful and affordable and like nothing else I'd seen. We went upstairs to a secret vault of sensory pleasure. It was his wife's creation. She is "a nose" or the Spanish word for someone who designs perfumes. Esrawe and his wife collaborated on designing this jewel box shop where you get to see how the perfume is made, the flowers which are the origin point and the incredible handmade packaging with artful details like pressed flowers and gauzy bags sewn together by hand.

Visiting their studio(s) was a dream come true for me because after being in the USA so long I think we are trained to wear one hat. I went to art school where I had to choose a major, was initiated into the "fiber" cult of feminists and activist art makers. I left the painting department which is very traditional and male. Then I started a wallpaper company and entered the realm of interior design to find that being an artist and a vendor of products was a bit confusing to people. They wanted me to tell them what I do, and I was pretty much like "I can make anything for walls," which confused the hell out of things. They wanted a textbook definition or to see my business card and understand I am the Owner of a Brand-- the end. However, now I'm an author. Sometimes I randomly take people on trips around the world, so thus I'm a cultural tour guide. Someday maybe I'll have an HGTV show and become the Anthony Bourdain of textiles. But, for now, I want to embody the boldness of Mexican creatives and do it all. I don't want to be defined by the things I make or the name of the company or my past work or my current work. I just want to be Erin, the artist. And that is the larger umbrella under which ALL other pursuits fall.

The Monkeys in my Mind

Fragmentation: *"Part of me wants to keep working at this 9-5 job for the benefits and the other part of me wants to quit and start a business."* You guys don't know how many times I've said this myself and heard other people stating things like this. We are not people with two parts and our brain isn't divided into sections. We are one person with conflicting goals or motivations. This person wants security but also isn't sure how risky it is to take a leap of faith into owning her own business. She acts like if she says "part of me" this and "part of me" that I will tell her to go with the first part and ignore the second part. It's all one brain thinking those thoughts. The real nasty truth of this type of excuse is that you are allowing yourself to be indecisive by fragmenting yourself.

Indecision is a form of inaction. It's a conscious decision to not do any deciding. When you do nothing, nothing changes.

So, you'll stay at the 9-5 and the benefits will make you feel secure, but you will always wonder "what if…?" Being daring and bold with your life is a learned skill. Jumping on the 3-2-1 blast off mentality is practiced and refined. Growing integrity with yourself using small decisions first, and then working your way up to larger life changes requires trust in yourself and faith that you're making the right move. But, hear me on this. Whatever you choose to do, you will not make your life easier. I'll state that in a different way. If you quit your job and leave your benefits and start your own business, you will in fact just create a thousand new problems for yourself. New problems which all require decision making skills to tackle. So, the laziest and safest thing you can do is to stay put being grumpy about your situation and wondering "what if…?" That's a state of inaction.

Comparison: We talked in Section 1 about why the comparison model always fails. If you're a woman, you've been comparing yourself to every other woman in your orbit for was long as you've been aware of your own limbs. You're either winning or you're failing in comparison to other women. In their height, breast size, jean size, wallet size, you name it. We will always find a way to compare ourselves. But here's the reason why that's a losing game. If you think that you can't start a business or go out on your own to make magic in the world because someone has already done it, you are assuming that there is only room for one chick with a hot ass to enter a room. That just isn't true. Think about it. The more attractive women in one room, the more variety. Some are tall, and there are men who love that. Some have tiny boobs and big booties. There are connoisseurs for that too. Some are dripping in make up and jewelry and fine brand label clothing, which attracts a specific type of man. So to assume that you won't be able to take up space doing what you love assumes that there isn't someone out there who needs what you are making. Who loves and is searching for it.

I used to think that all the textile designers in America started because they had family money. That they built their brands because they had husbands with fat wallets that wanted to give their wives something to do. So all of them were hobbyists and they'd become successful because they started with an investor. That was my own chip on my shoulder. It was because I had met one or two women who had told me that their businesses wouldn't have survived if their partner or parents weren't supporting them. And because I was a divorcee and single mom, I had this paradigm that I wouldn't last five minutes in this industry without a man. But, here I am, five years later and I lived to tell the tale. Comparison assumes that there is only one flame. If my candle has it, no one else's candle can be lit. If hers is lit, then mine is extinguished. But truthfully, there is space for all of us to succeed within our own niche. You may need to refine your niche and define yourself as different from what others are doing. And your candle can still burn bright even when so many others are doing the same thing as you.

Always/Never: Avoid these words. Avoid statements using these words. When you say, "I never get the good clients," or "My applications always get rejected" you are in essence limiting the possibility of those things happening. You are reaching a conclusion based on evidence you collected along the way. But just as Darwin once discovered diverse mutations of birds and animals, he was able to prove new theories to the outside world about evolution. If we thought that all situations would lead to us being broke then we get wrapped up in thoughts of scarcity. It impedes our ability to make sound judgements or be decisive because we feel doomed to fail or as if opportunity doesn't knock on our door.

Catching yourself using these scripts will allow you to reframe your statements by saying, "It's not my experience that good clients come to me," and work through why they haven't. Maybe you need a better screening process, like your website can say that you only accept homeowners with a $50,000 budget or higher! This necessitates a different level of marketing, and informs how you speak about your brand. If you do interior design, you may need images that relay a $50K remodel instead of taking on only your friends or cheap clients who don't have big budgets.

Someday: If you want to get better at something or start something the worst way to approach it is to hope that it happens. Reaching goals is rather simple, and I've been working on helping you train your mindset to be awake to the ways we limit ourselves and our time and our talent. To say that you hope to write a book someday is to not prioritize it. To not break down the real steps that it would take to write the damned book is to dream that the book will fall from the sky and land in your lap already done. I had to write "Write for two hours" in my agenda three times a week for about 6 months before the book sat on my lap. I knew it would be done someday not because I was being vague and saying "There's so much going on right now, I think I will start sometime soon." Being vague is a device for us to never get started. Once we start, we obviously also have to follow up and finish. Making each dream into a list, a task, a set of goals and actionable steps sounds easier than it is because in theory, you can do it. Making it happen requires determination. "Someday" is not the attitude of the determined.

I've been in relationships where partners wanted to talk about it later. They asked to finish the conversations that were hard when life wasn't so stressful. They wanted to tackle the emotions once they felt more centered. I often prodded and pushed until our conversations escalated to "arguments" or even "fights". "Someday" thinking is a lack of accountability in a business or partnership. Thinking of this in another way, if an employee told me that they'd get the work done "soon" or "later" instead of "by 5 PM today it will be on your desk" I would very quickly tire or grow annoyed with this behavior. I might get irate or give the work to another employee. I might even fire them if they kept this attitude up. In a relationship with yourself, don't fall back on this way of treating your creative pursuit. The CEO of your life knows that there's no better time than NOW. To get started, to break it up into small manageable tasks, to write it in the calendar, to pursue answers if you don't know how.

Ego: In defense of our own self-image, sometimes we let our ego get in the way of our work. When someone tells us that we can't or that we need to wait or that it's not our skill set, sometimes we use that as a reason to become defensive. Sometimes we are so offended that we start justifying our actions based on our wounded ego's puny cry for validation. Being defensive usually plays out in very unattractive ways.

In confidence, I once told my friend about a venture I wanted to pursue. It was to lease a commercial warehouse space in an industrial part of town, convert it into a co-working space for artists and host events there. The spreadsheet I'd put together was convincing that I could make money doing it. He advised me with some expertise as a real estate investor, "You're an artist. Stick to what you're good at. You don't need to become a landlord. Sounds like a huge headache. Just design wallpaper and do that, it's what you know." Wounded and defensive I wanted to sign the lease that same day just to show him I can do it. That women and artists can be powerhouses and landladies and bosses. *I made it about me.* I made his statement about how he thought I wasn't capable and my ego set out to prove him wrong. Doesn't he know how many skills I have other than just being an artist?! Doesn't anyone see how hard I work?! While me ego was peacocking around my house, my monkeys in my mind got drunk on a box of Franzia and hit the town. It wasn't pretty. The next day they had a hangover. This is what happens when your ego gets away from you. You've got to reign it in. Maybe my friend was right. Maybe being a landlord is tough work. I mean, hell, he has thirteen properties and hundreds of tenants. Maybe he was just trying to prevent me from the horrible hell of a job of simply keeping keys for that many units and signing leases with a bunch of…artists. Needless to say, I gave up on that opportunity and decided to write a book instead.

Eeyore: (AKA Poor Me), this grey donkey's tail is falling off… the cloud follows him around raining. He's an unfortunate character which none of us would like to admit we relate to. But, sometimes we all come up with excuses that sound like "poor me." We resign ourselves to a fate that is grim and dismal because we simply don't think we can do it. We really rationalize our Eeyore thoughts by saying things like "I don't even know who will read a book about artists thriving. It sounds like a dumb self help flop." We treat our ideas like a soggy rag and throw them in the corner to get washed. It's too hard. It won't make a difference. No one wants what I have. Those are common doubts that erupt when we are having a bad day.

I liken this to exercise once more. I've always kind of laughed at people who are doing cross fit. I don't know why, maybe because I dated a jock guy named Kevin who was big into the cross fit genre of working out and thought it was a ridiculous show of masculinity (as many sports are in my opinion anyway). Flipping over huge tires is not something that humans naturally do in the wild. We weren't even flipping over boulders to look for bugs to eat. We were sharpening spears to shoot deer and in our free time sharpening pencils to write poetry. So, this abject form of exercise always fascinates me. What's the point?! That said, so many people on Facebook seem to really be enjoying the comradery, the achievements and the competition when participating in this sport! For them, fitness should be achieved in ridiculous displays of strength and power. For them, stinky gyms are the go-to venue for bonding! And more power to the Kevin's of the world who are ranking top crossfitters. Exercise of any kind feels futile when you only do it once, or when you focus on the action itself. Lifting weights, sprinting, plyometrics. The hoops we jump through to make our bodies do things differently, when repeated over and over, actually strengthen muscles, help our minds release chemicals and signal growth, health, happiness and well being. For that reason, we do it.

If we saw things as Eeyore did, we might have the attitude of "this hurts!" and not want to lift huge tires. We would say "what's the point?" or "who does this even benefit?" without ever measuring the success of the activity when repeated over a length of time like a month or two. Simple actions are trivial. Even everything I've asked you to do up till now would be super pointless if you only ever did it once. Writing things down, positive affirmations. All of those exercises are futile if not repeated. So, when you're tempted to dismiss something, quit or resign your enthusiasm for a task just think back to the cloud above your head and ask Eeyore to keep going.

The Victim: Not far from donkeys with clouds over their heads are the martyrs and victims of the world. There is a subtle distinction between the two though. They have made the story all about them, their suffering and failure. Martyrs have died for their causes, a thousand times over. When we pour our time and money and love into something but it doesn't turn out, we can think of it as a failure and we can also create dramatic narratives about how no one understands us or appreciates our generosity or talent. Artists are particularly good at being servants to their crafts and falling on their own swords. I am guilty of this too (remember the old mantra "It isn't fair"?)

After grad school I entered a job market that was bleak. I felt I had no marketable skills, though I had talent and a toolbox full of things I knew how to do. My skills didn't seem applicable anywhere. "No one will hire me with a fine arts degree," I would say when someone told me to look on LinkedIn for jobs. I devoted my whole life to teaching and making art and then I had nothing, no future, *wah wah wah* went the sound of my tiny violin. Singing a sad tune. It was all about **me**, and how much I'd given, and less about ingenuity and trying something new and getting outside my comfort zone. I was basically complaining that no one knew how great I was, even though no one knew me, or what I do, or what I wanted to do, or that I lived in Chicago, or that I existed at all. I wasn't even putting myself out there so how could anyone hire me!? Poor me, right?

Elizabeth Gilbert spoke to me in her audible book called Big Magic when she urged artists not to dwell on their failures. "You don't have to do an autopsy on every failure," she explains. Figuring out why you failed isn't helpful. "Chop it up and use it for bait for the next project." I love that. It's not a waste. Whatever you tried and it didn't pan out, it was meant to be. A part of the bigger plan for you. A learning tool, a stepping stone.

Being a victim requires zero effort to change. It bases all of its assumptions on the past and your current circumstances, disregarding the future. It assumes that you will stay right where you are and not grow at all, and that if no one loves you enough it's because you're unlovable. Not because you suck at intimacy or are deeply codependent and tend to annoy your partner with obsessive texts and chatter. Being a victim is a decoy for being stuck in your ways and depressed about your life. There's no quick fix for this, I am afraid. But parsing out some of the why's and how's is the first step to going from martyr to hero. Therapy is a really good place to start. Also, see the glossary under "H" for Hot shower and "C" for Coffee and "G" for Get off your ass and Get started.

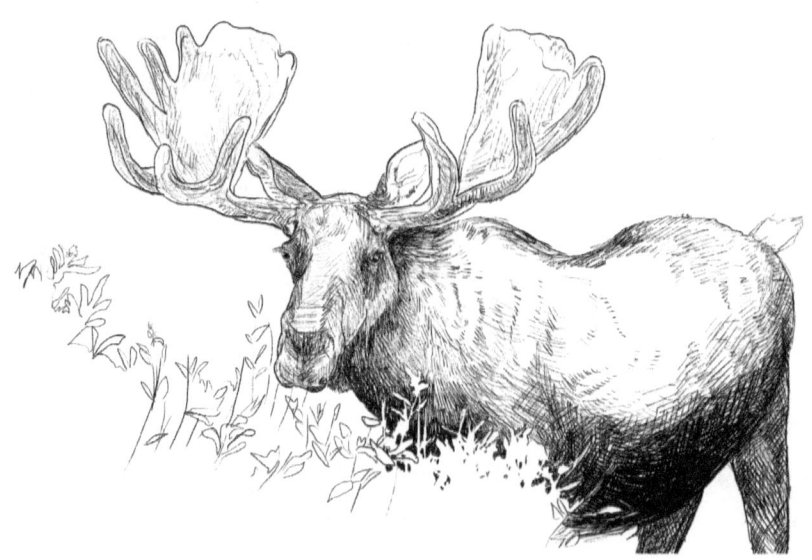

Fear is the Moose on the Trail

I once heard a podcast about Fear and Anxiety[21]. It summed up a few points that I'd like to mention here so that I can really drive home this message about the power of the mind. Fear was explained as a response in the body to a real live thing, such as a grizzly bear, or in my case, a moose. Having grown up in Utah I love nature and hiking. While visiting my mom one summer I took her and my two year old son to Brighton ski resort where there is a magnificent lake in the summer. The tops of the peaks are still covered in snow. The sun was shining and we hiked around the lake, taking our time because my mom's health was winding down. Not sure if she could make it around the lake now.

As we ended our circuit, we were about to go to the car. My son wanted to get out of the backpack he'd been in to stretch his legs. So I let him run around a bit on the grassy picnic area. My mom went to the car, but turned back to get the keys from me when I heard her shaky voice call my name. "Erin…?" I turned around to look at her to see what was wrong. Her finger was pointing at Anwar, my two-year-old. In his little red t-shirt, only about 3' in height, he was jogging around the grass and about to climb up onto a picnic table. He wasn't far from me, but right beyond us, emerging from a tall set of shrubs was an enormous moose. This moose looked like it was ten feet tall. It's antlers were the width of the picnic table and he was making eye contact with me. Moose are not gentle animals when they feel threatened or when somebody is encroaching on their territory. My son was not aware of the animal but I called his name. He looked at me and I tried to figure out a way to get him to come closer to me and farther from the moose without letting him know that imminent danger was headed his way.

---

[21] https://unfuckyourbrain.com/wp-content/uploads/2020/03/UFYB-Transcript-126.pdf

We were all frozen in time. I walked slowly towards him and picked him up. The moose and I still had our eyes locked. I whispered to my child that I had snacks in the car so that he wouldn't scream. I backed up slowly. My mom was perfectly still. Time stood still as the moose made its way slowly to the woods nearby and we walked to our car and buckled Anwar into his seat. That was FEAR staring me straight in the face. My heart was racing. My brow began to sweat. I didn't know whether to scream or run or nervously laugh or break down crying. But thank god it was over.

Fear is real. It's the moose on the trail. It's a car speeding towards you as you cross an intersection and have to slam on your brakes. It's something you have to react to very quickly to escape and your instinct takes the wheel. Anxiety however, is not. Anxiety is you in a public park imagining the potential grizzly bear coming through the bushes to eat you. There is no bear in sight! That might sound extremely judgmental to people who struggle with anxiety and even take medication for it. Anxiety is a real ailment. But the things that you are anxious about are not. The imagined grizzly bear is the reason many people avoid camping. For anyone who has been in a major car accident, it's why they avoid the highway or cars altogether. For someone who has watched a loved one die, it's why hospitals and doctors visits make them sweat and panic. For someone who fears other peoples' disapproval, leaving the house can seem like a nightmare. But those are imaginary fears. Fears that are not actually happening in the moment. They're made up by your human brain to "protect" you from harm. And it's a perfectly natural human response but it can be controlled. "The fear you let build

---

[22] https://www.amazon.com/Moved-Cheese-Spencer-Johnson-M-D/dp/0743582853

CHAPTER 11: ELIMINATING OBSTACLES & HAVING COURAGE

up in your mind is worse than the situation that actually exists.[22]"

Let's say you have anxiety that prevents you from doing things that might cause you to be successful. Like go to a networking event by yourself, knowing you will not know anyone. Or submit your resume to a job that you're not sure you're qualified for. What if moving to another city would ensure your quality of life would be better but all the unknowns prohibit you from making any plans at all? What if you've been asked to have a studio visit with a gallerist in town but you haven't made any work in months or years? Do you cancel the studio visit? The impulse to avoid a grizzly bear that was made up by your human brain is not always protecting you then, is it? Sometimes it actually inhibits growth. Anxiety can asphyxiate your momentum in life. It stomps on dreams before they're ever formalized. It runs from the moose that wasn't ever there.

How do you conquer anxiety? First, you must monitor your state. When you begin to start feeling worried or scared, you need to notice it and acknowledge the moose on the trail. In every situation you encounter, you must recognize him. Back up slowly. Make eye contact the entire time. Tell him "I see you, you son of a gun. I know you're not real. I reduce you to a negative thought and I resist you." You need to proceed with your life. Because it's not fear of failure that prevents you from moving forward. It's anxiety and it causes your complacency.

One way to calm anxiety is to take a shower or warm bath. Another way is to meditate and empty the mind of negative thoughts. One way is to just breathe and say "I can do this." The most compassionate way to diminish anxiety is to normalize it. The thing that most of us don't realize is that anxiety is something that all humans encounter to varying degrees. Lastly, if anxiety is ever present in your life, there are resources to seek help. You don't need to have me tell you that therapy and medication are options. There are books and podcasts and support groups for this. There are endless options for finding help, but please, don't tackle this part alone. These are the heaviest burdens and they need to be tended to before you attempt to start some massive creative venture or move across country or leave a toxic relationship. Don't think it's something you need to keep private and battle in the shadows.

Grief and Courage

I did a lot of *light* reading about grief while dating a widower. One book that helped me to understand where his heightened state of fear was coming from was Anxiety: *The Missing State of Grief.* We all know the other stages: Denial, Anger, Bargaining, Depression, and Acceptance. Author and clinical psychologist Claire Bidwell Smith explains that Anxiety is the stage we rarely speak about or acknowledge[23]. After losing someone you love, tragedy manifests itself deep within your subconscious mind as shock or the feeling of your world turning upside down. Your brain begins a heightened awareness of situations where you feel unsafe; your mind looks for opportunities to protect your body as if on high alert. Feelings of fear and dread are commonplace even years later after losing a person you love, but especially when you are triggered. Panic attacks are the pinnacle of anxiety's presence in your life and can render your body motionless, choking, frantic and feeling like you're having a heart attack. The irony about having a panic attack is that you begin to have anxiety about having another panic attack, thus perpetuating a continuous cycle of dread and fear; virtually panic about panic, anxiety about anxiety.

---

[23] https://clairebidwellsmith.com/anxiety-missing-stage-grief/

Triggers. We all have things that drudge up our "worst" or lowest self. At our best, we are resonating epic energy and light and creative magic. At our worst, we exemplify all the Jerry Springer, irrational, toxic behaviors that repel good humans out of our orbit. Some of it stems from lack of solid parenting as children. Some of it is our innate inability to cope with stuff that is hard. Some of our tricks that worked in the past start to not work for us and then what? We cave in, we turn our canoe back around and go back to physical reality or the hole we crawled out of. Figuring out what triggers your worst self is honestly the hardest "work" any human can do. It's the coldest shower you can take. It's the most miserable task and therefore I'm talking in vague terms about it because it's at the root of all our bad decisions, lying dormant like termites. Ready to eat the whole house we just built. Ready to crumble all our efforts in the external world with one devastating comment from a friend or colleague that makes us feel like a child again who is being told "You'll never be _____ enough."

Blame

Passing for a "bad day" or lunar cycle hormones is one way to squelch a moment for learning about yourself. Blaming an incident on another person's behavior is also a very common way to deny yourself a hard look in the mirror. In relationships (and businesses) that are toxic, no one in that partnership is an inherently flawed or evil person. They're just using strategies that aren't cut out for the enormity of our expectations. Shit hits the fan all the time and we are quick to dismiss a bad incident as the other person not doing the right thing. But you were in that moment triggered by a past experience that brought your vibration down. It made you so on edge that your fight or flight response reared its ugly head and sent you spiraling into a danger zone. You often feel horrible after this type of event and you wonder how to prevent it again. You avoid that person or topic of conversation or location anymore, allowing your tonality or sensation to forever be scarred. Instead what people with emotional intelligence need to do is figure out why those things happened.

Take responsibility for why the fight or flight mechanism in our brain caused us to act a certain way and then highlight it with a big fat yellow marker. When you find your triggers, you will know how to armor yourself for future encounters with traumatic topics or people. You will be able to protect yourself from situations where your boundaries are diminished, and you feel unsafe. You will be able to layer up some onion skins to make sure not to get hurt or damage a situation, especially a business relationship. You will notice a situation for what it is, instead of instinctually turning the other person into the 'bad guy' and blaming a negative outcome on the other person.

I have had a handful of experiences like this in my life, none of them I am proud of, where I was my lowest self. Where I felt very indignant about my own culpability in the situation because it felt so real and so palpable in the moment that someone else had done me wrong. Resulting in the loss of friendships, the inevitable apology phone call which is humbling or humiliating, or just a lingering sense of guilt that won't soon be resolved when you know you could've saved that fight from ending disastrously. But, the good news is, you have agency in your own life. You have to ability to:

a) not get involved in relationships lacking boundaries
b) express your needs, wants, concerns and desires
c) tell people when they've crossed the line

d) say sorry when you were wrong

These are like, *next level* adulting behaviors. If you are to run your life like a CEO, damn straight you have to master these. Brenee Brown hasn't been mentioned quite enough in this book, but her title Dare to Lead made a huge impact on me. She tasks us as leaders-- even if you're not managing a team, you are still running a family. If you're not running a family, you are still of influence. You don't have to have 150K followers on Instagram for me to consider you an influencer. Your generation is watching as you make a mess of your life. People are either having to pick the pieces up as you wretch around on the floor claiming it's not your fault, or they are putting you on a pedestal. Saying that they hope to be like you some day. What's the difference between becoming a leader and being hopeless? Grit.

> *"If you are not in the arena getting your ass kicked on occasion, I'm not interested in or open to your feedback. There are a million cheap seats in the world today filled with people who will never be brave with their lives but who will spend every ounce of energy they have hurling advice and judgment at those who dare greatly. Their only contributions are criticism, cynicism, and fearmongering. If you're criticizing from a place where you're not also putting yourself on the line, I'm not interested in what you have to say."*

What Brown is advocating for is at first, vulnerability. Secondly the courage to come forward and be a leader. Third, to ask hard questions like "what can I be doing better?" and waiting for your team, your family, and the monkeys in your mind to come forward with the truth. And to not back down when there's some hard work to be done.

We all have to set a goal to improve ourselves, stay open to feedback, make course corrections when necessary. Avoiding triggers is one thing, but that does not give you agency to hide under the couch and wait for the world to go by. You have approximately twenty-four hours to grieve small occurrences. You've got limited time on this Earth to make your impact. Want us to remember you for your gifts and highest self? Ready to step up to the plate to make that happen? Or are you going to cower in the corner and watch as others dare to lead and live their life artfully?

In psychology the definition of 'vulnerable' is someone who is thick skinned, open to being hurt, even a type of weakness. In Ontology, it's thought of as allowing the winds of life to blow freely over your soul. To let life in, on Life's terms. This sounds too fluffy to be truth, right? So I'll paraphrase someone famous in order to earn your

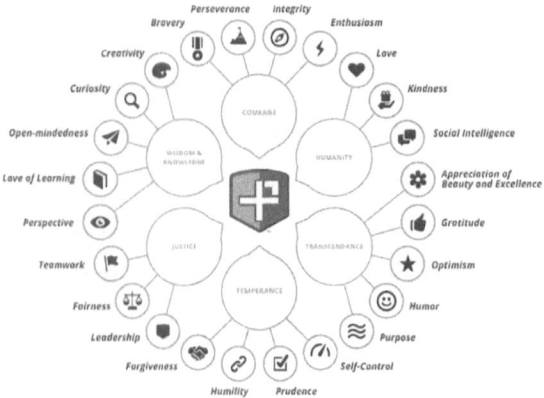

trust. The Dalai Lama is an eighty-five year old Nobel laureate whose people were driven out of Tibet in 1935. He said one of his greatest teachers was Mao Tse Tung known as Chairman Mao and founder of the People's Republic of China. The Dalai Lama marks the experience in his dealings with Chairman Mao as ones he learned the most from in his life. His enemy was his greatest teacher. When one faces adversity and struggle, it should cause them to grow. If we can remain coachable by life's lessons, we may learn through bad experiences and dealing with people who rub us the wrong way not as an inconvenience or something to be avoided. But as a way to better understand ourselves, our limitations and be able to see everyone through a lens of compassion and forgiveness. To shield yourself from the world is to diminish the capacity to flourish within it.

If Optimism Seems Fishy, Will You Believe Science?

Catherine Vader spoke in her TedX Talk about two kinds of thoughts. She states that it comes in two packages: Love-based and Fear-based. Love-based thoughts are impulses like generosity and kindness. Fear-based thoughts are anchored in resentment or self-doubt.

Fear-based thoughts trigger a part of the brain called the endocrine system, secreting hormones and causing insomnia. Cortisol is produced which decreases the immune system. The physiological response that negative thoughts can produce range from shortness of breath, spinning, panic attacks, etc. This is science.

In contrast, Vader teaches that love-based thoughts produce endorphins, thyroid hormones, etc. Her field is called "Positive Psychology" studies what makes us thrive rather than illness and mental illness, which does not.

Stay with me. Let's look at what makes humans thrive. There are

---

https://posproject.org/character-strengths/

twenty-four characteristics validated by hundreds of hours of research and verified by multiple scholars in different places around the world.

Kindness, Hope, Generosity, Humor, Curiosity, Leadership, Courage, Spirituality, Honesty, Zest, Perseverance, Teamwork, Justice, Fairness, Integrity, Enthusiasm, Perspective, Open-mindedness, Forgiveness, Humility, Prudence, Self-Control, Purpose, Optimism, Appreciation of Beauty and Excellence, Social Intelligence

Want to know how many of these characteristics—present in the very moments of us thriving—were rooted in fear-based thought?

None.

None of those involved things like:

Holding a Grudge, Stubbornness, Grinding and Struggle, Cynicism, Skepticism, Victimhood, Comparison to Others, Unworthiness, Complacency, Apathy, Worry, Anxiety, Protection, Revenge, Blame, Procrastination, Agnosticism, Doubt, Self-Limiting Beliefs, Power, Privilege, Supremacy, Judgement, Refusal, Abstinence, Deprivation, Defamation, Disruption, Anarchy, Destruction, Pessimism.

During the study that led to this research, Dr. Martin Seligman and Dr. Peterson in 2004 established a test for optimism and followed 15,000 people to see if they were outperforming those who scored high on the optimism test. By year two they were performing 50% higher in their fields than their peers who scored lower on this test. Optimism, they posited was then linked to success at work.

From the day we are born our parents aim to protect us from

things that are dangerous. Little do we know, our parents are just fucked up kids in grown up bodies, which we learn in therapy in our thirties. Their intention is to help us refine our sense of risk and danger and be able to be careful in making decisions. Decisions like running with scissors or jumping off a cliff into the ocean when on vacation in Hawaii. With a mother who worked nights in the ER for twenty-five years, I was particularly sheltered from anything and everything that might injure my body.

So when I was fully grown and, in my twenties, with a friend in Honolulu watching dozens of people jump from this cliff and survive I thought I'd try it. As I got to the top of this massive rock formation near the beach, I looked down and hesitated. My internal drive kicked in and years of training stopped me from going. I told my friend she could go ahead of me and she egged me on "Just jump!" I couldn't do it. I assessed how I'd look like the youngster who had second thoughts, retracing his path from the roller coaster to the entrance, bumping into everyone who was climbing up. I'd still climb down. The easier way was obviously to just hold my breath and jump. But I couldn't. I was paralyzed by fear.

My parents were strict for good reason. My mom had seen every bone in the human body broken and all types of horrific accidents. I just wanted to roller blade or jump on the trampoline but she was averse to risk; she had privileged information to inform her hypothesis that "Anything that can go wrong will." Most parents are telling their kids all day long to "stop doing that" or "No!" to the point that a child under two may believe their name was 'No' because they hear it on average 500 times that day. As kids we discover that a lot of behavior and activities are bad and dangerous, but as teens we figure out that we can do them as long as our parents don't find out. As adults we have to make our own decisions about what to say 'no' to and what to risk our efforts on.

How does this relate to being a thriving artist? Well several character traits are necessary to be successful at a creative pursuit. Number one, I posit, is courage. Even if no one else had been on top of that cliff and jumped before me, I could have leaped into the ocean and just hoped for the best. But there was evidence to support the argument with my own brain that it was safe. Hope is a close second. Because without a firm desire to see something succeed not knowing if it will or not, no one would ever try anything difficult. Having faith that you are making the right decision is crucial, especially when you are starting out. Perseverance is what this whole entire book is about and so I'll define that 180 more times before we're done. Though I think it ties with passion. If you're trying to start a business selling suits that you make from scratch but you have no passion for men's wear then you might have followed the wrong creative pursuit down the rabbit hole. You have to be willing to do something you actually love as your day job and you have to see it through despite all of the challenges that will indefinitely be along your path.

One note about optimism is that it should not be misconstrued for those who ignore reality and have their "head in the clouds." In fact, optimists are not avoiding reality or walking away from conflict. They're not some lucky demographic of people who have never had it hard in life either. It's not like they got lucky and never had to suffer and therefore they have a hunky dory attitude. "Character strengths aren't about ignoring the negative. Instead, they help us overcome life's inevitable adversities. For example, you can't be brave without first feeling fear; you can't show perseverance without first wanting to quit; you can't show self-control without first being tempted to do something you know you shouldn't."*

Real research proves that optimists are good at problem solving. I once read a whole book about how to learn the tactics of an optimist. (As it turns out, the wheel pictured above was created by the same person who authored the book, Learned Optimism). Optimists just become good at disputing the 'status quo' of thoughts. The automatic thoughts (our mind on default setting) are usually doubting, questioning and asking "What if _____?" and filling in the blank with a negative outcome. Standing on top of that cliff I didn't necessarily have the foresight to ask myself "What if I die?" but I just looked at the surface of the water and assessed that it was too far down for me to want to leap. "No way," was my first and only thought. I concluded that getting the fuck off that cliff was the best idea ever.

What would have happened if I'd challenged my brain instead?

As Seligman explains:

> "If you change your mental response to adversity, you can cope with setbacks much better. The main tool for changing your interpretations of adversity is *disputation*. Practice disputing your automatic interpretations all the time from now on. Anytime you find yourself down or anxious or angry, ask what you are saying to yourself. Sometimes the beliefs will turn out to be accurate; when this is so, concentrate on the ways you can alter the situation and prevent adversity from becoming disaster. But usually your negative beliefs are distortions. Challenge them. Don't let them run your emotional life. Unlike dieting, learned optimism is easy to maintain once you start. Once you get into the habit of disputing negative beliefs, your daily life will run much better, and you will feel much happier."

Research concludes that if you're a die hard pessimist, it's not your fault. Actually, 50% of it is genetics, 10% is situational but 40% is UP TO YOU. It's in your control.

If you're from the Clan of Pessimists, then you have to start with your own thoughts. For those who have a genetic predisposition to breast cancer as I do, we have a 60% likelihood of dying of cancer but 40% is up to us. Wouldn't you want to have an ounce of agency in trying to prevent the disease? Get the routine mammograms, do self-exams and think positively. Challenge your inner pessimist. He/she/they are not serving your ultimate purpose nor are they contributing to your overall happiness.

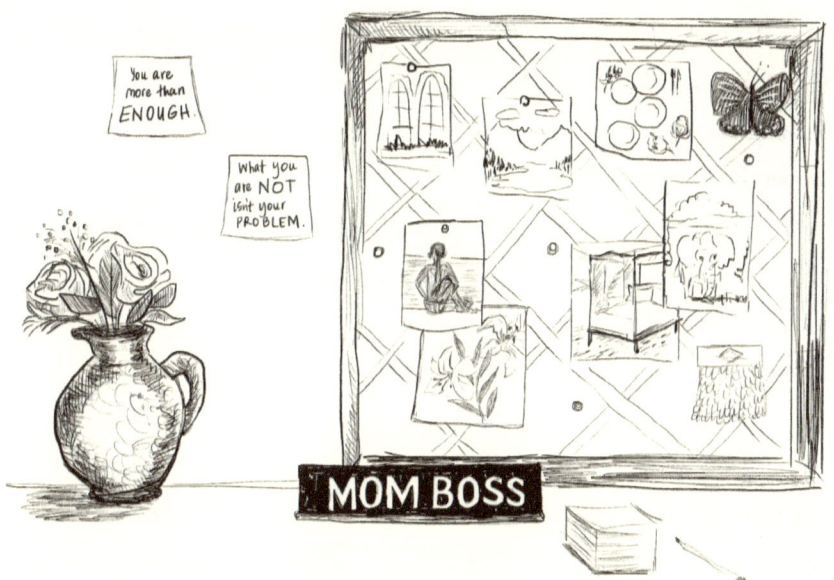

Chapter 12

Mastery

They say that it takes 10,000 hours to master any skill. That means that if you want to become an expert at typing and you spend twenty minutes a day on it, it will take you about one lifetime to achieve mastery. If you want to become a professional figure skater, I'd venture to say it might take longer than a year, even if you practice for two hours a day, even with an Olympic gold medal coach. Why then would it make any sense for you to believe that you could read this book, go spend a week or two putting these principles into practice, and then suddenly you'd have perfected the art of not sucking at life?

I am five years into my business, and I flounder all the time. It has taken a village to get me to here. I wanted Elle Decor magazine to call me the month I started my business and ask me to be on the cover. Four years in, I wanted an HGTV show of my own. However, as I sit down to give you "all the answers" to your burning questions about HOW to start, I realize that I need to prime you for the reality that is ahead. Things happen slowly. Every BHAG you set will be met with a long laundry list of SSS's. Small. Sweet. Steps.

A transcontinental railroad is laid one inch at a time. Rome wasn't completed in one day. A Rolls-Royce takes six months to fabricate due to intense craftsmanship, engineering and design whereas a Toyota takes seventeen-eighteen hours. Please consider this chapter a field guide to building your Rolls-Royce of canoes. Take it easy on yourself if it's not perfect after attempting to craft one piece, lend some patience and care (Go Slow and Be Kind to Yourself) while you construct it, and trust that if you build it, they will come. Elle Decor magazine, or whomever you wish to see your "thing" in all its glory. Fame and fortune rarely come to those who've mastered nothing or half-ass started ten things.

Manifestation vs. Demonstration

A note on visualization, inspiration boards, and positive memes on Instagram and Pinterest. No amount of willpower, wishing, hopium or prayer is going to build your canoe. You can channel your Native American ancestors, but those guys and gals can't come back with amulets or talismans holding your wisdom. You will have to take action to start, perfect, and finish every task on your mile-long to-do list. I don't care how much you are manifesting, girlfriend. The universe is based on energy. Positive and negative energy alike, those neutrons and electrons don't sit still. They move around. They are always in action. This is the distinct difference between manifestation and demonstration.

In order to demonstrate your ability to master something, you have to have a few key principles in place:

1) Change Takes Energy

Wanting to win the game is not enough. You have to exert a whole hell of a lot of energy if you want things to change in your life. Example: You want to lose weight. You wish and pray for things to change but you still eat the same, exercise the same and drink the same. You shame yourself when the mirror shows you the same figure day in and day out. You get discouraged easily, right?

What would be a more productive way to make a change? How could you do it more compassionately? More creatively? Think through the things that you have in your power to do right now with the resources you have. Too often we go out and buy a Peloton and spend $5,000 instead of just doing 100 crunches and 100 jumping jacks and drinking more water. Small sweet steps lead to gradual change. Gradual change will eventually be noticed in the reflection in the mirror.

2) Circumstances & Situations

Routines are great. Programs, regimens, plans. They're all swell, aren't they? Goals are meant to motivate us. All the podcasts and pep talks are also awesome. We think we're in control, but guess what? Sorry for bursting your bubble, but things change while you're trying to change. You're trying so hard to root yourself and ground yourself each day, and suddenly an earthquake or a forest fire up ends your efforts. Even the Earth we stand on is grounded to nothing. It's also just matter and energy floating in a vast universe. People whose visions were upended by unpredictable circumstances and situations, natural disasters may ask "how did I manifest this?" Even human-made disasters like riots, looting, vandalism, brutality-- these happenings put a damper in our plan for peace and progress. Let's adapt to survive. Make amendments to your earlier desires, plans or orientations to where you were going. *That is okay.*

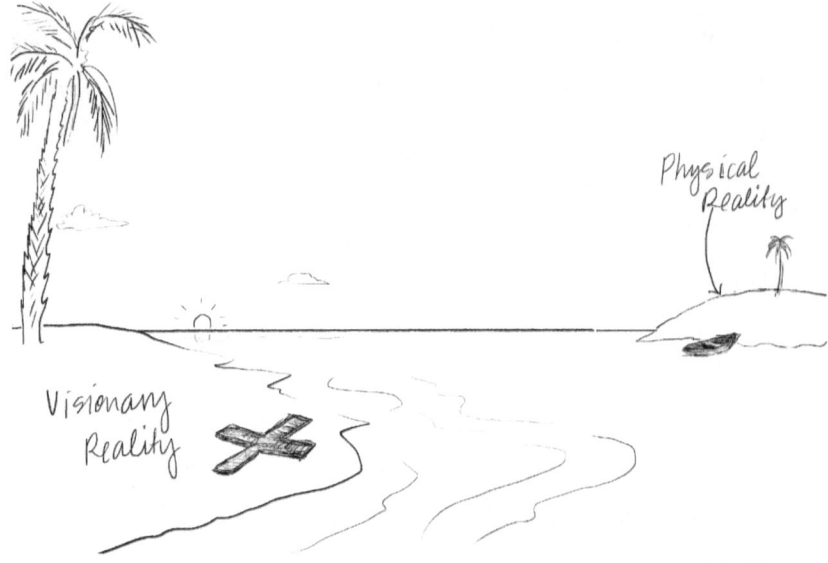

There is a disconnect for all of us when we are dreaming up our vision of how life will look once we've achieved something and how it is right now. That's called "visionary reality" vs. "physical reality." The two are separate planes or land masses or planets. Where you are right now is your physical reality and everyday life. The place where you want to be exists only in your imagination. You don't know how to get there, but you admit that it's not so far away. You also can acknowledge that there will be some bumps along the way.

CHAPTER 12: MASTERY

What happens about halfway through the journey, for most of us is what? We get scared about the potential moose on the trail. We let the monkeys in our minds get the best of us. We even want to give up and turn around. Time and time again we head back for our homeland because we convince ourselves that the journey is not safe, the struggle to paddle to the new world isn't worth it, or that we are just not cut out for this.

Here's how it shows up for me. I began writing this book with the intention of publishing it on Amazon in June. I thought if my kids could do e-learning with their dad Monday through Friday that I would have enough time to write six hours a week. For several weeks, I met with my editor on a routine basis. I blathered all my thoughts into a Google Doc and I was making good headway. About halfway through, something happened. I realized I was on a paddle board, naked. I had just told all of the inner workings of my mind, all the moldy, stinky milestones of my life to everyone. I'd even admitted my faults. I had involved my family and friends in my journey and told their moldy, stinky milestones too. What if…..?

What if they hate me for saying these things? What if the book makes no sense? What if no one buys it? Worse…what if important people read this book and they hate it or criticize it?! What if I'm not doing the right thing? Should I just run my wallpaper business and keep this shit in a journal?

I was second guessing my abilities, my voice, my audience, my purpose. I found every other task that desperately needed completion and did that instead of finishing my book. I got back together with my ex-boyfriend so we could repeat some of our prior fights, just in case they hadn't stung enough the first time around. I decided to redecorate my house. I bought bunk beds and spent late nights putting them together. I planned camping trips, and while making those memories with my kids was awesome, every single thing I did took me away from the goal. It made me further and further away from the completion of the one thing I'd set out to do. Summer passed. I broke up with my quarantine buddy again for the second or third time. I grieved one last time. It was brutal. I stopped writing, I stopped making art. I sabotaged all of my progress by letting the circumstances of my life take precedence. I don't feel bad about it, but I see it. The truth is I was procrastinating halfway from physical reality to visionary reality because I just didn't know if it was worth it to reach the other side. You never do. It was scary and new.

When you do something totally new, there is going to be *so much discomfort.* Our brains are wired to look out for danger. In a very primitive way, we are always looking for the moose on the trail, or worse, a saber tooth tiger who will devour us in one bite. That would be a fatal mistake. Maria Nemeth, one of my intellectual guides, says there are two fatal mistakes. <u>Number One:</u> Leaving the cave without looking around, spear in hand, ready to defend one's self. The fear of a negative outcome is enough for your brain to be constantly on the lookout for danger. <u>Number Two:</u> Leaving the cave without thinking. Fatal error number two is an untimely death. How this looks in real life? You leap into a new career and you failed to see that the company who offered you a generous salary actually needs you to work a million hours or sell your soul. You text and drive thinking nothing will go wrong and then suddenly you can't slowdown in time and hit a Mercedes (this literally happened to me).

I did no scientific research about the human brain in order to give you statistics about the psychology of the fight, flight or freeze mechanisms built into our internal wiring. There are volumes you can read about it though. I have no evidence but the situations in my own life where trouble at the border happens. Resistance, fear, excuses, procrastination, self-doubt, and dread. They all have happened to me at some point in my process of self-actualization, but my reason for mentioning this is that it is 100% normal and I want you to see it as it's happening to you. In that moment between Old World/Life and the New World/Life you have to observe the gray matter in between your ears working against you and keep paddling.

Perseverance requires ten times more energy than we expect it to. Like a rocket launch takes fuel and fire and inertia, so will your journey from one island to another. Here are a few things that will energize you while you're on your path:

Accountabili-buddies- Try to find one person who is also trying something new. Since you went on a diet from all of your energy vampire friends, find one person whose positive energy is a light in your life. They are the types who are accountable, have integrity and can help you see things clearly. They're not a coach. They're someone you can share goals with. You can say "My goal for today is to clean up my pile in the office" and they'll send back a high five emoji.

Enjoyment- If your small sweet steps or tiny paddle strokes are getting you closer to the goal but they are all dreadful, you will neglect one key factor in leveling up to the glorious new life. Having fun. You're supposed to enjoy the process. Now, I know lifting weights (or creating spreadsheets) is not easy or fun for most people, but the endorphins (or tax savings) alone aren't enough to "enjoy" the moment. Work Hard, yes, but also celebrate. Create a sticker board for yourself! Try to be creative about it and bring some fun into your process. Even if it's separate from the goals you're setting, please don't forget to live your life. Demand some joy throughout the journey. Turn it into "play" whenever possible.

If all we do is look at the goals we set as a destination, there is a measuring and quantifying happening. "How much longer will it take?" "When will I get there?" By the end of your life is when you will have reached the destination. Don't be in such a rush to get there. Enjoy where you are, even if there are squirrels in the attic.

"You Don't Know What You Don't Know"

People said that to me often when I was in the startup phase. Now I am feeling that so deeply as I'm contemplating launching my book online in a virtual space. I have no fucking clue what I'm doing. I don't have optics right now because it's like looking at a holograph. There are certain universal laws that govern 'Transformation' and one of them is Not Knowing. If you try to analyze all the possible outcomes, you'll burnout before you start up. The goal of starting anything is not to produce results immediately. Think about a caterpillar. He's been chomping along on all these leaves all spring long. Suddenly he's feeling queasy. His appetite ceases and he's tired. He has no clue that this is nature's signal that it's time to build a chrysalis. He just kinda goes through the motions setting up a cozy place to take a nap. He falls asleep and what happens? What happens isn't up to him! Transformation takes its course. If he knew that he was about to shape shift he might say, "Oh no. No way! I am not doing that. That sounds super risky and I like it right here in this fat worm body. I'm not changin' nothin".

If we all knew this in the beginning when we first started out, we'd feel much better about the process being painful, full of mistakes, and downright difficult. We'd go, "This is part of the process. This is what is supposed to happen." Instead our dumb lizard brain starts saying "Danger! Stop!" and we usually fail before we ever try. Keep with it.

Follow one path in the maze until you get to a dead end. Then, when you can't go any further, turn around and try a different route. That's part of this journey. Nothing is Purfict.

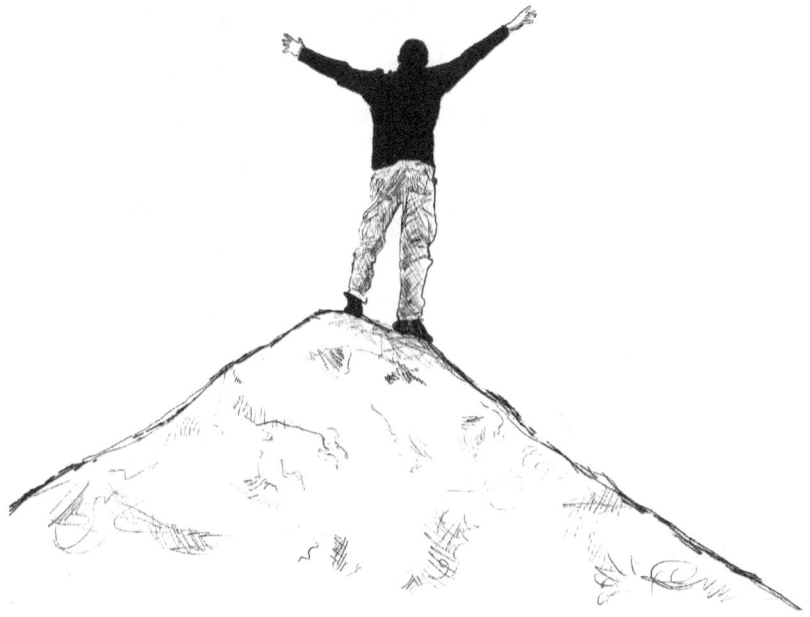

Believe it. Better Yet, Yell it from the Mountain Top

I'm going to talk to you about Branding and Marketing. But since these terminologies give you the hives I may as well lie to you and say you're going to be eating ice cream when really, it's tofu. What I've avoided saying until now is that you are going to be running a business if you do everything in this book. After you read this book and start taking small sweet steps towards your goals, you will be figuring it all out on your own. You'll be stuck in a maze wondering why the cheese keeps moving[25] .

---

[25] https://www.amazon.com/Moved-Cheese-Spencer-Johnson-M-D/dp/0743582853

See, people aren't as clever as mice. Mice, in a lab environment, make adjustments to their routines and get clever and sneaky in order to find their next meal. If the cheese isn't where it was yesterday, they'll run all around the maze looking for it and they'll remember which routes lead to no sustenance. Humans on the other hand are kinda dumb. They're like cows. Cows go back to the same patch of grass over and over, even after they've eaten all the grass. So many artists I talk to say things like "I posted my campaign on Facebook and only $50 was raised." They posted it on one platform. One time. And were confused why 1,000 people didn't see it. Why you still doing the same tricks, old dog? There are new things to explore, new methods that will yield new results.

Look, you already are running a business if you have a creative pursuit and I know it takes a little twisting of the mind to think about it as a business. Probably because it's "not in your nature" to sell stuff. It's not in your toolbox to market online. You've never even sold anything maybe, so you have a hard time wrapping your mind around earning or asking for money for your thing. But there are still some congratulations owed to you for this: You've read this far.

You're going to leave me thinking of yourself as the CEO of your Life, Inc. and your Creative Practice, LLC. You're going to find a team to delegate things to and you're going to use your time in the best and highest paying ways. You're building your canoe and you'll be adamant about it not sinking. The stakes are higher now. You are recognizing your inherent magic might be the key to your life's success, your dreams, your fulfillment. The priority needs to be "Profiting." You want to make money! We all do. Here's the biggest trick I have in my treasure trove. Making money doesn't have to be so hard!

CHAPTER 12: MASTERY

Making money is okay.

What we will talk about next is in most books referred to as marketing. I like to think of it as the guy dressed as the Statue of Liberty during tax season who was hired to shake a sign at the intersection. He's advertising one of the more boring professional services there is, accounting. But the most creative ones have headphones on, they're rocking out to Bon Jovi or Lord knows what ballad. They're dancing and it's drawing attention! People are taking notice of him; some are terrified and some find him humorous. That's a message that is worth yelling about. The one that takes all your energy. As if that guy would go broke by the end of the day or be taken out back and beaten and thrown in jail if he hadn't given it his all. He is shouting it from the rooftops.

The last remaining thing to do, after you've really homed in on your magical powers, is to announce them to the world. When you say it out loud, it becomes true. When you post it on Facebook, it becomes true for the world. Right? You need to try everything. Try calling people you know and saying, "Hey, I haven't talked to you in a while but let me tell you what I'm up to…" Try emailing very personal emails. Try group messaging old friends. Try posting on neighborhood mom boards on Facebook. Try a flyer in the Thursday folder that goes home to 1,000 parents at your kids' school (if the PTA will let you advertise). Take out a real ad. Put your face on a bust stop bench or billboard if you have the funds. Join a networking group. Make post cards and pass them out at the dog park. Tell every single person in your orbit how awesome you are and what a solution your "thing" is to their problem. Frame it as they need it. Tell them it is awesome and valuable and really will improve their life.

Pause. I know what you're thinking. "I can't do this. I am not good at this. I dread the sales part. I wish someone else could manage this so I can just do the creative part." Boys and girls. Here's the truth no one wants to tell you: if you don't sell anything, you'll never make any money. If you don't market the things you made (tell people what you do or what you've created) you can never sell anything. So, unfortunately, this step is unavoidable. Up until now, we have just been playing games inside our own brain. Mastery is about interacting with people in the world.

Let's pretend that the basic assumption for all things is clear and certain. Let's call it the "truth." The truth is, someone, somewhere wants what you have. They are excited to pay lots of money for it. Their lives will be improved by having what you made. You just have to find them.

Find them on the internet. Find them by buying a zip code from the US Postal Service and sending post cards to everyone in that area. Find them with an advertisement. Find them by networking. Find them on Facebook, or Instagram or going to a trade show where those people are going to be. Just FIND THEM. Virtually or in real time. But find them and tell them what you're making.

Sales Strategy: Just Tell a Story

Branding is just telling your story-- artfully. Telling your story is where the idea hops out of your brain (or the shoe box under the proverbial bed) and onto the page. Into reality that idea blasts. This is when you are responsible for justifying WHY it is so important. Marketing is selling to a given audience. You aren't a salesperson, I know that, but you can learn to be one. More importantly than learning how to sell though is to learn how to *tell the story* in a way that helps someone solve a problem they're having. Here's the very finite difference between just being a good storyteller and being good at marketing. The story is being told for the benefit of someone else. The art is also being made for the benefit of someone else.

Game-changing moment. I'm not just making art for self-expression? No, starving artist. That's what you've been doing up until now. Have you been making art just because it feels good? No. Art that only satisfies the maker is what I call "masturbation." Art that serves a party of one can be done alone in your studio. Burn it afterwards for all I care. That's private. No one needs to know what feels good to you. Think about someone else for a change. My nanny is a painter. She once said, "I know, I should just make blue paintings because they sell." She knew this information but continued to NOT make blue paintings. Who does that serve? Her masochistic ego?! It serves no one. She is purposely not making the things that she knows will sell. That is sabotage.

The story of the origin of the word 'sabotage' is quite comical. Once upon a time in a place called France there were factory workers who wore wooden shoes called sabots. In an attempt to interrupt production, some workers decidedly threw their wooden shoes into the machinery, clogging, bungling and destroying the factory's equipment. These persons became known as saboteurs. Is this you? "Hey, Pierre! Stop throwing your clogs into the machines!" It will work just fine if you play nice and leave your ego where it belongs.

What I propose in this section is that you begin making work that deserves to be shown to the world because it will add value to someone else's life. That is the type of art that needs a stage and a microphone! So tell the story. Tell them who you are, where you came from and why this work is important.

Solving Other Peoples' Problems

An ideal customer for me as the Lead Sales person for Relativity Textiles is: "someone bougie with bare ugly walls." It's someone who is ready to commit to positive tonalities where it intersects with luxury design. My expensive wallpaper solves their problem. Period. I don't feel bad about that because a lot of people want to buy expensive things. They'd prefer not to buy cheap, DIY, removable wallpaper. I purposely placed myself in this niche because I needed to be profitable. If you make Covid-19 masks that don't fog up sunglasses, you are solving a LOT of problems!

Create an avatar. I'm not talking about the ten foot tall blue people from James Cameron's animated movie. I'm talking about a caricature of the ideal customer for you. Get specific. Are they male or female?

How old are they?

What do they do for work and how much money do they make?

What do they eat and where do they buy groceries?

Do they read and, if so, what do they read?

What form of transportation do they take to work?

Are they living in a major city or a rural place?

Do they have children?

Are they college educated?

How many cars do they own?

How many homes do they own?

This is called demographic information. You can look up statistics if you want to be nerdy. You can ask others in your industry or someone who does what you want to do. You can look at the census information. You can observe people at the dog park and figure out by what they're wearing if they can afford a pet portrait for $100 or $1,000. Do some digging. When you figure out these details, you can create a marketing plan based on these factors. If they ride the "L train" to work, you can inquire about how much an ad costs, or you can stand at the busiest time of day with a stack of flyers and pass them out. Up to you. But, figure out your avatar, because if they're not exactly the same kind of person as you, you might not know too much about their buying habits. Maybe find a friend's mom to be your guinea pig and ask her if she'd buy a $1,000 pet portrait or what she would pay for it.

There's no wrong answer here, and I will reiterate what I said before about "you don't know what you don't know." You try something, and either it works, or it doesn't. Try a different font in your ad and a different picture. Try posting on Instagram at a different time. That's called AB Testing. You try two things and see which works better. Then you make a guess that there's something about the winning marketing piece that works. Keep doing that.

Looks Matter and the Story Matters

Think about the way in which your 'thing' is going to serve someone else. Brand it for them. The classic red and white Campbell's label tells you "Soup" is mmm mmm good. That's branding. You'll see. This is stupid and too simple. But it works. You don't need fancy language or metaphors or any heady complicated conceptual thrust. Just real talk. Tell people what you are doing and why. Make a little tagline or jingle. Be a little whimsical on this one. Be a little… cheesy.

If all of what I've just said makes you so stressed, it's okay. It made me stressed at first too. I remember sitting in the front row for several panel discussions at Design Chicago where my glamorous friend

Claire sat with her designer clothing and talked about how she built a following of 15,000 in the same time it took me to get 3,000. She was a journalism major and worked in marketing before switching to become an interior designer. She loved to write and started a blog. Pretty soon she earned the title "influencer" and brands started to offer her free shit. Like pots and pans, clothing, free wallpaper, you name it. She was advertising for them in her posts. She was using the free stuff in her clients' homes and charging them full price for it. She has a money mindset and the blog was a means to an end. The hours of pinning on Pinterest. The very particular Virgo strategy of the nine Instagram pictures in a grid and do they all look harmonious. This woman was on a mission to get high end clients. She wasn't out for fame or fortune. But she was driven to succeed. In 2017, Claire's blog was honored with an award for Best Design Writing by the Design Influencers Conference. She'd pitch her own stories to magazines instead of hiring a PR firm, and you know what? She got published. A lot. Now people fly her around the country to speak and design their homes. She's a brand ambassador for William Morris's wallpaper collection for Christ's sake. It's a dream come true for a pattern lover. She taught me to be persistent. She taught me some of the rules of the game, without me needing to pick her brain. She was giving this information away for free and I took notes.

Before you start writing your story, take some time to think about all of the artists or creators or brands or companies who are already doing what you want to do. Think about their themes, images, color palette, brand names, geographic region, the founder and their ethnicity or age, the charities they support or non-profits they founded, etc. Think about how they present themselves to the world. Most likely there are hundreds of people doing what you want to do already, but none of them are doing it as YOU would do it. What makes you special? What makes your creative product or service special? What would make a consumer or client chose you over them? What's your "brand" identity? Sometimes looking to your future competitors for inspiration (or just get really jealous of what they've achieved and want to have those things) is a great place to start. See what they're doing, what they're reading. Heck even reach out to them and ask to interview them on how they got started.

Here's the exercise that my very first web designer (I'm on website number five) had me do when we first met to strategize the look and content of my future website. Figure out your Top 5 Differentiating Factors. Here are mine:

1. **Artist-Owned Company**- I am the creator of all of the textile patterns that my company has in their collections of wallpaper. I am also the owner of the business. *That is rare.*
2. **Supporting Artists and Artisans**- In a time when anyone can take an image and repeat it and send it off to a company to print it digitally, I am purposely supporting mills in America who have artisans screen printing wallpaper by hand. It's done in the same way it was done since the 1970's and it's a dying art-form or craft. I like that it's old fashioned printmaking having a renaissance. I like that real humans are making it and there are small inconsistencies for that reason. It's not robotic or machine made. It also lowers the cost to be printed this way.
3. **Globally Inspired**- The theme of each design is a foreign country or textile printing technique from a region outside the "West." As someone interested in travel and translation of culture, I wanted to find a way to make the industry of interior

design a bit more culturally inclusive. By way of wallpaper, I am trying to introduce homeowners to places like India, Morocco, Japan or Sudan. And once they love the wallpaper and bring it into their everyday lives, I have subtly snuck my artistic ideas into their homes. They symbolically embrace a foreign culture or place just by owning my artwork on their walls. This is how I thought about the tagline, "Bring the World Home."

4. **User-Friendly**- Our Wallpaper is Wipeable, Fade Resistant and Removable. We are capable of printing Type 1 and 2 (residentially or commercially fire rated) wallpapers and vinyls; all are Class A. It's easy to install and easy to remove (depending on if you use the right kind of paste!) ~This is the technical side of my brand, but it is usually a huge "selling point" when you compare my wallpaper with that of other brands.

5. **Customizable**- Many wallpaper companies spend thousands of dollars to make these huge massive books with leather handles and dozens of pages. I however created tiny sample books that fit in your purse or desk drawer. I wanted to invoke an intimate conversation with the viewer and give them a taste of what is possible. That said, I can kind of make anything. Because I'm that small of a business that I can choose to stray from my SKU list and make a purple colorway if someone wants that. So I tell people that the sky is the limit (and sometimes that overwhelms a designer or home owner to know there are not rules or restrictions) and the more creative they are the more the wheels start turning in their head about

how they can choose anything they want on their "build your own pizza."

My tagline is #BringtheWorldHome.

Another way to really visually explain who you are and why anyone else should care is having sexy images. No, sicko, I don't mean make a porn or send some Richard pics. I want you to hire a professional photographer or videographer to tell your unique story [of your brand] in still or moving images. Make it short: four minutes long. Write a script using a dictation app on your phone. Time yourself. Dub some stock videos if you don't have good footage of yourself doing your thing. There are websites where you can download dummy videos of just about anything for only $15 a month, and if you're broke like I was, you can sign up for a 14-day-trial and then cancel after you hit the maximum downloads. I had four email addresses at that time, so I just kept doing it over and over until I had 20 videos or 30 downloaded. That is how a starving artist makes a Kickstarter video. Find the images to support the words or else the human brain will turn off by hearing too much without anything to look at. Even a text overlay will be a great converter for Facebook videos or YouTube. Don't know how to do that? Hire a starving artist who can.

Likely, yes, you will need to stage something. Like you pretending to paint while someone snaps your picture. Take photos of you at your computer pretending to look off into the distance, while completing a deep thought. And, yes, that is going to feel semi-inauthentic to take these photos because they're not happening real time, live and genuine. But, do you look better with a little lighting, hair and makeup, tidying up your space and smiling for the camera? Yes. Do you really want to load images onto your professional website and social media that someone took on their phone? No. okay, good. So this is part of the deal. *It's just a fact of life* as you move to the next stage of the game.

Do not skip this step.

Lastly, packaging is super important. If you have to ship things, maybe get a colorful tissue paper. If you don't know how to mail merge your shipping labels yet, google it. Then put your logo on the label somewhere. Logo and tagline can go anywhere. Come up with a standard set of fonts, colors and image sizes that you can use for pretty much everything. It can be your Facebook header image, your Etsy show profile image, at the bottom of your emails in your signature, etc. For the love of God don't deliberate forever about this. When I launched my company, my logo was horrible. This stuff evolves over time just like the caterpillar. Let it naturally grow up as your brand gets more mature. You can change it once a year, but don't change the name and URL and logo all the time because it's confusing to people. This will be your Style Guide. It helps the graphic designer, should you hire one, with precise details.

Okay that's great that you just spent a hundred hours crafting the mythology and narrative of your brand. You chose your words so carefully that they will be forever in your catalog. But, what about you? You are the creator. You're not getting away with this. You can't just sell the girl scout cookies without dressing in your uniform and knocking on the door! You're going to also have to introduce yourself. Think about the Shamwow guy on TV[26] . He has a personality that sells a mundane item! His story is incredible. Madame CJ Walker was an African American entrepreneur and female to boot, in a time when black business owners had a hell of a time getting traction. She was

---

[8] https://www.amazon.com/Moved-Cheese-Spencer-Johnson-M-D/dp/0743582853

her own spokesperson because her hair product "Madam Walker's Wonderful Hair Grower" helped her gain confidence to start her own business. She's her own case study. She talked about her own journey and that inspired other women to want to be like her. And her product name! Imagine if you could sell (Insert Your Name) "_____'s Wonderful Watercolor Paintings"!

So too will you have to write your bio, speak it out loud and broadcast it to the world. You don't have to tell where you were born, where you studied, all the ideas behind your work, etc. unless it's relevant to the thing you're making and selling. Nobody cares if girl scout cookies are made by elves or day laborers in Tennessee. They just want to eat delicious snacks and binge while feeling good about supporting the girl scouts. The bio of the creative person is important. Remember to *channel your magic.* Talk about it passionately and don't water it down. Don't downplay your skills. If you play trombone while painting with your toes, you'd better include those details! Wow people with your unicorn magic and get ready to receive their warm reception.

Self-Promotion

Finding support is a practiced skill. It's not the art of begging and it's not selling out. It's simple and effective when done correctly. But it's about creating your own net[work].

Here's what I mean when I say network: A safety net of qualified givers who care for you and your position in life. They empathize and serve. They listen and they effectively execute. They offer guidance and wisdom not shut you down when your plans aren't "based in reality." They catch you when you fall but they're not sitting there waiting for your failure. Promoting one's self means coming into your own as an artist; to do this is crucial to success by any definition. Networks can be divided into three categories: personal, family, and career.

I could have named my textile company Erin Minckley Chlaghmo Designs or Studios or Textiles. But I chose instead to name it after my initials, EMC. Like $e=mc2$ or the theory of relativity. Albert Einstein's theory made great sense to me as a metaphor about how we see interior design. His theory states that if I am standing still and looking at a mountain in the distance, and you are on a train looking at that same mountain, our vantage is relative to our proximity and our momentum. The mountain is getting progressively bigger to you. But, for me, it stays small because I am far away and standing still. How does that make sense to design? Well, depending on our age, race, style, and taste for things we will all choose different wallpapers! I may like bold colors, whereas you prefer gray and beige. Therefore, our preferences are relative.

What made it easier to have a brand that was embedded with the initials of my name but not my personal namesake is that I could view it objectively as a company or brand. It was not "me" that I was selling or "my artwork" as much as it was a product. Wrapped up in the identity of that product were all of my ideas, all of my time and devotion and the origin of each wallpaper was indeed my own drawings. Still, somehow marketing and promoting the product was easier as I considered myself just a salesperson or representative of the company.

CHAPTER 12: MASTERY

How Do I Profit?

Everything I ever learned about sales I learned from Girl Scouts. The iconic brand teaches young women how to sell. Their parents obviously play an integral role in how many boxes they sell, and some kids cheat and let their mom take the purchase order form to work at the hospital. All the doc's and nurses ordered three boxes, and thus my quote could have been filled. But I liked knocking on doors and introducing myself. It took some time to get over being shy about it. You know why it got easier? The brand speaks for itself. It didn't matter if it was me, my sister, my mom or another girl from another troop knocking on the door. When they saw that little green uniform, the homeowners got out their checkbooks and wrote me a check.

Why? Why do people love those cookies so much? Is it supply and demand? Like the pumpkin spice latte from Starbucks that only comes around once a year, so you feel inclined to stock up? Or is it because they have addictive ingredients? Or are some people so kindhearted that they'd do anything to help an aspiring entrepreneur with $8? Perhaps all of the above. What I do know with certainty is that the more you can make your art like the Girl Scouts make cookies, the better. Make art that appeals to other people. Make it desirable and enjoyable; the more others like it the more they'll likely pay money for it. If your work is so dark or abject that only goth vampires like it, you might have a tough crowd to sell to. Cookies are cheap; make art that is affordable to everyone (or don't, we'll talk about that later). But if you make art that is $40 perhaps someone will be able to afford three prints instead of only one. Then each sale has multiple units sold. Having a very limited quantity is another tactic called supply and demand. You can make diverse artworks or images from a focused source of magic (medium).

Draw, paint, make jewelry, knit socks, screen print band posters or have some of your unique typeface made into catchy coffee mugs and mouse pads. But, heavens to Murgatroyd, don't make ALL of those things.

I make wallpaper. That's it. Just like the girl scouts make cookies. I could have gotten into bed linens, throw pillows, fabric by the yard, etc. But I took the advice to FOCUS, focus, focus. I do wallpaper really well. Once I've established the name of the brand and the reputation on the street, that's when I can branch out into new territory. The wallpaper comes in many colors and patterns, just like the cookies do. Wallpaper is $400 a roll. How many do you want?

If you want to offer high ticket artworks, you can. You do so knowing not many people can afford a $14,000 painting. Your reputation better be stellar. Your network better be high net worth individuals. Your sales pitch or introduction letter or proposal better be 100% magical gold. If you want to start off a little lower in price, you can always work your way up. But, be weary of changing your prices too much once you are already known for being cheap because it's hard to make jumps to the luxury market once your wallpaper is already being sold at the Home Depot. Likewise, I am now somewhere near the $$$ range for the price of my items and if I discount it now, the reputation of the brand may suffer when the price tag drops in numbers. Decide where you want to be from the beginning and try to stick it out. There are many times I wish I made cheap wallpaper that was easy to install and DIY friendly! During the Covid-19 pandemic I'd have loved a dolalr for everyone calling me asking for peel and stick paper.

I pointedly chose to be on the higher end of the price continuum and also towards the far-right side of the x axis or style/taste continuum.

You got to spend money to make money. Ever heard that one? Here's a little more depth about how to price your work. How the

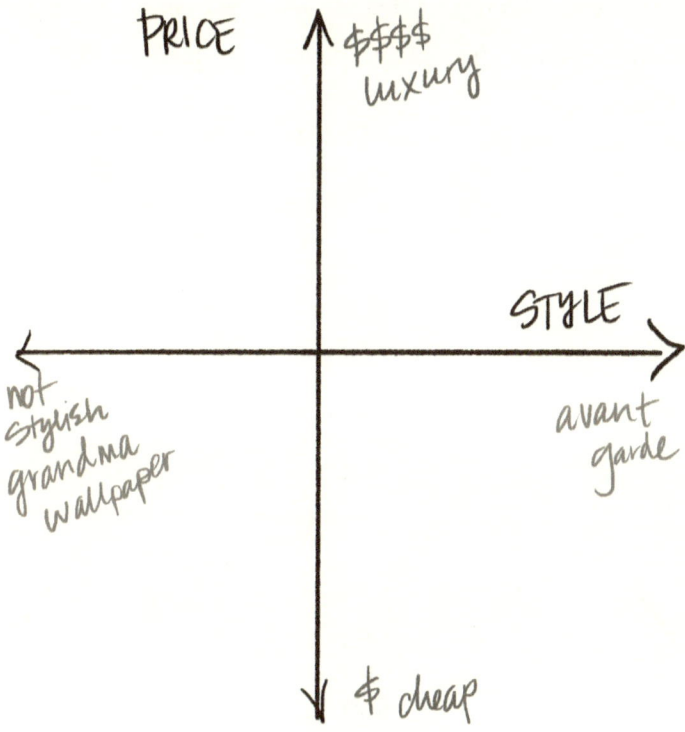

market determines the price of an item and the ecosystem where your artwork relies on to sustain itself.

"The ego is expensive." This is a quote that I was told by my accountant when he began grilling me about why I used luxury showroom reps to sell my work. I can't be in NY and LA and Chicago all the time to present my wallpaper collections to design firms in all the places. So I sent my samples out to many different showrooms from Austin to Denver to Raleigh in order to get them to place my wallpaper in the hands of their local clientele. With that came a whole bag of new dilemmas like supply and demand, regional taste habits, and of course, price.

What I didn't know was that my wallpaper needed to be priced to accommodate a lot of different people taking a piece of the pie. Here's how it shakes out.

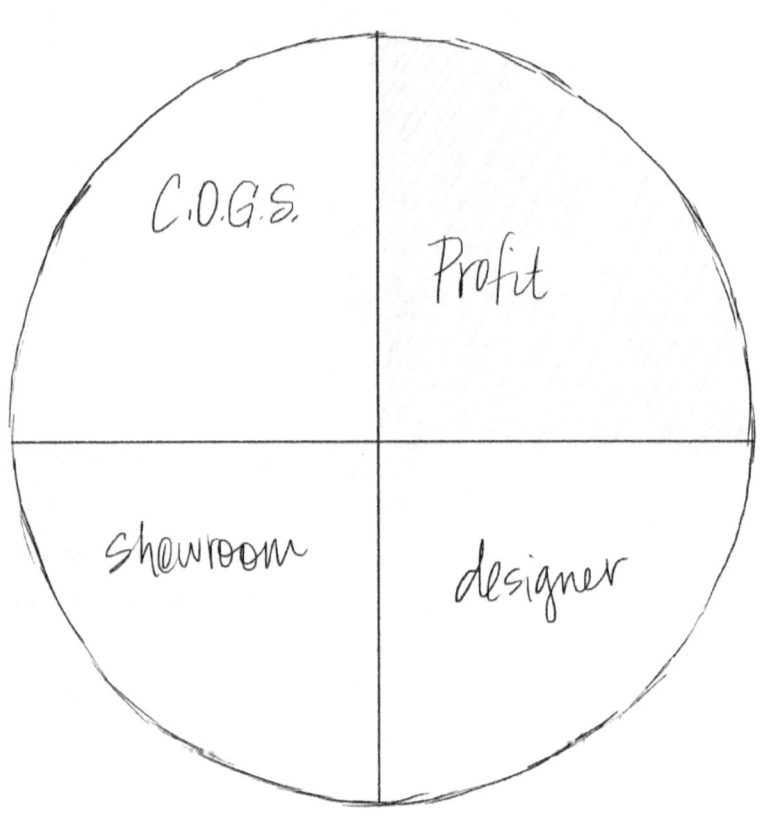

My profitability is based on a few things. Not only my time and the raw materials that it takes to create the product, the labor, the shipping, etc. All of that, (which without these key ingredients my product would not exist!) is classified as the Cost of Goods Sold or C.O.G.S. The COGS is different for each of us.

The next thing you have to do is base your art or service's price knowing that there are others who are going to resell it. With wallpaper, when I sell it to a luxury showroom, I have to sell it half price. They are then going to add a 25% margin and sell it to an interior designer. The designer adds another 25% and sells it to the "end user" or homeowner. Thus, the full pie from the diagram above costs $400. I made only $100 because it cost me about $100 to make. I sold it to the showroom (wholesale price) for $200 and they sold it to the designer for $300 (NET price). It in effect will be sold four times! To me, by the print manufacturer or mill, then to the showroom, then to the interior designer and lastly to their client. Lots of math, but it's honestly why I just took the COGS and times'ed it by four. Because I knew it would be sold four times, adding $100 each time. That's how I decided to price it at $400/roll-- easy math!

But I don't make enough money in this model to succeed in the long term. It's why all the textile designers I know are being bank rolled by husbands, parents or a part time job. Once I finally understood that, I called my accountant and told him I decided to write a book instead. He acted excited and proud of me. Neither of us know if this will be any more lucrative or promising than me designing wallpaper. "The ego is [so] expensive" that I have to keep trying. Is your creative pursuit really going to make sense from a cash flow perspective? Will writing the book make me rich? Nope. Will the sales of the book create wealth in the long run? Maybe. But the book will lead me to new opportunities.

It will make me an "expert." After all, I wrote the book on how to thrive as an artist. Now, I need to thrive so I can prove it. It also pushes me to make something of myself instead of staying in a state of "starving artist."

This stairway to wealth way of living is not the easy way. I'd like to point that out. I am doing everything b-ass backwards. This is why I could never write a business book. The sharks would pick apart my own personal strategy by saying it was two steps forward and one step back. With each stage I develop more skills, and I discover what I didn't know in the stage prior. My editor said she's never seen a book written this way… but that's the magic in the journey! *Everyone I know who runs a business is doing it in their own haphazard way, with all their messy emotions tied up in it, and with a lotta help from a lotta people.*

The ego is expensive, and expenses are real. When you even consider that the studio rent you pay needs to get divided up by how many paintings you sell, because without the physical space, you wouldn't have a way to make the artworks! All the bills you have for the purpose of making art are typically called expenses and they exist for any business whether you're selling millions or eking out $3,000 a year selling artwork as a "hobby." Gas to and from the studio, cardboard boxes and tape to ship things out, software programs, accounting tools, memberships for Google and Dropbox and email newsletter tools. The costs add up. Each month I have hundreds of dollars in non-negotiable fees just to be in operation and not even sell anything. So, don't purchase the stick before the herd of sheep, young shepherd. In due time you can save up for the new laptop or the industrial sewing machine. You need to land your first client before you can justify all the costs of running a full-fledged business.

Your Champions List

There are people who are going to help you sell your product and there are people who are going to buy your product. You need to begin to formulate a Top Ten or Top Twenty list. If you want to perform or speak on stage, you can add in contacts or venues and stages. There are organizations and conferences. Higher education institutions, craft fairs, churches, organized networking groups, chambers of commerce, etc. Think local and think global and start to compile a few people you really want to get in touch with. Put their name on the Champions List.

Once you have a clear picture of who you want to talk to, you are going to possibly need to do some outreach to them. Unless you believe that you can "manifest" them like the tooth fairy. Outreach can take many forms. Warm Outreach is when you have someone, in the seven degrees of Kevin Bacon, who is connected to them. LinkedIn and Facebook are a good indication of if you have any shared contacts. See if the person you know can email introduce you (or real time invite you both) to meet one another. It's warm because there is a living breathing connection. A Cold Outreach is like Cold Calling. You'll have to reach out to them directly without any reason. You don't tell them, "Hey you are on my Champions List." Make them an offer.

The people on your list will dictate how you reach out to them, just like when you're applying for a job you need a different cover letter for each potential employer. Likewise, pricing, program design, and marketing will shift depending on who you're contacting. Keep in mind, that if your Champion is the editor in chief of Elle Decor magazine, possibly she receives MANY emails each day and her email inbox is stuffed with pushy offers and pitches.

A warm outreach may look like this:

"Dear _____, it's Erin Minckley from Relativity Textiles. I hope you are doing well. Are you open to connecting in the next week or two? I've been working with local Chicago designers helping their teams develop custom wallcoverings solutions for their current/future projects. I'd love to get your feedback on the new designs I'm launching. Curious also what you're working on right now to see if there's any way I can support you. Please let me know if you've got thirty minutes for a Zoom call or a coffee in person. Thanks!"

This would be to a contact that you already know. If you're looking to have that person connect you to someone you don't know you could write something like this:

"Dear _____, it was great catching up with you this week at the networking event. I was hoping to have your assistance in connecting me to _____(the event coordinator for the ICFF, International Contemporary Furniture Fair). I have created a short bio for you to use, which hopefully makes it easy. I'm free any time to meet up or talk via phone. In case you don't have it, my contact information is at the bottom of the email.

'I'd like to introduce you to my friend Erin Minckley. She's a friend of mine from college and she's just written a book called "Artists Who Thrive." She's looking to present the topic of her book at conferences like ICFF in NY. I wanted to connect you to her in case you need speakers for this year's event. Check out her webpage: *www.profitableartist.org* and her email is *hello@profitableartist.org*"

When you are reaching out to someone for the first time and it's a cold call situation, here are some things to include in your email:

*Hello, I'm _____ (name).
* Here's how I came across you and why I was inspired (compliments or flattery optional but usually a good start if you've done some research about them).
* I work with companies/people just like you to achieve _____ (outcome you probably want).
* Now more than ever, having _____(what you want) without _____ (what you've been getting) is important because _____. Based on what I know of you it seems like you may want or need this.
* Can we set up a brief call so we can connect and verify that and see if I can help?
*Pertinent information about me, web links or social media. Don't attach eight PDF's with catalog and credit card authorization form, etc.

What is not second nature yet is your pitch. What they want is your product and you need to get comfortable with telling them that your thing/widget/artwork/creation/service. You have to literally tell them that having it is going to solve their problems. Without ___ denotes the thing that's holding them back from getting your product easily. Maybe it's weight loss without dieting, or maybe it's wallpaper without long lead times. Think of something you can offer to alleviate their worry.

There are one-to-one relationships to build and there are one to many relationships to build. Getting yourself and your creative magic in front of larger audiences might give you the hives but without being open to exposure, you should just stay home with your WalkMan. Get on a stage and pitch your product to a Shark Tank-like venture capital group. So what if you get turned down!? Go to an event where interior designers are congregating if you sell luxury home decor items. I once went to the Las Vegas Market and literally sat on the couch in the lounge where the free WIFI was. I had my samples out so that when the designers came in to rest their feet they could feast their eyes on pretty patterns. They asked, "ooh whose is this?" and I launched into my casual couch presentation. $5,000 worth of sales came from two days sitting on a couch. Find the one-to-many situations too.

Golden Goose

If you can find one ideal client who will buy from you over and over again, this is your golden goose. One off sales are great but can be hard to rely on because the stream or "pipeline" of sales is random (golden eggs). Foster the relationships with your one-to-many customers and figure out if you have one or two (or ten) who can consistently bring in the golden eggs for you. Having a goose who lays eggs is much better than hunting down the gradual, random, or one-off sales one at a time. It was suggested to me to foster these relationships with care. As you would someone you are really trying to grow and foster a relationship with, send them thank you notes written by hand. Give them gift cards to the movie theater. Buy them an iPad when they hit $1,000 in sales for you! Whatever it might be that your creative heart can come up with, find incentives to offer your golden geese so that they appreciate doing business with you. Whatever you do, don't send them a gift basket at Christmas. So many other vendors are doing this! The high-end interior designers I work with get so many cookies during the holidays that they end up taking them to homeless shelters and dropping them off. I'm not even kidding. There is an abundance of gratitude once a year so become cleverer than the prescribed formalities of other product companies and maybe send them a birthday gift instead.

When Your First Client Knocks on the Door

I interviewed an interior designer for a promotional video before this book launched. She spoke about how she got her first interior design client. It was her boss at her full-time job doing textile design. Word of mouth lead her to a second client who was a friend of theirs. When she finally left the company, she was doing textile design to start her own business, she couldn't help but blame her boss for giving her a love for interior design. I asked her how she got the gumption to leave full-time stable work for freelancing. She had brilliant advice: Go to every talk, every lecture, every event in the industry you want to be in. Sit in the front row. Offer to take pictures for the speaker and text or email them to her later. Then you have her contact info and can keep in touch. They'll always remember you for being so helpful and sitting front and center. She started to get referrals from more established designers who were tossing the entry level homes her way. They remembered her from the days of the front row. This advice isn't just for designers. You can attend webinars or special events in your field and connect with speakers who oftentimes are very gracious to rising stars like you. Ask to meet them for coffee and confide in them that you don't know where to start. They may have some golden nuggets of advice or words of wisdom.

While my company was still in start-up mode, I read a book called the *4 Hour Work Week* and got some ideas for how to package my design knowledge as "consulting." Two companies reached out to me on Instagram and said they admired my line and wanted to know how I got started. They wanted to pick my brain. Want to know what I told them? "I have options for you! I can teach you how to start your own line, and even skip some of the pitfalls that I fell into when I was starting!" I literally paid my bills with that consulting income for the first year I was in business since I had barely any revenue to speak of. I had no other job or money coming in while my ex delayed paying child support. The knowledge I put into practice as a "system" for others was then all written out. Three or four other brands who are more established than Relativity Textiles came to me for guidance on print design, manufacturing and launching a label. I obliged with a three-tier option.

Option One: I do a limited amount of hours per week. I teach you what you need to do (step by step instructions not included) and let you do the fumbling, ahem, I mean homework on your own. Come back in a week and check in to see how far you got.

Option Two: Skip the fumbling. I am going to show you my examples of a label with hanging instructions, how to create a purchase order for the mill, and how to make a "spec sheet" that shows your product's information. I'd create a timeline for the process and speed them through the process.

Option Three: I will do all the set-up for you. You don't have to learn or DIY anything. You basically hire me to take care of it all, in essence making me a member of your staff. Should not exceed "x" number of hours per month. If more hours and work are required in a given month, I will bill additionally $100/hour for the time.

CHAPTER 12: MASTERY

What I didn't even grasp at the time was that... it would work! I made the Option 3 equal in pay to my monthly rent. That way, I knew my bottom line would be covered. Then, I made Option 1 all of my other bills added together and averaged over twelve months. This would free me up to do anything I wanted with Relativity Textiles or my kids, just to break even was the goal. I picked up both clients, one at Option 1 and one at Option 3. They paid me to help them. They praised me up and down for teaching them, consoling them, and coaching them when it got really hard. I was a kind-bossy creator motivator and I carved out a little freelance niche for myself. What types of "services" could you offer right now that would improve the lives of one or many people? What would you charge for it? Could you offer an upgraded Gold medallion option? Is there a way to add value or service? Remember to help a person solve a problem that they're currently having. During Covid-19 everything from standing desks to blue light filtering goggles became a hot commodity. So many people made masks at first, but that is just one problem of a plethora of issues we've all come to know as the "new normal."

Listen to your audience. Ask them what they need. Ask them how you could provide extra value. They'll usually tell you! But don't let them set the price. You're not the Goodwill and you're not selling secondhand skills. You need to set your price based on the marketplace. That's right kittens, you need to look at other people who are doing that same thing in other places and see what they charge. Sign up for their email newsletter too so that you can compare (not copy) their content to the stuff you want to say to your audience.

I did dozens of Lunch & Learn presentations in the past five years and each time, the resounding response was, "Wow. You have an inspiring story. You should write a book." So... here I am. I listened to the feedback. I pivoted to meet the demand.

Remain Curious (Even if it Killed the Cat)

When a child is curious, they ask a lot of questions. "Where do people go when they die? What happens to their body? Why do they die in the first place? What does heaven look like? Do we have nine lives like cats? Does everyone die? Will you die someday?" Imagine answering these innocent curiosities of a child. He doesn't know why things happened and you can't help but say some cynical things about fate and God and how unfair it is. You try to summarize with mythologies like angels and wishes sent to heaven that will be heard, called prayers. You talk about life in abstract ways. You usually have a pit in your stomach because some answers feel like lies.

I once had to answer a question from two boys under the age of five as they talked loudly on a public bus. "Is Dan my brother?" my youngest son asked at the age of two and a half. "Not yet," I told him, "If Dan's dad and I get married then you would be brothers." They didn't seem satisfied with that answer. "Will James be my dad then?" he wondered out loud. Now people were really starting to listen in and awaited my clever response. Luckily for me, Dan answered him with his little kid logic. "You already have a dad," he told my son. "Erin will be my mom because my mom died." The forty-eight eyeballs on the bus were now fixated on me. "Step mom. Yep." And that was that. They understood, though the intricacies and logistics were irrelevant. The whole bus understood our situation, who I was, and which kid was mine in an instant.

Children don't care if curiosity is going to kill my buzz. Kids are brave enough to ask anything. They ask until their imagination has been satisfied and then they move on to more interesting thoughts. Kids are geniuses because they don't let the burdens of inhibitions weigh them down. They have some stereotypes, but when they're young and impressionable they will believe whatever you tell them. Letters go to Santa, or "colors don't have genders," as I like to say, "so pick pink if you like it. Nothing manlier."

When I first started my business, I did what many mentors told me to do. **Find a competitor.** Ask them to be my mentor or just pick their brain. Ask them an insane amount of questions until you find some answers and then try to replicate their formula. Or not. Maybe change everything; it depends. So I asked another wallpaper designer who had been around for twelve years. "How did you get started? What was it like for you when you were just getting your first collection together? How did you know what to charge for your work? How did you make decisions about ...[x, y and z]" The designer answered with vague generalizations like "...*it all came to be.*" It wasn't really couth to go around asking people the real things I wanted to ask! "Did your daddy fund your startup costs? Do you have a rich boyfriend? Did you max out all five of your credit cards?!" I needed to know how long it would take me before I left the realm of zero to breaking even, to making it, and eventually wealth! I needed real answers and the clarity I hoped to gain was so urgent, I couldn't stand hearing bullshit! I wanted to chart my course before I'd ever even ridden a horse.

I had to remain curious like a child on a bus. I researched every mill in America that makes wallpaper. I even asked stupid questions. "Why do you outsource the making of the screens? Couldn't you make more money doing it yourself?" and then they would educate me about why the commercial screen fabricators had old technology like a dark room and camera that was seven feet tall and seven feet wide. It required a specialist to make those screens and their staff was only skilled for printing the paper. They trusted the other guys to get the screens right. "Do you also print digitally?" Yes, they had converted their facility a few years back when wallpaper made a huge come back and the digital technology exploded. The mill owners were usually so excited to talk about themselves that they went on and on with details you weren't even curious about. Then I would just ask things that were pertinent, "How long have you owned the company?" I would find out the whole history of the mill owner, his family tree, etc. Sometimes they would name drop their competitors. I would hang up and call those guys and ask all the same questions.

I used to always ask textile designers where they printed their paper. Had they always used that manufacturer? Did they like working with them? Then it became less about me finding out their super-secret resources and more about their experience being in business. I would ask them things like what type of fabric they used and their favorite pattern they designed. I would ask why they started their line and usually it revealed either their Boiling Point or their past work experience.

I learn by other people's stories. What makes them tick might help me to make better decisions. Leaders are readers, so I read a lot of books. When I say "read" I mean that I listen to a lot of books on Audible. But, believe it or not 50% or more of this book is just reimagined information that I pulled from someone else's manifesto, things that resonated with me or I found helpful were shuffled into my "don't forget that part" document in my mind. But I ask people lots of questions and I compile a list of opinions, reviews, and second opinions on a given topic.

One wallpaper and fabric designer I met used to design for Prada and had a high-power job in NYC. It was very competitive and fast paced, so owning her own business was an upgrade in many ways to

CHAPTER 12: MASTERY

a slower lifestyle in the Carolinas somewhere and a day dictated only by how many shipping envelopes needed to be packed and how many emails to be checked. But her education was also in business. I often tried to figure out if people had a business background before starting their companies or not. That gave me confidence when I met several designers who had technical backgrounds in textile design or business degrees. Because the fact that I did not have any understanding of software when I entered the field, but learned it on the job, made me feel accomplished. The fact that they had an MBA and I had an MFA and we were hitting for the same team made me proud of myself for figuring it out with limited tools.

I always ask people about their start up stories. Especially people in other fields. Even if they've been in business 25 years, I would ask them how they started out. The fascinating thing is that people when they have that many years of perspective speak about things in a very thoughtful and reverent way. Having passed that stage of their business and made it without failing, they feel a sense of pride and accomplishment. This is a great way to build rapport with someone when you first meet. When you are at a networking event and don't know what to say to anyone, try asking them what they do, how long they've been doing it, what their biggest takeaway is from their time in their field or what they love most about their job. That usually opens them up to describing things in detail for you about how they too may have had to learn a lot on-the-job-training style. It helps you understand if they are doing well in their business now by the amount of serenity they have when they tell their start up story. If it's been hard the whole time, they'll tell you. If they almost lost their business, or had to pay off an investor to get free, they'll tell you. It's kind of cool that when you're talking business, you can feel like you're part of a club.

The 90% Rule: Just Press "Go"

It was daytime, sometime in mid-November when I had my edited version of the Kickstarter video uploaded on my Kickstarter profile. I held by breath. My project wasn't yet launched but I'd filled out my bio and my "asks" and incentive gifts were all created and ready to go. I hesitated. I thought all kinds of things like *"What if it doesn't work?..."* I contemplated putting it off another day until I was ready. But as my mind did another cartwheel from hopeful and stupid optimism to dread and thoughts of inadequacy I realized that no one is ever ready to jump off the ledge with their bungee tied to a harness. No one is ever ready or prepared enough for jumping out of a plane with their parachute on their back. No one is ever trained enough to dive from the high dive and do a triple back flip into the deep end. They just jump.

And I hit "SUBMIT."

And it was done.

Nothing earth shattering. The sky didn't turn dark, nor did the booming voice of God rain down *"what were you thinkingggggggg...?"* Literally nothing changed. I exhaled. And for the next 60 days my brain kept cartwheeling along from discouraged to excited and I realized that my life wouldn't change one single bit if the campaign wasn't funded. I would be no worse off than I was before I hit the button. So I kept promoting it even though I hated the self-aggrandizement it took to market my goal to the world (aka my 1,000 friends on Facebook). I hated that I got closer and closer to my goal because that meant that the gap between being a nobody and having achieved a huge BHAG was quickly closing in. I was closer to winning than to losing. But the part that pushed me forward every day to keep talking about my idea and pitching my company to everyone I met was that I had a crowd of people rallying behind me, lobbying for my success. They were encouraging me. They were proud of me, even if I didn't make it. They asked me how it was going, and they called me things like "inspiring" and "incredible."

No one had ever thought I would do something this big. Only one in seven people who launch a Kickstarter campaign raise the kind of money I did.

To tell you the truth, the video was not perfect. My logo was janky. My voiceover was done on my lunch break at work in the faculty office at SAIC and my sales pitch was amateur. The incentive gifts were a horrible idea: throw pillows, stationary, and wallpaper drop shipped to seventy different addresses. That alone ate up a significant part of my budget to spend money on. By the way, I also photoshopped the shit out of those images because I hadn't made one single pillow before I launched the campaign. But, no one knew that.

That's where a very sage piece of advice I'd once received in a graduate level art critique came in handy. Jose Lerma, a well-known contemporary artist told me "just lie." When I started telling him that my artwork wasn't done because I'd had a hard time with the colors, so I decided to start over, and I didn't really like it and it didn't seem finished.... He stopped me and said, "You don't have to tell the truth." He wanted me to edit out my mistakes and present my art as if I had intended it to be exactly as it was. Hanging on the wall with all of its imperfections, I would say, "I meant for it to be this way" and then just wait for people to give their feedback.

See, if you tell the whole story that led up to the thing and admit that it was only 90% done, that is how people will receive it. They'll consider it incomplete. And you can't critique a work of art that isn't done. You can walk through the Art Institute and likely find works of art that the painter intended to finish but then gave up or moved on to something more interesting or he died while the artwork was in progress! But you don't receive it as 90%! You just assume it was 100% what they intended it to be.

That is where I came up with the phrase: **The 90% Rule**. Crank it out. Get as much done as you can. Nothing is perfect. Nothing is 100%. If you can imagine that every invention there ever was never made it to market because it still needed the inventor to tweak it a little, we'd never have an automobile or a flushing toilet. We'd be walking and still pooping in nature. Okay? Let's get real. Nothing you do, especially on your first try-- like a business card, a logo, a website, a photo shoot, a sales presentation, a public speech, an Instagram story-- will be perfect.

Give up trying to produce everything at 100% completion. Put it out at 90%. Hell, put it out at 79% if you want. Just get it out into the world.

Whatever it is, don't overthink it. Don't over research how to do it, AKA Analysis Paralysis. Don't over plan the execution of it, meaning giving yourself two years to plan every step and strategize because you'll lose focus and energy. Don't overspend. Don't buy more than you need at first.

I spent one of my first $1,000 I ever earned on a gold foil press. It's a die cutting machine but I was going to letterpress all of my packaging with it. I bought gold foil tape and I set out to stamp all of the envelopes by hand. Problem was we couldn't go fast enough, and the press wasn't precise enough. We messed up about half of the envelopes/packages that we made. That was a hard learning lesson. I ended up outsourcing all of the envelopes to be made at Rohner Letterpress in Chicago and they finished 1,000 of them in one afternoon. It was an expensive mistake to think that I needed that press, that I could do it myself and that it would help my business thrive. It was impulsive in retrospect and I am better now about deciding what is absolutely necessary to keep running the business and what can be outsourced.

Press "Go" when it comes to asking for help or launching something new because it will never be perfect. There will always be bumps in the road, like when my first website went down after three days and Nate Berkus's office called to say they were interested in ordering wallpaper, but they couldn't find my website! Other than those major blooper moments, in general, no one will know the 10% margin of imperfection except you.

Besides, you can always tweak it later.

ARTISTS WHO THRIVE

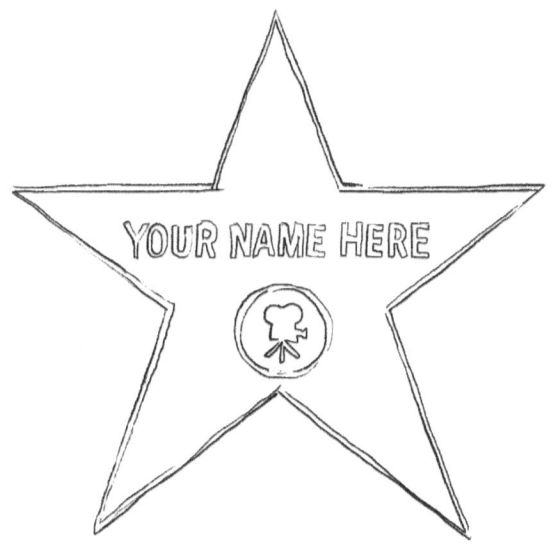

Chapter 13

Writing Your Legacy

Something I've been thinking a lot about as I write this book is my legacy. I used to believe that only noblemen and royalty had legacies, because they'd be entered into the history books. The thing is, nowadays there are so many success stories and so many famous people and so many myriad awards and industries where people are making an impact that I need to revise my definition of that concept of "contribution" to history.

In every industry there are thought leaders giving TedTalks and adding their research into the libraries of their field. There are scholars and change makers who are forward thinking enough to revolutionize the way we do things or our vocabulary around topics such as Black Lives Matter. There are dermatologists and children's book illustrators that if I brought up their names with those in that arena their faces would light up with recognition. Though I am not familiar with many industries but my own, I have a level which I aspire to be at relative to the well-known influencers in my own field. I can aim to surpass them or be offered a chair next to them at a panel discussion. I could collaborate with them on a fabric collection or co-author a coffee table book. What you don't realize is that you don't have to be the Prince of Whales to leave a mark. Nobility is not the only legacy.

In the present tense, I have two sons whose opinion I want to be highly regarded. I have my parents, sister, half-brother and a slew of other family members who are looking to my Instagram to see my success. I am sharing magazine articles with them where I was noted as a cultural contributor. I have my friends who I care about deeply and want to lend a helping hand or a listening ear when they need me. My customers and colleagues who I want to admire and revere my wallpaper brand as having standards of excellence in customer service and production of great wallpapers. But, beyond that, what will I be remembered for?

The types of humans who I look to for inspiration are thought leaders and revolutionaries. Albert Einstein's theory of relativity inspired my wallpaper brand's name. Martin Luther King Jr. is one whose quotes I often come back to when social justice sits on my lap and asks me, "What are you doing for the people of this world? How are you using your soap box, your privilege, your social network?"

CHAPTER 13: WRITING YOUR LEGACY

During the pandemic, we all have been asked to re-evaluate what is important in our lives. Once we sacrificed all of our intimate friendships and rearranged our work habits, what is left is time to pontificate about what is truly important. What will we go back to doing once the Corona virus is eradicated? What will we choose to keep about our "new normal"?

I for one am happy to never wear a bra again or dye my hair. I am happy for folks at the grocery store line to stay six feet away from me, because it always made me nervous that they were so close they could watch me key in my PIN number. I am a big fan of virtual meetings because it means I don't have to find childcare and race to a school council meeting or interior design presentation. Even trade shows are moving to virtual, which truly could save my small business thousands of dollars on airfare and hotel arrangements when participating as a spectator or exhibitor.

What it has given us space to do is to look inward. Not only at our deepest desires and dreams or to begin creating new ways to stay busy like baking bread or gardening, but, looking at ourselves for who we could become.

In psychology, the focus is on feelings and thoughts. (F+T=A). In theology, the central idea is knowing God. Cosmology is knowing the universe. What about Ontology? It occurred to me that I know very little about Ontology, which focuses on "ways of being." How do we create space for just being? It's a very heady concept that was presented to me during a four-day course. I am simultaneously writing this book and training to become a coach. This discovery made me very curious. I had spent so much time in the past five years (that is the time stamp for when my life really began anew) focusing on GOALS. Action plans. Strategy. But what I'd given very little credit to was my way of being while I was working on things. Was I stressed all the time, but productive? Was I cranky but an activist? Was I cynical and cited in magazines? Could there be a disconnect from the way I am living my life and who I really am? Finding my magic whilst being the Wicked Witch of the Midwest was not exactly the Visionary Reality I was striving for.

I have listened to twelve books on Amazon Audible in less than six months. That's really great for someone with attention problems. I have enlisted in therapy online, a two-day course for personal growth, a coaching system for growing my business, and decided to write a book, and publish it with the help of an indie publisher. I launched two websites. I directed six short videos. I made several paintings, displayed them in a showhouse, sold most of the artwork and donated the money to charity. I've collaborated with my publisher and a local chef to provide a globally inspired meal for those deserving. I've enlisted myself and friends to join a group of women building homes for Habitat for Humanity. I decided to let my gray hairs grow out, started working out using two apps, bought some home workout gear and got a subscription to deliver green smoothie powder to my door once a month. I'm alone in my house and it has made me transfer a lot of attention that I'd been giving away to other people towards myself.

When I had to sit with my thoughts, I realized that there is more to me than just being the "Wallpaper Lady." I never set out to be what my email signature reads: "Founder and Owner, Relativity Textiles, LLC." I set out to take my art and make a living doing it. I set out to not have to teach or work for anyone else. The whole thing was a pipe dream turned into a reality. I pushed it and molded it, and eventually it started to mold me. I saw my leadership peering through the uncertainty. I grew to love being the boss, getting recognition, and feeling like I was making an impact. I realized that my dreams had come true. What comes next is an impact that is even nearer and dearer to my heart. I am speaking to my eighteen year old self, my twenty-four year old self and my thirty year old self as I write these words. I am proving myself wrong because I never thought I could write a book. I've invested a lot of my own money and time into making this happen and it's coming easier now that I've already been the CEO of my life for some time.

Thus, I'm focusing on what I think is important and what will support me. These connect back to my list of values. The things I hold dear. The things I admire in others and the things I want to be remembered for. If you want to be remembered for loving kittens but you don't own a cat, you could volunteer at the animal shelter. It will help you link those internal desires with the open display of your values. The impact it will have on others will be seen, felt and appreciated.

Change, then happens first in the human mind. From the invention of the wheel to the Civil Rights Movement, one person had the audacity to try something. They enlisted many others with similar goals, vision and pride. To change the world in some small way and carve out a niche for yourself within a given social space, you have to act on your thoughts and ideas. You have to answer those deep-rooted desires that have been calling you. Stop letting them go to voicemail and saying "I'll get to that later." Don't dig for the approval of others. It's a mistake that we all make.

Audre Lord was an African poet, a civil rights activist, mother, lesbian, librarian, feminist and warrior who once coined the phrase "the master's tools will never dismantle the master's house." Lord defied society's definition of an 'acceptable woman' and highlighted that being poor, being gay or owning any other 'crucibles of difference' can be turned from a weakness into a strength. Our differences should not be our stumbling blocks. The fact of the matter is that being an underdog (as an artist) has distinct advantages! "Survival," she argues, "is learned not an academic skill." Our differences might allow us to temporarily beat our oppressor at his/her/their own game, but they will never enable us to bring about genuine change. Educating others is the most important strategy to dismantling the "master's house."

One must first be educated to educate others. "Empowering people who are doing the work [of making cultural change happen] does not mean using privilege to overstep and overpower such groups; but rather, privilege must be used to hold the door open for other allies.[27]" Racism, sexism, ageism, heterosexism, elitism, classism… all assert their inherent worth and use their domination as a powerful weapon. But what I want you to consider again is that your agency, your ability to adapt, your ingenuity during this time empowers you to make bold choices about how you live and how you define yourself.

The personal act is the most political.

What if, then you first believe in a world where we all were supported 100%? Where we all had the same access to money, resources, and time. Where we all were cherished and loved. What if that starts with you accepting yourself? Celebrating your talents and pushing yourself to achieve goals with your art form just might inspire someone else to do the same. What if you prove to yourself that you can? Show the world what you're made of. Show yourself. And what if with this radical act of self-love and self-appreciation and self-

---

[27] https://en.wikipedia.org/wiki/Audre_Lorde

imposed celebration, you begin to show others how to stand up and do something with their own lives?

Throw Yourself a Party

I launched the third wallpaper collection in 2019 and called it "La Tierra" inspired by my trip to Mexico City. I threw myself what could be considered the largest party of my lifetime. It was larger than my own wedding. I arranged for a local paint store called JC Licht to co-sponsor the event with me. We organized 250 goodie bags to be made and delivered and stuffed with paint fan decks and wallpaper samples. I coordinated the use of a luxury Canadian sofa company's beautiful lofted showroom space to be rented out (for free) for the night of Cinco de Mayo. We hired a taco truck to prepare food for our guests. We filled a margarita machine with tequila and mixers and hired bartenders. I displayed beautiful photos of the wallpaper in abstract still lifes around the room. I hired an all-female mariachi band. I organized all of my friends to come and join me, invited over 500 local designers and press.

As I got ready that evening, none of my clothing inspired me. It didn't yell out "Mexico!" so I made a last-minute trip to Anthroplogie at the mall outside the city. I hurried to grab some colorful things and waited for a dressing room. As I tried on my outfit and came out to look in a larger mirror, the sales associate stopped me. "Hi, I'm sorry if this is weird, but..." the shy look on her face made me worried if I'd done something wrong. "Are you Relativity Textiles?" Her question shocked the hell out of me. If I'd been sitting, I would've fallen out of my chair. I laughed and responded "Yes, umm, I mean, I'm Erin. But that is my brand." Turns out she used to work for a local interior design firm, and I had presented my product to them not so long ago. She'd since left to work in retail, apparently, and just wanted to say that she was a big fan of my work. I confided in her that I was throwing a party that night downtown, if she wanted to come for a margarita. I would be wearing this shirt.

Arriving to my own fiesta, I set out flowers and waited nervously. Many friends and some complete strangers filed in. By the end of the night it was a full house. I spoke for a few minutes about my inspiration for the collection and thanked all of our generous sponsors for the event and the liquor companies who had donated Mexican cocktails and beers. I thanked everyone for coming. I thanked my assistants and everyone who'd been a part of the launch. I really felt like the CEO of a large company. People clapped. I finally could relax and have some tacos, like a famished bride on her wedding night who'd spent hours going around and talking to everyone who came. I listened to the Mariachi band and sat down to admire all that had conspired because of me; I'd invited them to share in celebrating my artwork as a wallpaper, but it was a celebration of community and life. Almost 250 people gathered together in one place for globally inspired design, music, and food. People made new connections. People enjoyed themselves and got interested in the paint colors. We all became a community there in that sofa shop. We all became a little more worldly.

When you open the door, you never know who is going to come in. I have no fucking idea who is going to read this book. Up to now, only three people have made it past page sixty. Some friends are humoring me by looking it over, but by the time this book has hit your hands or ears on Audible, maybe I'm doing something completely different. The cool thing is that what you make goes on to live and breathe its own oxygen. It has an aura of its own.

My artwork, my wallpaper, my writing, my voice will all have a life of its own after I let it free. It's not my baby anymore. It's not a child that I have to protect, because if it was, I wouldn't leave it alone in the bathtub for fear it would drown. I wouldn't let it bike around the neighborhood for fear of getting hit by a car. I wouldn't trust the universe to care for it, so I'd have to protect it forever. That's what you do with babies.

This book will offer you guidance, but I wrote it for me as much as I did for you. I wrote it to get my thoughts onto a page. I labored over it as much as you will over your own work when it's ready to have legs and walk on its own. That's the thing: It's easy to keep your art unfinished or hidden. Sharing your art, though, is like writing this book. It isn't easy. See because if it was easy, everyone would do it.

So now it's your turn to make your own contribution to the world. If you want really intricate planned out steps on how to take your own business to the next level you can always find me. I'll have many podcasts, webinars, online courses and perhaps even one-on-one coaching available for you to pick my brain like monkeys pick fleas off each other and eat them. Pick away. It's your turn soon to do the thing. I believe in you. I want to come to your party and have a margarita and celebrate your accomplishments.

Surrender

I avoided writing this final chapter because it is still fresh. It's painful but it needs to be written. Life has a way of being the greatest coach of all. There are subtle, slow paradigm shifts where you mature gradually into a new way of seeing, much like teens mature into their new hormones and body shapes. Then there are the large life lessons that hit you over the head like a cosmic baseball bat. It's best if you can practice on the small stuff first like locking your keys out of your house. This one wasn't small.

I ended a two-year long relationship with a man who I still deeply love. More or less, we were not meant to be, though I wanted very much to spend the rest of my life with him. Our wavelengths are *too different*. Our traumas create a vast canyon between where we'd like to be (visionary reality) and where we are (physical reality) and it wasn't possible to cross the divide together. I am going it alone and so is he.

Aside from our differences, the experience of opening up my heart to love post-divorce has taught me huge lessons about myself and about life. Losing him has been one of the greatest motivators for me to pick up the pieces and figure out why I'm still here. Alone. What's the point of living a life full of money and success and vibrant, incredible adventure if you can't do it with the one you love? What's the point of having someone come onto the stage with you if they are just going to exit stage left too soon after they came? What lessons are being hurled at me by life?

Perhaps the most profound realizations of my lifetime, if not the most influential turning point in my life came from this recent relationship. Meeting James and his son Dan taught me how to love someone as if they were my own. I could have omitted this part of the book since I might get shit for exposing someone else's life in printed word. Even still, I feel it's important for some reason to bare my soul at the end here (though my mother calls that 'lifting your skirt up over your head' or an unnecessary show and tell). Perhaps it's my last-ditch effort to motivate you (and myself) to move forward with courage.

James is forty years old. He was married at age twenty-five to the love of his life, Eva. They have one son together named Daniel, age eight. Eva developed metastatic melanoma and died in the winter of

CHAPTER 13: WRITING YOUR LEGACY

2017. Dan was four years old. She left behind two sisters, her parents, and her husband and one beautiful golden doodle doggie Penelope (Penny for short). The family was heartbroken by her loss. Eva was a soft spoken, insanely beautiful woman who liked to garden, listen to vintage records, and take photographs. She owned many antique cameras and collected beer glasses and steins from places she'd visited; she built furniture and was active at church. Her and James's life was quiet, and routine and they rarely argued.

Fast forward to eight months after her passing. I met James on a dating app. He was tall and handsome. On our first date it rained uncontrollably and although I didn't plan to invite him inside (we had a glass of wine on my front porch) I didn't want him to get soaked. I had just moved into my new apartment, a coach house in the trendy neighborhood of Logan Square. That place was my only house in Chicago I had lived without my husband and I was able to afford it by the grace of God. It was the first week living there and I was still unpacking boxes. I had no sofa for the first few months and so James and I sat on the wood floor of my living room and finished the bottle of wine. He cried as he told me about his wife. I hugged this fragile man and listened to how much he loved her. I wanted to jump into his life and save him from this tragedy.

In the months and years to come, Eva's legacy became a part of my everyday reality. On Sundays, I went to the church where her funeral service was held and met the parishioners who knew her well. I talked with James's mother about her grief on the first day we met. Eva was so much a part of my life by the end of my two-year long relationship with James that I had no choice but to accept the fact that *she was always there*. I moved into his house with my two kids and we all shared two bedrooms like little cozy sardines. Rather than consider myself his mistress or resent his late wife for being the better partner, I began to love Eva instead. Her wedding dress hung in the hall closet, in the house that was once hers and was then mine. I was so in love and I wanted to support James and Dan. In retrospect, it was too soon. I didn't heed anyone's advice to take it slow-- because I live boldly and unapologetically and sometimes regret not having more caution or choosing my words more wisely.

James had his bouts of depression and a constant, silent grief. He manifested his sadness in every way possible-- physical ailments, sleeplessness, compulsive behavior. The need for control in every aspect of his life was a caveman's attempt to not make the Fatal Error #2. He has three life insurance policies and practices shooting at the gun range in case of a home invasion. His anxiety was a cloud that followed above his head. I often tried to soothe his anxiety or trick it into going away. I offered a comforting distraction sometimes and our intimacy was a welcome escape from the burdens of the other three quadrinities. The nagging emotions, the constant monkey mind drumming up the past. He was still terribly lost deep down. He told me repeatedly that he was "broken."

All of this is understandable since he'd lost his partner of thirteen years, his best friend, and his son's mommy. Where I was taking it upon myself to be the glue that held it all together, I stepped into a role play. Where I was filling a void for him, he also fit the bill for male companion, role model for my kids and bread winner. I kept holding out for the visionary reality but ignored the physical reality. I did not want it to be true. The fantasy version of him would wake up one morning and say, "I'm going to enroll Dan and I in that Grief Camp. I'm ready to really process this and move forward in my life." But that never happened. Instead I enrolled the two of them in Camp and they went away for four days to make tie dyed t-shirts and he thanked me for forcing him to go.

James kept his feelings locked inside and he grew tired of me always wanting progress and transformation. This little hamster in my brain made him tired. His caterpillar was still preparing for spring, chomping away…

The trouble with relationships is that cosmic timing is involved. Things progress on a timeline that is out of our control. We can't approach a boyfriend or girlfriend as we can a Kickstarter campaign. You just set a goal, work hard every day to make it known that you're trying to reach it, and then boom! Sixty days later, you've achieved what you wanted and you're fully funded. Everyone celebrates your success and you both ride off into the sunset like Price Eric and Ariel. I thought that I could mold us into what *I wanted*. The reality is, both people have to want to have a transformation. Both people have to be willing to do the work, talk about things openly and be vulnerable. Both people have to leave their past behind and consent to a new future together.

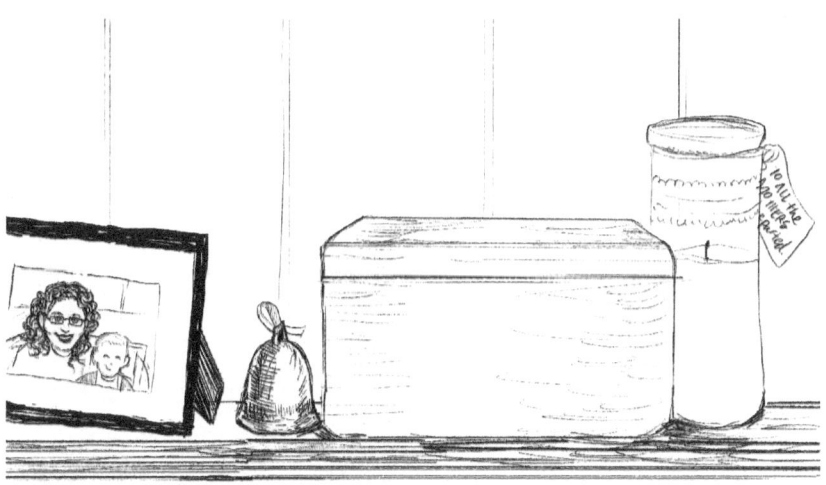

Both people have to be present to how their past trauma informs their behavior, and how in turn, that behavior alters how others around them behave/respond/react. I was guilty of letting my lover see the worst of me on so many occasions.

Eva's ashes sat atop the mantle at our house in a small wooden box. Her shrine had photos of her and candles for Mother's Day gifted by a neighbor. Everyone mourned her passing. I sat with the notion that I had never known her personally but felt like she was an old friend. I'd make eye contact with her photos and I even began to tell her "thank you" each day. For sharing *her people* with me. For giving me a place in this world that felt like home. I even considered her to be my guardian angel because she taught me patience and forgiveness. She taught me what it was to be devoted to something that I didn't know how it would end up.

The new life I wanted with James was to include Eva. No matter if we moved out of their house or got married. Maybe both of our wedding dresses could hang side by side in the closet?... I wanted children with him and a magical life where the world was our oyster. I wasn't awake to the fact that I'd inserted myself into a place that didn't quite have room yet for anyone else. It was like the children's story "The Mitten" where all the animals squish into a child's mitten together. There was no breathing room. It was eventually going to burst open and everyone would fall out.

Our differences were obvious. He wanted to 'wait and see' and I wanted actionable steps and a plan for the future (roaring marching band music playing in the background). He needed calm and quiet and I was galivanting off to Mexico City to be inspired and take pictures. I invited him to hike the pyramids of Teotihuacan with me and I could not understand why he turned down my invitation to come. He was taking things day by day and I could see twenty years into the future. I thought that if only I was "devoted" enough... that I would manifest the relationship of my lifetime. I had all the vision boards and all my tricks and tools. I was doing my best to parent the kids and decorate for every holiday, scrapbook all of our memories into an album for each year together. I even baked a cake for Eva on her birthday because I wanted Dan to celebrate his mommy's life instead of mourning her death. I wanted to be the Martha Stuart mother and wife, not an emotional caretaker. It was a confusing time to know the right thing to do.

There are no manuals for this.

You see, the Administration of Life has a way of distracting us from ever really having the big conversations like "Are we meant to be?" It wasn't for lack of trying. We sought couples counseling. I downloaded books about relationships, codependency, and grief. I urged him to get into habits of self-care or routines of taking vitamins or eating healthy. I bought Groupons for cryotherapy to freeze his nervous system and wake him up to the beautiful life I was creating. I tried leaving him alone in thought and giving him space. I began to feel so lonely in the relationship. I lashed out and threw all my resentment onto him every chance I could, like confetti, which only reinforced his stereotype of me as someone who was chaotic and unstable. He told me maybe I should grow up and be an adult and get some health insurance and stop messing around with my life. My propensity for risk was a liability to his safety net he'd built. And I almost quit-- I almost gave up my business for a desk job-- just to see if then he'd finally accept me as I am.

What made no sense to me was that supposedly James and his wife never fought. I came to the conclusion that *I was the problem.* Why could he live so blissfully with someone else but not with me? He told me that Eva wasn't one to get upset or loudly profess her emotions. In fact, when I met her older sister, she told me that in their nuclear family Eva was the sister who was the 'peacekeeper.' She'd always calm her folks and sisters down and mediate the family drama. She seemed to keep her feelings in, since she was quiet and likely introverted or introspective. Many of the thoughts I have about her are assumptions since I never met her. Since I can't ask her side of the story, I have to build a narrative in my own mind. I do know that she was often alone while James worked long hours during political campaigns. If they did fight, he explained that their way of resolving issues was that he'd leave for an hour to Home Depot and return with some items no one knew they needed. That hour was enough time to cool down. They would spend a few hours or days in quiet contemplation (AKA the silent treatment) before one of them would apologize. Then they'd make up and all would be well again.

I was in the backyard one summer tearing weeds from the rows of ferns when I sensed anger or energy. Maybe it was because I was mad. Maybe someone else's energy was present. I tried to listen for Eva's silent voice. I was blowing off steam after a disagreement by taking it out on the plants. Maybe the ferns were upset. Or maybe this was where she went to break down too. I believe the ferns absorbed my grievances. I clued into something very important that day in the fern garden. I kept wondering "How is it possible that a husband and wife never fought?" It dawned on me then that she could have been keeping her magic (or her discontent) inside her own mind and heart. I honestly don't know if she was burying some hurt under the surface to keep the peace. Maybe she buried it there in the garden. I can't say what her life was like because I didn't know her. What I know is that repression comes at a cost.

My relationship with James was deteriorating and we both tried half-assed to hold it together. Our differences in parenting styles and how we dealt with our finances added to an unstable foundation. Our ramshackle, conjoined home was crumbling before my eyes and my Brady Bunch fantasy disappeared. At the lowest valley, I sought my own therapist to try to mend the broken heart I held in my chest. I wanted solutions and a ninety-day plan for success. The pain was preventing me from creativity or positivity. The "second hand" grief I'd been inhaling had affected my spirit. My therapist was a holistic yoga practitioner. I told her about Eva and she gave me two pieces of advice that have stuck with me to this day.

1) I didn't need to compete with a dead person. I was winning. I got the man and the house and the kid and the car and the golden doodle that was once hers. ***I was alive.*** So I could stop competing with the idea that if she were to rise from the grave and return to the house, that he would pick her over me. That simply wasn't going to happen, so I could sleep soundly knowing that the future was mine even if the past belonged to her.

2) I was told never to share what I am about to say here with anyone. That's why I hesitated for a long time putting it into this book, but it's important because it has everything to do with thriving in this world. I am not writing this to be malicious or to hurt anyone, especially not James. Because a human life is not to be reduced to a lesson or a badge on my sash of wisdom. Eva's life was meaningful, and her memory is honorable. This is what the therapist told me:

"People who hold everything inside get sick."

My yogi shrink did not mean to imply that Eva was unhappy or unloved. She wasn't insinuating that she'd gotten cancer because of bottled up anger or sadness. What my therapist meant to tell me was that I would surely make myself sick if I continued in this way.

Eva's cancer spread to her brain. She had countless tumors by the time she died. She never got to say goodbye to her son. She died in a hospital room with her family surrounding her. What's left of her beautiful life is a box of ashes, a photo album, a white dress, a box of memories in the garage, and an eight year old boy with her eyes. We will never know her deepest magic now because she left this world too soon.

It's tragic. It's sad. It's horrible what happened to her.

I grieve as a bystander for the woman I never knew. Because in her, I see myself. I am a mother and I can imagine a life where my sons had to learn to ride without training wheels and I wasn't there to watch. Imagining I had not been present to witness their victories, devastates me. I am a sister; and I imagine a box of my clothes being donated because they don't fit my busty sis's size. I am a daughter; and I imagine my mother's grief as she looks through her phone at texts I've sent or voicemails she's saved from a time when I was still here on Earth. Listening to my voice over and over again when she misses me. The sheer amount of Kleenexes cumulatively used in my three-year tenure knowing James was a testament to the suffering everyone endured.

I am not Eva. But symbolically, *we are all Eva*. We will all die someday. We will all leave behind people and legacies and unfinished paperwork and a stack of old college papers and CDs that no one can play because the technology is expired. We will all be defined by the things that we leave behind. We'll be defined by the way we lived.

We will not be defined, however, by what we kept inside our hearts and never shared with anyone. Those whispers live in the garden with the ferns. That is why we must vocalize and verbalize our magic, our fears and our deepest desires. The way we live is an expression of who we are, no matter how imperfect. We must love like we won't lose everything, even if we do in the end.

I once wrote a eulogy for my grandfather who was an architect and a raging alcoholic. He loved Playboy magazines and playing pool. He wore a cowboy hat but was so small in stature I doubt he ever rode a horse. I omitted all of those details when I wrote about him because it was better to be poetic when his life was over. I am planning my own eulogy while I am still alive, and it's a little less perfected. It goes something like this:

Erin lived a vibrant life full of adventure and love. She was a joy to be around. Her empathy was her greatest quality. Her creativity was inspiring, and her laugh was infectious. She was never afraid to tell someone she loved them, and you never walked away from a conversation with her thinking "I wonder how she really felt." She always expressed her feelings, even if it got her into trouble. She fought for what she believed in. She was an extraordinary mother.

She was deeply flawed and usually late. Her studio was always a beautiful mess, filled with experiments and imagination. She hoarded fabric and finger paints and furniture for projects that she would start or finish 'someday.' She used to cry when she laughed too hard and she'd fart in her sleep. She hated very few things, but rats and large spiders were some of them. She loved orchids and rollercoasters. She had an excellent sense of direction even without looking at a map. She promoted her friends. She was a mentor and teacher to many. Most importantly, she loved her sons with all her heart. Their mother taught them how to pursue a dream and how to stand up for themselves to push through the doubts by proving people wrong. She also taught them how to peacefully walk away. They will achieve great things because she showed them how.

CHAPTER 13: WRITING YOUR LEGACY

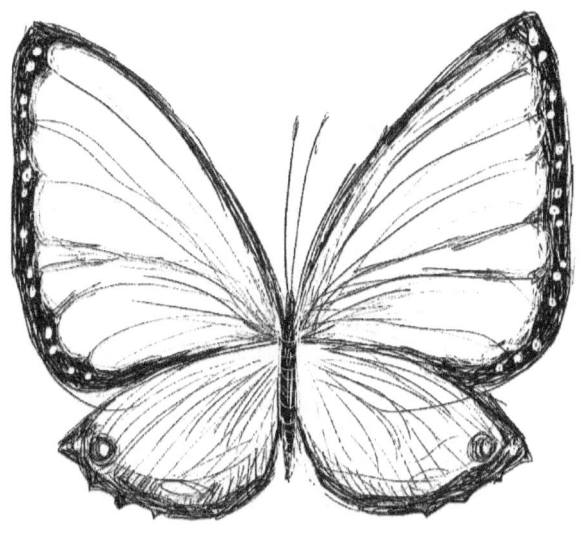

Butterfly Conversations

Our scripts are running the computer (aka our brains) on autopilot and it is easy to doubt the legitimacy of some artist chick named Erin who thinks she has all the answers. Truth is, I started with zero and grew a half a million dollar business in five years but I am still nobody and I'm still imperfect and holy crap I absolutely don't have all the answers.

Some people doubt themselves. They doubt their own worth and therefore couldn't possibly deserve the life of abundance and wealth and stable relationships we've talked about. The first part of the book is devoted to challenges of the mind, though I'd rather hold your hand and process it with you, you have to read words on a page.

Some people truly aren't coachable. Life is constantly trying to throw lessons our way, but we don't adapt or listen or observe long enough to see that little nuggets of wisdom are everywhere.

Some will let their feelings dictate their movements and momentum and they are paralyzed by trying to make the "right" decision instead of taking a leap of faith-- thus the critical outcome (Action) isn't happening. The equation goes around in a circle...Feelings + Thoughts = more f+t = F+T... instead of resulting in A for Action. Even the Dalai Lama nor Mother Theresa could motivate these people.

Some people, to put it simply, *don't want to change.* They don't want to unearth their flaws, for fear that like moths who have found their way inside a chest of drawers, little destructive holes litter everything that was once meaningful. For some their pain is too great.

Some might put the book down with a disgruntled skepticism and say "bullshit, lady!" and that's fine for me actually. I've come to grips with it only because of the wise words of my best friend Sydnee.

"Caterpillars can't have butterfly conversations."

You don't know the life that exists out there for you once you have wings, until you're flying. The perspective is totally different. You see so much more after the metamorphosis because you are no longer your former self. It is therefore pointless to try to talk to caterpillars about this change. They will have to experience it for themselves. The hard part is that once you are a butterfly, you need to fly around with other butterflies. I don't relate to caterpillars anymore. I have to try really hard to resist the urge to convince caterpillars of the light at the end of the process.

Sometimes this means leaving people where they are. Like energy attracts like energy. I'm sure Albert Einstein has a theory about this. He was one of the most brilliant creators of ideas, wasn't he? So, if you're one to believe in science rather than the Hippy Dippy School of Manifestation, then believe in Einstein. *Energy attracts.* Like magnets. The negative end of the battery repels the positive. Why is that?

CHAPTER 13: WRITING YOUR LEGACY

Because the people who are not meant to be in your life will slowly (or rapidly; in terms of a breakup or leaving a job) fall away from your life. Your newfound positive energy will attract others who have similar mindsets, motivations, and conversations. Heard the saying "misery loves company?" Same philosophy. I don't want misery in my life; therefore, I've had to experience very little company at times.

Those who are down attract others who are down, or they want you to speak about the lack in your life instead of the success because it makes them feel less envious or alone. Or they're more comfortable around those who are also loathing and pitying because they don't feel so ashamed in their presence. Let those folks repel away from you and rise above their negativity. Don't criticize them, just wish them well and reserve your sparkles unto yourself. Don't share sparkles with them.

Be conservative about one thing in this lifetime. Where you devote your energy. Make sure it's in the right place. Donate your time and heart sparkles to the right people. Divvy out your advice and give all the fucks to the right people. Make the work that feels like it makes a difference, comes from the heart, or is the hardest thing you've ever done.

In conversation with Tony, the knight, I offered yet another metaphor and visualization to illustrate this point. "You're in a dark room. Once your eyes adjust you realize that the room is filled with candles like the votives stacked in front of a Catholic shrine. You reach into your pocket for your lighter. What will you do?" Tony responded by saying, "I would have some fucking burned thumbs." I continue to express, "What if instead of spending all of your day lighting every candle in the entire room, returning to some that fizzle out, you pick one candle. Go to the edge of the room and sit down. You light it and you return your lighter to your pocket." Tony's aha moment is percolating.

See he calls himself a co-dependent but he's a people pleaser. He does that because he wants validation. He seeks it because he's not sure the light from his own candle is enough. "People enter the room, they select their own candle, and they light it with their own lighter. If need be, you can light their wick from your flame. Yours won't go out. But keep your lighter in your pocket."

I used to be like Tony, thinking that it was my job to educate everyone. Get them to see what they were missing. Go out and stick my views as a yard sign on their front lawn. But it is enough to have the sign on my own lawn. It is enough to light my own candle. Anyone who wants to know more will knock on my door. I don't need to become a Mormon missionary and knock on everyone else's door to give them an opportunity to see the light. If they're interested, they'll find me, sitting in the corner of that darkened room. And I will light their wick from my flame.

Be the hero of your own story and let those people go be their own hero, caterpillar, or negative end of a battery. Whatever they are, it's none of your business. The only thing that is your business, is being the CEO of your own damn life. Just "paddle your own canoe," as Nick Offerman would say.

As I have embarked on a journey to change my life the dismal truth is, I have had to let go of the tether of most of the people who are closest to me. My husband, my mother, my twin sister and my father, my beloved James and my almost-stepson Samuel. Eventually, I will have to let my children go out into the world and make all their own messy mistakes in their life. You know what? There's no way around that. The only thing that makes me feel a little bit easier is an idea my therapist gave me in a session long ago before I uttered the words "divorce" or "business." I was unhappy and I felt like I was dragging everyone around behind me trying to get to my ideal life. Nobody wanted to envision the future as I was and come with me, so like a ball and chain I just pulled them along. Stella, my therapist said,

> *"Life is like a play. You are the main character. We don't know how it ends, but what we do know is that you are the only cast member who will be here for the entire show. Some characters enter and stay for the entire time. And some will exit stage left."*

That gave me permission to let go. It freed me up to be the butterfly I wanted to be and fly where I needed to fly. I can't drag my caterpillars into the sky with me and I can't wait for them to transform. I can't talk them into it, like a sales pitch or a coach. I just have to embrace not knowing what it will be like without them and know in my heart that their heroic moment is coming. They'll find their own answers someday. But, for right now, it is my time to thrive.

Forgiveness: The Ho'oponopono Prayer

This last bit won't be as you expect it to be. You think I am going to tell you to forgive your mom and dad and ex-husbands or ex-boyfriends or ex-bosses for their wrongdoings. You think I'm going to ask you to make amends with all the people you've hurt so that you can feel free. But, I'm not. I am about to do something even more unconventional. Because it's not about them. It's about you.

There is a prayer or a saying in Hawaiian culture that allows forgiveness of the self. It's called Ho'oPonoPono prayer and it is meant for the times when you catch your language drifting. When you haven't been impeccable. When you've talked negatively to yourself or argued, berated or blamed another person for something. Even simply getting flustered or frustrated when a conversation doesn't go as you'd like it to. This is when you have to say four things to yourself.

1) **I'm sorry.** You're apologizing to yourself for letting your behavior slip. For not being your highest self. For not having composure and losing your cool. For letting your inner beast run out of its cage. "I'm sorry" is not directed at the person who made you upset, it's *the opposite*. You're apologizing to yourself.

2) **Forgive me.** Asking yourself for forgiveness may seem silly. But, if you actually say it out loud, you are instigating a moment with yourself that you rarely stop to think about. Your stubborn ass likes to hold a grudge. Say it to yourself, man. You have to cut that out. Say it. "Please forgive me."

3) **Thank You.** That's the response someone else would have if you apologized and asked for forgiveness, right? So you thank yourself for having the moral aptitude to do the first two steps. That shows maturity and growth. Even the fact that you can get this far in the prayer without labeling me an armchair guru shows that you are working hard on breaking your own patterns. Thank yourself for that effort. "Thanks, me."

4) **I love you.** Much like the love letter to yourself, you can heal a lot of minor daily dramas by just completing this loop. I love you is what you say after a fight with your partner or child when you know you lost your top and you didn't mean to hurt anyone's feelings. What about your own feelings? It's harsh to call yourself an idiot. It's just a gas light, and the mistake didn't

cost anyone their life. "I love you" is the way to remind yourself that you're lovable. Though flawed, still deserving of love. It's the highest vibration in the world, that of love.

You can say this prayer every day five times a day. It never gets old to me. I also say these things to others sometimes. Especially the ones who piss me off or make me envious. I am a hard knocks type of woman with a foul mouth, so I usually start off with "Fuck you, _____ (their name). I'm sorry for being mad at you. Forgive me. This ends resentment. You own your feelings. Thank you for letting me say this prayer to you. I love you (even if I totally hate your guts right this minute)."

The Fat Lady Sings

An artist is no different than any human being on this planet Earth. We are all created from the same spec of plasma and we all return to the same specs of dust. We all have hopes and dreams, doubts and demons. In Islamic ideology, there is one angel on each of your shoulders. The one on the right is recording your good deeds and the one on the left is tallying up your mistakes. Our lives are short and recorded only by our deeds, our actions, the love we gave away for free, the things we create and the monumental piles of bullshit we leave behind. Make sure the right-side angel runs out of paper and needs to re-order via Prime. That's how much great stuff you're doing.

Each of us has a very different QR code imprinted on us, a microchip embedded inside in case we get lost. We need to scan those internal sensors and download our gifts. Put a little time into them every day. Push our talents and ideas to the max. Share them with as many people as possible. Today could be the first day of your journey or I could have found you mid-way through the play. Be like your kindergarten self. Play dress up, get on the stage, sing to Whitney Houston as loud as you can. Dance like you're Paula Abdul circa 1988. Live boldly, colorfully, and don't be afraid to scare the neighbors.

Get over the dismal fear of promoting yourself. Your voice should be heard, because it could help someone else. The work you're making is an inspiration and a gift. You owe it to everyone who ever inspired you to pass it on to an unknown reader, viewer or admirer on Instagram. Speak as if you're the CEO of a brand, or speak as if you're the boss of your own life. You're the author of a very specific, very rich narrative, so please include your world view. Don't parade in vanity, just bathe in your unique identity.

Your crowd may not surround you right now, but they are out there. Dig deep, find meaning, tell people your dreams and write them into your calendar because we all know there's not enough time in a day for all the shit that's urgent/important to everyone else but you. Pinpoint the exact person you need to meet and be ruthless until you find him/her. Hand them your demo tape or email them your portfolio. Take huge risks, because that's how you get huge rewards.

Devote yourself to this pursuit and you will thrive. Know that there are so many others in this world who have broken out of their shell to expose their most vulnerable onion inside. And they made it. So will you.

What better way to pass your lifetime than to do what you love, get paid for it, and create a legacy you were born to leave behind?

About the Author

Erin Minckley is a visual artist based in Chicago, IL. Her paintings, drawings and sculptural fabric works have been included in many exhibitions and showcases around the country. She founded the luxury wallpaper brand in 2015 using her own drawings and the help of 226 friends on Kickstarter. Her wallcoverings are distributed and sold online and in showrooms around the world. Her hand painted murals are displayed around the country. The tagline #BringtheWorldHome embodies her love of foreign cultures and a deep sense of historical nerdiness about identity and cloth. She is the mother of two boys, a community builder, and an avid Audible listener.

For more information about online courses, one-on-one coaching, and artist retreats related to the Artists Who Thrive series please visit http://www.profitableartist.org or email hello@profitableartist.org

About the Cover

Salvador Dali is an important archetype of a thriving artist. His bold personality resonates with everyone who's ever thought of themselves as a freak, a clown, the creative misfit. He was no outsider to the world of culture and commerce and did anything he could to build his fortune and his legacy. Artists like him are celebrated for their success but their stories are not a dime a dozen. Few live as vivaciously, few prosper as much. His recognizable moustache and serious, fervent look on his face was my attempt to tap you all on the head and wake you up to your destiny. I myself, don't think I'll live up to the celebrity, audacity and charisma that Salvador Dali had but I can try to emulate his zest for life and hunger to live miraculously.

Notes

I have written a book. Honestly, I never even knew I wanted to write one. I never thought I'd write more than a caption on an Instagram or blog post.

I took this plunge with my lungs full of hopium. My heart open to opportunity. My mind free because I spewed all my vomitous thoughts out onto this page for you to read. You can love it or hate it or tear it apart. *But*, I did it. Not many people I know have written a book. Not many people I know have pivoted successfully or risked everything to see their dreams come true. Most people keep their thoughts to themselves and their feelings in a light pink diary with a small lock on the front. Two tiny keys in their underwear drawer are the only way to unlock the deepest inner workings of their heart.

I want to thank my publisher Jackie Camacho Ruiz for being the pilotina. For adding me into your library of talent and for introducing me to my lovely editor Michelle Kelly. Without you, my Italian stepsister, none of this would have made it to the page. Thank you for being my dramatically enthusiastic fan, my hard knocks writing coach, my accountability partner, and my very first guinea pig to the Results of a clean office, AKA Writing Studio.

To Maria Nemeth, for whom I am indebted to your life's work and teachings. Though I have never met you, but virtually, your spirit traverses your materials and tools and those have changed my life. I can't wait to coach with these materials and watch others transform their lives. To Allison, for being an integral part of this entire story. For being my champion, a shoulder to cry on and a big high five and rock and roll when I succeed, even at the smallest things. Wherever a Theta is, her sister is always welcome, right? Thanks for taking me under your wing.

I want to acknowledge the many authors who have been a constant guiding light for me as I've embarked on this journey into becoming a new person, not just an author. From the day I decided to get a divorce I was set on changing the trajectory of my life and reigning in control of who I wanted to be. A business was the birth of my new identity, but it was important to have the support of these voices and pages to gently nudge me in the right direction.

To the departed, Dr. Wayne Dyer who guided me in statements of "I am." I am spirit, energy, light, or God. I believe that though I am not a religious person and remain politely skeptical of all of this hocus pocus. Thank you for revealing the human brain as a conveyor belt of thoughts, where I can choose to pick one up and stare at it for a long time or I can decidedly put it back when it's ugly. Also, for teaching me that other peoples' opinions are none of my business. That freed me. To Eckhart Tolle, Esther and Jerry Hicks, and James Redfield thank you for opening me up to the power of being present to my life. Listening and looking for clues from the universal energy, my ancestors, the mystical powers that we cannot see. To Eric Riles, for writing the *Lean Startup*, Michael E. Gerber for the *E-Myth Revisited*, Chris Guillebeau for the *$100 Startup*, and Timothy Ferriss for the *4-Hour Workweek*. You guys taught me that work doesn't have to be so hard. That my business can be simplified and that I don't have to do everything myself. To T. Harv Ecker for inventing the *Secrets of the Millionaire Mind*, which I thought at first to be a load of crap, but it turns out to be a simple formula to leave "stuck" and thrive.

To Jen Sincero, Mark Manson, and Rachel Hollis: thanks for making me feel empowered. For being highly imperfect which allows me to do the same. For swearing and being unapologetic. To Stephen R. Covey and Jack Canfield for being old dudes with lots of practical tips.

Maximum Confidence is so cheesy and so brilliant that I refer friends to it often and I listen to it again and again. The saxophone music though, guys. To don Miguel Ruiz, thank you for reminding us to stand tall and be better. To Brenee Brown and Mel Robbins: you are witty and smart as two whips and my heroes. To Jerry Saltz: thanks for the anecdotes and puns, the melodic writing that puts novices to shame. To Elizabeth Gilbert for being forthright and reminding me that the story has its own heartbeat and breath and if I don't capture it and bottle it up it will find another voice to tell it.

To Jim Kwik: thank you for helping me hone in on my capacity and refine my broken brain. To Spencer Johnson and Kenneth Blanchard for that age old, short story that mocks us for being such dumb humans that we don't evolve quickly and starve because of it. To Gary Vaynerchuck for being such a douche that I strived to write all your clever messages with a nicer touch. To Sarah Thornton for exposing the ridiculous nature of the Art World, which helped me realize I didn't want to waste time trying to be part of the "in" crowd. To Steven Pressfield for reminding us of the muses of olden days. To Martin E.P. Seligman PhD for instilling optimism back into our lives. To Ramit Sethi for being an expert at being rich, which has inspired me to be a sliver as ambitious. To Chuck Kloswerman for your skepticism.

To Sheryl Sandberg for sharing your truth and reminding us that life goes on. To Daniel J. Siegel and Tina Payne Bryson for reminding me that my "big feelings" live upstairs and I can always just come down. To J.D. Vance for sharing your story of a hillbilly mother who threatens to cut people off but still turning out alright, since I feel a kindred connection to that story. To James Clear for getting our lives in order and teaching me new tricks. To Claire Bidwell Smith for helping me understand what grief is like and how anxiety is an unwanted visitor.

To J.K. Rowling for being a single mother and starting an empire with not a whole lot. That's so badass. Hats off to you. Also thank you for hours of entertaining my oldest son with your imagination. Thank you, Roald Dahl, for writing with such detail and humor that maybe somewhere very deep down I'd wanted to write a book like you.

To my family for teaching me patience and perseverance. Without you I would have been fucked up by some other lot of weirdos. Glad it was you who molded me. Thanks for being a part of my journey, though you've been far away for a while now. I wish you each peace and an end to your suffering. I wish for you lots of success and happiness. Thanks for not disowning me when this book comes out.

To my ex-husband, thank you for giving me the two best gifts that I've ever received. Through twenty months of baking in my belly and fifty-one hours of labor, cumulatively, these boys came into the world. It has been a wild ride! But, without you I wouldn't have had the opportunity to become a mother. So, thank you. Thank you also for teaching me how to grow up and live alone and thrive with nothing. For starting our first business, because I met so many wonderful people through cultural tourism trips. Thank you for giving me the gift of my second home, second family, second name, Hayat. I got to camouflage into a Moroccan household like I was one of the family. Many funny memories will be cherished from those days when we spent hot, sweaty summers in Sidi Slimane.

To JPH, although we were oil and water, I loved you with every inch of my heart and soul. Thank you for teaching me grace. I had a funny way of learning it… but through the mess, the anger, the chaos, and the pain we found ways to have bits of joy and family. Thank you for loving me in return. I wish you love. I wish you peace. I wish you protection.

To my guardian angel thank you for the lessons you taught me. For being present to show me the way and for giving me another egg in my nest of boys. If even for a short time. To all my spirit guides who never let me forget who I am, thank you. Keep pushing me to stay open and awake to all that is amazing in life.